The Radical Isaac

SUNY SERIES IN CONTEMPORARY JEWISH LITERATURE AND CULTURE
EZRA CAPPELL, EDITOR

Dan Shiffman, *College Bound:*
The Pursuit of Education in Jewish American Literature, 1896–1944

Eric J. Sundquist, editor, *Writing in Witness: A Holocaust Reader*

Noam Pines, *The Infrahuman: Animality in Modern Jewish Literature*

Oded Nir, *Signatures of Struggle:*
The Figuration of Collectivity in Israeli Fiction

Zohar Weiman-Kelman, *Queer Expectations:*
A Genealogy of Jewish Women's Poetry

Richard J. Fein, translator, *The Full Pomegranate:*
Poems of Avrom Sutzkever

Victoria Aarons and Holli Levitsky, editors,
New Directions in Jewish American and
Holocaust Literatures: Reading and Teaching

Jennifer Cazenave, *An Archive of the Catastrophe:*
The Unused Footage of Claude Lanzmann's Shoah

Ruthie Abeliovich, *Possessed Voices:*
Aural Remains from Modernist Hebrew Theater

Victoria Nesfield and Philip Smith, editors,
The Struggle for Understanding: Elie Wiesel's Literary Works

Ezra Cappell and Jessica Lang, editors,
Off the Derech: Leaving Orthodox Judaism

Nancy E. Berg and Naomi B. Sokoloff, editors,
Since 1948: Israeli Literature in the Making

Patrick Chura, *Michael Gold: The People's Writer*

Nahma Sandrow, *Yiddish Plays for Reading and Performance*

Alisha Kaplan and Tobi Aaron Kahn, *Qorbanot*

Sara R. Horowitz, Amira Bojadzija-Dan, and Julia Creet, editors
Shadows in the City of Light: Images of Paris in
Postwar French Jewish Writing

Alana Szobel, *Flesh of My Flesh: Sexual Violence in Modern Hebrew*
Literature

Ranen Omer Sherman, *Amos Oz: The Legacy of a Writer*
in Israel and Beyond

Adi Mahalel, *The Radical Isaac: I. L. Peretz and the Rise of Jewish Socialism*

The Radical Isaac
I. L. Peretz and the Rise of Jewish Socialism

ADI MAHALEL

Published by State University of New York Press, Albany

© 2023 State University of New York Press

All rights reserved

Printed in the United States of America

No part of this book may be used or reproduced in any manner whatsoever without written permission. No part of this book may be stored in a retrieval system or transmitted in any form or by any means including electronic, electrostatic, magnetic tape, mechanical, photocopying, recording, or otherwise without the prior permission in writing of the publisher.

For information, contact State University of New York Press, Albany, NY
www.sunypress.edu

Library of Congress Cataloging-in-Publication Data
Names: Mahalel, Adi, author
Title: The radical Isaac : I. L. Peretz and the rise of
 Jewish socialism
Description: Albany : State University of New York Press, [2023]
 Series: SUNY series in Contemporary Jewish Literature
 and Culture | Includes bibliographical references and index.
Identifiers: ISBN 9781438492339 (hardcover : alk. paper) |
 ISBN 9781438492346 (ebook) | ISBN 9781438492322 (paperback)
Further information is available at the Library of Congress.

10 9 8 7 6 5 4 3 2 1

To my mother, Nava (Sheyndel) Mahalel, a devoted social worker
To Dovid Shneer z"l, scholar and mentor

Contents

List of Illustrations	ix
Acknowledgments	xi
Introduction: Intellectual and Historical Backdrop of Peretz's Early Work, Outline, and Methodology	xiii
Chapter 1 Education, Professions, and Literary Proclamations: Peretz between Warsaw Positivism and Proto-Socialism	1
Chapter 2 A Radical Shift: Becoming a Social-Protest Writer	35
Chapter 3 "To Be a Fighter with Both Fists!": Peretz the Radical Hebrew Writer	69
Chapter 4 On Love and Class War: Peretz's 1890s Hebrew and Yiddish Poetry	117
Chapter 5 Between Liberal Satire and Socialist Roots: Peretz's Hasidic Creations of the 1890s	161
Conclusion	207
Appendixes	213
Notes	217
Bibliography	267
Index	287

Illustrations

I.1	Peretz on the cover of a Cuban edition of his works entitled *The Legend of Peretz*	xiv
I.2	Peretz in the late 1880s	xv
I.3	Marszałkowska Street in Warsaw, ca. 1912	xvi
I.4	Peretz card with his minibiography in Yiddish	xxx
1.1	Postcard featuring I. L. Peretz	33
2.1	Jack Gilford plays Peretz's character Bontshe Shvayg on US television, 1959	38
2.2	Cover of the Yiddish version of the 1881 brochure "Kto z czego żyje?" (By what do we live?) by the prominent Polish socialist Szymon Dickstein	42
2.3	Illustration from the Soviet edition of "Weaver-Love" (Moscow, 1947)	45
2.4	Cover of the *Yontef bletlekh*, second edition, 1913	57
2.5	Dovid Pinski (1872–1959), Peretz's main partner in creating the *Yontef bletlekh*	59
3.1	Peretz's Hebrew journal *Ha-chetz* (The arrow; 1894)	73
3.2	Peretz's prose debut, the Hebrew short story "The Kaddish" (1886)	99
4.1	Cover page of the Hanukah volume of the *Yontef bletlekh*	135
4.2	Cover of an issue of the groundbreaking journal *Yontef bletlekh*, featuring an original poem by Peretz	144
5.1	Bundist demonstration in 1905	179
5.2	Peretz's mugshot, 1899	193

5.3 "If Not Even Higher" became one of the most famous
    Yiddish stories of all time   197

6.1 Collection of photographs from the opening of Peretz
    Square in New York, 1952   210

6.2 Illustration from the Yiddish daily *Forverts*: "Today Mayor
    Impellitteri Opens the Peretz Square near Second Avenue"   211

6.3 Peretz Square Park in lower Manhattan   212

Acknowledgments

I would like to thank my advisors at Columbia University, Jeremy Dauber and Dan Miron, who turned me on to I. L. Peretz early. I would like to thank my colleagues at the Meyerhoff Center for Jewish Studies at the University of Maryland for their support in completing the manuscript, notably: Charles Manekin, Rachel Manekin, Hayim Lapin, Maxine Grossman, Bernard Cooperman, Paul Scham, Yoram Peri, and Marsha Rozenblit. I am grateful to the people at SUNY Press for helping me realize this project, Rafael Chaiken, James Peltz, and Jenn Bennett-Genthner. I would also like to express gratitude to the Joseph and Rebecca Meyerhoff Program and Center for Jewish Studies, as well as the Littauer Judaica Publication Fund for their generous support.

I thank anyone whom I talked to about the subject over the years who commented or gave me feedback, notably: Sheila E. Jelen, David Roskies, Nancy Sinkoff, Hannan Hever, Bruce Robbins, Mikhail Krutikov, Dovid Fishman, Rachel Rojanski, Uri Cohen, Yitzhaks Lewis, Ken Frieden, Jan Schwarz, Ofer Dynes, Saul Zaritt, Dovid Shneer, Alyssa Quint, Shoshana Ronen, Alina Molisak, Nick Underwood, Jessica Kirzane, Madeleine Cohen, Sunny Yudkoff, Gideon Kouts, Sharon Bar Kochva, David Mazower, Marion Aptroot, Daniel Mahla, Yoav Peled, and to anybody else I am forgetting here, thank you.

I would especially like to thank my family: my wife, Laura, who was an ardent reviewer, and my children, Ahuva and Melech, for their patience and tolerance throughout the long process of working on the "P-man."

Introduction
Intellectual and Historical Backdrop of Peretz's Early Work, Outline, and Methodology

Yitskhok Leybush Perets, better known in English as I. L. Peretz (1852–1915), was a major leader of Eastern European Jewry in the years prior to the First World War. During this period, Yiddish was the most widely spoken language of the Jews in Europe. While he was best known for writing in Yiddish, Peretz was in fact a prolific bilingual writer in Yiddish and Hebrew. Through his work and his deep involvement in Jewish communal life and politics, Peretz earned great respect during his lifetime and continues to be revered to this day. Numerous studies have been issued on Peretz;[1] nonetheless, a very central component of his life remains severely understudied, though it offers the potential to better understand his body of work and communal involvement overall.

This book strives to illuminate a key part of Peretz's life and art that has often been neglected in recent years: namely, his close alignment with the needs of the Jewish working class and his deep devotion to progressive politics. In the mid-1890s, he began to visualize the Yiddish-speaking working class as his target readership. I show that Antonio Gramsci's concept of the "organic intellectual" applies to Peretz, and I call this period "the radical years of I. L. Peretz." By offering close readings of Peretz's work from this period and by analyzing his Yiddish journal, *Di yontef bletlekh* (The holiday pages), I seek to recast the way political activism is understood in scholarly evaluations of Peretz's work. Peretz's journal revolutionized the means of artistic production. In my analysis, I employ a partially chronological, partially thematic scheme, following Peretz's radicalism at its inception and then the various ways in which it was synchronically expressed through its initial intense decade. In this introductory chapter, I first discuss the historical and cultural context for Peretz's radicalization, then I move on to review the previous scholarship on the subject of Peretz's politics, and I conclude by outlining the book's chapters.

Figure I.1. Peretz on the cover of a Cuban edition of his works (1951–52) entitled *The Legend of Peretz*. Steven Spielberg Digital Yiddish Library.

The Backdrop of Peretz's Proto-Socialist Phase (1888–92)

Like his good friend and collaborator Nahum Sokolow (1859–1936), Peretz was inspired by Aleksander Świętochowski (1849–1938), one of the founders of the Positivist movement in Poland. Świętochowski preached for a swift adaptation of society to progress and argued that true progress could only be accomplished through a change in religious traditions.[2] In 1890 Yitskhok Leybush Peretz (sometimes known as Leon Peretz), son of middle-class family of merchants, left his hometown of Zamość, a small town in southeastern Poland of fewer than fifteen thousand people at the time, about half of whom were Jewish, like the family of Rosa Luxemburg. He then established himself permanently in Warsaw. He was a lawyer by profession and known in the literary world as a Hebrew poet. In Warsaw, he began to form relations within the intelligentsia. Sokolow describes his transformation and his integration, noting that Peretz became "more Polonized": "He used to speak Polish then; and he used to use this language with us and at his home, and anywhere he went. Mainly he read Russian literature, but he also used to read a lot in Polish, and I remember that Świętochowski influenced him a great deal."[3]

Figure I.2. Peretz in the late 1880s. Reprinted from I. L. Peretz, *Briv un redes fun Y. L. Perets*, edited by Nachman Mayzel (New York: IKUF, 1944), p. 100. Steven Spielberg Digital Yiddish Library.

Figure I.3. Marszałkowska Street in Warsaw, ca. 1912. Wikimedia Commons.

In the Jewish positivist circles, the attitude toward the Yiddish language, the dominant vernacular of Eastern European Jewry, was purely practical. The Jewish masses needed information about crafts and trades (*melokhe*), personal hygiene, and the sciences, and to be understood such information would have to be in Yiddish. Peretz stressed in a 1888 letter in Hebrew to the Yiddish author Sholem Aleichem (1859–1916) the great need "to enrich [Yiddish] literature with science books."[4] However, despite plans to establish a popular-science library in Yiddish, among the positivists the feeling was that it would not be tragic if the so-called Jewish jargon (how Yiddish was referred to back then) eventually disappeared.[5] Already in 1886, Peretz confessed his affinity to Yiddish ("the language of Beril and Shmeril") in his Hebrew poem "Manginot Ha-zman" (The melodies of the time):

My fellow writers,	אחי הסופרים,
Do not hold a grudge	אל תטרו לי איבה
If I am fond of	אם לי שפת בריל
The language of Beril and Shmeril—	ושמריל ערבה—
And I would not say with contempt	ובבוז לא אקרא
"Inarticulate" regarding their tongue	"עלגים" ללשונם.
For it is the language of my people	כי לשון עמי
I shall hear it coming out of their mouths!	אשמע מגרונם!
Not the holy tongue.	לא שפת הקדש.
Not the language of the prophets,	לא לשון הנביאים,
But the language of the exiled.	אך שפת הגולים.
The language of the "Hebrews"![6]	לשון ה"עבריים"!

This plea to his fellow Hebrew writers not to be hated for writing in Yiddish was characteristic of nineteenth-century Yiddish writers, who all felt a need to excuse their linguistic preference to other members of the Jewish intelligentsia.[7] Peretz had been a Hebrew writer since the 1870s, although he was also capable of writing in Polish. He first expressed his ideas concerning writing in Yiddish in his aforementioned letters to Sholem Aleichem. He told his friend about the inseparable connection he felt between nationalism and language.[8] In another letter to Sholem Aleichem in 1889, Peretz expressed an ambition, also shared by other writers at the time such as Sholem Yankev Abramovitsh (1835–1917; known as Mendele), to form a standard Yiddish literary language that would unite the different Yiddish dialects. Through this nationalist practice of standardization, it would be understood by Jews in different parts of Eastern Europe. He saw the need to constantly expand Yiddish so that it could be a fertile field for writers to develop.[9]

In his 1891 article "Bildung" (Education), Peretz emphasized the functionality and the usefulness of writing in Yiddish for spreading modern ideas, as he had previously written in his personal correspondence. At the same time, he deemphasized any intrinsic value that the language possessed: "We want to encourage our people to write in Yiddish, because we have about three million people who understand only Yiddish. But we do not consider jargon to be holy. We sympathize very openly with those who wish to substitute Yiddish for a spoken state-language . . . we sympathize even more strongly with the adherents of spoken Hebrew."[10]

Peretz here does not fully break away from the Jewish Enlightenment's agenda to eradicate Yiddish in favor of European state languages and Hebrew. Thus, he sympathizes with Safa Brura (Clear Language, 1889–91), a society for the promotion of Hebrew as a spoken language, which Peretz was associated with.[11] Instead, he offers a temporary tactical compromise: the Yiddish language should be developed in order to *promote* modernizing the millions of Jews who only speak Yiddish. In the long run, Yiddish would run its course, and other dominant languages would take its place, an inevitable cost of progress.

Initial ideologies aside, through the creation of Yiddish literature and by participating in related projects, Peretz played a key role in producing a modern standardized textual Yiddish language, despite Polish being more natural to him as a spoken language. At the popular literary salon he hosted, discussions were held in Polish rather than Yiddish.[12] Yudl Mark contends that Peretz's Yiddish became much more refined and richer during the last fifteen years of his life (1900–1915) compared with his earlier language.¹³ But the birth of his Yiddish productivity, alongside his political transformation, clearly happened during the earlier years and therefore demands special analytical attention.

As opposed to a kind of territorial nationalism that puts its emphasis on the need for sovereignty, Peretz's nationalism was first and foremost defined in linguistic and cultural terms: it is a folk nationalism, which centers on the issue of class, meaning that Peretz's is a nationalism of the common people, of the Yiddish speakers. The latter group became his professed muse, the "folk" was for him "the only genuine source of national creativity."¹⁴ Peretz believed that what the Jewish folk needed most at the time was modern education (*Bildung*).¹⁵ "Chauvinism is awful!" Peretz wrote,¹⁶ even as he was in the process of establishing an ideology that incorporates some basic nationalist thinking.¹⁷

On the surface, Peretz's version of *Bildung* encompasses a whole nation: a large group of people that, through the use of modern means of communication (mostly the press), becomes able to imagine their commonality. He wrote that his choice to use Yiddish stemmed from both the need to "educate" the people and of "knowing" the people.¹⁸ Peretz needs Yiddish in order to establish his nationalist project, and to do so he must imbue it with the power to accurately reflect "the people," who are capable of unlocking its spirit and truly knowing its essence.

The role of Yiddish becomes even more acute when taking into account that Peretz's brand of nationalism lacked a territorial component. Der Algemeyner Yidisher Arbeter Bund in Lite, Poyln, un Rusland (The General Union of Jewish Workers in Lithuania, Poland, and Russia), known as the Bund, whose establishment, I argue, Peretz played a key cultural role in, were influenced early on by the ideas of Austro-Marxists Karl Renner and Otto Bauer, who had conceptualized the model of nonterritorial autonomy.¹⁹ The national-cultural autonomy platform for Eastern European Jewry, who were scattered over vast areas among other groups, stood in contrast to the proto-Zionist nationalism of the time, which was based on the narrative of "return" to the historical territorial homeland of the Jews in Palestine. Regarding the option of Jews migrating westward, to Western Europe or America, Peretz in 1891 thought it was an unfeasible solution for the poor masses since any country would eventually limit the entry of masses of people without any capital. Most Jews, according to Peretz, did not possess even the small capital needed for travel.

Peretz did not believe that Eastern European Jewry could ever acquire a modern education through Hebrew: "In Hebrew we lack even one science," he wrote (8:10). On the one hand, he broadened the *maskilic*

(Jewish Enlightenment) themes of knowing the state language (Polish in his case) plus Hebrew to include Yiddish ("three million people live in it"[20]). On the other hand, he confronted what he called "nationalist chauvinists" who adhered strictly to Hebrew (the "holy tongue") and would throw out the "nanny" (i.e., Yiddish) before it had completed its modernizing task. Peretz, as was common in his time, has personified and feminized Yiddish, the homely *mame-loshn* (mother-tongue).

Economic development in the Russian Empire and the relative tolerance exhibited toward Jews since the mid-to-late nineteenth century sparked massive waves of Jewish migration to the cities, such as Warsaw, Lodz, Bialystok, and Odessa, from outlying provinces. A new social class was growing within the Jewish population by the end of the nineteenth century, made up of working-class, Yiddish-speaking Jews.[21] According to the lowest estimates, there were about 400,000 Jewish wage workers in the Pale of Settlement in 1898. Interestingly, 60 percent were handicraft workers, and the rest worked in agriculture or were day laborers or factory workers. They were almost exclusively employed by Jewish employers.[22]

Jan Bloch (1836–1902) was a philanthropist, financier, and railway giant who belonged to the Jewish plutocracy of Warsaw, which dominated the board of the Warsaw Jewish community.[23] He also became well known for his passionate advocacy for pacifism, arguing that a future armed conflict would have disastrous consequences for all participants.[24] Bloch financed both the statistical expedition to the Tomaszów region that was represented in Peretz's major early prose effort in Yiddish, *Bilder fun a provints rayze*, and the first two volumes of the almanac *Di yudishe bibliyotek* (1891). For the expedition, he recruited members of the Jewish intelligentsia like Peretz and Sokolow to gather information about the Jews living within the Pale of Settlement. Jews were restricted to living in the Pale according to czarist laws dating from the early nineteenth century.[25] However, as Jacob Lestschinsky writes, "the rapid growth of capitalism in Central and Eastern Europe during the 19th century . . . forced the Jewish masses to change their living places as well as their social appearance; forced them to seek a new place in the world and a new occupation in society."[26]

During the latter part of the nineteenth century, when the economy was unstable, Jews feared that the discriminatory May Laws of 1882 that were already in effect in the Pale (which prohibited Jews from the countryside within the Pale, thus further limiting their economic opportunities)[27] would be applied to Jews in Poland as well. Such laws would block the road for Jews wanting to integrate into the changing economy.[28] The goal of the expedition was to prove by scientific methods that Jews in fact do contribute to the general economy, that they work the land, and that many of them, in contrast to the common stereotype, are impoverished.[29]

Up until 1893—when he strengthened his ties with Jewish socialist activists as they were taking their first steps in appealing to Yiddish-speaking workers[30] and with socialist intellectuals such as Dovid Pinski—Peretz served as a middleman between the capitalist Bloch and lower-class Jews through his cultural productions. His target readership was middlemen as well, and his professed goal was to create a middle-class Jewish intelligentsia. Their mission to prove that Jews were contributing to the modernization of the economy served as a way of advocating for the modern economy itself. Peretz's sense of doubt toward alternatives to the contemporary economic system was evident from his writings.[31] One can speculate that Peretz's commitment to his patron prevented him from suggesting any radical social solutions at this stage. Sokolow described the relationship between the economic elites involved in Jewish communal affairs, like Bloch, and middle-class Jews, like Peretz: "The heads of the community thought about it, and an idea began to flow regarding the use of Peretz's strength for a spiritual purpose." In other words, the "Blochs" would use the "Peretzs" to keep the simple Jews in "spiritual" check. The idea of *Di yudishe bibliyotek*, the first Yiddish almanac that Peretz created, was born out of those meetings.[32] The participation of the middle-class Jews in Jewish politics gave birth to a proto-nationalist stage in Jewish politics.[33]

A valuable testimony regarding Peretz's state of mind at the time surrounding the expedition through the Pale of Settlement is found in Sokolow's essay years after the fact, "Yosl the Crazy (Sketches from My Memory)." In it, one gets a glimpse of the transformative value of the expedition, which I argue played a role in pushing Peretz to embrace socialism:

> Our private goal was to sail in the Jewish world, to renew what we knew from our childhood, and in order to observe new impressions. . . . We both had seen beforehand that advocacy is an effort in vain, that it's about as useful as a pair of glasses is to a blind person, or physical therapy to a corpse; but Peretz the poet, in the beginning, awoke, became angry, and afterwards froze while in rage. For both of us the work was the purpose and not a means. I was then heavily occupied in literary and public work; I wanted to shatter the walls of my

prison and break out, to get some fresh air; similarly Peretz jumped out of his hiding for the same multi-varied trip around the Jewish communities, like Jewish travelers in the Middle Ages before us. . . . Going quickly from city to city, from one small village to the next, it was an expedition of Jewish Don Quixotes, even more interesting than the literary visions of Mendele the Book Peddler with his strange twists.[34]

Peretz is portrayed here as poet first and foremost (his main claim to literary fame at the time), somewhat out of touch of regular people's lives and who increasingly became angry and frustrated by the reality of poverty he witnessed. The pessimistic feeling of two late-nineteenth-century Jewish influencers going on a hopeless battle that Sokolow expresses here also appeared in Peretz's first literary account of a visit to the shtetl in 1887, several years prior to the statistical expedition. The Heine-inspired Hebrew poem "The small town" contains many motifs that Peretz would later develop in the Yiddish prose of *Bilder*: the deteriorating marketplace, the economic struggle for survival, the hunger, the fires, the dybbukim, the isolation from the world, and the meeting of the shtetl Jews with the modern urban Jews. The character of the modern Jew is portrayed as having a hard time communicating his position to the shtetl Jews. He is a man modernly dressed and mannered, but still he wants to prove to traditional Jews he is a Jew like them. The protagonist tells them,

"Oh, brothers, calm yourselves,	"הה, אחי, הרגעו,
I am not a gentile,	הה שמעו שמוע!
And not a wealthy person	אינני בן נכר
The short uniform	ולא אדון ושוע.
Gave the wrong impression;	המדים הקצרים
Only one faith,	אך שקר בי ענו
Only one God between us."	אמונה, אך אחת,
As soon as they heard	גם אל אחד לנו".
Away they dispersed,	אך שמעו נפזרו
"Or a heretic or a baptized Jew,	לכל עבר ורוח,
Or an instigator seducer!"	"אפיקורס או מומר, או מסית מדיח!"
They dispersed, from afar	נפזרו, מרחוק,
I would still hear the curse . . .	עוד אשמע הקללה . . .
Is this supposed to calm down	הזאת המרגעה
A troubled soul?[35]	לנפש אמללה?

The last question is asked after the speaker starts the poem expressing the hope of finding some relaxation in the shtetl ("The town here is small, / Here I will rest my soul"). Dan Miron describes the unnerving shtetl reality that is revealed to the modern protagonist as "a frightening Darwinist image . . . an economic jungle, where everybody is so busy in the war for survival, that that becomes essentially the content of his existence."[36] In reality, Peretz himself was barely out of the shtetl at the time he wrote *Bilder*. The statistical expedition was the first undertaking that Peretz engaged in after moving to Warsaw in 1890.[37] Peretz ran a thriving legal practice in the late 1870s and during the 1880s in Zamość, representing prominent Polish and Jewish clients. During this period, he lectured in a workers' evening school and was active in other civic affairs. After a decade or so of practicing law, he was stripped of his license in 1887 for allegedly promoting Polish nationalism and socialism. Unable to resume his legal practice, he moved to Warsaw the following year.[38] Thus, Peretz had only arrived in the big city from the large town Zamość a few months before setting out for Tomaszów, a region about thirty kilometers from where he had grown up.[39] Reconnecting with traditional Jews cannot have been as difficult for Peretz, the son of shop owners in Zamość, as he portrayed it in *Bilder*. The sense of pessimism and frustration, and of "[freezing] while in rage" ("קפא תוך כדי התגעשות"), expressed in these early Yiddish texts represents a phase of exposure to the reality of poverty while not yet embracing the activist solution of class organizing and socialist struggle.

The overall significance of Peretz's evolving political consciousness as a result of being exposed to poverty and to socialist activism on the Jewish streets was that it led him to produce cultural works relevant to the socialist cause. If in the years 1888–92 Peretz was functioning as a committed agent of the hegemonic class, from 1893 onward he made an effort to establish himself as an organic intellectual, committed to the interests of the Jewish working class. According to the Italian Marxist Antonio Gramsci, every exploited social group needs to develop its own cadre of intellectuals in order to help shape its people's culture and way of life according to its own interests rather than according to the interests of the bourgeoisie.[40] These "organic intellectuals" articulate class perceptions and aspirations for the group in its own language.[41]

Peretz himself did not belong to the Jewish working class, but, as I argue in this book, he consciously bound himself to it, thus becoming a critical source for Jewish proletarian culture. As Gramsci writes, "an intellectual who joins the political party of a certain social group is merged with organic intellectuals who belong to the group itself, and bonds himself tightly with the group."[42] Peretz, as I show throughout this book, indeed joined the ranks of the nascent Jewish Labor Bund in spirit. An early Bundist activist in Warsaw called it "a kind of moral bond between the socialist Jewish youth and Peretz" created through a series of meetings beginning in 1893–94.[43] In later years, the Bund would become the biggest Jewish Marxist party.

The Bund

Founded in Vilnius in 1897 by Jewish Marxists, the Bund's initial goal was to recruit Eastern European working-class Jews to the emergent Russian revolutionary movement. The use of Yiddish—rather than Russian or, later, Polish—would help create a mass movement of Yiddish-speaking workers. Through strikes, Jewish workers were organized to seek better working conditions at their workshops. In 1905, the Bund added national-cultural autonomy to its platform, on top of advocating socialist revolution and civic equality. At the time, the Bund claimed approximately 35,000 members in 274 branches and was the largest and best-organized Jewish political party in Eastern Europe. However, in the Soviet Union, the Russian Bund was eventually liquidated by the authorities.[44] Between the world wars, Poland became the party's center of activity. It enjoyed legal status as a political party, and its candidates were chosen for municipal positions. In opposition to Zionism, Bund leader Vladimir Medem sharpened its ideological commitment to *do'ikayt* (hereness): the belief that the future of the Jewish people lies in the Diaspora they reside in and the commitment to change and improve that place of residence.[45] The party positioned itself as the guardian of secular Yiddish culture, opposing attempts to cultivate Hebrew culture at the expense of Yiddish. The Bund supported the Yiddish school network TSYSHO, active in more than one hundred communities, and it played a central role in the development of Jewish newspapers in Russia and Poland. By the mid-1930s, the Bund had become the dominant Jewish organization in Poland, leading the struggle against antisemitism. Until 1949, the Bund continued to carry out activities, but the organization was eventually wiped out when Poland adopted the Stalinist line. The Bund as an organized political party ceased to exist in Eastern Europe while maintaining chapters in the decades that followed in places like the United States; France; Melbourne, Australia; and Tel Aviv.[46]

Regarding the relations between Peretz and the Bund, I rely on the work of Yoav Peled, who in his book *Class and Ethnicity in the Pale* (1989) examined the rise of an "ethno-class consciousness" amongst Jewish workers in the Russian Pale of Settlement. The same year Peretz was starting to publish his radical work, 1893, was also the year when the Jewish social democratic *intelligenti* (active in Lithuania since the late 1880s) went from working in small, elite workers' circles to agitation on a mass scale, "appealing to the workers on the basis of their immediate material needs."[47] Following Peled, who examined the emergence of the Bund using analytical tools borrowed from political economy and sociological discourse, I argue that Peretz played an instrumental role in helping the Bund develop a Jewish, culturally unified ethno-consciousness.

Various theories exist regarding the emergence of the Bund. The traditional view based its reasoning on the socioeconomic realities of Jews, while Jonathan Frankel emphasized the role of politics.[48] Frank Wolff emphasizes the transnational character of the Bund from its inception but tends to essentialize such elusive concepts such as *yidishkayt* and *mishpokhedikayt* (family-ness) as a basis for a secular Jewish identity (inherently national).[49] Recent scholarship by Roni Gechtman uncritically adopts the Bund's own anti-nationalist rhetoric, utopian aspirations, and self-characterization. Gechtman also tends to lump Peled with other Israeli historians, assuming Peled's scholarship suffered from "the tension between the goals of Zionist historiography and the Bund's political and ideological commitments, namely the party's radical opposition to nationalism in general and to Zionism in particular."[50] But did the Bund "radically oppose nationalism"? Is Peled's scholarship part of the project of "Zionist historiography"? It's much easier to show how the Bund clearly opposed territorial Jewish nationalism and statehood in the form of Zionism but actively promoted Yiddish schools and Yiddish letters in Eastern Europe, because even "national cultural autonomy is rooted in the theoretical home terrain of nationalism"[51]—and to show how Peled's scholarship is critical of nationalist projects in all their forms.[52]

In his examination of the formation of the Bund and the rise of an "ethno-class consciousness" among Jewish workers in the Russian Pale of Settlement, Peled places the Bund's usage of (Jewish) "ethnicity" as a symptom of a split labor market. In a split labor market, the concept of ethnicity is used both by the hegemonic group as an argument to ensure its dominance within the society and by the minority group as an organizational tool in its struggle for equality.[53] While later Bund historians shed light on many other aspects of the Bund's history and ideology, it is

Peled's focus on the ethno-class consciousness that provides a particularly powerful lens through which to explore the ways Peretz's work during these years participates in redefining ethnicity in radical terms.

Previous Scholarship on Peretz and His Politics

The first Peretz scholar who emphasized Peretz's socialist art and devotion to working-class Jews was Shakhne Epshteyn in his long essay *Y. L. Perets als sotsyaler dikhter* (Y. L. Peretz as a social poet), published in 1916. Epshteyn states that, contrary to Peretz scholarship's emphasis on Peretz's "artistic significance," he wants to focus on the "social content of [Peretz's] works."[54] Epshteyn overemphasizes literary content without discussing the means of artistic production and form. While I also analyze the content of Peretz's literary works and examine their commitment to progressive politics, I am not less interested in the means of art production. Revolutionary artists must also revolutionize the means of producing art, as Walter Benjamin taught us, in order to make it more accessible to more readers, and thus they create new class relations between themselves and their audience.[55] Moreover, I disagree with Epshteyn's misleading dichotomy between "artistic significance" and "social content." In contrast, I am exactly interested in the interplay between the two elements, which, weaved together, can give birth to groundbreaking political art such as Peretz's challenging and multidimensional socialist literature.

The idea that Peretz made a radical turn in the mid-1890s was first compressively presented in a 1934 book by the Soviet literary critic Ayzik Rozentsvayg entitled *Der radikaler periyod fun Peretses shafn: "Di yontef bletlekh"* (The radical period of Peretz's creative work: *The Holiday Pages*). Rozentsvayg's excellent effort emphasized the content as well as the production of the *Holiday Pages* (the journal Peretz produced in the mid-1890s) and Peretz's class position, and it puts forth the demand from the artist to commit to social realism, in line with the Soviet hermeneutic doctrine of the time. I do not demand from an artist any commitment to a certain genre or style of writing, nor do I present any negative attitude toward modernist trends in art. Therefore, I refute the long-standing convention in Peretz scholarship that his interest in new literary styles—specifically his shift to neoromantic Hasidic stories and away from his earlier social realistic and naturalistic writings—coincided with a rejection of revolutionary politics.[56]

In contrast to Rozentsvayg, who was also restricted by official Soviet guidelines of literary criticism, I argue in this book that Peretz's stylistic shift reflected his ongoing search for new ways of expressing his radicalism. I analyze Peretz's radical-creative spirit through a holistic lens, which might still point to contradictions but is free of Rozentsvayg's somewhat mechanical relationship between the work of art, the mode of production, and social class—an approach that does not adequately consider the possibility of sincere internal ideological struggle.

In the process, I also refute other notable prewar and mid-century Peretz scholars like H. D. Nomberg,[57] and more so Shmuel Charney,[58] who emphasized Peretz's psychological personality portrait as a so-called noncommitted seeker, always on the look for new ideas and philosophies. Therefore, due to his restless character, Peretz was unable to fully commit to any political party. Charney acknowledges that a shift occurred in the mid-1890s in Peretz, since he began interacting with Jewish socialist activists—and, as I argue, that Peretz, as a result of those meetings, began seeing working-class Jews as his target readership. However, Charney feels obligated to stress that "Peretz did not become a socialist in the partisan sense of the word, and surely he did not become a Marxist-proletarian socialist."[59] Charney's claim about partisanship is anachronistic, because Peretz played a key cultural role in the *formation* of the Bund among proto-Bund groups, before the party was actually founded. And one cannot speak of official membership in a party that throughout Peretz's lifetime was forced to operate underground because the czarist regime deemed it illegal.[60] Regarding Peretz not becoming "a Marxist-proletarian socialist," judging by his various works and activism and considering the government restrictions he operated under, I do see Peretz as a socialist who was heavily influenced by Marxian thought and politics, embodied by the proto-Bund and the Bund. From "Bontshe Shvayg" to his Hasidic short stories, to essays and cultural production, I show in this book Peretz's unambiguous commitment to serving the needs of the Jewish working class. However, my strongest disagreement in this book is with later Peretz scholars.

If earlier scholars mainly debated the extent of Peretz's progressivism, postwar American and Israeli Peretz scholars began to reinterpret Peretz's legacy from a conservative perspective. In the mid-twentieth century, the rich progressive tradition of Peretz critique that emphasized Peretz's socialist work and his deep affection for the socialist cause and toward working people began to give way to work that sought to deemphasize Peretz's relation to the labor movement. Interpreters such as

Chone Shmeruk (1921–97), who was head of the Department of Yiddish at the Hebrew University in Jerusalem (1970–82), presented Peretz as an ardent anti-revolutionary, constantly in a state of doubt and despair, resistant to any fixed political ideal, and certainly never committing himself to the socialist cause.[61] Similarly, Ruth Wisse (1936–), the distinguished Yiddish professor at Harvard (1993–2014), argues that Peretz's texts from the 1890s display a "constant tension between radical and conservative impulses."[62] She suggests that Peretz was "used" by socialists for their purposes rather than acknowledging that he was an alert and willing participant engaged in a process of mutual inspiration.

In fact, as I argue in this book, Peretz's work from that period is characterized by a clear affection for the cause of the proletariat, and Peretz was actively engaged in stimulating Jewish workers to action, until his 1899 arrest for a speech he made at an illegal workers' gathering despite his awareness that undercover police were in the crowd. I discuss in this book at length examples of his Yiddish social-protest literature from this period, but moreover I argue that in later years he continued to produce, though less intensively, socially oriented literature, including his so-called Hasidic stories.[63]

One of Peretz's major sins in the eyes of his American neoconservative interpreters was that he held negative views toward Zionism, which at his time was taking its very early steps. Already in his lifetime, Peretz was vehemently attacked in the Zionist press for expressing such views. The criticism included booklets parodying his work, written by Peretz's contemporary David Frishman. At the time, Peretz polemicized with his attackers with full rhetorical force. Posthumously, the most vicious attack against his views came from Wisse at the end of her book *I. L. Peretz and the Making of Modern Jewish Culture* (1991). According to Wisse, if Jewish national power, as expressed by the Zionist movement and the current State of Israel, had existed during World War II, then the Holocaust would not have occurred. Wisse's neoconservative Yiddish scholarship not only rejects Yiddish Diaspora nationalism but attributes to it, and to Peretz as its inspiring messenger, a degree of responsibility for the destruction of European Jewry.[64] While Wisse unquestioningly supports Israeli statehood and military power, Peretz maintained his belief that "all states were coercive and culturally reductive."[65] Until his last days, Peretz viewed "freedom of conscience, human culture and ethics" as the "only conditions for a free life and victory."[66] One of my motivations to write this book was the scant up-to-date Peretz scholarship accessible in English and the centrality in the field given to Wisse's neoconservative Peretz scholarship as result.[67]

Rozentsvayg divided Peretz's creative journeys into three central ideological periods: a preradical Peretz up until the mid-1890s, followed by a radical period from 1893 to 1905 and a reactionary period during the last decade of his life, characterized by his closeness to bourgeois nationalist and decadent ideals.[68] Rozentsvayg's periodization does reflect much of Peretz's wonderings. Its main fallacy and my point of disagreement with him in this book concerns the so-called late reactionary period. I argue that Peretz never had a period past 1893 of utter rejection of radical socialist politics. He expressed doubt on occasion, but to the end of his life, since he was exposed to the ideas of Jewish socialists, the latter group remained his cultural-political milieu, his point of reference, his base of support, his base of affection.[69]

With all that in mind, one can undoubtedly state that, first, after 1893 a radical socialist twist did occur in Peretz's writings. He invested himself in those years with an unprecedented intensity in writing social-protest literature in various genres and styles. And, second, in later years, even while he continued to produce radical work (though far less intensively), these works were occasionally accompanied by works that openly criticized socialists and socialist ideologies.

Outline of This Book

The first chapter in this book discusses the proto-socialist stage of Peretz's writing career through his major Yiddish essays and literary work, from the time he settled in Warsaw in 1890 up until 1893, when the radical shift occurred. Most of his early cultural productions in Yiddish were published in the almanac *Di yudishe bibliyotek*, which he also edited. It was published only twice due to lack of commercial success.[70] Though some awareness of social-class issues appears in his early writings as well, Peretz did not actively associate with Jewish labor groups. Moreover, his target readership was not working-class Jews but middle-class "enlightened" Jews, in an effort to create a national intelligentsia.

In the second chapter I show how Peretz's new sense of commitment to the interests of the Jewish working class was expressed not only in his many essays, works of prose and poetry, and speeches in front of working-class audiences but also, and maybe first and foremost, through the radical new ways he has produced art itself. This radicalization of the means of production is evident in the radical Yiddish journal *Di yontef bletlekh*. Its content is examined throughout the second chapter (including further discussion of its relation to the nascent Bund) and beyond.

Peretz's Hebrew work receives special focus in the third chapter, where I analyze his ambitions to write radical literature in Hebrew. I show also that in his usage of Hebrew Peretz had ambitions to be innovative and that he left his mark on that language's literature. I examine his genuine attempts at producing radical Hebrew literature both in light of earlier attempts at producing Hebrew socialist literature and with respect to his radical works in Yiddish. I show that the inner contradiction of producing radical socialist work in Hebrew while the language of Jewish workers was Yiddish led Peretz to experiment only for a short time with writing radical Hebrew work. I also examine in this chapter, through a look at his essays and satires in both Hebrew and Yiddish, Peretz's regard toward Zionism, which was mainly negative. Peretz strongly opposed the program of the influential Zionist philosopher Ahad Ha'am, who proposed creating a Jewish spiritual center in Palestine. Peretz saw such a plan as elitist and completely alienated from the true needs of Eastern European Jewry.

In the fourth chapter, I look at Peretz's early writing career as a Hebrew poet and at his 1890s Hebrew poetry while giving attention to the poetry he was producing during that decade in Yiddish. Poetry in Yiddish was a new medium for Peretz, as was writing in Yiddish altogether. Examining his Yiddish poetry from his radical period, I will ask to what degree this poetry can truly be called radical political poetry. Peretz's poetry serves as a critical bridge in accessing his development as a writer and producer of Jewish proletarian culture in both languages.

The fifth chapter shows how Peretz's Hasidism-inspired works, both in Hebrew and in Yiddish, used the Hasidic metaphor in varied and complex ways. Peretz's Hasidic stories were often misunderstood and mistaken as reactionary by orthodox Marxist literary critics. Similarly, they were often mistakenly viewed by nationalists as simple Jewish folk tales. Both misinterpretations neglect the socialist core of many of these stories. I view in Peretz's Hasidic work an attempt to construct a mythological base for the Jewish labor movement and thereby have an important effect on the radical reader. My analysis also considers additional philosophical influences and aesthetic aspects that enrich and inform these stories.

Through my work about Peretz, I hope to give the reader a better understanding of his development as a writer, of his engagements with radical politics, and of the resulting radical literature that was the vivid expression of his alignment with the needs of working-class Jews in

Figure I.4. Peretz card with his minibiography in Yiddish. Israeli National Library.

eastern Europe. I also hope to provide the reader with a deeper understanding of the cultural productions that became the cultural foundation of the nascent Jewish Labor Bund in eastern Europe. But my hope is that my work will also contribute to scholarship in fields beyond Jewish studies by helping to decipher the complex relationship between radical movements and the cultural productions and cultural agents associated with them. Similar to the uncovering of the silenced radical Martin Luther King Jr., who tackled in his later years issues of poverty and warfare and was described by Cornel West as "the most significant and effective organic intellectual in the latter half of the twentieth century,"[71] I aspire to uncover in this book the neglected radical Peretz and his role in the Jewish labor movement.

Chapter 1

Education, Professions, and Literary Proclamations

Peretz between Warsaw Positivism and Proto-Socialism

In the editorial comments to the second *Yudishe bibliyotek* (1891) casually entitled "What's up?" (*Vos hert zikh?*), Peretz wrote about the working class and its worsening condition, which might read as sympathetic to its plight:

> Every day new machines are coming out that replace human labor. The workers in the meantime are increasing in number and from day to day have less work and even less income, because competition reduces the cost of labor. In all of the European countries, as is in the United States of America, the working class is restless, unsatisfied, and constantly rebelling. Governments fear rebellions and wish in any case not to let the size of the proletarian class grow.[1]

Later in this essay, it becomes clear that Peretz is writing mostly in order to discourage emigration to the United States rather than to identify with the working class, as one might conclude from the last passage. In a letter from around 1887–88 to Moyshe Altberg, his cousin and childhood friend, Peretz explains why he was banned from practicing law. This rejection was certainly a catalyst for the development of his Jewish national sentiment, and it paralleled the experiences of many other middle-class Jews of the time who suffered similar discrimination and arrived at the same conclusions. According to his letter to Altberg, Peretz believed that he was banned from practicing law because his competitors falsely informed the government that he was a socialist. He describes his futile attempts to convince the authorities that he was not a socialist:

> For a long time I have been very restless. I had to put up a tough battle with those who do not support me, who told the authorities that I am a socialist. Are you laughing? Nevertheless, I was very scared. The battle itself was a tough one, and in addition, I managed the struggle in great secrecy, so the matter wouldn't become known to anyone. My parents, my wife, and the people close to me didn't know a thing. I bit my lip and kept silent, knowing all the while that the danger is great. Now, praise the Lord, the struggle is over and, praise the Mighty One, I fell in battle. I couldn't clearly prove that I am not a socialist, nor an enemy of the government, nor a hater of the church. I don't defend any trials of revolutionaries . . . well, they made me out to be a socialist. Even though I have *not yet* uttered out from my mouth any word and *not yet* written any word against the order of the world. And thus, they swallowed me like a freshly ripe fruit at the beginning of summer.[2]

The twice-repeated use of the phrase "not yet" (my emphasis) plants the seed of Peretz's radical outspokenness through much of the 1890s, suggesting a more radical perspective was already fomenting in his heart, even though at the time he considered the idea of being a socialist laughable. Remember that the *Bibliyotek* as well as the statistical expedition were funded by the capitalist Jan Bloch, a fact that made any open call for class struggle problematic. However, in a private letter, Peretz could reveal his true thoughts and feelings, and in this one he did not significantly diverge from the positivist, middle-class-oriented mindset of the *Bibliyotek*.[3]

In his Yiddish essay "Bildung" (1891), Peretz had put forth a platform of education and outreach to the Yiddish-speaking masses of Eastern Europe. In *Iber profesyonen* (About professions; also 1891), he encouraged Yiddish-speaking Jews to take on useful modern professions so they would not be left behind by the socioeconomic changes sweeping Poland at the time. While he wrote in a straightforward manner in his essays, this subject received a more nuanced treatment in his major debut in Yiddish prose: the short story "In postvogn" (In the mail-coach) and the longer *Bilder fun a provints rayze* (Pictures from a travel journey). In these key texts, published between 1890 and 1891, Peretz wished to elevate the low symbolic status of Yiddish into that of a modern European Jewish-national language. Still, these texts did not express an alignment with the working class, nor did they embrace socialism. However, I show in this chapter how these texts, examined carefully, contain the seeds of Peretz's ideological transformation of the mid-1890s toward socialism. Through different manifestations of expression and sentiment, one can see signs he was beginning to recognize the idea of conflicting class interests, albeit vaguely. Examined together, they are key to understanding the formation and the genesis of the radical Peretz.

Bildung for the Masses, Professions for the Common People

> Our program is *Bildung*: education; we want to educate our people, turn the fools into smart people, turn the fanatics into educated people, and turn the idlers into workers who are useful and respectable, capable of working for their own good and in this way for the general good.
>
> The Jewish professions at times are so specialized that their equal in the twenty-first century would be that when one specialist would lift up the upper eyebrow, the second would push down the bottom one, and a third would examine the infected eye.
>
> —I. L. Peretz, 1891[4]

The first quotation opens Peretz's essay "Bildung," which was featured in the Yiddish almanac *Di yudishe bibliyotek*. This almanac and this essay in particular represent a desire to create a public sphere in Yiddish, one that aspires to be both modern and Jewish.[5] This is a new public sphere, in which Jewish intellectuals of all sorts, located across the European Jewish geography, can rationally discuss society's problems, and do so in Yiddish. Early on, Peretz imagined his Diaspora Jewish community in progressive terms. Unlike the mainstream Zionist current, which was taking its very early steps at the time, Peretz saw the positive effect of exile on the Jewish consciousness:

> Because we are in exile . . . our egoism is the purest human-love! Because we feel that as long as human-love does not prevail, as long as there is jealousy and hatred, as long as there are rivalry and wars, life won't be good for us. For this

> reason, we constantly seek peace. For this reason, our hearts are like a sponge for all the newest ideas. For this reason, we have a heart, and we have feeling and compassion toward the unfortunate. We share a connection with the expelled and displaced, with the persecuted. (*Ale verk*, 8:4)

Here, Peretz was constructing a Jewish identity founded on the principles of seeking universal social justice and peace and solidarity with the underprivileged. In his view, progressivism and living as a minority in the Diaspora benefited Jews much more than creating their own army and competing in this world of "rivalry and wars." Complimenting and praising (albeit through essentializing) Diaspora Jews for being open "for all the newest ideas" was Peretz's way of convincing Jewish intellectuals that the Jewish masses would be receptive to the *Bildung* platform. The focus on education was not innovative, since education was also the focal point of the Jewish Enlightenment (the *Haskalah*) preceding Peretz.[6] Shmuel Feiner, relating to the early *Haskalah* in Western Europe, notes that "the *maskilim* placed a special emphasis on the moral rehabilitation of the Jews, and internalized the educational ideal of the *Bildung*, one of the hallmarks of the German Enlightenment."[7] In Eastern Europe close to a century after the *Haskalah*, Abramovitsh's (Mendele's) first published article was the Hebrew essay "Mikhtav al dvar ha-khinukh" (A letter regarding education). It focused on the need for Jewish children to learn Russian and professions and suggested Jewish educators should worry about their own professionalism before complaining about their unmotivated and underachieving pupils.[8] But Peretz's article was innovative in its use of Yiddish as a serious political tool.

Bildung in German literally means a process of building oneself, or self-improvement through culture and education. Within the *Haskalah*, the concept of *Bildung* was always used to mean creating, through education, a rational (i.e., modern) individual, a person capable of organizing their life rationally and successfully. Ideally, this individual would also develop moral and aesthetic sensibilities. Peretz offers his version of the concept: "We want *Bildung*, but we don't mean the *Bildung* that people used to speak of. . . . We mean the *Bildung* that makes factories, trains, highways; *Bildung* that teaches you to work for your own benefit and for the benefit of the world, the *Bildung* that also makes a person honest and good" (8:12). Peretz distinguished a broader and deeper version of *Bildung* from the superficial *Bildung* of the Jewish Enlightenment. That "old *Bildung*" worried about appearances and concerned itself with useless diversions such as the study of languages for their own sake. In contrast, Peretz's *Bildung* is more practical (better suited to the demands of the job market), more beneficial for society (concerned with infrastructure), and more ethical (concerned with how people treat each other). His version of *Bildung* resonates with the Warsaw Positivism strand of thinking with its emphasis on cultural and economic development. A socialist writer would have added an emphasis on democratizing the economy and put out a plan to achieve it. Peretz here is still struggling in matching the progressivism of Jewish Diaspora and its openness to new ideas (as he envisioned it in this article) with a full-on progressive platform. It is curious that Peretz used the plural "we," as if a group of people is standing behind his project, although he had not yet gathered a following. Even if by "we" he meant the collective of Yiddish writers, his mini manifesto would still have applied to only to a very small group of people. One of his few readers, fellow writer and future collaborator Dovid Pinski, wrote, "In his article 'Bildung' he addressed 'all honest educated persons' to help educate the people. He called on them to return to their people, whom they had abandoned. He wanted them to come and help bring his version of *Bildung* to the people. It seems to me that his call did not reach any further than my circle of people in Vitebsk. No one responded from anywhere, and nothing began to happen."[9] When Pinski stresses his small "circle," he is reviling the elitist top-down outreach strategy at hand here: the way to reach people was not through targeting mass readership but rather through strategic targeting of informal networks of intellectuals. Moreover, even among those targeted, merely a handful of people were willing to sign up for Peretz's plan. The lack of enthusiasm toward Peretz's calls speaks to the fact Peretz did not offer the intelligentsia any meaningful productive message to bring to the masses. Besides receiving access to information about modern professions in their own language, he is not providing the masses a compelling path to improving their lives. Modern professions per se are insufficient if workers do not receive a living wage and have zero job security, all of which require social struggle and political organizing to obtain. The article is devoid of such issues and was thus doomed not to generate excitement and enthusiasm. However, through portraying Diaspora Jews as a group aligned with progressive values, Peretz was indirectly (and likely unintentionally and unconsciously) implying that Jews (including himself) would be receptive to the new progressive socialist agenda on the horizon. In a major way, choosing to write in Yiddish over other languages signified a progressive cultural choice of writing in a linguistic medium the working class shared.

"Bildung" was sealed by the open wish that "the main thing that ought to be seen, as much as possible, is that the people should have a livelihood" (פרנסה),[10] emphasizing a central feature of the *Haskalah*: its dubious slogan regarding the "productivization of Jews." In the long pamphlet article *Iber profesyonen* (About professions), initiated by Peretz's Jewish positivist circle, Peretz followed the agenda of making Eastern European Jews "productive." He proposed that Jews need to acquire productive occupations and integrate themselves in the modern industrial production process in order to extricate themselves from the poverty they were experiencing. Historically, because Jews could not own land, they were occupied as artisans, handicraft workers, traders of goods, and in general the manufacturing of finished goods (like tailoring) as opposed to producing raw material. These occupations were increasingly becoming outmoded due to new methods of production.[11] Peretz was focusing here on how Jews can adapt to industrialization in Poland.

Peretz describes the changes capitalism brought to Eastern Europe, including the terrible poverty it brought for Jews. The traditional preindustrial occupations of the Jews were dying out. Their roles as commercial middlemen between farmers and landowners were less in demand due to improvements in transportation and manufacturing. Peretz predicts, "Three quarters of Jewish professions will fall away and all must start to produce, to practice craftsmanship, to work in the factories" (*Iber profesyonen*, 14). The source of these numbers is the same as sources in charge of the statistical expedition.[12] Peretz acknowledges here the rise of the working class as a major factor in the economy, yet he still does not adapt his political platform to this new economic reality.

Similar to *Haskalah* literature, which repeatedly cited the places where the Talmud and Midrash speak in praise of craftsmanship and handicraft workers, Peretz also made an effort to back his agenda with evidence from traditional Jewish sources: "The Talmud for example had perceived artisans in a different way: 'Whoever doesn't teach his son a craft, is like he taught him theft!' 'Great is the craft, it gives the person respect!' 'Love the craft and hate the rabbinate!' 'The Torah can't exist without the craft!' The few words shown here are enough to prove that past generations had praise for those who work with their own hands not with someone else's" (*Iber profesyonen*, 4). Also, in his compiled booklet about the cholera epidemic, which he based on German and other sources, Peretz tried to show how most of the hygiene rules have a basis in ancient Jewish tradition.[13] This usage functions as a precursor to Peretz's use of coded "traditional Judaism" in promoting a radical socialist agenda, as I discuss in chapters 2 and 5. A significant part of *Iber profesyonen* is devoted to distinguishing between the Christian worker and the Jewish worker, which Peretz bases on well-known stereotypes of Christians and Jews. While the Christian worker divides his hours in an organized fashion between work and rest, "You [the Jews] do not," he accuses his Yiddish readers.[14] Nevertheless, Jewish workers, according to Peretz, do possess many advantages in comparison with Christian workers:

> You drink less!
>
> You are (in the provinces) more educated, in any case all of you can pray, a lot. You can write a bit, you come out of some form of traditional Jewish education.[15]
>
> You are more easygoing, more relaxed, and live better with your family. (*Iber profesyonen*, 22)

Peretz's assertion that a Jewish worker has a better family life than his Christian counterpart stems from the stereotype of gentile workers held by Eastern European Jews.[16] One can strongly argue such stereotypes serve to discourage cross-ethnic/religious working-class solidarity. For example, according to Peretz, the grave advantage Christian workers possess against their Jewish counterparts is their love of work for its own sake as opposed to the Jewish affection for money and laziness:

> A Christian worker loves his occupation; you [Jews] work for the most part to get time off, to get the task over with; you never have in mind the work but your earnings; you barely have a bit of money and you work less; you get a lot of money, you throw away your craft and become merchants, saloon owners and the like. . . .
>
> People say "Jews are thieves"; that is totally true; as much as a Jew steals money from himself, a Greek and a gypsy don't steal from one another . . . our handicraft worker have unfortunately a very bad name, and not for nothing you earn such a name! (*Iber profesyonen*, 22–31)

Ironically, Peretz's expedition to the provinces portrayed in *Bilder* aimed to dispel such biased accusations that Jews were lazy, unproductive money-lovers, but still Peretz repeats these stereotypes in his own writings.

Such typical charges against underprivileged minorities often stem from members of the dominant group, though they can also be echoed by "collaborators" within the minority, albeit in a more moderate manner. Peretz is not immune from this stereotyping, and his elitist preachiness here is representative of his lack of contact with actual Jewish workers or socialist activists at this time. Moreover, due to his lack of acknowledgment or awareness of the universal dire state of workers under capitalism, he substitutes with essentializing claims about manner of work according to ethnicity. We will see in the chapters that follow how Peretz, once he embraced socialism, would not repeat such preconceived assumptions, as he grew to abstain from talking down to working people. Another example of punching down in this article is when he lays forth points to which Jewish handicraft workers need to aspire:

> Our handicraft workers should better learn their craft.
>
> Our handicraft worker should work on time, regularly . . . thus he will be healthy and fresh at work. . . .
>
> Our handicraft worker should be, as much as possible, not a merchant, not a broker. . . . His livelihood should become a respectable livelihood. . . .
>
> Our handicraft worker should be an honest man . . . not deceiving, not based only on how best to fool the customer!
> (*Iber profesyonen*, 43)

Jewish workers have a lot to improve according to this text. This rhetoric echoes the Warsaw Positivist concept of "organic work," albeit dressed in Jewish clothing. It represents the out-of-touch character of the Jewish intellectual, in effect alienated and distant from the needs of working-class Jews. However, this article does prove the degree to which Peretz was preoccupied with issues of labor and the place Jewish workers had in the job market, which would make his imminent change of allegiance from capital to labor all the more powerful. Cluelessness as to how to get Jews out of poverty and uplift their socioeconomic status, alongside signs of transformation, also characterize Peretz's major efforts in prose from his proto-socialist phase. But in prose his cluelessness is even more emphasized and serves as a tool to undermine the positivist optimism expressed in his articles.

Peretz's Yiddish Literary Proclamations of the Early 1890s: "In Postvogn" and *Bilder fun a Provints Rayze*

Examining a selection of Peretz's early Yiddish essays showed an intellectual who talks down to working people of his ethnic group while not offering them a meaningful ideological platform to better their lives. The irony is that as much as he tried to appeal to simple folks through Yiddish pamphlets educating people about modern professions and the cholera epidemic, what strikes most from his early works of Yiddish prose fiction is his sense of alienation and lack of answers. True, he wrote in "Bildung" about the need of Jewish intellectuals to "go to the people," but the sense of urgency and psychological and ideological transformation of the individual intellectual who actually goes to meet this enigmatic construction comes across only in his art. The short story "In postvogn" and the longer work *Bilder fun a provints rayze* are Peretz's first major Yiddish literary achievements in prose and thus give us a platform to grapple with the art of the preradical Peretz.

"In Postvogn": Creating a New Path for Yiddish Literature

The release of the short story "In postvogn" (In the mail coach; 1890) signaled that while Peretz emphasized the usefulness of writing in Yiddish for spreading modern ideas in "Bildung," his use of Yiddish in an artistic medium dispels by its very definition any reductive argument of using Yiddish strictly for this usefulness. This text represents the genre of Yiddish literature that Peretz saw as vital to promoting a new nationalist agenda. The spatial dialogical premise he uses, of two Jews talking in a mail coach, corresponds to a larger Jewish literary topos of Jews meeting and talking inside a mode of transportation (cart, train, etc.). The twofold encounter introduces two characters who tell their stories to their travel companion, a modern Jewish writer. The two narrative segments complement each other, collectively exploring Peretz's ideology of nationalizing Jews in the Diaspora. It is a nationalist political project that was first and foremost defined in linguistic and cultural terms, in contrast to the territorially focused Zionist movement.

Like his contemporary Sholem Aleichem, Peretz believed Yiddish literature needed to be saved from the vulgarity of the time and should express more Jewish nationalist concerns. Sholem Aleichem accused popular Yiddish literature of not being truly representative of Jewish life nor sufficiently concerned with the fate of the Jews. He and Peretz both resisted the dominance of *shund*,[17] and by resisting they each carved out their own literary path.[18] In addition, Sholem Aleichem and Peretz agreed the elitist Jewish literature of the period (mostly in Hebrew) needed to be confronted as well, for it addressed an exclusively male and *maskilic* elite.[19]

Sholem Aleichem had his own idea of how to appeal to both male and female readers and to stay "true to Jewish life." His conception of the Jewish novel was devoid of any romantic or erotic elements, a common novelistic component. He believed these elements were foreign to Jewish life and thus should not be a part of a "Jewish novel."[20] Good literature, as was the convention in the Russian literary circles that influenced Sholem Aleichem, should depict society realistically and reject the fantastical. It should let the common Jew speak without morally judging his behavior.[21]

Peretz's early Yiddish literature was targeted at the Jewish intelligentsia. He innovated by placing the modern man's individual consciousness and psyche at the forefront of his narrative voice. His fiction highlights the modern person's inability to communicate with Jewish masses from the shtetls, underlining the distance from country life. In contrast, Sholem Aleichem and Abramovitsh, though they were both modern city people fluent in the state language (Polish or Russian), made a deliberate choice to narrate their fiction through the voice of literary personas of small-town, Yiddish-speaking Jews. As noted by David Roskies, "Peretz had no desire to pass himself off as a naive folk-balladeer, any more than he would adopt the voice of an itinerant, erudite Jewish book peddler à-la Mendele, or imitate the ebullient, irrepressible, ever-present, extremely talkative Mr. How-Do-You-Do ('Sholem Aleichem')."[22]

Peretz's modern man is not merely one character who is part of a panoramic, literary representation of Jewish society, as previous literature went; rather, he is the absolute, dominant voice both outside and inside the narration.[23] With Peretz's mentoring, many new talents in Yiddish literature followed his modernist lead; among the most distinguished of them are Hersh Dovid Nomberg (1876–1927), Avrom Reyzn (1876–1953), and Sholem Asch (1880–1957). When Peretz started writing in Yiddish, the Yiddish literary market was still far from reaching its full potential.[24] To give an illustration of the scope of this market in 1889, Abramovitsh sold 5,000 copies of his novel *Di kliyatshe*, Sholem Aleichem sold 4,100 copies of his novel *Stempenyu*, and Shomer sold a record 96,000 copies of his thirty-five titles![25] In 1889, Peretz already had major plans for entering the Yiddish literary market, which he elaborated in his correspondence with Sholem Aleichem, but his plans had not yet materialized.

State of the Nation on the Road

"In postvogn" is a combination of two stories told inside a mail coach, a spatial setting signifying movement and communication, and a perfect place for new encounters. As mentioned, it was also by then an established Jewish literary framework and the premise of one of the more famous Eastern European Jewish jokes.[26] The narrator listens in turn to the stories of his two male traveling companions. As an engaged listener who shares his own impressions with the readers, the narrator plays an active role in the stories of both men and thus functions as a central character in the story.

A short Hebrew story by Abramovitsh from the same year, entitled "Shem and Japheth on the train" ("Shem ve-Yefet ba-'agala," 1890)[27] takes place in a similar setting. The listener-character in Abramovitsh's story, Mendele, listens to the story of Moyshe, the tailor, while they spend a train ride together. Like "In postvogn," Moyshe's story deals with Jewish and gentile relations during the rise of antisemitism in Europe. But if Peretz's characters are utterly modern and middle class, then Abramovitsh focuses on the low socioeconomic strata.

Both characters in "Shem and Japheth on the train"—one a Jewish tailor, the other a Polish gentile cobbler—start off, as in "In postvogn," on a friendly basis. As immigrants in Prussia, they were both driven away by the Prussian government, but the Jewish character was driven away before the gentile. In retrospect, this contributed to the fact that, for a period of time, the gentile character was himself carried away by the antisemitic rhetoric that campaigned for deporting the Jews from Prussia. The two characters eventually team up again in Poland and bury the hatchet between them; the gentile even becomes a close family friend of the Jew. The story suggests that solidarity between Jews and non-Jews can be based on shared poverty and misery. It also suggests that, regarding misery, gentiles have something to learn from the Jewish experience of exile, and it reminds its readers (originally Jews) that the seven laws of Noah apply to gentiles, too.[28]

Like Abramovitsh, but unlike the listener-character in Sholem Aleichem's more famous *Railroad Stories*, written about twenty years after "In postvogn," Peretz's listener plays an active role in the story. Both Peretz's and Abramovitsh's listeners sometimes function as intermediates of the storyteller, asking leading questions and drawing "proper" conclusions from the two stories. However, Abramovitsh's listener is a book trader and only semimodern in his consciousness, whereas Peretz's listener is a modern fiction writer. In addition, while in both cases the listeners have an emotional reaction to the stories they listen to, Peretz's listener has an even more intense emotional involvement in the plot (he is a former friend of the second storyteller), while no such relation exists in Abramovitsh's story.

In the first monologue within "Postvogn," the companion traveler is a traditional Jewish man, Haim, who gives an account of his relationship with his wife. He tells the narrator how his wife complains to him of her boredom and her desire to read. "Polish, German . . . let it be Yiddish; main thing is to read,"[29] Haim relates of her request. He views her complaints as a sign of idleness, which, he claims, is a privilege that traditional Jewish men do not share because they are constantly occupied with the study of holy books written in Aramaic and in Hebrew. In reality, Jewish men were preventing women—who were mostly literate only in Yiddish or non-Jewish European languages—from having access to this knowledge.

The story seems to protest the inferior status of Jewish women compared with that of Jewish men, but the producers of modern Jewish knowledge in the story, including of modern Yiddish literature, which was accessible to women, are still exclusively Jewish men. "The obligation of every Yiddish [male] writer," according to the story, is to include Jewish women in his targeted audience (*Ale verk*, 2:75). What comes out of this conversation between two men is that the status of Jewish women is an issue to be discussed between Jewish men, while the women here are present only as "symbolic means in the policies of men."[30]

In the second story, we find out that even this limited feminist agenda is restricted to Jewish women who remain within the imagined collective, within "the Jewish people." The narrator—now traveling alongside a gentile passenger who shows romantic interest to a Jewish woman—views Jewish women who move outside of the collective as victims of a demonic seduction by a non-Jew. His "concern" for women is a progressive disguise for the well-known chauvinistic and ethnocentric goal of protecting the nation's women from "abusive" foreign men, a view that both Peretz and Sholem Aleichem expressed in their writings. In these stories, gender equality can only be truly realized by, and is conditioned upon, promoting the unifying nationalist agenda.[31]

The first monologue highlights the case of a woman who wants to study, which, if it were permitted, would promote national unity between Jewish men and Jewish women. Contemporary popular Yiddish literature, Peretz tells us, fails to serve as a nationalizing tool for Jews, for it does not meet the needs of male Jewish readers. It literally puts them to sleep, according to the narrator. In reality, Jewish men enjoyed reading Yiddish sentimental novels but viewed doing so as an insignificant distraction or entertainment.[32] Presumably, if women were educated, men and women could both enjoy a higher literature, building a common bond that would foster the nationhood of the Jewish people and dissolve gender boundaries within the Jewish community.

The second monologue aims to define the Jew in contrast to the non-Jew. It uses a Jewish woman's story to define the boundaries that distinguish the Jewish nation from the Christian one. However, its criticism of racism creates an opening to further the progressivism of Peretz's brand of nationalism, for in this representation of reality both the Jew and the non-Jew speak the same language (they converse in Polish in the second segment), share the same mail coaches, and share a common history. If minor differences are present from time to time, it does not amount to the total Jewish divorce from Poland that Zionist thinkers and writers often postulated.[33]

In order to create a sense of Jewish national community in the first monologue, Peretz uses two Jewish characters: Haim, the traditional husband who tells his story, and a listener-character who is a nonorthodox, modern man. The conversation between the two Jews in the mail coach, who are strangers, flows naturally, for they both belong to the same (Jewish) nation: "He told me everything at once, in a single breath; within minutes I learned that his name is Haim, that he is Yona Hrubeshover's son-in-law, Berl Konskivoler's son, and that the wealthy Merenstein from Lublin is related to him, an uncle on his mother's side. This uncle of his has almost a goyish household; non-kosher food he doesn't know if people eat there, but eating without washing first—he saw it for himself" (*Ale verk*, 2:67). In contrast, in the second story, Peretz stresses the Jewish character's prior relationship with the Christian Janek Polniewski (a Polish version of *Joe Smith*), which is a prerequisite to a meaningful conversation developing between the two characters. In an age of increasing ethnic tensions, a Jew and a non-Jew had to be represented as alien to each other, an image which is only strengthened by the fact that these two foreigners were in fact childhood friends, as we learn in the opening lines of the second segment:

> Another passenger joined me in the coach; and in the morning light, not only could I see him clearly, but I even recognized him. He was an old acquaintance. As children, we used to slide on the ice together and often played at making mud pies;

we were kind of buddies. Later, I went to the filthy and dark Jewish religious school, the *kheyder*, and he went to the bright and emancipated gymnasium. . . . Polniewski recognized me and embraced me, but before I even had time to speak with him, he immediately asked what I thought of the vile antisemitism. (2:75–76)

This second conversation justifies the first one's quest for inner unification (modern Jews with orthodox Jews, male Jews with female Jews) because it explores the difficulty of reaching outside the "imagined community."[34] The ironic-humorist tone of the first segment (the Haim segment) portrays problems inside the nation as solvable and not too terrible. It is followed by a harsher, borderline violent tone in the second segment (the Janek segment; the irony in the depiction of the schools is dark), which implies that issues between Jew and non-Jew are bitter and difficult to resolve.

The criticism of Haim for refusing to visit his poorer relatives while caring more about observing religious law (keeping kosher, handwashing) are the typical criticisms for a secular nationalist (the narrator) to make of a more religious and traditional counterpart. The setting of the story in a secular public space is inherently advantageous to the modern writer compared to his more religiously observant traveling companion. The polarity between the secular, nationalist Jew versus the "old," religious Jew, however milder, is no less vital in constructing the modern imagined community than the inter-national tension. In fact, it reveals an inner power struggle within the Jewish community for leadership.[35]

The stress on common language and costumes, which existed among Eastern European Jewry in the forms of the Yiddish language and the Jewish religion, weaves a common thread between urban middle-class Jews and the impoverished Jews of the little towns. The class system is not challenged here but rather restructured with the mediating help of the intelligentsia.[36] To overcome the inherent tension created by conflicting class interests, Peretz adds an interior monologue wherein the narrator expresses some bewilderment about how Haim recognized him as being Jewish despite his modern appearance: "until today I don't know how he recognized me as a Jew . . . perhaps I gave a Jewish groan? Perhaps he felt that my groan and his groan are one groan?" (מיין קרעכץ און זיין קרעכץ זענען איין קרעכץ?; 2:68).

Haim and the narrator share another exchange concerning the ethnic attributes of Jews that cannot simply be hidden by a change of clothing.

This time, Haim is bewildered to discover that his travel companion is a writer. "From this you make a living?" he asks. "I answer a truly Jewish answer: 'Feh!'" Shortly thereafter, Haim asks rhetorically, "What doesn't a Jew do for the sake of making a living?" (2:69). The humor functions here as a naturalizing tool of nationalist ideology. It suggests a shared peoplehood among Jews exists, and not just a shared religion. This motif of Jews being recognized as Jews even if they wear modern clothing, also significant in *Bilder fun a provints rayze*, is a tool in the construction of a modern Jewish identity in which *dos pintele yid* (the "little Jewish dot"[37]) is an organic part of his biological being.

Storytelling

אַז מע זאָל שרײַבן אמת פֿאַלט אים גאָרנישט אײַן That one writes the truth doesn't occur to him at all.)

—Peretz, "In postvogn"

The humor of the story also helps grapple with cultural-political questions, including the social status of the writer. Through its dual-monologue format, the text poses aesthetic questions of representation, narration, and the profession of the fiction writer. A major duality in the story is the one between high-minded modern literature ("Peretzian" literature) and widely popular and "interesting" lowbrow literature. The writer character considers how he could adapt Haim's oral story to a written one that people would actually read:

> I must admit, he began to interest me. A story about a young man from a small town and his bride who was raised in Warsaw and detests the small town . . . something might come out of this, I think. I must get more details, add something of my own to the plot, and I will have a novel. I will put in a convicted robber, mix in a few bankruptcies, throw in a dragon for good measure; this way I will also be interesting. (2:68)

This quotation is a pungent mockery of the popular Yiddish novels of the period, like Shomer's *Half Man, Half Monkey* (1888), the sensational title of which speaks for itself. Peretz himself never wrote a whole novel, so in that sense he was trying to attribute a low artistic value to a genre that he never mastered. The mockery by the Peretzian character (the listener) of the novel echoes Sholem Aleichem's critique of the Yiddish novel and his demand for a more "Jewish realistic" novel. While traditionally women were the main readers of Yiddish literature,[38] Peretz's goal, which he expressed explicitly in his essays, was to create highbrow literature that would also inspire modern Jewish men to serve as a national Jewish intelligentsia. This goal Peretz did not share with Sholem Aleichem, who wrote in 1889 that he wrote for the common people and about the common people and that only gradually could a highbrow Yiddish literature be established.[39]

Throughout the conversation with Haim, the tension between the writer's desire to be widely read and his desire to produce work that succeeds in delivering new aesthetic and political ideas to the people shines through. There are the "interesting" novels, and the need to make a living (Haim is certain the writer won the lottery if he can devote his time to thinking of stories), and there is the voice of the modern intellectual who looks at it all with a clear sense of irony ("this way I will also be interesting"). Peretz would solve these inconsistent goals in his later socialist writing, in which, I believe, he successfully combined accessibility with a meaningful progressive political agenda, but the tension is also present in this early text.

The modern conceptualization of literature, according to Terry Eagleton, was born out of the Romantic period of the nineteenth century, in the sense of being synonymous with the "imaginative." He writes, "the word 'imaginative' contains an ambiguity . . . it has a resonance of the descriptive term 'imaginative,' meaning 'literally untrue,' but is also of course an evaluative term, meaning 'visionary' or 'inventive.'"[40] Peretz rejects the "imaginative" as untrue and suggests that unlike his own works, the popular novels of his time lack any real vision or inventiveness. This concept "literature" is still incomprehensible to everyday people like Haim, just like the technology that enables incubators still perplexes him. Haim asks, "What are the stories good for, for the public? What's the point of them? What do people write in those booklets?" (2:69).

Haim's imaginative solution to the problem of "literature" is to feminize it. He claims it is "solely his wife" who is interested in literature out of boredom because she does not work outside the home or study. It is exactly this kind of gender-cultural division of labor, which both Peretz and Sholem Aleichem attributed to Shomer and his "unmanly novels," that Peretz wished to challenge; he aspired to develop his own concept of literature for Yiddish readers regardless of their gender.

Haim's wife can read several European languages as well as Yiddish. If she is not able to satisfy her cultural needs within a Jewish language, there is fear that a strong cultural force will distance her from "her tribe." Consequently, the fate of the Jewish nation is dependent upon the development of modern Yiddish literature—a literature that can interest both Jewish men (educated in traditional Jewish texts) and Jewish women (well-read in modern European literature). But if the "Jewish genders" can potentially become united under one Yiddish roof, this is naturally not the case for the outsider gentile, liberal as he may be. Liberal values of the prenationalist era are also put to the test.

Liberalism Revised

The Pole and the Jew of the second segment share a past that includes *lezen* (reading) texts of science and western classical literature during the period when Warsaw Positivism dominated the intellectual scene (1860s–1880s). The Jewish character (the same writer of the first segment) gives us a glimpse into his state of mind as he reminisces about his optimistic childhood plans and dreams: "I wanted to invent such a gun powder that would shoot really far, for hundreds of miles, for example a balloon that would fly up to the stars, so we could bring order there too!" (2:75). If there is a nostalgic tone to this telling of the past, it is delivered with a dose of irony (combining technology and destruction). The writer contemplates a theory of history in which the rising classes will need to find new methods to ensure their rule: "There are two kinds of periods in history: sometimes the best and the brightest person leads the masses, and—sometimes the masses drag the best and the brightest people down . . . as soon as bread and water become scarce, the ship-slaves rebel and they lead! First someone must be slaughtered, both to eat his meat and in order to still the murderous fury" (2:77). The text reflects a society at a crossroads: its liberal values are being put to the test. In Poland since 1863, liberalism carried with it a promise that if its economic plans were adopted, a new era of universal prosperity and harmony would arrive.[41] An era of prosperity did come, and by the end of the nineteenth century, Congress Poland was the most economically developed part of the Russian Empire.[42] However, its economic gains were concentrated in the hands of a select few, making for a perfect recipe for social disaster and opening the door for the rise of hate-filled nationalism in which the

Jew served as a cultural "other."[43] Such an atmosphere breeds a sense of despair, undermines the belief in the progress of humanity, and most often fosters antidemocratic tendencies in the society, tendencies that, according to "In postvogn," Jews are themselves not immune from.

In a sophisticated manner, Peretz lets his Jewish writer use the same antisemitic and racist rhetoric that the non-Jew Polniewski condemns. Before Polniewski even speaks, the writer presumes that his gentile friend has become an antisemite who believes Jews today are the "warts" that should be "cut off from Europe's pretty nose" (2:76). The Jewish character is subsequently caught by surprise upon hearing a strong, outspoken condemnation of antisemitism by Polniewski:

> "Antisemitism is an illness.... Politics uses antisemitism; a stone flies into the air, so Bismarck's assistant directs it at the window of the synagogue; if not, other windows would shatter. A protesting fist is raised, so they shove an emaciated, stooped, Jewish shoulder under it; if not, other bones would crack.... Who generally succumbs to illness? Weak children, old and feeble men and women, sick people. Who succumbs to a moral epidemic? The child of the masses, the effete aristocrat, and a few madmen who jump out of the crowd and lead the ailing in a wild dance! Only healthy minds endure!"
>
> "How many healthy minds are there among us?" I ask.
>
> "How many? Very few, unfortunately," answers Polniewski.
>
> We both remained sadly silent. (2:77)

Peretz here defamiliarizes and reverses the stereotypical roles: it is the gentile in the story who holds fast to his progressive values of equality despite a rising jingoistic wave in the public opinion, while the modern Jew rejects these values. The Peretzian character suspects that his Christian childhood friend, now an adult, married pharmacist, is not revealing the entire truth regarding his relationship with a young Jewish female patient of his. Polniewski credits the woman with curing him of fashionable Jewish hatred. The character of the modern Jewish writer offers the following stunning interior reflection on Polniewski's relationship with a Jewish woman:

> Who knows a person? Who knows what he's made of? I'm beginning to think that I have in front of me a Christian skunk, who sneaks into a Jewish chicken coop. He wrangles too much

over the fortune of Jewish women, too long he's looking for matches; he's ashamed of something! Why doesn't he want to "talk at length"? Why doesn't he want to tell me everything as it occurred, with all the details? Who knows what kind of a role he played in this thing, if not *the old role of the snake in the Garden of Eden!* What's the meaning his conscience wouldn't let him? Such a thing! A young Jewish married woman, why not! Once it was considered a duty to baptize [Jews], today he feels obliged to at least turn a Jewish woman against her God, her parents, her husband, and—her entire life.

This is the meaning of liberalism, to go into a prison, bringing with you a wave of fresh air, a bundle of sun beams, to wake the prisoner up, give him a piece of candy, and then to disappear . . . not to see how the prisoner gnashes his teeth when the rusty key turns back the lock; how anguished his face becomes, how stuffy the air becomes, how spasmodically he breathes, how he tears his own hair and flesh from his body, or how he moistens his moldy mice-bitten piece of bread with tears, if only he could still cry. . . .

Waking up a dark, sleepy, repressed Jewish woman's heart, so a sweet romantic tone would cling there, so a new, wild, unknown, or long-forgotten emotion would arouse; to kiss and then afterwards adieu! Shut the door! So her life would be sour and bitter. (2:82)

What a reader of modern Jewish literature might expect from an antisemitic gentile or from a reactionary rabbi, he gets in these lines from a supposedly modern and enlightened Jewish character. This character equates liberalism with an illusory candy for a prisoner, not as something granting him any genuine freedom. The non-Jew who confesses to his friend that he developed some strong emotions toward a young Jewish woman is demonized by the Jew as a predator who preys on young Jewish chickens. The gentile is further equated with the seductive biblical snake from the Garden of Eden. This interior reflection presents primal, tribal instincts of protecting one's own, serving as a watchdog of the Jewish nation, and rejecting the bourgeois myth of romantic love (which Sholem Aleichem felt a Jewish novel should reject), in favor of national loyalty.

The great irony Peretz masterfully produces here is that this anti-liberal interior reflection by the Jewish character comes in sharp contrast to his non-Jewish travel companion's insistence on *not* abandoning liberal values. In a way, Peretz confronts his own personal struggles with his past beliefs. In "To a Jewish Maiden Who Alienates Herself," a poem in Hebrew published five years prior to "Postvogn," he directed his arrows toward Jewish women for being "foreign" and condemned them for going out with a "corrupting goy" (a common motif that existed previously in the Yiddish and Hebrew *Haskalah* literature, and one that later reappeared in his career[44]). To whom is she foreign?

She is foreign "us," to the entire Jewish collective. She is accused of not using her Hebrew name, deceitfully using a goyish one; of conversing in French and not in her people's tongue (most likely Peretz is referring to Yiddish); of reading "Love poems, melodies of lust / They are not for us, sister, not for us!" Out of the poem's six stanzas, the following two stanzas deal with a similar theme to the one in the story, namely the biological survival of the Jewish nation:[45]

The best your parents have chosen for you	אלוף לנעוריך לך בחרו הוריך
An educated and honest young man,	נער משכיל גם דגול מרבבה
From his pretty eye a pure soul was reflected,	מעינו היפה נפש טהורה נשקפה
On his forehead floats a thought.	על מצחו מרחפת מחשבה
But alas, Hebrew maiden,	אך הה, עלמה עבריה
To your fiancé you are foreign.	את לחתנך נכריה!
[. . .]	[. .]
For a drunken goy, a nobody,	כי שר חמשים שכור, חדל אישים
As a solid peg he is stuck in your heart	כיתד נאמן תקוע בלבבך
For your heart desired golden buttons,	כי ליבך תאב כפתורי הזהב
He is your dream in the night when you sleep,	הוא חלומך בלילות על משכבך
Ha, Jewish maiden,	הה, עלמה עבריה
To us you are foreign!	את לנו נכריה!

The dichotomy here is so simplistic it could easily be read as parodic. The first type is a pure, educated man who comes from a similar background as the poem's addressee, someone your parents approve of. The second type is of a greedy non-Jew with an uncontrolled drinking problem. The latter is borrowed directly from the very common stereotype among

Eastern European Jewry that regards non-Jews as drunks who beat their wives. These are the clear choices for a young Jewish maiden. Matching up with non-Jews means "giving in" to both financial and sexual desire. "The nationalist discourse about women," writes Parush, "thus functioned as both a pretext for and means of appropriating the space of women and gaining mastery over it."[46]

This direct rejection of liberal values would be revisited and questioned throughout the conversation between the two traveling companions in the second segment of "In postvogn." An anti-Enlightenment sentiment exists among Jews, Peretz tells us. Largely, this sentiment is a direct response to persecution. While a cultural look inward has some merit, it is dangerous to draw excessive distinctions between peoples and make exclusion a value, lest it degenerate into racism. As the writer character alarmingly attests immediately after expressing his own chauvinistic thoughts, "we ate our fill so much with poison, with malice, with hatred, that when we are given bread with salt, we are also certain that it is poisoned . . . may our hand shiver out of pity, may a tear of compassion hang in our eye, and on our lips—consolation. . . . It's hard to believe! We are also infected; the epidemic is upon us too" (2:82). This distancing from the hint of Jewish racism at the end may be a first step in the creation of a progressive and culture-focused version of nationalism, also referred to as Diaspora nationalism. This movement drew extensively from Peretz's new Yiddish cultural project, through which Peretz sought to establish a respectable and modern Yiddish literature, a literature that was also suitable for men, to expand the base of Yiddish readership at the time—which mostly consisted of women. Both conversations in the mail coach are between male characters who discuss Jewish women. While this text shows that Peretz questions the anti-liberal sentiment that was present in the Jewish streets in terms of ethnic relations, women in his new national project have not yet gotten a seat in the "male coach."

From the Province to the City and Back

מיר גייען פֿון הויז צו הויז, פֿון נומער איינס אָן. איך ווייס אַליין, ווי ייִדן און ווי נישט־ייִדן וווינען, איך קוק נאָר אין פֿענצטער אַרײַן. פֿאַרגעלטע פֿענצטער איז אַ סימן פֿון "אתה בחרתנו," בפֿרט נאָך אויסגעהאַקטע שויבן, פֿאַרטרעטענע מיט קישעלעך און זעק . . . פֿאַר דאָס—בלומען־טעפּ און פֿאָרהאַנגען זענען סימנים מובהקים, אַז דאָ וווינט שוין אַזוינע, וואָס האָט נישט אַזוי פֿראַווע אויפֿן דלות ווי יענע . . .

—Peretz, *Bilder fun a provints rayze*[47]

Bilder fun a provints rayze: In Tomashover povyat um 1890 yor (Impressions of a journey through the provinces in the Tomaszów region around 1890; 1891) was the major Yiddish belletristic text Peretz produced during the early part of the 1890s. It drew an atmospheric image of despair and doubt, aimed to reflect the extreme alienation between the modern Jewish intelligentsia and small-town Jews, who were of the intelligentsia's "own people." Inspired by his participation in a statistical expedition deep into the Jewish Pale of Settlement, Peretz's work signifies the new "reportage" genre in Yiddish literature.[48] At the center of the drama is a Peretzian protagonist, the reporter acting as an agent of modernity, who encounters the "inferior provincials." The result of these encounters is a "tragic-comic drama of alienation."[49] I argue that his close encounter with Jewish poverty made Peretz doubt his ready-made positivist set of answers and sparked within him the notion that a different approach was needed to fix these social problems.

The failure of the modern national intelligentsia to lead the Jewish people into modernity was a message also related to Peretz's own problems reaching out to the intelligentsia.[50] The role Peretz assigns his protagonist is one of a failed mediator who exists between tradition and assimilation, between the shtetl and the big city, and between the assimilated Jan Bloch and the observant Jews who provided the subject matter for his research.[51] Peretz depicts one encounter between his modern protagonist and two young men at the house of a kosher butcher as one of sheer astonishment and foreignness toward him: "on their young faces appeared a kind of wonderment-fear, as if they have actually fallen down from one world into a second one."[52] The expedition has "discovered" Jewish poverty, as was its stated mission, but the protagonist questions the utility of his tool of scientific recording of data for *solving* the problem—thus subverting his own sense of optimism, forward looking, and essentially faith in the system that he expressed in his essays (in "Bildung" an alienated urban intelligentsia is useless in creating mass social change, but the effectiveness of their platform is not questioned). Before delving into the text itself, I will briefly examine how *Bilder* fits into the literary tradition of writing about poverty.

Representing Poverty

Writing about poverty was common in nineteenth-century fiction. Iconic European writers such as Dickens, Hugo, and Dostoyevsky (and Abramovitsh in Jewish literature) set standards for this theme. Accurately representing poverty was a major goal that was generally dealt with through realist fiction, a style that set out to represent social realities as they were rather than through rose-colored lenses. The genre was a corrective for works that were strictly occupied with the lives of the aristocracy.

In Yiddish literature, Sholem Aleichem became occupied with the ways Jewish poverty was being represented very early in his career. He thoroughly addressed this topic in his article "Jewish poverty in the best works of our Yiddish writers" (1888).[53] He opens by citing Nikolai A. Nekrasov (1821–78), the radical Russian poet and editor of Dostoyevsky, who had a great influence on Yiddish and Hebrew poets, with verses about the poor Russian masses.[54] The anarchist Yiddish poet Dovid Edelstadt (like the socialist B. Gorin) reworked some of Nekrasov's poetry into Yiddish, transferring its content to the reality of working-class Jews in America in the 1880s.[55] Sholem Aleichem, through Nekrasov, was setting the standards of what he expected from Yiddish writers: realistically depicting Jewish life, which, according to him, equated with depicting poverty.

Sholem Aleichem praises the early works of Abramovitsh (in particular his novella *Fishke the Lame: A Story of Jewish Poor People*, 1869) for depicting Jewish poverty in a realist way and not through a rosy lens, as the Yiddish writer Mordkhe Spektor does, and for not "degrading" his works by infusing them with stories of crime and intrigues, as popular novelists tend to do. Abramovitsh's poor may act cruelly, but they don't lack in feelings or in heart, for even a warm and good heart could be frozen by living a life of pressing poverty.[56] Moreover, Abramovitsh's poor protagonists are even more capable of achieving genuine feelings of romantic love than the modern, enlightened, "rationalist" Jew.[57] Sholem Aleichem also criticized writers who made distinctions between the Jewish and non-Jewish poor based on cultural stereotypes such as the "drunken goy." He asserts that the only difference between those two groups is that poverty among Jews is simply greater than anywhere else[58]—perhaps true regarding czarist Russia. But throughout his discussion, Sholem Aleichem pays little attention to the question of the poor's potential as agents of progressive social change (the discussion of the repressed emotions of Abramovitsh's poor stands out).

Patrick Greaney claims that discussion of the poor needs to simultaneously grapple with the question of their potential. Regarding nineteenth-century fiction, he makes the following argument:

> In the nineteenth century, the poor were associated with power. They were destitute, but they also embodied productive and

destructive forces. Their labor power and revolutionary potential situated them in the center of any wider consideration of Europe's political and economic reality as well as any reflection upon its future. The link between the poor and power also made them a focal point for the modernist aesthetic concern with the representation of potential and virtuality. If the treatment of the poor in literary and philosophical texts was to be faithful to their "powerful" constitution, they had to be represented not only in their actual state but also in relation to their potential.[59]

One wonders whether the notion of the poor as a force is to be found in Peretz's text, for he was certainly influenced by these artistic currents. Does Peretz show the potential of the poor as agents of progressive social change in *Bilder fun a provints rayze*, alongside the image of poverty? Consider for example the following passage taken from the segment in *Bilder* entitled "A yingele?" (A little boy?):

> A few small houses are standing stone blind. There goes a piece of dry bread, with or without herring. And maybe—night-time prayers are said without any supper . . . in one of the small houses stands the widow, who needs so little, and she pounds herself on her meager little chest while giving a long final confession. . . . My orphan has something else in mind. Dancing with his little foot, he lifts up his little head to the moon, which swims silly-aristocratically from out of one small flat inside the second one. He moans. Have you seen a star falling?—No:
> Oy—he says—I would have liked, that Messiah would come!
> What do you mean?
> I want the moon to become bigger! Mercy on it! It has indeed sinned, but to suffer for so long . . . it's been six thousand years already. . . .
> All and all two requests: from our father on earth—an additional onion, and from our father in the sky—that the moon would become bigger! An enormous desire gets a hold of me to tell him: relax! Your local father will soon marry; you will soon get a stepmother, become a stepchild, and will cry for a piece of bread! Waive the onion, forget the moon, think about bread! But I barely restrained myself.[60]

We read here the contradiction between the poor, skinny widow, who has accepted her fate and is patiently awaiting her death, and the orphan boy, who asks for more onion (reminiscent of Dickens's famous orphan), for redemption, and for the moon. Does Peretz address the potential of the poor through the character of the orphan? Moreover, does it constitute *revolutionary* potential, which would tap the power inherent in the poor? In the closing lines of the same segment, the following exchange between the orphan and the protagonist appears:

"Why," asks the boy, "Did God create such a way that each and every one of his creatures would eat something different?"
"Kid, if everybody would have gotten to eat alike, then everybody would have been equal."[61]

The word *glaykh* in Yiddish means "alike" but can also mean "equal." So, in the original Yiddish, the protagonist uses the same word for the amount of food and for the status of people. The orphan wonders about the injustice of the world and receives a somewhat cynical reply from the protagonist. The latter is willing to offer the poor the potential of climbing the social ladder (though not to abolish it), given the proper guidance from educated urban Jews like himself. The protagonist's views towards the orphan's ambitions are revealed in the interior monologue ("relax! Your local father will soon marry; you will soon get a stepmother, become a stepchild, and will cry for a piece of bread! Waive the onion, forget the moon, think about bread!"). He sees the boy's ambitions as unrealistic fantasies that only divert him from finding practical ways of getting bread (that is, real food and a living) for himself. His anger tempers the hope that the poor will imagine revolutionary change. Here, his critique is in staunch contrast to the satirical arrows Peretz directed just a few years later against his passive character Bontshe the Silent, who was incapable of asking for anything but a piece of bread.

The Journey to the Provinces

Peretz, the modern city Jew, traveled from the metropolis through the Tomaszów region of Poland. Being within Polish rule, this region had slightly better economic and social conditions than the Russian-controlled Pale of Settlement to the east.[62] Peretz was sent under the sponsorship of the financial giant Jan Bloch to study the Jews of the Pale. Bloch had close ties to the imperialist czar, was active in Jewish diplomacy, and later developed a relationship with Theodore Herzl.[63] Why was Jan Bloch interested in sponsoring a study about poor Jews?

On the surface, Bloch hoped to refute various antisemitic accusations against Jews, to promote liberal policies toward them, and to oppose discriminatory legislation. Allegedly, Bloch was interested in poor Jews because he shared a common origin with them. But under the auspices of helping minorities or defending moral and religious principles, the powerful frequently wish to expand their control over underdeveloped regions.[64] The suffering of Jews in peripheral countries could be wielded as a political tool in Jewish diplomacy. Under the patronage of the Jewish plutocracy, public and organizational activity was developed and directed toward the Jewish middle classes.[65] In this climate, an aspiring cultural leader such as Peretz, a middle-class Jew who was fluent in the national language (Polish) as well as Yiddish, was valued for his abilities to communicate with both the Yiddish-speaking "natives" and the authorities. Through his autobiographical protagonist, Peretz plays the role of the foreigner. Trying to appeal to the Jewish intelligentsia, he writes in the short introduction to *Bilder*, "People were turbulent. Libels over libels were pouring from all directions. It was decided among ourselves that one must acquaint himself with the regular everyday Jewish life, to see what is really going on in the small towns; to understand what people hope for, from what people live, what people do" (*Yudishe bibliyotek*, 2:54; *Ale verk*, 2:119). This paragraph uses the reportage style, reminiscent of a personal journal, to normalize the existence of Jewish nationhood.[66] It wishes to create a sense of community and intimacy among the Jewish intelligentsia ("among ourselves"). The intelligentsia, which needs to get "acquainted" with the "regular" life of small-time Jews, is placed here in the same boat of victimhood from antisemitic libels as the shtetl Jews. This nationalist-communal tendency is even strengthened in the later version of the text, when a line is added at the end of the introduction: "what the people say!" The word "people" here, "Dos folk," comes in the sense of nation or folk.[67] In a later part of *Bilder* entitled "Asekurirt," (Insured; segment 15), the protagonist is expressing his thoughts in anticipation of visiting another small town. He portrays himself as becoming better acquainted with shtetl life and simultaneously feeling more doubtful about his mission. He claims that he now knows what to expect in regard to accumulating data:

> Early in the morning I will begin writing down—I know beforehand what will be: if not 36 rubles a year, the earnings

will be 33 and 32. . . . I will find many professions and few blessings; factories of potash, many empty houses. . . .

I will meet abandoned children, who bathe themselves together with geese and ducks on the edge of the swamp; babies in their cradle tearing their lungs crying, the sick helpless in their beds, young husbands living with their in-laws and studying traditional books, young wives with raw silk wigs modest or immodest . . . with torpid eyes, carrying—a trough of fruit, a sack with onions, or an infant together with a sack of onions. . . .

But what about the statistics? Can one answer the question: how many empty bellies, empty teeth; or from how many people does [the appearance of] a thin piece of bread pull the eyes out of their sockets as if with tongs; or how many people actually died out of hunger—turns out an impropriate tavern, a thief and a horse thief? Whereas medicine wisely invented a machine which can measure your pulse and your heartbeat, statistics plays stupidly with numbers.

Does statistics know how many times or how—every time—how deep and how strong the heart pounded by a grandson of noble Spanish descent, the son of a great rabbi, or a landlord, before he committed a wrong for the first time? And how long afterward did it bleed?? Do statistics at least count the sleepless nights before and after? Does it calculate how many days of hunger, how many times the kids quivered with cramps, how many times you became physically ill with the first pouring of a glass of tainted bootleg liquor?

. . . I throw myself on the bed, I shut my eyes, and the good old rabbi's wife from synagogue appears in front of me. But,—she says with her childish silver voice—but, if after all is said and done, if it would turn out to be all right for you—would you, my child, cite the saying: *ve-amkho kulam tsadikim*? And are all your people righteous? (*Yudishe bibliyotek*, 2:123–24; *Ale verk*, 2:171–72)

In this choppy and erratic internal discussion about poverty, social injustice, and the brutal new economic playing field, Pertez redefines what is lawful and what is criminal and ties it all at the end to the national question, thereby politicizing it. The shtetl Jews are as ghosts to him, haunting his consciousness with images of human suffering and of want. No accumulation of more cold data or "statistics" would suffice in acutely expressing both the total human experience of living in poverty and the inner emotional world of the outsider ("of noble Spanish descent"? Peretz had Sephardic ancestry) encountering such suffering. The protagonist here is the urban writer arriving at the underdeveloped periphery, struggling to grasp what he sees, struggling to produce artistic content under such incomprehensible circumstances. Unlike the actual report he submitted to Bloch, he is writing this text in the "third world" language he shares with the "natives." Its segmented travelogue structure differentiates from the works produced strictly within the metropolis. By its Yiddish and journalistic nature, it simultaneously reports on the locals and produces a literary work that is accessible for the very same community of people it documents.

In this transitional work between positivism and proto-socialism, Peretz lacks any comprehensive solution to the poor Jews' problems, and he does not structurally and systematically address the problem of unequal economic development of his time.[68] One might argue that isn't his task in the first place but rather the reader's. However, by not suggesting any meaningful alternative, he is in practice suggesting working within the system, promoting an integration of Jews in the current world order. That said, by producing fine literature rather than any essay in sociology, he is able to stir emotion toward reality as a first step toward grasping its structural mechanisms and eventually confronting them. It is through literature that he can create empathy among readers toward their compatriots and stir anger toward the social reality that is responsible for people's misery.

Marc Caplan argues that the fragmented narrative structure of *Bilder* ostensibly suggests a negation of modernization or modernity and a resistance to nationalist ideology.[69] He maintains, not without justice, "that Peretz in the *Rayze-bilder* explicitly rejects the optimistic, progressive assumptions underlying the actual journey it ostensibly records."[70] But he goes as far as portraying Peretz as a stigmatic, Schopenhauerian pessimist, not taking into account that even if Peretz were influenced by Schopenhauer (through Polish mediation), there are various ways one can incorporate his ideas. I see pessimism in *Bilder* not as negating the hope for a better social order but rather—in line with Horkheimer's reading of Schopenhauer—as suggesting that the suffering can serve as a basis for revolutionary drive.[71] *Bilder* shows a protagonist whose limited, liberal, middle-class assumptions are shaken through the narrative of a series of intimate encounters with people of low socioeconomic strata. I see *Bilder* as a narrative of transition and transformation: Peretz's transition toward proto-socialism. Still fermenting and of low awareness at this point, he can only express his developing ideology through aesthetic rather than essayistic means. Therefore, the artistic techniques Peretz used—including the aforementioned interior monologue showing the writer's anticipation of the shtetl that he would see the next day and the reportage-like style of narration—merit further discussion.

Fire and Insanity in the Shtetl

The reportage style of *Bilder fun a provints rayze* gives a narrative structure that at first glance seems broken and fragmented.[72] The text is divided into twenty-four short segments, and often each segment corresponds to an encounter with a different character in the shtetl. This division into "personal segments" reflects Peretz's more atomized consciousness, but in fact each individual's story is just one example of the overwhelming social crisis that he encounters.

Insanity

The title of segment 19 in *Bilder*, "Der meshuge" (The crazy person), implies this singular crazy person is alone in this condition, rather than a whole society, but he could also be perceived as a representative character of a broader social condition. Crazy Yoyne sneaks into the protagonist's chambers:

> "Don't you want to write me down?" he asked softly. I didn't know what to answer. He assumes that silence equals confession, and already stands in the middle of the house. Scared and even more bewildered, I don't take my eyes off of him.
> "Write it down!" he said impatiently. "Should I hand you ink and a pen?" Not waiting for an answer, he pushes me toward the sofa, to the small desk with the writing material. "Write, please, write!" (*Ale verk*, 2:180)

The poor beggar—who begs for dinner, when his children are still in *kheyder* (2:182)—demands through the protagonist to be documented and heard. He wants his story to be written down; he seeks recognition. The physical act of writing, of documenting under imposition, is what Peretz was hired in real life to do for Jan Bloch. In his literary work, he reverses this situation of class subordination, making his Peretzian protagonist become the agent of the underprivileged, working for them, so to speak, rather than for the capitalist. This class reversal is parallel to the mental reversal—the upside-down perception of the world by the insane character, who expresses in psychological terms what is taking place socially.

Crazy Yoyne tells the protagonist how he was stoned by other people in the shtetl, until one stone that hit him in the head cost him his sanity: "Two or three times a day I have the dybbuk in my stomach,[73] then I speak out of my stomach. . . . I crow like a rooster. . . . I can't help myself at all, in any way" (*Yudishe bibliyotek*, 2:133; *Ale verk*, 2:181). The dybbuk literally forces you to stand in somebody else's shoes. Peretz uses it as a metaphor indicating the grave challenge it takes to show true feelings of sympathy and compassion toward the "others." Through these encounters between the modern and the underprivileged, Peretz tries to generate compassion, to advance social sensitivity and, moreover, national solidarity. Like "Crazy Yoyne," the protagonist himself goes through a profound transformation. His own gradual path toward insanity along the *Bilder* cycle is manifested by the shtetl ghosts he senses around him at the ending segments. The shtetl ghosts represent his attachment to and identification with the suffering characters he meets face-to-face in his journey. These dybbukim haunt him, and they should haunt his urban readers since they are all part of the same collective, the Jewish people.

Fire

The motifs of insanity and fire appear often in shtetl literature; a literature that was created by writers who left the small town in favor of the cities. These themes project images of social destruction and decay in the world they left behind. The small towns in *Bilder*, writes Miron, "are waiting for the first spark to burst into flames and for the first breeze to carry away their ashes."[74] It is the fire that wakes up the *Bilder* protagonist from his vision of being surrounded by shtetl ghosts who pay him a visit. By the end of the segment "Asekurirt," a fire in a house next door wakes up the protagonist.

The next segment, "Der nisref" (The burned), is the story of a person whose home was burned to the ground. For Peretz, this is an opportunity to redesign and reimagine the Jewish socioeconomic structure. For this purpose, he uses the "twisted mirror," or "grotesque analogy" technique to point out the impotence of the real world compared to the legendary and the mythical.[75] As the *Bilder* narrative progresses, we see the protagonist increasingly turning to the mythical style of storytelling, as a way of coping with the harsh social reality he encounters. The life story of the fire victim who lost his property in the tragic accident is framed as a story of "shtetl upward mobility." Through this framework, Peretz shows how pathetic the possibilities of professional advancement are in the backward shtetl economy. His agenda is to offer the alternative of real, *urban* upward mobility as a nonillusory possibility, with worthy social values to embrace. He ironically describes the shtetl social ladder in mythical terms:

> A Jewish livelihood can be such a ladder as Jacob our father saw in his dream. . . . How deeply is it buried in the ground, only the worm that lies under its feet knows. How high does it stand, only the stars that light it from above can know. We look up and we're dizzy. We look down, evermore deeper and deeper, and our guts turn and our faces become forever green.
>
> On this ladder angels go up and down . . . humans desperately climb up with their last bit of strength and fall down. A Jew, when he manages not to break his neck, and makes the blessing after escaping a great danger, no longer has the strength to climb up again. (*Yudishe bibliyotek*, 2:127; *Ale verk*, 2:175–76)

The social ladder portrayed here is better suited for angels and mythical beings than for humans. It is rooted in biblical tales and the mythology of the Jews becoming a people. But real people, living Jews, are incapable of climbing it. They remain closer to the worms under its feet with no possibility of going anywhere. The Jewish society in the shtetl is a dead-end society. Under such circumstances the *nisref*[76] lived his life. He "crawled" on such a ladder, as his personal story tells us:

> He "ran" in the village, and the ground burned under his bare feet. This Cain doesn't hear his brother's blood, only the cry of a woman and child crying: Food! But God helped. For a few years in a row he bought fantastic bargains; after a few years—he advanced from a "runner" to a "walker." At home there was ample food supply for a whole week, the mind became calmer, and he had time to feel that his feet have become swollen, that a father of six kids has to walk, not run, if he wants his feet to carry him at least until their bar mitzvah. . . . And God (with Ha-Shem's help) helped further; he is already a village

merchant! Which means he walks from one village to the next only when no opportunity comes up for him to earn meager pay. But when an opportunity comes up for him—he goes by vehicle.

God, blessed be He, helped further; after a couple of years he has his own horse and cart! And time doesn't stand still, he doesn't rest, God, blessed be He, helps—a horse becomes a couple of horses, the wheeled cart—a barouche. After that comes his own barouche driver! He is by now a crop merchant; first he trades with farmers, afterward—with landowners! And when God helps, people start to like you: first the lowest rank maintenance guy, afterward the steward, afterward the superintendent, afterward the lackey of the courtyard, and at the very end the count himself. Oh! Then he becomes a "settled" person in the shtetl. From being a barouche driver, he becomes a house servant, sells his horse and wagon, and in his pocket lays the earl's receipts. . . .

What is he now? In the shtetl he seems like the sun, around which the stars circulate; the smaller are merchants, and the larger comets are brokers. He shines and lights the whole shtetl with credit. To an antisemite[77] he seems like a spider sitting in the middle of his net, while the count is one of the flies who become entangled. . . . All of a sudden (in any event—for the shtetl) the count went bankrupt and our "sun-spider" or "spider-sun" suddenly lost everything. . . . Today I note one word: "*nisref*, burned"! I can add though: A man of eighty-two years, swollen feet, a family of seventeen persons. . . (*Yudishe bibliyotek*, 2:128–29; *Ale verk*, 2:176–77)

This highly ironic description of the socioeconomic structure of the shtetl and its "growth potential" is meant to appeal to Peretz's readership, many of whom are young adults in the process of leaving behind this world. Compared to every pathetic and useless aspect of shtetl society, the modern metropolis functions as its implicit mirror image. In the city, one can move up, the economy is growing, *real* jobs are available in modern professions. It is everything that the shtetl is not. This text is equally patronizing and ironic. It was this biting ironic style that later readers did not always grasp, mistaking Peretz for a writer of simple folktales. This strong sense of irony also dominates later additions made to *Bilder*,

Figure 1.1. Postcard featuring I. L. Peretz. William A. Rosenthall Judaica Collection, College of Charleston Libraries, Lowcountry Digital Library.

such as "Di toyte shtot" (The dead city). In that late segment, the level of the grotesque rises above anything in the original *Bilder*, as ghosts of shtetl Jews outnumber the so-called real Jews in this town. It is easier for dead Jews to survive than for living Jews, for the dead need no physical nourishment.

The Hebrew version, "Ir ha-metim" (City of the dead), contains some variations compared to the Yiddish one, and it includes a reference to the Yiddish *Bilder* for those who wish to understand the context of the first sentence: "Beshikvar hayamin, belekhti lemasa'i lekabets misparim" (Once upon a time, when I was going for my trip to gather numbers). It also contains a passage at the end that was omitted in the Yiddish version in which the storyteller rants against the inhabitants of the dead town. He tells how if somebody from the outside arrives and wants to address the larger questions of the day ("hunger and famine, Argentina and Palestine, 'wise' assimilationists, and 'pious' nationalists"), before he would even open his mouth, the stench and the decay would kill him, "and he would rise and walk in the world of the dead" (literally, "the world of fantasy," *olam hadimyon*). In Yiddish, Peretz wished to tone down this kind of elitist criticism against lower-class Jews, and it also didn't fit to come out of the character of the old Jew.[78]

The protagonist repeatedly tells his readers how the trip transformed him. He adopts the idiom of the shtetl inhabitants (like using the term *nisref* and not a Germanized Yiddish word), in the process becoming a "national" writer who leads the people to modernity. As a national writer, Peretz in *Bilder* is concerned primarily with Jewish suffering (in keeping with the mission of the expedition) and ignores the non-Jewish presence in the shtetl, as was typical in Yiddish literature of the time. The distinctive economic function of the Jews as middlemen between the landowner and the farmer, as a "people-class" of mostly merchants,[79] supported a separate Jewish language (i.e., Yiddish). As the language of a separate Jewish life, Yiddish formed the basis of a Jewish consciousness separate from its environment. This distinction in languages would form a basis for a strand in Jewish politics that would become a primary force for social justice. After *Bilder*, Peretz was now on the verge of becoming one of the early forebears of this cultural-political strand.

Chapter 2

A Radical Shift

Becoming a Social-Protest Writer

> I write for myself, for my own pleasure; and if sometimes I remember the reader, then he is someone from the highest level of society, a man who has read and studied in a living language.
>
> —I. L. Peretz in a letter to Sholem Aleichem, 1888

> You haven't suffered the agony of the workers and yet you wish to describe them. . . . I don't ask for firsthand experience; you need not be a worker yourself; if only "you would not turn away from your own flesh," you will feel like the worker and you will live his sorrow. But that time has not yet come for you.
>
> —I. L. Peretz in a letter to the young writer Yitskhok-Yankev Propus, 1899

You Know That You Can Count Me In

When Peretz became acquainted with Jewish socialists during the early to mid 1890s, he was inspired to create literature primarily devoted to exploring social relations and exposing the suffering in society. He committed many of his artistic productions during the rest of the 1890s to political aims. He sought to give a voice to the voiceless, and he encouraged others to speak up and challenge the existing social order, but he was never one to give readymade solutions to his readers. Peretz's sense of excitement about the new organizational ideas brewing among urban Jewish workers is reflected in his writings of the period. These were the Jews who had been recently uprooted from rural towns like those Peretz visited during his statistical expeditions. The rise in popularity of Marxism, the strike wave in the Jewish trades in the early 1890s in the northwestern region of the Pale, and the use of Yiddish would all help to create a mass movement of Jewish workers[1] and to attract and radicalize parts of the Jewish intelligentsia.

While some of Peretz's texts might correctly be perceived as being aimed at helping people recognize political agitation was in their self-interest, Peretz was aware of the danger of losing his artistic credibility due to excessive partisanship. And, in fact, he was also influential in his uncompromising artistic approach. The Yiddish writer and Bundist pioneer B. Gorin (1868–1925, also known as Yitskhok Goyda) credited Peretz for influencing his writing, acknowledging that under Peretz's influence "the pamphleteer element had totally disappeared from my belletristic work."[2]

Peretz's transformation from a pro-capitalism liberal positivist to leaning toward socialism—caused, to some degree, by the *Bilder* experience and his increasing relations with Jewish socialist activists (proto-Bundists) in Warsaw—inspired him to produce the valuable and important Yiddish literature of social protest, which is the focus of this chapter. The chapter also examines Peretz's radicalism as an editor, especially in his journal *Di yontef bletlekh* (The holiday pages), which included his own writing and works by others. In this chapter I argue that through the *Yontef bletlekh*, Peretz was a cultural producer who aligned himself with the Jewish working classes. He was his own publisher, and, together with Dovid Pinski, he established a distribution network that was part of an alternative production technique to the capital-driven publishing business. While these endeavors did not last long because their economic base was too weak to sustain itself, Peretz's efforts cannot be overstated in this regard. His cultural productions during those years laid the foundation for the establishment of one of the most important modern political parties to emerge out of the Eastern European Jewish world—the Bund.

Bontshe Shvayg: The Workers Will Not Be Silent

The first major textual representation of Peretz's radicalism can be found in his Yiddish short story "Bontshe shvayg" (Bontshe the Silent; 1894).[3] The story was first published in an American newspaper, *Arbeter tsaytung* (Workers' paper), and only later in Eastern Europe. Such a progression for a Yiddish text from the New World back to the Old World was not an uncommon phenomenon given that the Yiddish press was forbidden under czarist rule until the early twentieth century. In Eastern Europe it was published in *Literatur un lebn,* one of Peretz's almanacs of that period.⁴

"Bontshe shvayg" deals with the perpetually downtrodden yet silent and passive character of Bontshe, who dies and goes to heaven, where he is received with great honor for the first time in his existence. The dramatic action unfolds in the heavenly courts, where Bontshe's sorrowful life is judged favorably by the angels, and he is ultimately granted his every wish as a reward. But Bontshe famously responds that all he really wants is to receive every morning "a heyse bulke mit frisher puter," a hot roll with fresh butter.⁵

This story has frequently been misread. For instance, Zionist leader Berl Katznelson viewed Bontshe as "the epitome of the small-town Jewish poor and the Jewish apprentice,"⁶ whereas the modern urban experience is key to "Bontshe shvayg." One of the keys to the story is that a cold and hungry Bontshe was driven from his small town to the big city in search of work:

> In a deceiving, wet spring night, he arrived in the big city, entering as a drop of water into the sea, and although he spent that same night in prison . . . he was silent, he didn't ask why, or for what. He went out and looked for the hardest work! But he was silent!
>
> Harder than the work itself was to find it—he was silent! . . .
>
> Splashed from another's mud, being spat upon from others' mouths, chased from sidewalks with his heavy load down in the streets between carriages, carts, and tramways, looking death in the eyes every minute—he was silent! (*Ale verk*, 2:417)

The scene Peretz depicts here is firmly located in the modern experience of urbanization and proletarianization, a setting that is quite different from the view of modernity found in his earlier major Yiddish prose text *Bilder fun a provints rayze*. There, he referred to the alleged promise held out to small-town folk that if they would just adapt and become modern, then their situation would fundamentally improve. In "Bontshe," just wanting to work is insufficient: jobs are scarce, and, for the few who do find work, conditions are grueling and demeaning.

There is no trace in the story of any existing social institution (Jewish or otherwise) able to adequately assist the masses of Bontshes. Instead, the burden of support falls entirely on the shoulders of the suffering individuals themselves. During those early years (1890 through 1897), various socialist Jewish groups were emerging in Eastern Europe, including in Warsaw. The General Union of Jewish Workers in Lithuania, Poland, and Russia, known as the Bund, was established in 1897 in Vilna (now Vilnius). Over the years, the Bund adopted a platform that prominently stressed a Jewish-nationalist agenda,[7] but one that would ultimately lead to a form of class-nationalist politics, not a nationalist-chauvinist agenda. Peretz was also close to Jewish socialists who were active in the Polish Socialist Party (PPS, founded in 1892–93), such as the brother-and-sister team Julius and Esther Golde. He went to some of their meetings and gave talks there.[8] The PPS also issued its propaganda material in Yiddish, addressing the same readers as the Bund. Unlike the Bund, which sought one Jewish social democratic party for all the Jews in the Pale and was closely aligned with Russia, the PPS was a Polish party that pushed for Polish national independence as a basis for its socialist agenda.[9] Peretz presents all of these emerging groups with the challenge of Bontshe.

Figure 2.1. Jack Gilford plays Peretz's character Bontshe Shvayg on US television, in the middle segment of *The World of Sholom Aleichem*, in 1959. More than anger toward the passive Bontshe, as in the original text, Gilford's post-Holocaust portrayal generated empathy for the innocent European Jew. Video still from "Sholom Aleichem—Zero Mostel, Nancy Walker, Gertrude Berg, Charlotte Rae," uploaded to YouTube by Alan Eichler, 2017.

In "Bontshe shvayg," Peretz bemoans the passivity of his main character. He ends the story with the Persecuting Angel bursting out in laughter considering Bontshe's oddly modest request. In order to relate to his semitraditional readers, Peretz staged his call for a revolt of working-class Jews against their oppressors in a familiar Jewish setting, namely the heavenly court, filled with biblical characters and the angels. This setting, which also helped Peretz divert the censors, led some of Peretz's readers and critics to ignore the critical subversive aspects of the story. A known example was the dramatization of "Bontshe" in mid-century New York, designed to fit the American stage during the McCarthy era, by a cast and production crew who were all banned from appearing in movies and on TV due to their leftist political views. In their play *The World of Sholom Aleichem*, the cast and crew used the silent Bontshe to show that they would not remain silent. Nevertheless, even in their adaptation they wove in a sense of empathy toward the passive character.[10]

Nahum Sokolow correctly described the story as reflecting a "general idea but with a local hue."[11] Sokolow's interpretation opposes the idea that Peretz had intended Bontshe to be purely a representation of the Jewish people, in which case his tale would become merely a protest against Jewish passivity.[12] But in fact, as Sokolow argues, Peretz himself was dismissive of readers who were sure that Bontshe was an allegory for the Jewish people. Jacob Dinezon's memoir tells us that

> when Peretz published "Bontshe Shvayg," he received a letter from one of his readers, with warm thanks for the pleasure and, by the way, the reader explains, that he soon understood that in "Bontshe Shvayg" Peretz meant the "Jewish People," which becomes so hunted and tormented—the poor thing. . . . Peretz then handed me the letter with the words: "That's *litvakes* for you! It's good that I still live and can swear to your *litvak*, that I didn't have in mind the Jewish People; whom I did have in mind, you obviously know."[13]

Rozentsvayg adds that the worker-reader understood very well whom Peretz meant: not the Jewish people, but the working people. The censor of Vilnius understood this, too, and chose not to permit the story to be published as a separate book, for fear that it would stir revolutionary fervor.[14] But what was is it about "Bontshe" and its radicalism that elicited such strong reactions from the authorities? Why does this allegorical story, which Rozentsvayg claims belongs to the *kamf-genre* (struggle-genre), play such a crucial role in the development of the working-class Yiddish reader? In Peretz's turbulent times, within a radical milieu, to be born silent, live silently, die in silence, and when buried become even more silent was a much-critiqued way of life. The message is thus: to resist oppression, Bontshe would need a voice.

Peretz's story can be adapted into many languages and cultures without diluting its message: oppressed people whose dignity has been shattered must take a good look in the provocative mirror that Peretz laid before them and start to claim their rights. For even the finest lawyer of the heavenly court cannot assist one who remains passive and silent, lacking any consciousness of their condition. In this call for action and activism, I see the launch of Peretz's radical socialist period.

Weaving the Revolution

In the years after "Bontshe shvayg," Peretz strengthened his relations with Jewish labor activists and added works to his radical repertoire that explicitly dealt with labor activism, such as his short story "Veber-libe: Dertseylung in briv" (Weaver-Love: Story in letters). The story was first published in an American socialist paper, *Ovnt blat*, in 1897 under a pseudonym and only later circulated back to Eastern Europe.[15] It is an epistolary short story written from the viewpoint of a modern working man, a weaver, who sends a series of letters to his older, more traditional future brother-in-law, a simple shoemaker. In his letters, the protagonist lays out his frustrations about his low socioeconomic status. He articulates the plight of workers in general, thus providing a kind of a crash course in labor-capital relations. The weaver complains that poverty hurts the lives of everyday people and expresses anger toward the economic system that created such injustice. His letters discuss his attempts to change the system by forming labor organizations.

Written in a simple Yiddish that the traditional shoemaker would understand, Peretz is effectively communicating socialist ideas to working-class readers in a language that resonates with them. The epistolary structure, interwoven with a romantic plot and a great deal of irony, is what makes this text a work of art rather than a simple political pamphlet or essay. Arguably, "Weaver-Love" is Peretz's most radical literary text, and he insisted on reading it at an illegal workers' meeting despite the text being still under the censor's review.[16] The weaver's active radicalism represents the opposite of Bontshe's passive nature and lack of class consciousness.

The story itself took much of its socialist agitation material from the brochure *Kto z czego żyje?* (By what do we live?; 1881) by the prominent Polish socialist Szymon Dickstein (1858–84). *By what do we live?* is one of the most celebrated Marxist publications to appear before World War I—a kind of a popularized version of Marx's *Das Kapital*. The Yiddish translation from Polish, *Fun vos eyner lebt?* (1887), appeared in London and was reprinted and disseminated numerous times during the prewar years, particularly by the Bund and the Polish Socialist Party.[17] Its significance is vividly conveyed by the way the Warsawian socialist activist Yitskhok Mordkhe Pesakhzon describes enthusiastically reading the brochure alone in a room in 1892 as an eye-opener to Marxist teachings.[18] The brochure makes the solution to social problems very clear: following Marx's platform, the answer is that "the entire land" and "all the factories in the entire country should be owned by all the workers; it should be their joint property."[19] But how exactly to implement this solution the brochure leaves as an open question to the reader.[20] It seems that this lack of a specific answer bothered Peretz. And, indeed, "Weaver-Love" challenges the ease with which this question—which even the brochure itself considers to be "the most important question" ("di vikhtikste frage")—is left unanswered.

In taking weavers as an example, Peretz was likely influenced by Gerhart Hauptmann's popular naturalist German play *Die Weber* (written in 1892 and performed on stage in 1894). The play depicted a workers' revolt based on the historical weavers' revolt in Schlesien in 1844. Peretz did not adopt Hauptmann's unique method of creating a drama of "social characters," in which the whole social class of working people is represented as one character rather than as individual victims.[21] Instead, continuing with the approach he took in *Bilder*, Peretz here adopts the individual-protagonist format. Like Hauptmann, Peretz also deals in "Weaver-Love" with the less sympathetic, less desirable, and sometimes violent aspects of his characters that such social struggles contain, in part because of the woes of the weavers themselves (the weaver tries to convince his home-base crowd of workers of the merits of nonviolent social struggle, but that does not gain him popularity among them).

"Weaver-Love" was published the same year that the Bund was officially founded (1897), and in it, I argue, Peretz shows support for the Bund's ideological line. The specific task of the Bund at its founding was

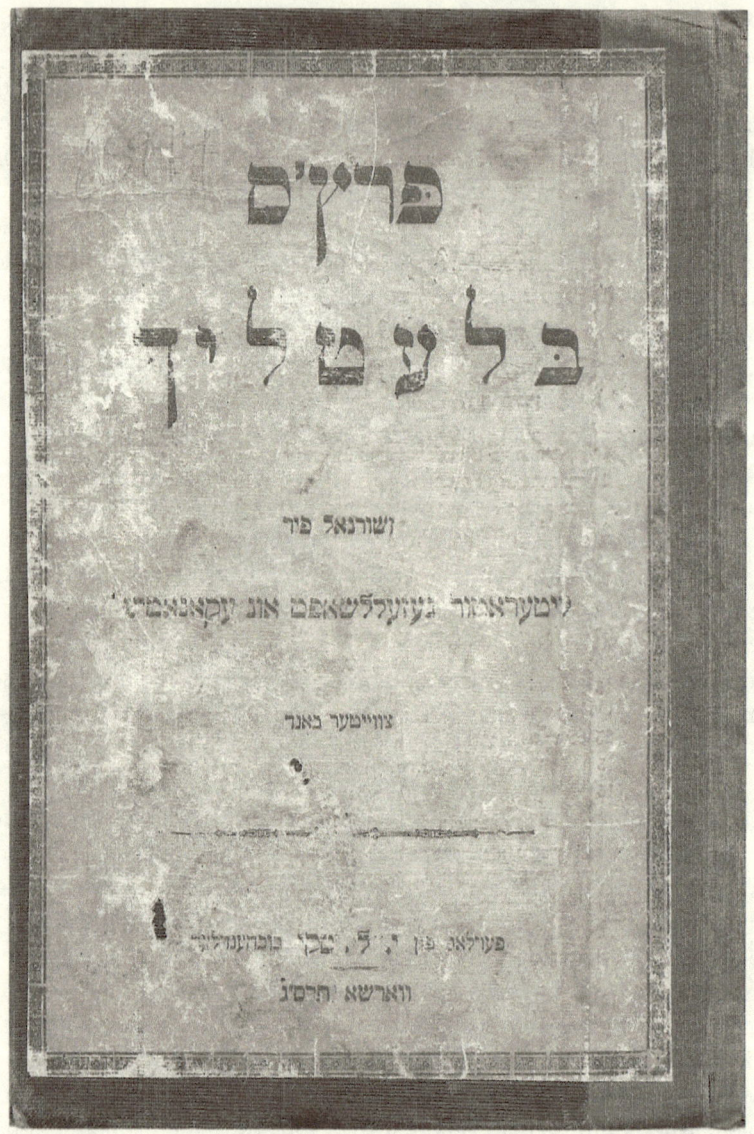

Figure 2.2. Cover of the Yiddish version of the 1881 brochure "Kto z czego żyje?" (By what do we live?) by the prominent Polish socialist Szymon Dickstein. It was one of the most celebrated Marxist publications to appear before World War I—a kind of a popularized version of Marx's *Das Kapital*. The Yiddish translation, *Fun vos eyner lebt?* (1887), appeared in London and was reprinted and disseminated numerous times during the prewar years, particularly by the Bund and the Polish Socialist Party, and it in turn influenced Peretz. Steven Spielberg Digital Yiddish Library.

"to lead the struggle for equality of civil rights for the Jews" and to be "an autonomous organization within the future Russian party . . . [that] would have a certain degree of freedom in issues relating specifically to the Jewish proletariat."[22] The unique platform and identity that the Bund offered to the Eastern European Jewish masses is described in this passage by Yoav Peled:

> The bonds of social solidarity . . . tied Jewish workers to neither their class nor to their ethnic group in an unproblematic manner. Their identity, therefore, was that of an *ethnic class fraction*, connected in both solidarity and conflict to the non-Jewish working class and to the Jewish community at the same time. This complex identity can explain . . . why the Bund, which sought to represent the political consciousness of Jewish workers, was committed both to a class struggle within the peripheral Jewish ethnic group and to a forceful defense of that group's cultural identity vis-à-vis the larger society.[23]

In "Weaver-Love," Peretz writes a story about the struggle of Jewish workers against exploitation, in a sense illustrating the Bund's nascent ideals. Historically, the general strike of Jewish weavers of 1887 is credited as marking the beginning of the Jewish labor movement in the Pale.[24] Thus, in this story, Peretz transports the reader to those formative days that eventually led to the movement's actual founding in 1897.

The Yiddish language is mentioned in a story within a story contained in "Weaver-Love" that expresses great disappointment with the promise of new prosperity that came with capitalist development. This inner story recounts the destructive invasion of a "capitalist sorcerer" into a premodern pious shtetl; as the narrator mourns the dissolution of the community, Yiddish figures as a marker of spiritual value: "And when people sold out everything, the sorcerer took power and began to torment the shtetl with diseases and all sorts of illnesses. . . . And nothing exists to save you, no mezuzah on the door, no amulet on the window; no Yiddish word at home!" (*Ale verk*, 2:502). By validating the spiritual value of the Yiddish language through pointing to the absence of the "Yiddish word at home," Peretz injects a modern-language-centered ideology into his imagined traditional Jewish world. In political terms, he has added a nationalist flavor to the emerging anti-capitalist sentiment. Thus, the direction Peretz pursues is not one of a strict internationalist class struggle but instead, as the Bund advocated, one of struggle for the ethno-class faction, the Yiddish-speaking working class.

In fact, the term *bund* even appears in "Weaver-Love." The phrase "to bind a broom" (*tsu bindn a bezem*) is repeated several times in the story, as in the following example: "If every lone weaver is, taken separately, a weak, soft twig, whom the worst contractor wraps, if he wants, around his finger, everybody together could have been a terribly strong broom to sweep away and to throw out something even bigger than the contractor with the garbage; but with what does one *bind* a broom?" (נאָר מיט וואָס בינדט מען דעם בעזעם?; *Ale verk*, 2:510). The phrase *tsu bindn a bezem* stems from the Italian word *fascio* (literally, a bundle of sticks), which meant in nineteenth-century politics "strength through unity" (representing the unity of politics, industry, and labor). The word symbolized the contrast between the fragility of one stick on its own and the conjoined strength of a bundle.[25] And *bezem* also alludes in this case to the new movement's name—the Bund (literally, bond)—and to its socialist, working-class ideal of unity. The struggle for human unity is apparent in "Weaver-Love" when the story refers to the workers joining together to resist the outsourcing of their labor to a middleman (*der loynketnik*).

The struggle for human unity also reveals itself in the private realm through the romantic intrigue that is interwoven in the plot concerning the workers' struggle. Throughout his letters to his future brother-in-law, the shoemaker, the weaver attempts to maintain his romantic ties with his fiancée, Miriam. Because he cannot afford to marry her, he uses a series of excuses to postpone or avoid the deed. This happens to the growing dismay of her brother, who is left to support her himself. The fundamental stalling technique the weaver uses initially is his stories about the labor struggles, through which we understand the shoemaker responds to the protagonist's letters and might even be convinced by his arguments. The end of the last letter the protagonist writes to the shoemaker weaves together the social struggle with the romantic plot that underlies the entire story:

> The whole time that you didn't receive letters from me, I was in prison doing time, and God knows why? Only later, when they found out for certain that I stayed away from violence and guts slashing, I was released. But I was told to go out of the city for a couple of years ... a weaver, they say, needs to sit and work, not to jump on tables and speak. ... Bad, but

Figure 2.3. Illustration from the Soviet edition of "Weaver-Love" (Moscow, 1947), an epistolary proletarian story. Steven Spielberg Digital Yiddish Library.

two things comfort me! I've planted a seed and I am certain that it will grow. [...] And second, darling Miriam's wish will be fulfilled and we will see each other ... see each other very soon. ... Just prepare a bit of salt, to rub me on my shoulders; they were slightly hacked... Yours... (*Ale verk*, 2:514–15)

For Peretz, the modern capitalist system fails to deliver human unity or social cohesion: it prevents marriages from being fulfilled, and it only strengthens the animosity between people. This outcome of the unfulfilled marriage underlines the story's social content and represents a relatively modern message for its time. Perhaps the weaver believes that he has planted the seeds for the future workers' uprising but that his own seed will not be planted. This ending expresses a sense of optimism that is atypical to naturalist fiction (such as "Bontshe shvayg") but that is also a well-recognized feature of Hauptmann's naturalist play *Die Weber*. Both weaver stories portray people who struggle against oppression and bear great suffering but whose souls are not stifled.[26]

Aesthetically, unlike in Hauptmann's drama, in Peretz's text the voice of the individual is at the very center of the narration. Almost all the letters are written by one protagonist. Furthermore, the epistolary genre itself was important in constructing the individual subject. It represents the increasingly sophisticated ways in which fiction presented individual psychology, and the genre is significant in the history of third-person narrative.[27] Peretz's particular use of this genre in "Weaver-Love" shows that the working class is developing a subjective consciousness of its own, as well as a class consciousness.

The cause of the Jewish weavers serves Peretz in "Weaver-Love" as a literary laboratory for examining the merits of pro-labor Jewish politics that use "Jewishness" as the organizational framework in the struggle for equality. The text shows some ambivalence toward the fight itself, mainly because any fight might involve violence, and because the fight would exact a dear price from its participants. However, in the last account, Peretz's text demonstrates sympathy for the moral cause of fighting for the rights of the working class. "I've planted a seed and I am certain that it will grow" ("ikh hob a zomen gevorfn un ikh bin zikher, az er vet vaksn"), writes the weaver-protagonist toward the end of his last letter, leaving readers with a sense of optimism.[28] The struggle for human dignity lies at the heart of "Weaver-Love," and this struggle is thoroughly desirable even if it fails.

Anger Is an Energy: Jewish Women in Peretz's Work

In his stories centered on Jewish women, Peretz protests the injustice of their lower social status in a progressive tone. One can ask, though, does he present ideas that are truly revolutionary, like his writings regarding labor issues and the plight of the poor? Or does he fall short in this regard? Ruth Adler, for example, presents the more common perception on the matter when she describes Peretz as "a champion of women's rights . . . [who] distinguished himself by *identifying* with woman in his efforts to combat the social ills of his day and particularly . . . in his psychological struggle for personal identity."[29] In contrast, Dan Miron claims that Peretz did not express ideas that the *Haskalah* literature has not already presented before him—namely, the heavy influence he received from the poetics of the great *Haskalah* Hebrew poet Yehuda Leyb Gordon (known by his acronym, Yalag; 1830–92).[30] However, I argue here, somewhat in between Adler and Miron, that although they are not revolutionary (one can find linkage of the status of women to broader social ills in the work of pervious Jewish authors as well), one can read in Peretz's stories centered on female protagonists, particularly after 1893, an innovative edginess that is unique to Peretz and is half a step beyond the *Haskalah* writers. Take Peretz's Yiddish story "A kaas fun a yidene" (Anger of a Jewish woman; 1893), which includes criticism of the oppressive Jewish gendered division of labor. Indeed, Peretz's message, borrowed from Yalag, should be interpreted in a *maskilic* vein rather than as socialist.[31] However, I argue that the story's ending with its possibility of a future change does give it a radical edge.

In a personal letter originally written in Russian, Peretz adds his very own Yiddish translation of the famous Hebrew *maskilic* poem by Yalag that dealt with the low status of women in traditional Jewish society, "Kotso shel Yud" (The tip of the Yud; 1878). Its opening stanza in Peretz's Yiddish translation resonates with the way he will later describe Bontshe: "Jewish woman, he knows your life; / You are born in silence, you are lost in silence" (יודישע פרויא, אים בעקאָנט איז דיין לעבן\ שטיל ווערסטי\ געבוירען, שטיל ווערסטי פערלוירען.).[32]

In "Anger of a Jewish woman," Peretz establishes a setting of Jewish poverty: in a tiny, dark house with worn furniture, broken dishes, and barely any food lives a poor couple with a baby. The husband does not work or provide for the family but instead studies Jewish religious texts all day. Like the *maskilim*, Peretz was adamantly opposed to idle Jewish men who eschewed work in favor of studying holy texts and for whom gaining a livelihood was considered *bitl toyre* (contempt of the Torah). As a result of the couple's quarrel, the husband angrily leaves the house for the *bes-medresh* (the study and prayer house). What happens next can be viewed as an attempt by Peretz to examine the *Haskalah* ideal of the woman setting the moral tone for the family. In the center of "Anger of a Jewish woman," Peretz puts an undernourished, breastfeeding woman who prefers to take her own life (an act which constitutes a major sin according to Jewish law[33]) by hanging rather than suffer the torment of living with her idle husband. Only her baby's cry makes her untie the rope around her neck and breastfeed her child: "'Bastard! He doesn't even let me hang myself! Not even to hang myself peacefully! He wants to breastfeed . . . to breastfeed he wants . . . oh! Poison you would suck out of my breast! Poison! Take, glutton, take!' she screams in a single breath, and shoves her skinny breast inside the skinny kid's mouth. 'Here, suck, bite!'" (*Ale verk*, 2:234). In this story's ending, losing one's mind and attempting suicide are explained in part by social categories of poverty and gender inequality, not strictly by one's private individual experience or genetic flaw.[34] While the husband tries to show his superiority through his knowledge of sacred books and by wielding the threat of ancient violence (he threatens her with the Jewish mythological ways of killings, the "arba mitot bet din," or "four legal methods of execution," which are punishments for contempt of the Torah, thus expanding the family story into Jewish-epic proportions), the wife proves that she intuitively understands those same scholarly discussions. She tells him that his idleness is in effect equivalent to idol worship (a sin that, according to Jewish law, you are permitted to take your life in order to avoid), thus refuting his claim that gainful work is a rejection of the Torah. Her decision to continue living to feed her child and not take him with her to the grave expresses a bold willingness to fight in the face of an extreme challenge. Herein lies the possibility of resistance. Since anger is the strongest drive for political action,[35] Peretz's angry female character is not passively accepting her fate; instead, she is actively protesting it. This unlettered "market wife" may well be one of the most radical characters in any of Peretz's stories.

Proponents of *Haskalah* regarded women's work outside the home as something that would lead them to abdicate their maternal obligations and abandon their children to their own devices.[36] However, Peretz emphasizes here that it is the husband's idleness in the face of the wife's reliance on him that threatens the health of both the wife and her child. The watery milk the baby gets from his angry and suicidal mother at the end of the story is the fuel that will help him grow up into an angry adult who is capable of social revolution.

The edginess of "Anger of a Jewish woman" becomes sharper when one compares it to the older, Hebrew version of this story entitled "Eshet khaver" (A friend's wife; 1890).[37] First, one sees that the powerful word "anger" (the political motivator) is not part of its title.[38] Second, in the older version, the social context of poverty and economic pressure is weakened as the central plot driver because the reasoning of a genetic flaw is added (the wife's uncle had hanged himself as a result of mental illness, a fact that both the husband and the wife mention). And third, in the Hebrew version, the wife gives her crying baby her "skinny finger" to suck on, and not the "revolutionary milk" the wife feeds him in the later Yiddish version. The latter difference applies also to the poetic version of these stories, the Yiddish poem "R' Khanine Ben-Dose" (Mr. Hanina Ben-Dosa; 1891), which includes many of the same motifs as the stories in prose but concludes with a passive, cynical tone rather than an active, angry one. Both earlier versions give a strong indication of the radical shift Peretz experienced after they were first written.

Another example of Peretz's protest literature against the oppression of women is his epistolary short story "Ha-isha Marat Khana" (The wife Mrs. Hanna; published in Hebrew in 1896 and in Yiddish in 1901). It consists of a set of letters addressed to the female character Mrs. Hanna by her relatives, who constantly try to deprive her of her rights. Her husband is named Menakhem Mendel, just like Sholem Aleichem's famous protagonist from his epistolary novel *Menakhem Mendl*, which featured the comic correspondence between Menakhem Mendl and his wife, Sheyne Sheyndl.

The character of the wife in Peretz's story is a kind of female Bontshe Shvayg because her own letters are not published in the story, meaning her own voice is not heard. In effect, she is silent about being exploited by her family members. Peretz was not copying Sholem Aleichem by using the name Menakhem Mendel as a protagonist in an epistolary story (the epistolary genre in Yiddish literature predates Sholem Aleichem by one hundred years). Also, even though a great many of Sholem Aleichem's monologues are given by female protagonists, Sholem Aleichem never gave a woman as much of a voice in his stories as Peretz did here and in other works.

When one first compares the gloomy "Anger of a Jewish woman" with Peretz's Yiddish story "Sholom Bayis" (Domestic peace; 1891), one might think that they strongly contradict each other. In "Domestic Peace" we find the portrait of a traditional couple, smiling and loving despite being struck by poverty. The husband asks his wife, "How many times do the kids give you trouble? I myself become angry at times. . . . Nu, do I hear a curse word from you, as others do from their wives?" And to that his wife answers, "You are nevertheless a good father, and a good husband." Then, "the couple looks into each other's eyes so nicely, so warmly, and so wholeheartedly that it seems as if they are newlyweds again. . . . They become even happier by the table" (*Ale verk*, 2:103).

While it is true that it seems there is no tension, complexity, frustration, or anger in this earlier familial portrait by Peretz, things are not as simple as they appear. The couple's relationship is strong despite their poverty. The secret to their successful relationship lies in their good sexual relationship ("zey kvetchken zikh"; 2:101). Their sound relationship serves as a testimony that, for Peretz, the sensitive working man (the husband in the story is a porter) is even more capable of leading a good family life and of achieving intimacy than a traditional man who sits in the study house or the petit bourgeois storyteller. A similar scenario to the one in "Domestic Peace" of the unhappy storyteller who tells the story of a happy couple also appears in Peretz's Yiddish story "Der feter shakhne un di mume yakhne" (Uncle Shakhne and Aunt Yakhne; 1895).

The idea that a good sex life is key to a good relationship also surfaces in Peretz's ironic Yiddish story "Mendl Braynes" (1891). In this story, the wife spoils the husband so much and gives him her all until she dies. But she never resents him, even though they become penniless. She forgives him because he does one thing right: being a "stay at home" sort of person who is available to fulfill her desires (*Ale verk*, 2:87).

In his stories, Peretz's edginess manifests in touching upon issues of Jewish sexuality in ways that were unprecedented in modern Yiddish and Hebrew literature. The Yiddish short story "A Farshterter shabes" (A spoiled Shabbat; 1892) is an important psychological example of Peretz's innovative viewpoint. In it, a control-freak, traditional mother named Serl lives with her weak-minded daughter Miriam and Miriam's young, busy, clueless, and not pious husband, Zerakh. Serl does everything she can to inject fears about sex into her daughter's mind. The daughter, mentally controlled by her mother, does not wish to move to the big city, where she would "sin" by letting her beautiful blond hair grow back in (religious Ashkenazi women shave their heads after they marry and keep their heads covered out of modesty). By moving to the city, Miriam also feels that she would be deserting her mother.

Influenced by her mother's readings from traditional moral guidebooks such as *Taytsh-khumesh* (a Yiddish adaptation of the Torah stories for women) during the Shabbat,[39] Miriam becomes sexually dysfunctional. This motherly campaign began while the young couple were still engaged, after they were caught together alone on a few occasions, a behavior which is forbidden by Jewish tradition. Serl, determined to sabotage the sexual life of her daughter during the weekdays, permits Miriam to have sex only during Shabbat. But it is already too late: Miriam gets her period, a time "when a woman is full with demons" (*Ale verk*, 2:214), in Serl's words, and during which the sinful husband becomes especially attracted to Miriam (according to Serl). When Zerakh returns home from prayers, he finds Miriam already fast asleep. Her watchdog, Serl, shouts at him just for kissing his sleeping wife hello, calling him "a criminal against the God of Israel!" The husband is left deprived of any sexual activity, hence the title "A spoiled Shabbat"—a phrase the mother utters in the story.

"A spoiled Shabbat" was characterized as a "humoresque."[40] The story is grounded in Jewish laws that concern the responsibilities of women during menstruation (*niddah*) and can be considered satirical. In certain ways, it continues the *maskilic* confrontation between human emotions and a rigid, inhumane interpretation of Jewish law. But "A spoiled Shabbat" is not a satire of the traditional laws themselves but rather, like in "Anger of a Jewish woman," of the neurotic people who adhere to them.[41] This is the most significant point about "A spoiled Shabbat": the human triangle portrayed in the story sexualizes and personalizes the previous *maskilic* social confrontation without losing its critical edge in the social realm. The ways in which the story innovates in the sexual-psychological to criticize traditional mores has no precedent in *Haskalah* literature.

Criticizing traditional mores in these realms also occurs in Peretz's Yiddish short story "Muser" (Moral; 1898), which portrays an unconventional family. "Moral" is structured as a dramatic dialogue between two female characters: Grune, a widowed mother of three girls, and Khane, a so-called friend of Grune. As expected in a patriarchal society, the death of Grune's husband means a death blow to the family's livelihood, plunging them into severe poverty. During their talk, Khane tries to push Grune to be stricter and more restrictive with her three girls, for—in her view—they are "misbehaving."

One daughter was seen going out with a man in modern dress, an action likely to damage her chances at making a match with a well-off (traditional) man. Grune kept this daughter strictly inside the house—where the daughter found only misery and isolation. When the second daughter worked outside the house, she did so under slave-like conditions. The third daughter is an assertive factory worker, who works sixteen hours a day.

The basic conflict for all three girls is grounded in the "house" versus "work" contradiction. Peretz portrays the industrial working woman (the third daughter) as someone who has prospects and a potential to grow, unfettered by the old social norms. It is through this character that Peretz highlights the bright potential of the poor.

Grune, the single-mother protagonist, functions as a marginal social "other" who understands the changing times. She becomes tired of being preached at by her conservative and unsympathetic community, and she angrily reacts to Khane's nag of "What will people say?" Instead, she lets her daughter go out with boys. Grune says to Khane,

> "People should first have pity on poor orphans, not work them like donkeys for no reason! People should have hearts and not hold poor people to be squeezed as lemons. . . .
>
> And God? God, blessed be he!"
>
> And Grune stands up and yells, as if she wanted God in the sky to hear—
>
> "*God first* should have worried about those other people . . ." (*Ale verk*, 2:531)

Peretz tells his readers that the important struggles are those against disunity in society and against poverty, not the struggle to uphold outdated morals and a repressive, patriarchal social order. In "Moral," Peretz conveys his modern message in a conventional form of dramatic monologue, where the psychosexual tension is not as vibrant as it is in "A spoiled Shabbat." In the Yiddish story "Khasene gehat: Detseylt fun a froy" (Married: As told by a woman; 1896), Peretz uses a female first-person narrator. Like "Anger of a Jewish woman," it tells the story of a family falling apart due to poverty. While "Anger" dealt with a familial life decaying because of poverty, "Married" deals with the life of a young woman from a poor background before marriage. The protagonist in "Married," Leah, is torn between two men, each of whom offers her a different life. She could be the fourth wife of Zaynvel, a seventy-year-old rich man who may have abused his third wife to death,[42] or become the wife of a young assistant pharmacist who sings Yiddish songs beautifully but is not wealthy.

"Married" paints a believable picture of how poverty rules over the life of a whole family and shapes their actions. In the story, Leah's father is without a job and in bad health. Their family suffers constantly from hunger. These facts drive the plot forward.[43] Rozentsvayg claims that in "Married," "the problem of the woman's lack of rights is presented as a social flag,"[44] but he ignores the strong personal-psychological elements in the story, which Peretz introduced here to modern Yiddish and Hebrew literatures for the first time.

In "Married" Peretz introduces new literary romantic types to the conventional *maskilic* conflict that pits romantic love against a traditional arranged marriage. Peretz sets his female protagonist in "Married" between two male figures. One is the secular Yiddish nationalist (the assistant pharmacist). He represents a new literary type, who, by remaining nameless in the story, strengthens his status as a social category rather than a unique individual.[45] Her other option is embodied by the rich old Reb Zaynvel, a choice that reduces Leah to a mere commodity. Leah's marriage to Zaynvel would offer a crucial economic benefit to her family and give her the chance to save her sick father's life (*Ale verk*, 2:483).

The father makes no attempt to hide the sheer business aspect of this arranged marriage. Leah will be able to pay her brothers' school tuition, yet the possibility of her getting an education is not even considered. In fact, the situation in this scenario is worse than it seems: Leah is also threatened with being tormented by the new husband, as her friend and her mother warn her. Leah's mother and Leah's friend Rivke try to see the bright side in the short life expectancy of a seventy-year-old man (*Ale verk*, 2:486–88). Leah's moral dilemma between her family's shot at escaping poverty and her own shot at personal happiness is explored via the bad-angel and good-angel figures who try to push Leah in opposite directions. Thus, Peretz strengthens the inner psychological drama that lies at the heart of the social conditions he wishes to criticize.

Peretz also exploits a recurring dream motif in "Married" in order to strengthen its basic format as an internal drama that takes place exclusively in the psyche of its protagonist, Leah. Leah dreams that on her wedding day the young man appears instead of Zaynvel. In her dream, a young man tells her that he lured Zaynvel into the forest, put him in a sack, tied the sack to a rock, and threw him in the river (*Ale verk*, 2:484–85). Leah rationalizes her violent fantasy to the readers, telling them it is identical to a story that her mother once told her. In this way, Leah toys with the radical option of violent struggle against gender oppression, but this remains nothing but an unrealized fantasy.

Beyond its portrayal of women, the story "Married" is significant also because it introduces a new kind of national subject in Yiddish literature:

the romantic character of the Yiddish nationalist—the Yiddish folk hero, if you will. Before then, Yiddish *Haskalah* literature made modern young characters speak either Germanized Yiddish or in pure German. In "Married," Leah's mother states that the young character's speech is under foreign invasion: "he always throws in a few words in Polish" (*Ale verk*, 2:473), meaning that this modern Jew speaks a Polishized Yiddish instead of a Germanized one. This change of focus is not only a reflection of the strengthening of Polish nationalism at the time but also stresses its innovative element with respect to past romantic figures in Jewish literature. Our young pharmacist's mastery of "plain Yiddish" is surprising, as Leah says: "He came to me, took me by the chin, raised my head up and said in none other than plain Yiddish: 'a beautiful maiden like you shouldn't go with raggedy hair and doesn't have to be shy in front of a lad!'"(2:474).

The woman in the story is drawn to the young man and is surprised that someone like him, an educated, modern person, would sing in Yiddish, the people's language. The young man embodies the type of national intelligentsia Peretz strove to establish since his essay "Bildung." By this point, his idea has become a fully developed literary representation. The irony at the end of "Married" is that the young man is found dead in Warsaw, while the old Zaynvel has been married to Leah for five years. The deep sense of irony adds an outstanding naturalistic touch in this story. Peretz shows us the ills of traditional society and especially women's place in it, a sad state in comparison to women's intense involvement in the nascent Jewish labor movement.[46] In "Married" Peretz presents secular folkist nationalism as an intriguing alternative to the way traditional society relegates women to the status of a commodity. Yet, noble ideas aside, Leah and her family gain more material benefit by sticking to traditional ideals and staying close to old shtetl wealth than by choosing the uncertain ideals of romance, physical attraction, and what is considered to be folk culture.

The Yiddish songs the young man sings in "Married" show how far the Jewish intelligentsia has advanced toward the folk, as compared to their stance at the beginning of the decade. In *Bilder* and "Bildung," the modern Jewish intellectual was portrayed as being alienated, far from the people, and thus unable to play a dynamic role in influencing or leading them. Peretz's presentation of the "warmer intelligentsia," aligned with the folk and their language, goes hand in hand with the role Peretz himself was aspiring to play of an "organic intellectual," someone who has committed themselves to the interests of the Jewish working class. At the time, Peretz in his daily life was enthusiastically collecting Yiddish folk songs.[47]

And he even changed the ideal of *Bildung* into *folks-Bildung*, meaning education for the common Jewish people, the populace. The aristocrat, he wrote, hates *folks-Bildung* "because he knows that the smarter the people become, the smaller his fat share [of the pie] will become."[48]

The story "Married" was published in one of the last issues of one of the most important Yiddish literary and political journals of the decade, *Di yontef bletlekh*, which played an important role in the years leading up to the Bund's formation as a Jewish socialist party.

Revolutionizing the Means of Artistic Production and Radicalizing the Jewish Calendar in the *Yontef bletlekh*

> It will be an organ through which we will speak month by month to the Jewish masses. It is a portent of our happiness, that the thin *Bletlekh* are destined to play a big role in the development of our literature and in the education of the Jewish worker masses.
>
> —Dovid Pinski, regarding the goals he and Peretz set out for issuing *Di yontef bletlekh*, 1945

In his 1934 essay "The Author as Producer,"[49] Walter Benjamin writes about a revolutionary artist's need to revolutionize the techniques of artistic production. Writing about this essay, Terry Eagleton explains what Benjamin thought it meant to be a revolutionary artist. For Benjamin, the revolutionary artist should not uncritically accept the existing forces of artistic production but must instead develop and revolutionize those forces. In doing so, the revolutionary artist creates new social relations between artists and audience; he makes art available to the many and overcomes the limits that constrain art to the private property of a few. The revolutionary artist's task is to develop new media—cinema, radio, photography, musical recording—as well as to transform the older modes of artistic production. It is not just a question of pushing a revolutionary message through existing media; it is a question of revolutionizing the media themselves. The truly revolutionary artist is never concerned with the art object alone but also, critically so, with the means of its production and distribution.[50]

In the case of the *Yontef bletlekh*, radical artistic content was inseparable from the radical way in which it was produced. Having achieved a position as an independent publisher, Peretz was freed to produce radical art. While he was not bound by the constraints of an editor or publisher, the czar's censors limited him. Consequently, the radical content of the journal had to be cloaked in a traditional Jewish garment as a clever ruse to evade the anti-progressive censorship of the czarist authorities. Because the government made it impossible for Peretz to issue a daily newspaper (or any other kind of regularly published periodical) in Yiddish,[51] he cleverly settled on an idea that would enable him to bypass these restrictions. His idea was to issue an informal monthly journal that would be marketed as a series of short almanacs in honor of the Jewish holidays (including Passover and Purim) and other special occasions connected with the Jewish calendar.[52] As a result, Peretz's radical and socialist messages were transmitted via a traditional Jewish framework—namely, the supposedly harmless and apolitical Jewish calendar.

Originally designed in order to bypass censorship, his approach affected the entire format and content of the journal and had an unintended consequence for its readers: it made its radical messages easier to digest for the modernizing Jew who still had one foot in the traditional world. Simultaneously, it intensified the power of the progressive messages by imputing them within the structure of an ancient authority.

Despite the holiday patina Peretz put on the publication, the radical tone of the *Bletlekh* did not make it easy for Peretz and Dovid Pinski (1872–1959)—Peretz's main partner in creating the *Bletlekh*[53]—with the authorities. The editorial by Pinski "Ma-nishtone?" (What has changed?) from the first volume of the *Yontef bletlekh*—the first *Bletl* (*Lekoved peysekh* [In honor of Passover], 1894)—was, in his words, "mutilated" by the censor.[54] The editorial spells out the power of using ancient language and customs to express revolutionary messages. "And we were slaves to Pharaoh in Egypt," Pinski opens, in the style of the Passover Haggadah, "but we were even greater slaves by habit. Accustomed to slavery, we were barely torn out of there" (*Lekoved peysekh*). Peretz reacted to that censorship incident by adding a short article entitled "Passover is coming" as a sort of compensation that also served as an introduction to the *Bletlekh*. The article says a lot about the tone of the *Bletlekh* themselves but also a lot about Peretz's uncompromising spirit vis-à-vis the authorities. This is the full article:

> Passover is approaching, and I entreat you to invite me to the Seder.
> I won't cost you much; I don't eat knaidel! Take me!
> Don't treat me to bitter herbs;[55] I was born with them!

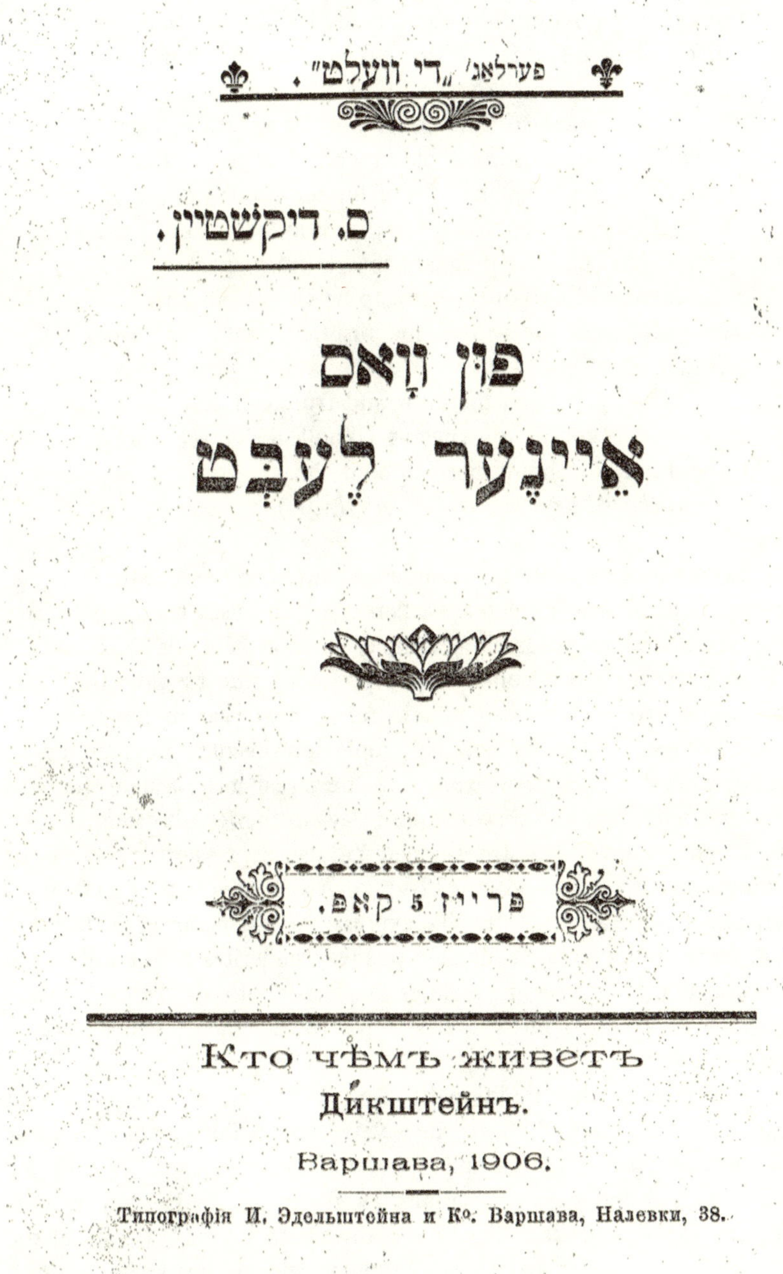

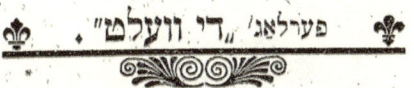

פערלאַג׳ „די וועלט״.

ס. דיקשטיין.

פון וואס
איינער לעבט

פרייז 5 קאפּ.

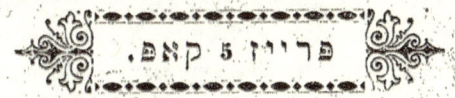

Кто чѣмъ живетъ
Дикштейнъ.

Варшава, 1906.

Типографія И. Эдельштейна и Ко. Варшава, Налевки, 38.

Figure 2.4. Cover of the *Yontef bletlekh*, second edition, 1913. Steven Spielberg Digital Yiddish Library.

> Don't tell me to count plagues either! I have forgiven the Egyptians a long time ago. Plainly it's like "beating a dead horse,"[56] because so far no one has become sick from written plagues.
>
> Release me also from "pour out thy wrath". . . . I am still too young; don't poison my blood with revenge. . . . I hope for better times, and even an idol worshipper I don't want to curse.
>
> I don't even want to say "next year in Jerusalem!" because "people don't become pregnant merely from speaking"!
>
> Meanwhile I only want to wish for you that next year you forget the whole "ma nishtana" with the "avadim ha'inu" . . . and—
>
> When you open the door and truly call, not like today in Aramaic: "kol dikhfin yitey ve-yikhol!"—Nobody will come in, and nobody should need to come in!
>
> (*Lekoved peysekh*, in *Ale verk*, 8:103)

This text is extraordinarily rich, condensed, and highly sarcastic. In a passage rich with Passover references, Peretz artfully uses traditional terms to convey his radical ideas. For example, he plays here with Hebrew and Yiddish by putting two contrasting expressions side by side: the highbrow and festive Hebrew call to celebrate—"next year in Jerusalem!"—against a coarse Yiddish expression, "people don't become pregnant merely from speaking." The Hebrew expression "next year in Jerusalem" (*leshono habo birusholaim*) is said on the holiest days in the Jewish calendar, Yom Kippur and Passover eve. The rhymed Yiddish expression "people don't become pregnant from speaking" (*fun zogn vert men nisht trogn*) effectively punches the air out of the first expression, underscoring the fact that words alone do not create action. In this way, he writes off the unfulfilled Zionist aspiration, expressing feelings that mesh with his critical position regarding the proto-Zionists circles at the time, which I will discuss at length in the next chapter.

Peretz uses the traditional wish "Whoever is hungry would come and eat" ("kol dikhfin yitey ve-yikhol!") during the Passover Seder eve as a call for a complete end to human hunger. He calls for an end to fighting between nations by rejecting the Hebrew expression "shfoykh-khamoskho" ("pour out thy wrath"), which is said at the Passover Seder in order, according to popular belief, to invoke God's wrath on the enemies of the Jewish people. Peretz's biggest parody here is his plea to his readers to "forget," a request that is in direct opposition to the central Passover commandment to remember. Traditionally, Jews are commanded to remember the Passover story and to retell it year after year. Instead, Peretz entreats his readers to forget the common phrases from the Passover Haggadah such as the "ma-nishtone?" ("Why is this night different from all other nights?") and the "avodim-ho'inu" ("we were slaves"). As an alternative, he invites them to join the "Bletlekh-seyder." *Seyder* literally means "order," and thus Peretz is playfully hinting at the realization of a new social order of justice and peace.

Figure 2.5. Dovid Pinski (1872–1959), Peretz's main partner in creating the *Yontef bletlekh*. From the postcard collection of Benny Swartzberg.

In the second *Bletl*, dedicated to the Jewish holiday Lag Ba-Omer, Peretz addresses the children who get out of the traditional classroom (the *kheyder*) once a year and into the outdoors to celebrate Lag Ba-Omer. He asks rhetorical questions laced with heavy insinuations to convey his message to these children:

> Just tell me who among you would grow up to be an honest worker, who would live from his own sweat and blood, tell me, who among you would live at his own expense, not be a slacker who lives at somebody else's . . . tell me who, and I'll give a few fine, good books to him to read that would surely come in handy to him! [. . .] Oh! I will tell him a few prettier stories and give as a gift—it is as you know Lag-Ba-Omer—a truly good bow and arrow. (*Der fayl un boygn*, 1894)

The promise at the end perfectly exemplifies the usage of traditional language and customs to inject radical ideas. Peretz is inviting his readers to learn from him about revolution; he promises to arm his young pupils with modern weapons adequate for the fight. A bow and arrow are what traditional Jewish children play with on Lag Ba-Omer to commemorate Bar Kokhba's revolt against the Romans in the second century CE. But here Peretz invites his readers to a modern-day struggle for social justice. Peretz could not spell out pure socialist ideas and rhetoric because of censorship, so he invites his readers, like a modern-day Rabbi Akiva, to learn in secret the true meaning of his writings.

On one of the first of the many feuilletons Peretz published of the *Bletlekh*, "Europe with a Bow and Arrow" (1894), he signed with the pen name "Not an Idler" (*nisht keyn batlen*). But Peretz was certainly not an idler in those mid-1890s years. It is safe to say that the years 1894–96 were the most prolific years of his career, both as a writer and as a public intellectual and cultural producer. Besides the seventeen *Bletlekh* that he issued, he also published the almanac *Literatur un lebn* (1894), the third volume of the *Yudishe bibliyotek* (1895), and more in other languages (mostly Hebrew).[57] But, by far, the *Yontef bletlekh* was the publication that helped set new standards in Yiddish journalism.

The *Bletlekh* was a radical journal not only in its content but also in its format and price. It was significantly shorter than other literary almanacs of the period. Peretz's *Literatur un lebn*, for example, was more than two hundred pages, and the second volume of his *Yudishe bibliyotek* was more than four hundred! During its first year's run of ten issues, the average *Bletl* volume ran only sixteen pages.[58] Because of their shorter length, the *Bletlekh* cost much less than the thick almanacs, just five kopecks an issue, thus rendering them significantly more accessible to the low-income readers it was intended to reach. To put this amount in perspective, consider that Peretz's *Literatur un lebn*, which was widely loved and read by socialist circles, cost thirty kopeks, and *Di yudishe bibliyotek* cost one ruble and twenty kopeks a volume.

The most crucial factor that made the *Bletlekh* revolutionary was the method of distribution. They were distributed by the network of jargon (Yiddish) committees, which produced many popular science brochures, published other works by Peretz ("Shtraymel") and Dovid Pinski ("Khayim Meshores") in low-priced formats, and established small Yiddish libraries in small cities where the labor movement had just begun to sprout.[59] Eventually the committee became a distribution center for illegal socialist material, and it helped lay the groundwork for the Bund's project of producing Yiddish literature.

It started off with workers' reading circles that used to gather in Vilnius during the Sabbath prayers in the morning or later in the day after a meal to read brochures provided by a proto-Bundist group. These secret underground groups of Jewish social democrats would meet in a member's attic or garden. The activist Kalman Marmor (1876–1956), who led such circles, preferred to select texts from Peretz's *Bletlekh* rather than the official brochures that were provided by the group. And despite his fears, he was backed by popular demand in doing so: "my listeners were very pleased by the reading from the *Yontef-bletl* and ended up bringing many of their worker friends to the next meeting of the reading circle," he pointed out.[60]

Pinski noted that "the *Bletlekh* seemed like a gift from the heavens for the leaders of the propaganda effort.... After the fourth *Bletl* ... I was notified that in Vilnius people wanted to become better acquainted with us. I soon went off to Vilnius. It was summer and I didn't have classes to attend."[61] In 1894 the young Pinski set off to Vilnius, then the center of the Jewish socialist proto-Bundist groups. The jargon committees were founded based on meetings in Vilnius in 1894 between Pinski and Jewish labor activists. They constructed a plan to join forces and distribute the *Bletlekh* through the rising network of Jewish socialist activists in Eastern Europe. Their goal, according to Pinski, was "to publish and to distribute literature for Jewish workers, and indeed immediately to take upon themselves the distribution of the *Yontef bletlekh* and all of the other publications of I. L. Peretz."[62] Pinski met there with Shmul Gozhansky

(1867–1943?), a political leader and Bundist theorist. Just a year prior, Gozhansky's pamphlet "A letter to agitators," together with Arkadi Kremer's "On Agitation" (both written in 1893), was a central motivator for change in the Vilnius circles' tactics from promoting propaganda (conspiratorial work and comprehensive education of small circles of workers) to agitation (disseminating fewer political ideas to larger groups of workers).[63]

Following Kremer's analysis, Gozhansky stressed the crucial importance of raising class consciousness and political awareness among Jewish workers. He argued Jewish revolutionary leaders should be more responsive to the specific needs of the Jewish workers they attempted to organize and represent.[64] Beyond publishing the brochure in Yiddish, which was a novelty back then, Gozhansky argued the Jewish labor movement should train its agitators partly in Yiddish in order to ensure their effectiveness in speaking to the workers whose Russian was poor and who were fluent only in Yiddish.[65]

In Vilnius, Pinski met with many other important activists, including the socialist activist and poet A. Lyesin (1872–1938), who would become a major figure in the history of the Yiddish socialist press in America.[66] Lyesin writes in his memoirs how he was heavily influenced by his meeting with Pinski, who caused him to see in modern Yiddish literature an opportunity to synthesize socialism with nationalism.[67] Pinski met Moyshe Terman (1872–1917), who led reading groups for workers and later in the decade was involved with Bundist groups in Paris, London, and New York. Terman was also one of the translators of Marx and Engels into Yiddish.[68] Pinksi also worked with Avrom Amsterdam (1872–99), an important figure among the autodidacts in the Vilnius group of social democrats who created the Bund in 1897.[69] Pinski also met with A. Litvak (1874–1932), who would soon come to be known as an important Bundist and was very active in forming the jargon committees.[70] Litvak pointed out an inherent tension during the meetings between the social activists and political ideologues and their more culture-focused literary counterparts from Warsaw.[71] But these tensions proved to be enriching more than anything else, for both sides.

Pinski made connections on his journeys and helped establish more jargon committees in places like Minsk, Bialystok, and Vitebsk. In Moilev the effort to form a jargon committee was shattered by informers from within the Jewish community who reported on the group's activities to the authorities.[72] Establishing the jargon committees significantly strengthened the nationalist wing of Jewish socialists into a critical group that would ultimately develop into the Bund. Litvak wrote in his memoirs about the first *Bletl* that arrived in Vilnius and noted that the socialist tendency was barely visible in the first *Bletl, Lekoved peysekh*, but by the second *Bletl, Fayl un boygn*, "the socialist character was already more distinct," and by the third *Bletl* for Shavuot, "they waited for it as if for a dear guest."[73]

In the first *Bletl* appeared Peretz's short story "Di royz" (The rose)—a text characterized by its sense of romantic irony. Litvak writes that "ever since [reading 'The rose'] we got used to racking our brains over a Peretz text, as over a complex course of Talmudic debate, or as over a tough spot in Marx."[74] He even received a postcard from Peretz, who answered that "the rose is a young woman who falls under life's burden."[75] However, despite the activists' enthusiasm, the financial resources of the jargon committees were sparse and relied on membership fees and on small revenues generated from an evening in which the works of Peretz and Pinski were being read. The *Yontef bletlekh* stopped coming out at the end of 1895. "First," writes Litvak, "there wasn't any money; second, the censor began to monitor them carefully, so it became impossible to maintain their earlier character."[76]

The jargon committees existed just three years, not much longer than the *Yontef bletlekh* themselves. They put out many popular science brochures and eventually became a center for distribution of illegal socialist material. The Bund's project of putting out Yiddish literature continued by other means (like bookstores and the publishing company Di velt). But the pioneering efforts of the jargon committees, advanced by the works and personalities of Peretz and Pinski and especially by the *Yontef bletlekh*, revolutionized the means of artistic production and distribution and gave birth to Yiddish socialism.

The relationship between Pinski and Peretz was that of mutual influence. Pinski was influenced by Peretz since he read Peretz's article "Bildung," and Peretz was equally drawn to Pinski's radicalness and youth: Pinski was only twenty-two years old when the *Bletlekh* came out, while Peretz was already forty-two. Peretz confessed in a letter that "my cherished cohorts are: Pinski, Pinski, and Pinski . . . sometimes Frank, Freyd . . . and also—I myself as: Y. L. Peretz, Dr. Shtitser, LTSFR, 'Prankster from the Editorials Office,' and so on and so forth, I forgot already how many names I have, about a hundred and eighty."[77]

Peretz counts here the numerous pen names he used at the time, of which there were at least eleven.[78] *Dr. Shtitser* means "Dr. Supporter"; *LTSFR* is an acronym for *Lets fun Redaktsye*, which means "Prankster from the Editorials Office," which was itself one of Peretz's pseudonyms. The use of pen names had multiple purposes: they were a tool both to make it harder for the censors to track him down and to cover up the fact that Peretz was writing much of the journal himself.[79] It was the common practice of nineteenth-century Yiddish writers to use pen names in order to hide the fact that they were writing in Yiddish, but this was not the primary motivation for Peretz by this time.[80]

In the article entitled "The New Movement," published in 1895 in two consecutive *Bletlekh*, Peretz took it upon himself to present to his readers the new social movement rising in Western Europe. The SPD in Germany (Sozialdemokratische Partei Deutschlands) was by then a significant political force; the Austrian pacifist organization was founded in 1891 by Bertha von Suttner; and while Peretz did not mention those movements by name, it is clear he is referring to them there.[81] Peretz's tone towards this new movement is one of enthusiasm and excitement. Its moral aspect appeals to him, and if we read between the lines imposed by the censorship constraints under which he was writing, it is clear that he fully supports the movement. He attacks the philosophical strands of Spencer, Darwin, and Lippert, who, according to Peretz, view history as a series of endless wars, without any utopian sense of hope. He begins by announcing the new movement and its core beliefs:

> In Western Europe a new movement is becoming noticeable. . . . Over a wild-sparkly sea flies a dove with a green leaf of peace. . . . Moral societies arise everywhere, societies that want the endless war between religions, peoples, races, and classes to stop; people should put their murderous weapons away from their hands, everybody should put away their cold evil, their egoism. . . . They believe in solidarity . . . that doesn't adhere to the clenched fist and which doesn't go hand in hand with self-interest, chauvinism, and religious hatred! ("The New Movement," *Shabes oybs* [Sabbath fruit], 3–5, in *Ale verk*, 8:93)

Peretz did not spell out the name of the movement he was writing about. But because, beyond its dovishness, he went on to mention the failure of the liberal individualistic ethos, to criticize a system that is based on narrow interests as opposed to broader social ones, and to use the terms "ego" and "self-interest" in a negative way, it is reasonable to infer that Peretz is referring here to the SPD. He claimed the theories of "survival of the fittest" are anything but new, describing them as a reframing of the ancient "theory of the fist," which is captured in the old Talmudic phrase *kol de-alim gaver* (whoever is strong prevails). Peretz takes on these beliefs and attacks their social worldview of "endless war, endless competition between individuals, peoples, and races" (*Shabes oybs*, 21–22, in *Ale verk*, 8:99).

These strong and clear words by Peretz attacking the free-market jungle and its intellectual backers are the most radical words to appear in a Yiddish legal publication at the time. His writing style is urbane, direct, edgy, and knowledgeable about world affairs and present-day political and philosophical trends to a degree that was unprecedented in Yiddish letters. Its content is unabashedly subversive, and it expresses a sharp discontent with the way the world is run. This time, his deadliest arrows are directed upward, toward the powerful, and not as in *Bilder fun a provints rayze* and "Bildung" toward the nonnationalist intelligentsia, or as in *Iber profesyonen* toward the Jewish workers and their "low" work ethic. Peretz wrote to a Jewish readership in a Jewish language, but his attitude in this passage is not at all insular. He applied universal thinking and world developments to the Jewish society he was simultaneously helping to create. He wanted to lead his readers, to bring them up to date with the most relevant political currents, and to imagine a Jewish society striving to be a morally driven society like those rising groups in Western Europe.[82]

While Peretz's worldview is broad, he directs his words inward toward Jewish society. He criticizes what he sees as the absurdity of Jews supporting the existing uncompassionate system of government. He wonders, "Are we, we poor, scattered people, the weakest people on earth, beginning to believe that the ideal of people is endless war between people and nations, races and classes . . . ?"(*Shabes oybs*, 6–7). Peretz equated this belief by Jews—which he saw as a self-defeating agenda—to American slaves aligning with the Southern forces against those who came to liberate them and to old Polish farmers who would still rather work in a feudal order than pay taxes.

If in "Bildung" Peretz came out strongly against the alienated Jewish intelligentsia, in "The New Movement" the Jewish intelligentsia is criticized differently. First, the tone is universalist and based on class differences rather than national ones. He comes out strongly against intellectuals who "sold out," more interested in receiving petty crumbs from the rich than in promoting justice and aligning themselves with the lower classes. He calls them "old experts" who "have dried-out brains . . . toadies, who live for a few bites that are thrown to them from the table of the rich. They must constantly . . . dance around strangely on brushes to clean the rich man's floors, so people won't see the stains of sweat and blood." He contrasts them with the new movement of the "young, educated world [that] is filled with joy at these new societies of pure morality" (*Shabes oybs*, 8–9).

Peretz feels a great degree of intellectual freedom positioning himself against intellectuals who are aligned with the ruling class and must therefore accommodate its interests—not dissimilar to Peretz himself when he was working for Jan Bloch, though Peretz here does not openly acknowledge this fact. It is interesting that this language was omitted from later editions of Peretz's collected works:[83] at the end of the original text, Peretz envisions how "the old system explodes . . . over the altar of sweat and blood rises the axe" (*Shabes oybs*, 9).

Just a few years after Peretz wrote these passionate words, when Yiddish author Avrom Reyzn (1876–1953) was compiling his first big almanac, *Dos tsvansikte yorhundert* (The twentieth century; 1899), he received a vastly different kind of advice from his mentor. From Reyzn's memoirs, we learn that Peretz advised the young progressive idealist (some of whose early poems Peretz published) to let Reyzn's benefactor Yosef Dovid publish his poems and additional texts of his in the almanac in exchange for his financing of the publication.[84] Peretz also did not hesitate to advise Reyzn to bribe the censor so he would overlook a few passages that were "too progressive."[85] It could very well be that Peretz was talking from his own experience with his *Yontef bletlekh* and his other subversive almanacs from that period. In 1895, Peretz wrote to Litvak in Vilnius that "your stories are very good. Unfortunately, they cannot be published on account of the censor." (Litvak was happy to read the news because it proved that his text was indeed very revolutionary, and it gave him a sense of being a martyr and a victim for the cause.)[86]

But in "The New Movement," and in the *Bletlekh* in general, Peretz was aiming at the ideal of a young and free-thinking group working together to promote a moral society. In the aforementioned feuilleton from the second volume of the *Bletlekh*, "Europe with a Bow and Arrow (A Political Feuilleton)," Peretz mentions both the socialists and the pacifist movement, and he takes an interesting anti-imperialist stand. Writing cynically about the "London Consensus" of his time, Peretz is mocking power and exposing the way it operates to strengthen and advance its interests. He writes about the apparent contradiction between capitalism's need for peace and stability to conduct trade and the factually violent nature of the capitalist forces spread over the globe, conquering new markets. He cynically remarks that the English would have loved for the entire world to disarm, except, of course, for the English themselves.[87]

Peretz might not have been able to pledge his allegiance to the Socialist Party due to censorship, but he reports about the socialists and offers them as a political alternative. He is presenting socialism simultaneously as a plan for the distant future, as the movement that would bring true peace to the world, and as a current threat to power because of its rising popularity. In another feuilleton by Peretz in the *Bletlekh*, "Vos zol ikh veln?" (What should I want?), Peretz makes fun of both the position of the philanthropist ("If I had been able to be a philanthropist, people would have pelted me with flowers and greeting cards while I'm still alive"[88]) and the concept of "peace": "I fear only peace! . . . Peace is between thieves, when they are preparing themselves to do their job. . . . Oh, no! Peace is a terrible thing . . . peace is the lie itself. No, I don't want to ask for peace!"[89] For the radical Peretz, the concept of peace means not attracting fire by toning down radical statements and compromising the truth, a way for the powerful to pacify the powerless who might threaten their hegemony. Litvak writes that in Vilnius, his Jewish Labor circles used to read and reread this paragraph about peace, stressing especially those last quoted lines.[90]

The *Yontef bletlekh* were a combination of short stories, poetry, and short articles. Much but not all of the literature that Peretz published in the *Bletlekh* had been written before and was not composed especially for this publication.[91] So, while one can assume Peretz would not publish material dramatically different in tone from his *Bletlekh* articles, it is also important to note not all stories contributed by Peretz to the *Bletlekh* carry a radical socialist tone. Take, for example, the story "The Miracle of Chanukah" ("Nes khanike"), which appeared in the eighth *Bletl*. Ruth Wisse claims this story, which carries a secular-nationalist tone, proves Peretz's constant political ambivalence, and to strengthen that point she downplays the fact the tone of the journal was clearly influenced by censorship. I argue his work from this period is characterized by a clear affection for the cause of the proletarian and by a strong desire that "the future general granary will feed all the hungry equally."[92]

To claim Peretz's "uneasy attempt to balance nation and class resisted any fixed political idea"[93] mirrors the Soviet criticism of Peretz and of the Bund more generally. This kind of criticism does not consider the Bund's unique ethnic-class foundations. The ways in which Jewish tradition manifested itself in Jewish socialist circles does not express ambivalence toward internationalist class struggle.[94] The *Bletlekh* were used, with the full acceptance of both Peretz and the proto-Bundists, as an agitation tool for proto-Bundist circles, and they clearly played an important role in developing the desired ethno-class consciousness of the Bund.[95] Proto-Bundist circles developed their unique blend of nationalist ideology throughout the 1890s, basing their program of "cultural autonomy" on modern Yiddish literature; much of it relied on Peretz's body of work and cultural legacy.

Benjamin shows in "The Author as Producer" that however revolutionary a political tendency appears, it can function in a counterrevolutionary manner if the writer experiences his solidarity solely with the proletariat ideologically and not as a producer.[96] I have argued in this chapter that through the *Yontef bletlekh*, Peretz was a cultural producer who aligned himself with the Jewish working classes.[97] As a publisher, he established with Pinski an alternative distribution network to the profit-focused publishing business. While these efforts proved to be short-lived, their significance cannot be overemphasized. His cultural production efforts during those years laid the foundations for an array of Yiddish-oriented progressive Jewish groups,[98] most notably the Bund.

Chapter 3

"To Be a Fighter with Both Fists!"
Peretz the Radical Hebrew Writer

To the Reader!

I did not come to for an afternoon chat; nor did I come to please you.

I have no desire to be your pleasure-reading and entertainment, nor your sleeping pill.

I am not a glass of wine in which to drown your worries or waste the time which you failed to use.

I am no potion for strengthening the bones, no healing drug to calm the nerves, and not the hope of lazy people, which deceives, which plays with the dusk shadows, to weave from them all that your heart desires!

I am no false witness for hire, to wave my head for all of your twists of thought; and not an advocate for the blood that will be found on your clothes; and for no reason will I purify the wrong which will be in your heart in the lake of delusions. . . .

I desire the opposite, to throw myself on you and to rule over you.

I desire to cleave your heart, to crush your brain, to stir all of your nerves, and to deprive you of your sleep. . . . I desire to tear down your blinders with the strength of my hand, to add bitterness to your anguish and to give a great sound—the sound of the bell ringing in your conscience, until you become shocked and astonished from hearing it. . . .

This is my wish and my desire.

—The Arrow

—I. L. Peretz, in the opening page of his Hebrew journal *The Arrow*, 1894

Radical Hebrew Arrows

Following the success of his radical Yiddish *Yontef bletlekh* journals, Peretz attempted to produce a new publication that would be similar in tone and format, but this time in Hebrew. He released the journal *Ha-chetz* (The arrow) only once, in May 1894. It was a low-priced, thin volume, mainly composed of literary prose, poems, and essays contributed by Peretz himself, who was also the editor.[1] The initiative came from his friend, the Hebrew publisher S. B. Shvartsberg (1865–1929),[2] who was inspired by the success of the *Bletlekh*. Dovid Pinski, Peretz's co-creator of the *Bletlekh*, wrote about their attempt to produce a Hebrew version of it:

> When [Shvartsberg] came to Peretz with his plan, Peretz was enthusiastic. Both languages were one in him. To derive satisfaction simultaneously in both languages, such joy! Such a thing! To be a fighter with both fists! In the shortest possible time he assembled a *bletl* under the title *Ha-chetz*. The title echoes the militancy in him. But in the Hebrew world, *Ha-chetz* did not receive as much of a response as the *bletl Fayl fun boygn* [vol. 2 of the *Bletlekh*, 1894] did in the Yiddish world. The inspired Shvartsberg quickly cooled off, and a second volume was never published.[3]

If in Yiddish the radical Peretz found some political backing from the nascent Jewish labor movement, in Hebrew his radical streak rendered him an odd bird, as Pinski implied. In Hebrew circles, Peretz's political enemies included the proto-Zionists, who were becoming increasingly dominant in the Hebrew cultural field they inherited from the tail end of the *Haskalah*. Displeased by Peretz's radical publications, the Zionists launched a war against him in Hebrew, through publications such as David Frishman's mock-*Bletlekh*, which satirized all Peretz's publications, including *The Arrow*. But even this singular attempt gained some attention from Hebrew writers with a conservative agenda. An anonymous writer for the Hebrew daily *Ha-melitz* wrote a double cover-page review article of *The Arrow* with the title "Demanded to contribute to the calf and provide," which had a threatening, witch-hunt tone to it. The author threatened to expose the names of the benefactors who allegedly funded Peretz's publications like the *Bletlekh* and *The Arrow* because, he argued, they were themselves financially unsustainable. That anonymous attacker writes about *The Arrow* and compares it first to the Yiddish *Bletlekh*:

> The new Yiddish books are many, and we can find in them many examples showing how they are fueled with burning anger, anger to burn the soul and encourage wrongdoing. . . And that is why we should hold it in favor of one of the creators of these "Bella letters," for he gave us its gist in Hebrew, and *The Arrow* is a collection of all that is written in these new Yiddish books . . . smeared with the poison which is in those books, and its deathly lightning is the deceitful light which is this new Yiddish literature.[4]

The anonymous writer suggested that a journal like *The Arrow* is out of place in Hebrew literature and would be better suited to Yiddish literature. In his mind, *The Arrow* is a poor translation from Yiddish literature, and it is intolerable to express such radical ideas in Hebrew, whose readership is conservative and pious. This anonymous allegation prompted Peretz to respond a week later on the front page of *Ha-melitz* under the title "Denial" as follows:

> In the main article of *Ha-melitz* it has been said of my publications . . . that they have a hidden goal (insinuated in the article), that they don't have any readers, and thus if it weren't for the help of the benefactors that they couldn't be issued. The writer of the article threatened these benefactors, implying that if they won't cease from supporting my books, he will denounce them by name for everyone to see. And all this is untrue. The little books *Yontef bletlekh* I published at my own expense without any outside assistance . . . and the purpose of all my books is strictly the distribution of straightforward knowledge among the people. All my books have sold in the thousands. Signed: Y. L. Peretz.[5]

Peretz's self-description as a distributor of "straightforward knowledge among the people" defines his essence as a radical intellectual: he popularizes complex ideas, making them accessible to the uneducated. This is Peretz aligning himself with the interests of the Jewish working class. Jewish socialists, who were starting to organize worker circles using the Yiddish material produced by Peretz and Pinski in the *Yontef bletlekh*, took notice of the attempt to create a Hebrew radical counterpart to the *Bletlekh*. According to testimonies, workers loved hearing the material written in Hebrew—when it was translated for them into Yiddish. Litvak, the proto-Bundist pioneer of the jargon committees, described the reaction to *The Arrow* when it came out toward the end of 1894:

> Our semi-*inteligentn* [Jewish intellectuals not fully assimilated in non-Jewish societies and who did not go to prestigious universities] were strong opponents of Hebrew; however, we still read everything new which came out in that language. We immediately threw ourselves at Peretz's *Ha-chetz*, which contained a poignant article against the Palestinian idea. . . . In the same collection of books there were two nice revolutionary stories by Peretz, "The Thought" and "The Harp." . . . I used to tell them with my own words in workmen's circles, where they always enjoyed a great success.[6]

Some interesting insights into the Yiddish-Hebrew cultural-political dynamic are revealed in this passage. First, it is clear Peretz succeeded in creating in Hebrew the same radical spirit so admired by Jewish labor organizers as he did in Yiddish. The second, more obvious point is the affirmation of the fact that Hebrew was inherently much less accessible to the masses than Yiddish was. Just like in Jewish religious circles, Hebrew required cultural agents who could mediate its content to most working-class Jews. A third point is that although the Jewish labor circles were starting to adapt Yiddish and a *yidishist* platform, only the very first signs of the Hebrew-Yiddish split were beginning to appear in the 1890s among the Jewish intelligentsia.[7] By the 1920s, the split between Yiddish and Hebrew was already an established fact. It was so much the case that Litvak reluctantly admitted in 1921 that they read everything that came out in Hebrew as well.[8]

The politics of translation also plays a role here: because Peretz's authentic Hebrew version was inaccessible to working-class audiences, Litvak had to spontaneously tell the tale "with [his] own words." Yet Litvak's ability to spontaneously translate a Hebrew text into spoken Yiddish shows how tightly Hebrew and Yiddish cultures were still intertwined within his "semi-intellectual," lower-middle-class milieu. And in any case, Litvak stressed the fact that this milieu "read everything" that came out in "that language."[9]

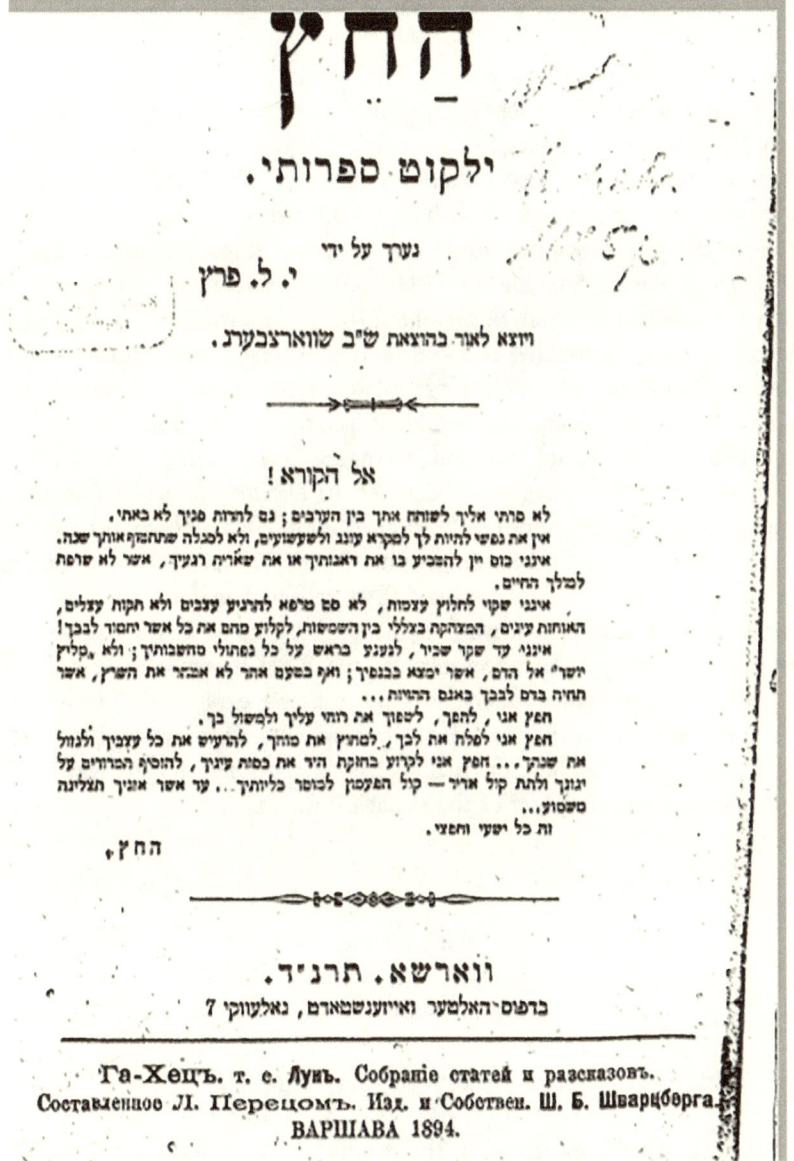

Figure 3.1. Following the success of his radical Yiddish *Yontef bletlekh* journals, Peretz attempted to produce a new publication similar in tone and format, but this time in Hebrew. He released the journal *Ha-chetz* (The Arrow) only once, in 1894. It was a low-priced, thin volume, mainly composed of literary prose, poems, and essays contributed by Peretz himself, who was also the editor. Google Books.

Socialism in Hebrew before Peretz

Socialist writing in Hebrew was not a novelty in Peretz's time. Peretz could build on a preexisting Hebrew socialist tradition. Although contemporary Hebrew literature was less accessible to the average worker, socialist Hebrew literature predated socialist writings in Yiddish: the Hebrew literature of the *Haskalah* dealt with issues of Jewish poverty and suffering.

Socialist writings in Hebrew can be found at least since the 1870s.[10] The writer Peretz Smolenskin (1842–85) gave voice in his acclaimed Hebrew monthly journal *Hashakhar* (The dawn; 1868–85) both to the nascent Jewish nationalist thinking and to socialist and radical worldviews. This journal became the first platform for Peretz's Hebrew poetry, where it appeared along such works as Yahalal's (1844–1925) pioneering socialist Hebrew poem "Kishron ha-ma'ase" (The ability to act; 1875). Each of the poem's chapters is devoted to a different profession, from the poverty-stricken autodidactic man ("Poor I was, no food or clothing, / All my friends did nothing to help"/עני הייתי אין לחם ובגד\כל יודעי מכירי\ עמדו מנגד;[11]); to the simple worker ("An artisan I was in craft and factory / There I worked with no shame. . . . / I know I will not starve"; אמן הייתי במלאכה וחרשת\ ובה עסקתי, לא ידעתי בשת. . . . \ אך מרעב אגועה אדע[12] כי לא), who eventually understands he is being exploited ("From dusk till dawn I work hard / And for a person who didn't work I give my share";מבקר עד ערב אעבוד יגע\ ולאדם שלא עמל אתנה[13] חלקי;); all the way up to the capitalist who lives off of the sweat of others:

> My hand accumulates—but it does not toil [. . .]
>
> And tens of thousands work for me,
>
> And I paid them for their work
>
> Only to get enough strength so they won't starve [. . .]
>
> And only for me go all of the profits.[14]

The voice of the capitalist here is the voice of utter exploitation. The moral upper hand belongs to the lower classes; their rebellion against their employer is morally justified. In a simple and direct way, Yahalal's poem exposed the core of socialist thinking—namely, class war.[15] The pioneering efforts in Hebrew by the journalist and publisher Aaron S. Lieberman (1843–80) and the poet and essayist Morris Vintshevski (1856–1932), in the periodical *HaEmet* (The truth; three volumes), helped promote socialist worldviews among a particular group of the traditional Jewish lower middle class.[16] When asked in 1877 why he chose to write in Hebrew rather in the language of the masses (Yiddish), Lieberman admitted that his choice was mainly due to the czarist legal restrictions over the use of Yiddish.[17] Vintshevski was a prolific socialist writer in Hebrew and in Yiddish who authored influential Hebrew feuilletons under the name Ben-Netz. After the authorities in Vienna (and later in Berlin) arrested Lieberman in 1877 for his activism, Vintshevski founded the Hebrew socialist periodical *Asefat khakhamin* (Sages assembly; eight volumes), where he published his poems, stories, and essays.[18]

Socially oriented stories in Hebrew appeared during the 1890s. Among the most notable of these was a short story by Yitskhok Goyda (a.k.a. B. Gorin) called "The Enlightened Carpenter" (1892). Goyda based his working-class protagonist on the figure of the socialist activist and Yiddish poet A. Lyesin.[19] The works of Alexander Ziskin Rabinovich (1854–1945)[20] and others, many of whom published their works through the publisher Ben-Avigdor, were also notable examples of Hebrew literature with a socialist bent. Thus, *The Arrow*, Peretz's attempt at producing a socialist Hebrew journal, appeared within a framework of like-minded content in Hebrew.

The Prose of *The Arrow*

The two "nice revolutionary stories" that Litvak mentioned, "The Thought" and "The Harp: An Arab Legend,"[21] are allegorical short stories, and it is worthwhile examining Litvak's claim that they are "revolutionary." Set in the Middle Ages, "The Thought" tells the tale of a daughter born out of "the spark from the eyes of the prophet" who wants to move from the provinces into the big city in order to preach the message of equality and "love for all mortals." She makes her point through symbolic language: she tells the narrator to listen to the sigh of the moon, who utters, "I am poor, meager, and small.". The narrator replies with a tale based on Isaiah 30:26, in which Isaiah (a biblical prophet who appears frequently in Islamic sources) describes the transformation that will take place in the messianic era. The narrator tells her,

"According to the legend of the Hebrews, God will fill the light of the moon, and its light would be like the light of the sun."
"And the light of the sun?" She asked.

"Will grow seven times as much!" I answered.

"Then" she sighed quietly "there will be much more light, but what is broken would not be repaired!"[22]

She carries this prophetic message of *tikun olam* (repairing the world) utterly naked (representing the sheer naked truth) into the city, where she encounters outright hostility. The city guards wrap her in a curtain; they block her from the city and physically torture her. The image of her being carried away out of the city, bleeding on a "Sodom bed," is a clear allusion to the Song of Songs[23] and to other tortured martyr figures. It recalls the image of Jesus on the cross, but also it alludes to the imprisonment of the biblical prophet Jeremiah. Both the prophet and Peretz's heroine strive to avoid bloodshed, and both end up incarcerated.

The other story Litvak refers to, the "Arab" legend by Peretz, was written when proto-Zionists were just beginning to colonize Palestine. Aḥad Ha'am, the leader of cultural Zionism, was sending letters from the Land of Israel that included criticism of the way Palestinians were being treated by the Jewish newcomers. In 1891, he wrote,

> We must be cautious with the way we interact with this foreign people among whom we come to live with, to treat them with love and respect, and, needless to say, with justice and the rule of law. What do our brothers do in the Land of Israel? The exact opposite! They were slaves in the land of their exile. And suddenly they find themselves living in endless freedom. . . . They treat the Arabs with hatred and cruelty, unjustly trespassing into their lands, disgracefully beating them for no good reason, and even bragging about it, and there is no one to step in and stop this disgraceful and dangerous inclination.[24]

One cannot avoid the thought that Peretz, who also referred frequently to Aḥad Ha'am in his writings,[25] was relating to these currents in public life by writing a story about the prophet who warned against destruction and exile and was imprisoned for doing so (Jeremiah). Peretz modified the tale and retold it from an Arab Muslim point of view. In both stories, his Arab protagonists quote from Hebrew sources as well as from Arab ones. Its message applied to Jewish politics and contained a warning against the inherent destruction of the colonization project. Its revolutionary element lay in the way it revealed the baldly violent and oppressive character of the authorities. It does so by displaying the contradiction between the authorities and the ideal of an egalitarian society based on morals, as represented by the torturing to death of the female prophet.

The second story, "The Harp," tells the tale of a poor man who is granted a miraculous gift: King David's harp. He receives the harp after he tells the prophet Elijah how, at night, animals mocked him outside his home, while the dead rose up from their graves to dance and join the mockery. Elijah then tells the man's troubles to King David in heaven, who decides to give him the harp out of pity.[26] The music that the poor man plays on his harp kills those who hear it, and he is sentenced by the *qadi* (a Muslim judge) to be committed to a mental institution and to give David's harp to the king's wife.

Both stories show the inability of the prophetic or heavenly messenger to fulfill their mission, whether they are a person or a musical instrument. Both are received with violence by the authorities, although in the second story the instrument itself also produces violence. The contradiction in both stories between the heavenly creative spark and the state's authority is probably the reason Litvak referred to them as "revolutionary." When he wrote that workers enjoyed listening to him retell these stories in Yiddish, he contradicted what the Hebrew literary critic Yosef Klausner wrote about this story. According to Klausner, "even . . . an educated reader who is familiar with the European style" will have a hard time understanding this story, "and the simple folk won't ever understand it."[27] Peretz wrote about the oppressed simple folk "not because of his democratism" but rather because "he has a warm and easily impressed heart."[28] Klausner wrote these words upon the publication of Peretz's collected Hebrew works.[29] They reflect his tendency to detach Peretz from his political leanings—to depoliticize his work, especially those parts that made Klausner, a Zionist critic, feel uncomfortable.[30] More convincing here is Rozentsvayg, who stated that "in *The Arrow*, Peretz took as his target all of the patrician-Hebrew sanctities."[31]

Peretz's main achievement in *The Arrow* is in successfully combining political and artistic innovations in Hebrew. According to Hamutal Bar-Yosef, Peretz published one of the first modernist manifestos of Hebrew literature in *The Arrow*.[32] In his text "The birth of Moses, the Giver of the Torah," the motif of a new prophetic message that the authorities receive with violence reappears. In this message "Peretz suggests to his readers a new literary path as if it meant the redemption of the nation and the world."[33] Writing in a style that evokes biblical Hebrew, Peretz described the new literature that was entering the world as "an echo of a new poetry [*shira hadasha*], coming down to earth from the sky penetrating the hearts of people."³⁴

The Arrow included a polemical article concerning Jewish nationalism entitled "The creators of chaos," written by Nahum Sokolow but signed under the pseudonym Amittai.³⁵ The article criticized Zionism and the distorted way in which it was defining Jewish identity.³⁶ Sokolow saw the (proto) Zionist circles as imitating the German version of "extreme nationalism and delusions of the superiority of race and homeland" (הלאומיות הקיצונה והדמיונות אדות יתרון הגזע והמולדת), and he regarded this nationalism as nothing but a "German statue dressed in a Jewish prayer shawl" (הלאומיות הזאת הלא היא פסל גרמני מלובש טלית-קטן עבר).³⁷ To Sokolow, the Zionists were creating a land-based version of Judaism, and for them this land was exclusively the Land of Israel. A footnote added by the publisher on the first page of the article read "The Land of Israel? But it is also the cradle of the Canaanites and the Philistines and the Samaritans!"³⁸ This article, which was edited and published by Peretz, was indicative of Peretz's own negative stance toward the early Zionist circles he encountered during the 1890s.³⁹

"Beating Their Heads against the Wall": Satirizing the Choveve Tsiyon in Hebrew and in Yiddish

Our national goal is cosmopolitism, and there is reason to fear that when we arrive in the Holy Land we will lose our enlightenment and our free spirit and become fanatics and reactionaries.

מטרתנו הלאומית היא הקוסמופוליטיות, ויש לחשוש שבבואנו לארץ הקדושה נאבד את השכלתנו ואת רוחנו החפשי ונהיה לקנאים ומורדי אור

—Peretz, 1891

In 1893, Peretz published in Yiddish an allegorical sketch called "Hekht" (literally, a pike fish; figuratively, an important person) as part of a series of stories entitled "Little stories for big people." The story tells of the live pikes and carps that were bought by a Jewish household to prepare for a festive meal. The pikes beat their heads against their glass-wall prison for a long time before they realize the fatal destiny set out for them. They pray against the spell that fell upon them, but then they remember that they have not prayed for an exceptionally long time and now they can't remember the words. When the two (Jewish) pikes fail to remember the words of the prayer (the *ashre*), one of them moans loudly, "Oy, I have an urge to pray . . . so do I, admits the second one, but after all, we are as you well know nothing but fish!" (דעןסוףכלסוףזענןמירדאָראויךנאָרפיש ..; *Ale verk*, 2:289).

When the pikes figure that out, they try to produce an escape plan for themselves and for the carps, who had long ago accepted their destiny. Their plan is to jump out of the bowl and "go back home" to the river. They repent as Jews do on Yom Kippur, bemoaning the fact that their own "homeland" is forgotten; "a sin" and "an outrage," they call it. Of course, any such plan would be by definition suicidal, and indeed the pikes command the carps to jump out of the water bowl they are both in, commanding them, in fact, to go meet their maker:

> and [the carps] are lying neither dead nor alive.
> I didn't know, says the second pike, that you are such an inspirational speaker; honey is flowing out of your mouth!—
> Meanwhile, the carps groan—
> Push yourselves! Commands the first pike
> The carps jump only a little bit further.
> Oy—they groan,—no river is yet to be seen, and our bones are breaking, and we are out of breath . . .
> Push yourselves; pull together your remaining strength! It's not far now, give another jump!
> But the carps cannot hear anymore. (*Ale verk*, 2:290–91)

What comes to mind, reading these lines about the "pike commanders," is the Yiddish proverb *der hekht shtinkt fun kop* (the pike stinks from its head), meaning the source of the problem lies at the top, in the people in charge. Who is Peretz alluding to as sending their "troops" on suicide missions to go "back home"? Who is telling the people that it is impossible to live where they currently do and with sweet words urges them to jump toward their freedom in the next world?

Workers' reading circles in Vilnius during the mid-1890s asked themselves the same questions. Kalman Marmor, who led such a reading circle of workers, told the story of how he and the workers were all in agreement regarding the meaning of nine of the ten stories of the series "Little Stories for Big People," but only in regard to "Hekht" they were in strong disagreement. Marmor wrote,

The majority interprets it as the war between work and capital. I'm not in agreement with them. I say that I. L. Peretz means very simply "The Choveve Tsiyon" [meaning "the Zionists"]. None from the majority would accept my explanation, because none of them know this particular movement as I do, which I have read about in Hebrew publications.

Unable to agree with the majority, I volunteered to write a letter to Peretz asking him what he had in mind in this particular story.... We waited a long time for his answer. There were people who made fun of us for expecting that the great writer in Warsaw would answer us with what he meant in one of his texts. But we didn't wait in vain. His answer was: "Mr. Marmor, you have guessed correctly. I. L. Peretz." Those few words made a strong impression on us.[40]

Marmor described how Peretz had satirized a movement whose name was still mostly unknown outside of narrow circles within the Jewish intelligentsia. In his satire, Peretz portrayed the Zionist plan as a suicide mission. Masked by a thin layer of traditional language (despite a secular leadership), dealing with dubious funds (monetary corruption is also involved in the allegory), and mobilizing agents talented in the art of speech, this movement—ridiculous and disastrous as its goal may seem—might still get its way. Peretz ends the story of our "brave heroes" the pikes when they debate between themselves just how many more live offerings will be needed to complete their plan, while the carps are dying on the floor:

> Both admit that given a correct jump it is possible to come back to the river. But one of them says that for this one needs other fish, not vile carps, which can only jump in water and cannot endure a couple of hours without breathing and eating, that one needs for this—electrical fish! ...
>
> And the second one thinks that actually only carps can do it! But one needs many, many carps! And if 100,000 will jump, one will succeed, and when one will succeed, ha! Ha! (*Ale verk*, 2:291)

The willingness to send people to die for a hopeless cause and the desire to breed a new kind of fish, a modern fighting fish, is how Peretz wished to caricature the nascent Zionist movement in 1893. That said, Peretz may have unintentionally advocated poorly for Diaspora nationalism as well: the fish are doomed whether they jump out of the water to die in the air or stay in the containers to be slaughtered by the people in the house. We can easily deduce from this allegory a sense of all-around despair, which it seems was not Peretz's intent. In any case, at least since 1890, Peretz was expressing doubtful and negative views toward the Zionist plan. The Hebrew publisher Ben-Avigdor mentioned quite a few incidents where Peretz spoke passionately against the Choveve Tsiyon and got into intense arguments about this issue (Ben-Avigdor himself was an ardent Zionist). In 1891, at a Hebrew Passover ball with female Hebrew students, Peretz was lecturing in Polish "in praise of cosmopolitism and against the Choveve Tsiyon."[41]

In general, Peretz negatively viewed the immigration idea as the solution for Jews, be it to Palestine or to Argentina (a common idea at the time). One can read it in his opening article "Vos viln mir?" (What do we want?) in the almanac *Literatur un lebn*, where "Hekht" was also published. There he writes,

> At the time when hard-line ideologists and cunning charlatans promised [the Jewish people] monumental help, a radical means for all its diseases and pains ... in a few years a Jewish state would be established in the Land of Israel, or a Jewish republic in Argentina would be founded ... the poor wretched people believed, and all other issues were put aside, all of the common human interests ... the crowd packed up in a hurry to go, the old drum of "we are the chosen people" thundered, Zion's cymbal rumbled, and the old rabbinic bat spread its wings over the confused crowd.[42]

In 1895, Peretz published another satirical text in Yiddish regarding Zionism entitled "One guy swindles the other," in his eleventh *Yontef bletlekh* volume *Kol khamiro*. In it, the narrator listens to the troubles of Gavriel, a poor Jew whose ten kids had died, four in one week! Gavriel is trying to do the reverse trek from the Land of Israel where he settled back to his home in Eastern Europe in time for Passover. Gavriel does not understand what the Eastern European Zionist propagandists achieve by sending Jews like him to the Holy Land, when they do not profit financially out of it like others do. When three messengers for the Zionist idea came to his hometown, Gavriel looked at them from afar and thought, There goes another group of *daytshn* (literally, Germans; figuratively, secular Jews, proponents of the Jewish Enlightenment), who came to make fun of pious Jews. But to his surprise they acted differently:

> these strange German types were very different . . . they washed . . . blessed . . . ate with their heads covered . . . spoke of the holy Torah and of the Land of Israel.
> He thought that it's a comedy; they play him like a fool . . . they want to deceive him. Though he sees that this is serious, their eyes aflame, their nostrils aflaring, always another one jumps up and gives a whole sermon, that the Land of Israel is eternal, the Torah is eternal, and Israel is also eternal—and politely interweaves all of it—at least start kissing the binding of Torah![43]

And eventually it did the trick; Gavriel has opened to them. Peretz was mocking here what he saw as a great weakness of Zionists: their cooperation with religious leaders, how seemingly modern people cynically adopt pious language and customs to advance their political goals—a method Peretz himself excelled in, which he forgets to mention. Gavriel's fear of the rumors that Jews are being beat up there hold him off a bit from the plan, but when he is reminded of the fact that that poor Jews were being persecuted in Eastern Europe, it reignites his plan to move to the Land of Israel. The narrator reads to Gavriel a hilarious mock version of a romantic Zionist poem. Told through the voice of a Russian man, the poem's message boils down to "Jews out!" while the Russian word "prakhvost!" (bloody swine) is used to describe Jews. It frightens Gavriel very much, and he wishes he will never have to hear this word again:

> You want to assimilate? Oh! I forgot—
>
> You want to help me put on a costume—
>
> I don't need a partner to eat a pig
>
> And a *kamarinsky*-dance I can dance without you!"[44]

Peretz mocks here also his own Hebrew poetry from the 1880s, some of which surprisingly had clear proto-Zionist tendencies. For example, in the long poem "Manginot ha-zman" (The melodies of our age), he wrote lines such as "This is your consolation! Oh, the lips / That a hero's poem, a song of redemption they sang / When the Jordan River backed away and as a wall stood the water, / Or songs of Zion, glorified in holy."[45] The source of Zionism, Peretz writes in this satire, is a narrow circle of wealthy, assimilated Jews who, wishing to further assimilate in their European host countries, plot to send away as many poor Jews as they can in order to advance their own aims. All the others, including the messengers, are ones who read fantastical letters describing a rosy view of life in Palestine. Even Gavriel sent letters back home telling his wife only good news from the Land of Israel so as not to upset her. But the letters are read by more than just his wife, thus inspiring others to immigrate to the land as well. The Zionist business network operates based on self-deception: "Everybody fooled himself; and it cost us so much blood and money, because for a long time no one had the strength to admit that people fooled themselves. . . . And today? Some still fool themselves . . . many love to fool themselves . . . many are already too far stuck in it."[46] As I mentioned earlier, Peretz published not only works that mocked Choveve Tsiyon but also works that praised the proto-Zionist group. In fact, Peretz may have even been active in establishing a chapter of the Choveve Tsiyon movement in Zamość, before he settled in Warsaw. One bit of textual evidence to this fact can be found in his pamphlet in Hebrew "Even ve-even, eyfa ve-eyfa" (Stone and stone, double standards), in which he described how he was going around among rich Jews asking for contributions. He requested a contribution from one Dr. Gentis for this new Choveve Tsiyon chapter. Here is Gentis's response and the exchange that followed:

> You as well—he wondered—dwelling in dreams, and your heart was taken by enchanting deceit? What will you do with this money? Isn't it time to forget all this nonsense? . . .
> —Why?—I asked—in wonder!
> —Are we a People?
> —Do we not have a unique belief system!? . . .
> —Superstition, fanaticism.
> —A unique education system!
> —An education system of big and small *melamdim* [traditional teachers].
> —A unique literature!
> —Of Beit Midrash dwellers!
> —A history . . .

> But talking didn't help; the Doctor turned his shoulder and went into the other room, and I remained with my question.[47]

It is clear from this passage that although Peretz was playing the part of the Choveve Tsiyon advocate, he was not fully convinced of their arguments himself. In his arguments, he did not defend the idea of settling in the Land of Israel specifically but rather the general idea of nationalism. However, the Zionist model of nationalism would later conflict with his commitment to a diasporic version of nationalism.[48] In 1892, merely a year before the publication of the satire "Hekht," Peretz published in Hebrew the text "Manginat ha-zman" (The melody of our age),[49] a text considered to be pro–Choveve Tsiyon.[50] "Manginat ha-zman" is a short allegorical sketch that consists of a dialogue between Miriam the clavichord player and David the poet. Contrary to Peretz's Yiddish satires from the same time, here, the longing for the Holy Land is as real as can be, and forgetting Zion is equated with the most severe sin.

David and Miriam are experiencing a relationship crisis, since Miriam is upset by David's lack of attention to her melodies. A "new wind" has captured him, he says, a wind that was born not in this world. "What happened to me?" he asks, then explains, "Through the window of our temple I observed the life . . . of our people and saw . . . its troubles!" "Yes! Forgive me, David! she called, and fell into his arms."[51] David challenges Miriam to express this newly discovered nationalist sentiment through music; he yearns to hear the sounds of "stress, hunger, thirst, contempt and disgrace, humiliation, subjugation."[52] The desire to give voice to human misery through art, a theme that Peretz himself was struggling with at least since his *Bilder fun a provints rayze*, takes on a particular outlook in this story. The melody that Miriam manages to produce expresses "a sea of tears," and it reminds David of Yom Kippur and of the Wailing Wall. The melody eventually becomes hopeful, "full of an innocent's worry, a hope for justice, and the faith of an honest heart."[53]

This story is infused with a messianic mood, pseudotraditionalism, and a back-to-the-earth feel through its call back to the Holy Land, with all its potential for sexual and national revival. The radical Peretz came out against these ideals during that decade, but here they are *the* solution for the suffering of Jews in Eastern Europe. Such romanticism is quite typical of the sentimental proto-Zionist Hebrew poetry of the 1880s, commonly referred to as the Ḥibat Tsiyon poetry. Ḥibat Tsiyon poetry was meant to stir an intense level of emotion in its readers for the sake of Zion while bemoaning the poor state of Jews in exile. One of its most famous examples is the poem "Tikavatenu" (Our hope), written by twenty-two-year-old Naphtali Herz Imber (1856–1909). The first two of its original nine stanzas were later reworked and became the national anthem of the State of Israel. Its seventh and eighth stanzas go as follows:

> As long as pure tears there / From the eyes of my people are shed / To cry at night for Zion / Awake every midnight
>
> As long as the feeling of love for the nation / Beats in the heart of the Jew / We could still hope today / That the God of wrath would pity us.[54]

This combination of Zion and tears was abundant in the writing of Hebrew poets during the 1880s. But it is not what we have come to expect from Peretz. Possibly, he wrote "Manginat ha-zman" just before he was influenced by social radicalism, or years before then. But still, how does one explain this inconsistency? Did Peretz present one stance in Hebrew and a different, more progressive one in Yiddish?

The choice of language is not necessarily significant regarding the different voices of Peretz, as indicated by the existence of his radical Hebrew journal *The Arrow*, but it certainly played a role. In a pamphlet in Yiddish, published in October 1894, entitled "What should I want?" ("Vos zol ikh veln?," in the Sukkoth edition of the *Yontef bletlekh, Hoshayne*), Peretz explained some of his inconsistencies. In this text, he expressed negative views about the path the Zionist movement was taking, contrasting his feelings about the current movement with the affection for the movement he felt in the past:

> I once had a beloved.
>
> I loved her even though she was poor and bare. . . I loved her, because I am, as I have said more than once, a hopeless romantic. . . for a period of time she was my muse. . . With time my beloved became corrupt! [. . .] Now she befriends rabbis, *melamdim*, and yeshiva students, and goes from house to house with a charity-box, collecting coins for the dowries of orphaned girls. [. . .] I don't want to keep her name secret. . . The lady is called "Choveve Tsiyon." And when I see her, my heart dies of pity, and my gallbladder pours out the bitterness of anger. . . and I can't help it. . . I don't even have the slightest hope! (*Ale verk*, 8:76–78)

The socialist Litvak regarded this text as very radical in its time.[55] But this text does not undermine core Zionist ideology. It wants to restore the Zionist practice to "the right track," which means here breaking the alliance with the religious establishment. Peretz here gave voice to the ideological divide within the Choveve Tsiyon movement that led to a substantial weakening of the movement in the late 1880s and early 1890s. The movement managed to attract major rabbinical figures to its ranks, but the questions of whether or not to follow Jewish religious law and what kind of rationale (more traditional-religious or more secular-nationalist) should be given to the colonization process created an ideological split within the movement.[56] In this article and others, Peretz expressed a disappointment with Zionism that put him on the fence but still closer to the secular end of the Choveve Tsiyon movement.[57]

Peretz's frequent attacks against the proto-Zionists became spikier as he grew closer to circles of Jewish socialists during the 1890s (as in "Hekht").[58] His Yiddish feuilleton "The Argument"[59] from the same period portrays two young people conversing in Yiddish in a public park in Warsaw. One explains to the other his relationship with the Zionist idea. Here again, Peretz criticized Zionism for being fully embedded in the traditional religious world, receiving from it its conceptual vocabulary, while modern, enlightened people should reject Zionism. However, Peretz avoided here an outright attack against Zionism and was careful not to mock it. The speaker, who reminisced about his childhood years, defined himself as "not a Zionist" but declined to call himself an "anti-Zionist." He explained his past attraction to the movement:

> I used to pray seriously once . . . and praying is—all "Jerusalem and Jerusalem! The Land of Israel and the Land of Israel"!
> But I don't know whether Jerusalem and the Land of Israel were not forgotten because people were praying so much; or were people praying all the time because they could not forget Jerusalem and the Land of Israel? (*Ale verk*, 8:127)

Jewish religious indoctrination includes daily chanting of a series of texts, in which the words "Jerusalem" and the "Land of Israel" frequently appear, not as strict geographical locations but as metaphorical and spiritual havens. When a modern political movement with a name that evokes "Love of Zion" sees these terms as concrete real-estate prospects, how can the adult who sang as a child about "the land of milk and honey" not get excited over it? Traditional Jewish education embodies a split spatial consciousness, "a half a soul here, and a half there [in the Land of Israel]") (אַהאַלבעענשמהדאָ, אַהאַלבעדאָרטן; *Ale verk*, 8:131). This text seems to be an honest attempt at analyzing the roots of attraction toward Zionism in the Jewish streets, including being envious of the national power of other nations (the narrator reminisced how as a kid, seeing an army march, he used to think with tears in his eyes, "Where is my military, my music?" [וואו איז מיין מיליטער, מיין מוזיק?; 8:128]; in his fantasies he was a soldier in the Land of Israel, guarding the Jewish holy sites).

At the end of "The Argument," a poor man appears, a former colonist from the Land of Israel. He did not digest the milk and honey so well, and his appearance serves as a harsh testament that Zionism is fundamentally a failing project. In Peretz's essayistic writings of the period one can find recurrent accusations that Zionist institutions wasted money on fantasies instead of investing in the Jews living and suffering in Eastern Europe.[60] In the Yiddish article "In eyrope un bay undz hintern oyvn," Peretz equates the Choveve Tsiyon's practice of selling lands in Palestine to lower-class Jews in Eastern Europe with practices in Chelm, the Jewish town of fools. The news from the Land of Israel described a beautiful grove growing on the plot—in which 100,000 francs were invested—and such gardens are presented as the only way to achieve redemption. But when someone inspects the plot, he sees it is nothing but "rocks and bones!" ("shteyner un beyner!").[61]

Although neither Peretz nor Ahad Ha'am believed in mass migration of Jews to Palestine, Peretz harshly disagreed with the latter's idea of creating a spiritual center for Jews in Palestine. He called this idea "foolish," "artificial," "far from the life center of the people," and illusionary.[62] Peretz's belief in Eastern Europe being the center of the Jewish people and where the Jewish intelligentsia should overwhelmingly focus its educational efforts is perhaps the strongest and most serious reason for Peretz's lack of support for the Zionist plan starting in the 1890s. Peretz expressed this view years later in a letter (1906/7) to the Hebrew poet Haim Nachman Bialik (1873–1934). He called on Bialik to "go out to the people," leave Ahad Ha'am's small house of elitist learning, and write in Yiddish.[63] But other reasons played a part as well.

As indicated earlier, Zionists' cooperation with religious factions bothered Peretz immensely. He described the Zionists as bowing down to rabbis and turning against the humanistic ideals of the Enlightenment.[64] Ahad Ha'am, who "always rubbed Peretz the wrong way,"[65] was supportive of cooperation of nonreligious Zionists with the Jewish religious establishment, as long as both sides were tolerant toward the opinions of the other, because both sides sought the well-being of the Jewish people, each according to its own way. Aḥad Ha'am did not believe in the abolition of religion, nor in reforming religion (as the *maskilim* preached), but in its "natural development"—meaning the belief that the changed material conditions of the Jewish people because of the realization of the Zionist plan would eventually lead to developments in religious matters.[66]

Although Peretz objected to cooperating with the religious establishment, he addressed religious Jews in his writing through his usage of a language and motifs taken from the religious world. Aḥad Ha'am hoped the Zionist project would work, thus tolerance between its different factions was key to him. Aside from this particular point was Peretz's stated more serious and fundamental critique of Zionism: being far for the heart of the people, wasteful, and suicidal. The most colorful anti-Zionist text by Peretz was the satirical feuilleton *Literature and life* (1894). In it, Choveve Tsiyon is depicted as a multiheaded dragon on its way to take control of the Jewish people, using its physical capacities wisely to spread its often-contradictory messages. "Defeating such a dragon could be done only by cutting off all of its heads at once!" he writes.

> And if there is a difference between a dragon and Choveve Tsiyon, it lies only in that the dragon had only one belly, one belly for all of its heads and thus he needed less, while in a human fraternity every head has its own separate belly; every head must separately bite, eating at his own separate expense, and therefore—every fraternity is so expensive! [. . .] I will risk my life and stand up against the biggest animal and beast . . ., but with a dragon, forgive me, I can't sustain a war! Because a dragon with a few dozen heads, one cannot catch in a lie! [. . .] Thirty-five heads are shouting: run, fly, snatch, flee to Palestine . . . milk and honey flows there for you, the Turk is waiting with open arms, the Arab is dying for you![67]

Following the same model of the contradictory messages coming out of the dragon heads, Choveve Tsiyon was accused of having double standards in its relationship with the Jewish religious establishment (its members needed to choose whether they wished to be pious or modern, progressive people). They were criticized for their dual relation to their Europeanism (on the one hand, they say they want their own culture, but on the other hand, they are all European in their conduct). And again, they are condemned for their mixture of Orthodox and modern Jews. All the above made the movement indistinct and "multiheaded" in its character. Peretz wrote that contrary to the argument that the dragon is a made-up story, Choveve Tsiyon is as real as you can get. But there was no difference between the two, in the sense that both were entirely false and therefore both could hurt only those who believed in them.

Peretz used such spiky rhetoric and colorful imagery to advance his cultural-political wars and to roundly reject both the ideology and the practices of Choveve Tsiyon.[68] He also mocked the movement's appropriation of progressive socialist jargon for its project.[69] In Europe, when an industrialist thinks about the question of the workers, "his hands and feet are shaking"—he knows that the workers claiming their rights will become expensive for him since the worker just might come to the "dreadful" understanding that "the industrialists are competing at his expense, and that three-quarters of the merchandise comes from his blood and sweat." But in the Jewish streets, such a social struggle manifests itself in "supporting the workers in the Land of Israel."[70]

He noted that sending charity to workers in Palestine had become a tool of self-promotion for those who want to have their name in the papers and a source of income for the paper that sold the advertisement space for such ads. Peretz concluded that this behavior could not be called socialism since it did not contain any element of class war. On the other hand, in the Eastern European Jewish Diaspora "there are many poor craftsmen. For that same money you could have built them workshops and bought them new machines."[71] As expected, Peretz was vehemently attacked in the Zionist press for expressing such views. The criticism included booklets parodying his work,[72] and at the time he polemicized with his attackers with full rhetorical force. Posthumously, even a hundred years after these articles were written, the attacks on Peretz for his stance toward Zionism continued. Although other prominent Hebrew writers were also very critical of Zionism—from the Hebrew poet Yalag, who warned as early as 1870 that if ever there would be a Jewish state, then the rabbinic establishment would take it over, and it would become a fascist and a religious state; to the Hebrew prose of Abramovitsh from the 1880s in stories such as "In the days of commotion" and the already discussed "Shem and Japheth on the train"[73]—they never received the same backlash that Peretz and his legacy endured.

"The Audacity to Demand Realism": Peretz and the New Wave of Hebrew Literature

In 1903, Peretz published a short satirical text in Hebrew mocking three famous figures in the world of modern Hebrew and Yiddish publishing. There Peretz depicted his longtime collaborator from the *Bletlekh* days, Mordkhe Spektor, and the figure of Ben-Avigdor (the pen name of Avraham Leyb Shalkovitz, 1866–1921). He began with an attack on Ben-Avigdor:

> And one beggar was an odd sod...
> He was born half a slave and half a free man...
> And he became half a writer and half a business man, meaning: a beggar business man; according to rumors, he didn't have much...
> He went and wrote tiny booklets, and he distributed them widely...
> And with his load of booklets he traveled to where Jews live, and called out: "buy, for the sake of Zion, for the sake of he who resides in Zion!"
> And they took the books.[74]

In this text, Peretz mocked a figure who stood at the center of the Hebrew publishing world in Warsaw for over two decades and helped it become the world's largest Jewish publishing center by the end of the nineteenth century.[75] In his early days, Ben-Avigdor devoted his time to writing as much as he did to publishing, helping to modernize Hebrew literature by introducing realist and naturalistic trends into it. The goal of Ben-Avigdor and his movement, referred to as the "New Wave" (*ha-mahalach he-chadash*, after the German *Der Neue Kurs*), was to emulate the success of Yiddish literature and try to bestow on Hebrew the same folk credentials that characterized modern Yiddish literature. They did so by focusing almost exclusively on narratives set in the present day, challenging the accepted norm of producing Hebrew literature that was set in the mythical past.[76] In so doing, the New Wave openly confronted the harsh socioeconomic reality experienced by lower-class Jews. In the Eastern European Jewish context, many in the Jewish labor movement believed that they were incapable of mobilizing people and creating a mass movement for social change using Hebrew. With spoken modern Hebrew in its very infancy, any contemporary manifesto for the people would have to be issued in

Yiddish. Ben-Avigdor's new realist movement in Hebrew literature was meant to challenge the association of Hebrew with the privileged and learned classes.

Linguistically, the movement employed a more secular Hebrew language and avoided the customary references to traditional Jewish texts, which had been the norm in modern Hebrew literature. Their texts included many Hebrew expressions that were directly translated from Yiddish, representing an intensification of the trend started by Abramovitsh in the 1880s. Most of the dialogues clearly reflected speech translated directly from Yiddish. For example, the Yiddish curse *tsen mises meshunes af im* (may he die ten violent deaths) became in Hebrew *eser mitot meshunut alav*, and the Yiddish expression *vey mir un vey tsu mayn mazl* (woe is me and woe is to my luck) became *oy li ve-oy le-mazali*.[77] The end result is that the language of the New Wave is a nonbiblical, Yiddishized version of Hebrew. Their nonreferential style distinguished them from past and contemporary writers.

Rejecting referential language surely meant a rejection of the style of *Haskalah* literature. But it also meant embracing a style different than that of the Hebrew prose of Abramovitsh (despite the shared "Yiddish influence"), whom Bialik referred to as "Yotser ha-nusaḥ" (the inventor of the style).[78] Abramovitsh's innovative style strove to blend various historical layers of the Hebrew language, including biblical Hebrew, Mishnaic Hebrew, and Talmudic Aramaic (some of which was sourced from the Hebrew-Aramaic component in Yiddish). This blended Hebrew became the norm for European pre-Israeli Hebrew fiction.[79]

The "Odessans," Bialik and Abramovitsh, believed that an intense usage of Aramaic vocabulary in Hebrew prose would somehow compensate for Hebrew's lack of folksiness compared to Yiddish. But as Ken Frieden shows, more often than not, Abramovitsh failed, and his Aramaic often "heightened" rather than "lowered" his Hebrew prose style, for his Aramaic was understood only by the elite circles who were educated in Ashkenazi yeshivas (as were Bialik and Abramovitsh).[80] Frieden focuses on Abramovitsh's Hebrew novels from the first decade of the twentieth century, meaning a decade after the appearance of the New Wave. A look at the language style of one of Abramovitsh's earlier texts, such as "Shem and Japheth on the train," shows an extensive usage of Aramaic vocabulary from Yiddish (like *milse-debdikhuse*, a joke, p. 50).[81] But he does use whole biblical phrases (like his playful use of *pri bitni khatat nafshi*, "the fruit of my body for the sin of my soul," p. 52; Micah 6:7; and *hadar hacarmel ve-hasharon ma'ase elohenu*, "the splendor of the Carmel and the Sharon created by our God," p. 46; Isaiah 35:2), phrases from the commentaries (like *nigzar terudin*, "sentenced to deportation," p. 56; Midrash Genesis Rabba:2), and other fixed expressions from traditional sources. Thus, even though Abramovitsh was also considered at his time to be a realist, and was praised for it by Sholem Aleichem, his language style was different than Ben-Avigdor's, for it was still referential.

The New Wave repackaged Hebrew literature in an affordable format embodied by Ben-Avigdor's *Sifre-agora* (Penny-books) project (1891–94): a series of low-cost pocket books (five kopeks a volume), a phenomenon that was just beginning even in European publishing at the time.[82] In 1891, Ben-Avigdor issued a manifesto "To the Lovers of Hebrew and Its Literature," stating that Hebrew literature was lacking in "literature for the common people" where "the life of our people [will be] reflected as if in a mirror." To enlarge the number of Hebrew readers, he wrote,

> I am initiating a great and valuable project. . . . I am going to publish "penny-books" for the people, little booklets sold cheaply, which will find many enthusiastic customers, even from the stingy public, the Hebrew public: A. Thanks to their low price. B. Thanks to their pleasant and useful content. The booklets will contain: stories, pictures, scenes, from people's lives, plays, poetry and epics and more . . . and after the people get used to spending money on books, belletristic writing will bloom. There is hope that one of these days our literature will become a part of the people's needs, for slowly, slowly a Hebrew public will be created.[83]

Ben-Avigdor is putting forth here the business plan for the creation of modern Hebrew literature, stating clearly that a Hebrew public as well as a new Hebrew literary language must be invented for this purpose. Its inspiration was drawn from the rise of modern Yiddish literature, as it similarly strove to recreate a vernacular Hebrew language as a *folksshprakh*, or a people's language, as Yiddish was commonly termed. Specifically, it took inspiration from a Yiddish publishing initiative started by Peretz and his close friend and collaborator, the Yiddish writer Yankev Dinezon. In Warsaw in 1890, the pair published a collection of three short stories in Yiddish by Peretz under the title *Bekante bilder* (Familiar pictures). These texts, which embody psychological complexity by employing the form of internal monologues, are considered a significant development in modern Yiddish fiction.[84] Three stories were published in this volume. "The Messenger" (*Der meshulakh*) tells the story of the dying traditional Jewish-shtetl economy in which Jews frequently acted as the middlemen between the aristocrats who owned the land and the peasants who worked the land. It does so through the story of an old man suffering from chest pains when carrying a sum of money and a contract that he needs to deliver through extreme weather. As he travels, he is reminiscing and hallucinating about his life. The story "The Crazy Idler" ("Der meshugener batln"; in English it was translated as "The Mad Talmudist") consists of an internal monologue of a person suffering from a split personality disorder, as does the less important story "What Is Soul?" ("Vos heyst neshome?").[85] Frieden states that in these stories "Peretz did not yet aim at social ends."[86] But while it is true that Peretz was not yet radicalized in these stories, he nevertheless carried a social message in them, namely the positivist ideal of embracing urban modern professions (very clear in "The messenger").

The introduction to these stories (written by Dinezon) resembles the later Hebrew literature manifesto written by Ben-Avigdor, which is unsurprising giving that each side was highly aware of the other. (In his memoirs, Ben-Avigdor cites a conversation he had in 1891 with the Yiddish poet Yehoyesh, who casted doubts on Ben-Avigdor's "penny-library" initiative. Yehoyesh doubted that it would be possible to distribute even cheap books in great numbers "because Mr. Peretz also hoped it would be possible to distribute his booklet 'Familiar Pictures' in thousand and tens of thousands, and yet he lost his own money in it."[87]) That said, the texts move in somewhat opposite directions.

Dinezon states, as Ben-Avigdor would later, that the goal of his booklet is to be the first in a series called *Groshen bibliyotek* (Penny library) "to give the reading public low-priced stories from our Jewish life in our Jewish language (i.e., Yiddish), so that everyone will be able to buy, read, and understand them."[88] But they move in opposite directions regarding the prestige they wish to bestow on their respective literatures. Whereas Ben-Avigdor wished to "lower" Hebrew to the everyday life of lower-class Jews and their language, taste, and concerns, and thus compensate for Hebrew's elitist status, Dinezon sought to introduce his readers to something as yet scarcely known in Yiddish literature—namely, highbrow literature.[89] In so doing, Dinezon wanted to compensate for the reputation of Yiddish literature as being vulgar and trashy (*shund*). Dinezon noted in a condescending manner that "Mr. Peretz does not write in order to suck up to the vulgar taste of the lower-class reader; the opposite, he wants to refine him and to correct him," and he regards this series as a contrast to the "most interesting novels" (meaning the *shund*) that poured like rain and created "lots of mud" in the Yiddish literary scene.[90]

Both Dinezon and his rival Ben-Avigdor attempted to introduce new capitalist means of literary production in their respective "national print-languages," a move they both viewed as a democratization of the literary book market.[91] Both were attempting to create a new "readership public" (both texts use the word *publikum*—rather than *der oylem / der kool* in Yiddish or *kahal* in Hebrew—in order to stress the modern imagined nationalist community, as opposed to the traditional one), wherein they would play the role of the bourgeois nationalist intelligentsia. Both paved the way for Peretz's revolutionary *Yontef bletlekh*, which began to appear in 1894. To give a concrete example, both Ben-Avigdor's penny-books and Peretz's *Bletlekh* were sold for the low price of five kopecks a volume. B. Gorin (Goyda) had a similar ambition regarding establishing a Yiddish parallel to Ben-Avigdor's penny-books, but it never materialized in any substantial way.[92]

Ben-Avigdor's demand for "realism" as expressed in his manifesto and in his programmatic story "Menahem the Writer" (1893)[93] triggered angry and cynical responses from Peretz, but also some cooperation since some of Peretz's Hebrew works were published in Ben-Avigdor's "penny-books" series and in other related volumes.[94] Part of Peretz's cynical response grew out of his criticism of the Choveve Tsiyon movement. Ben-Avigdor himself was active in Choveve Tsiyon. Like Aḥad Ha'am, Ben-Avigdor served for a while as the secretary of the society Bnei Moshe, which promoted a secular Jewish education in the spirit of Aḥad Ha'am's platform of "cultural Zionism."[95] On the one hand, asserts Peretz, the demand for realism in Hebrew literature came from the literary circles of those proto-Zionist groups, but on the other hand this Zionist literature depicted the Land of Israel in a very rosy, nonrealist manner. In his Yiddish feuilleton *Literature and life*, he commented at length on this inconsistency.[96]

While Peretz was critical of the Zionist plan in *Literature and life*, he himself mimicked the racist anthropological theories that claimed the cultural inferiority of native peoples, writing of Arabs and Turks that their "women are being whipped with bamboo sticks."[97] One can find also prejudiced passages about Persians in his popular-science booklet about the cholera epidemic in 1892:

> The speed [of the spread of the epidemic] is thanks the new train, which was finished in 1888, that attached Europe to middle Asia. The train, as all trains, did trade a great favor, but undermined our health, because it connected us with the Persians, an extremely unclean people, in addition to being terribly fanatical, and believing wholeheartedly that because the epidemic comes from God, it is forbidden to seek any cure or any advice against it, and if the doctors have somewhat of a cure, they contend the Master of the Universe with the help of demons . . . along with that they possess a good habit of eating with unclean hands and—the whole family from one bowl! And so it happens that if one falls ill the entire family falls with him. Thanks to the train the distance from them to us became short.[98]

These ill-conceived theories legitimized the colonial and imperial rule of the European empires over the "wild east."[99] At times these theories were espoused by Jews who wished to see themselves as being an integral part of Europe, aligned with its conquering aspirations.[100] Even in "The Harp," Peretz did not raise explicit moral concerns that the Land of Israel / Palestine might in fact belong to its inhabitants. He did raise awareness, as Aḥad Ha'am before him,[101] to the fact that other peoples lived there. Already in "Bildung," Peretz noted that "the land of Israel . . . is not available for us, because there is a people and a government there who also have an opinion. Our claim on the land is more ancient . . . but our lawyer has only his mouth to speak, while against us there is an armed force."[102] But his observation was made in the context of voicing a practical limitation—namely, that the presence of others might make it hard for Jews to settle in the land.

For Peretz, the writers' distance from the land increases their distance from realist depictions. What Peretz does offer those Jewish writers who wish to write "realistically" is a kind of a literary *doikayt* (a focus on the "here"): a commitment by Jews to their local society wherever they reside. The term *doikayt* was later be coined by the Bund as its ideological foundational guideline. For Peretz, if "you live for example in Vilna—describe the filth! You are in the Jewish study-house—study the cockroaches, or the wife of the sexton in a synagogue, who pours in drinks through the little window!"[103] But Peretz not only did not believe that those Hebrew writers were living up to their realist pretensions; also, for him, "genuine realism" in itself was less attractive as a literary style. He was more interested in modernist genres of writing, including symbolism and decadence.[104]

In a literary essay in *The Arrow*, Peretz expressed concern that Hebrew literature was sorely lagging behind what he referred to as the world of "general literature" (meaning non-Jewish Western literature), where "the sun of materialism has already set." Meanwhile, in Jewish circles, realism was "a new slogan that creates enthusiasm in the hearts of the people."[105] Peretz related here to decadent literature as one of his preferred modernist genres. The term *decadence* refers to a literary movement formed in late-nineteenth-century France, inspired by the writings of Baudelaire. The movement emphasized the autonomy of art (i.e., its independence from moral and social concerns as preached by the nineteenth-century French author and literary critic Théophile Gautier), the hostility of the artist to bourgeois society, the quest for new sensations, and the superiority of artifice to nature.[106]

Decadent literature was met with an ambivalent response in the Hebrew literary circles of the time, where the nationalist "Revival literature" enjoyed dominance from the mid-1890s onward, taking its lead from the *Haskalah* (the "Revival literature" included the New Wave but also figures such as Bialik, Tchernichovsky, Berdichevsky, and others, who were not part of the New Wave, besides minor efforts by Bialik[107]). It was hard at that time for Hebrew writers to identify with a literature whose founding assumptions were not linked with the idea of national revival.

In traditional Marxist literary interpretations, including the Yiddish-Soviet critical tradition, decadent literature was considered a reflection of a decadent society. The decadent writer was "playing along" with society's capitalist norms rather than criticizing those norms, as these critics believed the great nineteenth-century realist writers used to do. Sartre convincingly argued a counterpoint to these trends in Marxist literary criticism, which is useful in understanding Peretz's exploration of decadent elements in his writings:

> Either we accept an utterly naive and simple Marxism. . . . Or we say: "a decadent society poses new problems for a writer, tortures him in his own consciousness and in his creative activity." Otherwise, would there be any progressive people in a decadent society? Thus we must certainly consider that this society, which contains and produces the artist, also conditions him; but we are not by any means compelled to think of this author strictly as a decadent. On the contrary, he can

be recuperated by a new society; and there is no certainty that, in his struggle against his own contradictions, he may not have invented the forms of the ideas which will be used by the liberated society.[108]

Following the work of Bar-Yosef, we established that Peretz's writings in *The Arrow* introduced decadent trends into Hebrew literature.[109] The shattering of the foundations of faith, rather than "a stable depiction of reality" (the realist-naturalist convention), is one of the characteristics of the decadent style of writing. Thus, at least in *The Arrow*, Peretz—a progressive writer in a "decadent society"—was inventing "the forms of the ideas which will be used by the liberated society," in Sartre's terms, and should not be considered to be decadent himself. Bar-Yosef refers to Peretz's notion of decadence as "inconsistent and incomprehensive mainly regarding his views toward nationalism."[110] But it is based on her false attribution to Peretz of Sokolow's article "The creators of chaos" (signed Amittai), where Sokolow (and not Peretz) attacked decadent historical thinking. Decadence for Peretz was a crucial tool both artistically, in his efforts to modernize Hebrew literature, and in his political battles against Zionism's territorialist nationalism, a tool against "Realism and Love of Zion"[111] alike. And, in this regard, in *The Arrow* Peretz was consistent.

Can more examples of such challenging modernist works be found in Peretz's Hebrew prose of the 1890s? Did they indeed challenge the "new" realist-naturalist trends as set forth by Ben-Avigdor and the Hebrew New Wave? Or are his other Hebrew prose texts of that time (i.e., not those published in *The Arrow*) more conventional than the modernist trends he calls for in his essays? Where do these texts stand with respect to his major achievements in Yiddish prose from the same period? The next section will explore these questions through a close reading of Peretz's major Hebrew prose stories from the 1890s.

Peretz's Major Hebrew Prose and 1890s Creations: The Poor Will Remain Silent

Peretz's prose debut was in Hebrew, with the short story "The Kaddish" (1886), one of four short stories in Hebrew that he released that year.[112] It took him five years to publish another work of Hebrew prose, while he was commencing his Yiddish writing career. Not until the 1890s, when he was highly prolific in Yiddish literature, did he bring the modernizing spirit so prominent in his Yiddish work to his Hebrew writings. The 1890s were the last decade in which Peretz created original prose in Hebrew.

As we have seen in the previous chapters, Peretz often placed female figures at the center of his stories, like in the Yiddish stories "A spoiled Shabbat"(1892), "In the basement" (1893), and "A woman's wrath" (1893), and also in the Hebrew story "The Mute" (1892).[113] "The Mute" was published as a part of the *Sifre-agora* series, alongside the short story "Manginat ha-zman." As in Ben-Avigdor's story "Leah, the fish-monger" (1891) and other Hebrew New Wave stories, Peretz's story "The Mute" is a sentimental depiction of the lives of lower-class Jewish women in the shtetl. They are "the lowest of the low": the protagonist is a low-class Jewish woman who is also mute. As much as Peretz ridiculed Ben-Avigdor and his demand for realism, in this story Peretz seemed to follow Ben-Avigdor's manifesto: he used a "thin" nonreferential Hebrew and "low language" (meaning a Yiddishized version of Hebrew), he depicted lower-class Jews, and he devised a plot set in the present time that was devoid of any fantastic elements. Many of the conventions of nineteenth-century naturalist fiction can be found in this story, which is also characterized by tragic irony and the helplessness of the protagonists against external dominant forces.

What differentiated Peretz's story were the modernist elements he introduced, namely the mixture of narration styles and the use of the fragmentation technique,[114] the same techniques he employed and perfected in his Yiddish fiction.[115] The fragmented narration is built through three different elements, which move in a circular motion. The first element is a narrator, who tells the story with a constant flow of commentary. Second is the lighthearted and humorous dialogue at the beginning and

Figure 3.2. Peretz's prose debut, the Hebrew short story "The Kaddish" (1886), in the paper *Hayom*. It is one of four short stories in Hebrew he released that year. Jewish Historical Press.

end of the story between the two *yidenes* (literally "Jewish women," stereotyped as being talkative), who explain the current status of Chana, the mute (as she is thirty years of age), and who function as the story's choir. Finally, there is the central inner story surrounding the miserable life of Chana from the age of fifteen.[116]

The story's treatment of the poor was sentimental, not as a revolutionary subject: the story was set in a nonindustrialized shtetl reality, not the urban reality of the proletariat. There was class conflict in the story, between the protagonist Chana and her upwardly mobile beloved Yaakov, but it was blurred by the dominant narrative discourse of romantic love.[117] Still, since "The Mute" did expose the hypocritical norms of the nascent bourgeois Jewish society,[118] this Hebrew story can be considered a transitional story for Peretz. It fits neatly between the positivist nationalist stand of his Yiddish story "In the Mail Coach" (1891) and the more radical socialist stand expressed in later Yiddish stories such as "Bontshe the Silent" and "Weaver-Love" (1893–97).

The story tells of Chana, a young woman, who became mute after seeing her beloved Yaakov in flames. The cruel irony is that Chana lost her speech because of the trauma, but Yaakov not only survived it but bloomed afterward. At first, he remained faithful to Chana despite her muteness, but eventually he moved on with his professional career as a doctor, and we are led to understand that while at university (outside the familiar shtetl), he moved on romantically as well. Yaakov's father tells Chana that his son "stopped being sad and staying at home, because he was invited to a ball [*neshef-kheshek*] at the home of a very rich man, where he danced with all the women and the young ladies."[119] This, and the news that huge sums of money are offered by fathers who want their daughters to marry Yaakov, leads Chana to a total mental breakdown. To add to the bitter, Zolaesque irony, Yaakov now acts as her doctor but handles her in the same insensitive manner with which he treats the rest of his poor patients. Shaked correctly asserted that Peretz inherited this theme of "miserable love" from the *Haskalah* literature before him, but that in contrast to the *Haskalah* literature, here the source of destruction of the family lies not in backward religious laws but in the social condition.[120] Chana, who even before the fire was referred to as "Chana the Pale," is now obliged to marry the good-hearted but physically repellant Zaynvel, the *melamed* (a traditional teacher of Hebrew). Shenfeld views the unflattering description of Zaynvel's shape—he is a hunchback, with a thick, crooked nose and a big wart on his left cheek—together with the detailed accounts of the material environment, the petty social conditions, and the strong fatalist elements, as representing the naturalist elements in the story.[121] But the figure of the "ugly *melamed*" is also a literary convention that is familiar to readers since the *Haskalah* period (like in the works of Smolanskin), long before the naturalist trends entered Hebrew literature. It is impossible to find in modern Hebrew and Yiddish fiction a *melamed* character who happens to be handsome.

The plot contains many twists and turns; most of them include the mental and physical death of individuals and of the family unit, collapsing under the pressures of socioeconomic hardship: both Chana's father and Zaynvel die; she had two children by Zaynvel, and her fate is not a cheery one. Chana is a voiceless figure who stands in for the Jewish women, who are all mutes. She is the title and central character, unlike in Peretz's Yiddish story "In the Mail Coach," where women are merely discussed by men but do not make any actual physical appearances. The bold description of Chana's sexual encounters with her physically deformed husband are in effect a literary depiction of marital rape:

> Every night a dark dread befell her, and she would run out of the house into the yard, and she would stand at the gate immersed in her many thoughts. Then when her father would take her from there and bring her home using great force, all her bones were shivering out of fear and she couldn't stand on her feet, and against her will she fell on the bed. But no matter what, she wouldn't permit him to undress her. Instead, she screamed and bit and ripped her father's face with her nails and the faces of the neighbor women who helped him, but by the time her husband Zaynvel approached her she had no strength left and she didn't continue to struggle. She lay as a log on the bed moving as little as she could. Her thoughts became confused, and she stopped knowing what was happening to her . . .
>
> Since the day Zaynvel came into the house, scarcity did not trouble them as before.[122]

Peretz is clearly criticizing here the barbaric treatment of women, depicting how the female body was sold for material gain. It is not radically different from the enslaved women in nineteenth-century America, who "lived with the constant reality of rape because they were the property of their white male masters."[123] Like those enslaved women, who "did not easily give up their rights over their bodies and tried to keep some form of perceived control over their bodies and their lives,"[124] Chana also struggled as much as she could but was incapable of single-handedly defeating such a coalition of men and women who were out to subordinate her to the will of the male provider. The material gain turned out to be all too temporary and later failed to save the family from destruction.

Linguistically, Peretz's Hebrew did not stray from Ben-Avigdor's aesthetic demands. He emulated the (Yiddish) speech of lower-class Jewish women by using a "quasi-*Yiddishi*" Hebrew speech, which included many direct quotes from Yiddish. For example, the term *merak ha-zahav* (Yiddish: *gildene yoykh*) means "a wedding soup," and it ironically referred here to Chana's ugly Zaynvel the day after their wedding. Some of these direct translations appeared in the Hebrew version with quotation marks and thus stuck out even more. As a rule, this Hebrew style of prose was heavily influenced by Yiddish, a fact that Peretz tried to tone down in later versions of the story.[125] The language was "thin," meaning it did not make references to traditional Jewish texts. Instead, it followed Ben-Avigdor's aesthetic demands that the words should stand on their own.

Roland Barthes maintained that the language of realist literature—in this case, the nonbiblical, Yiddishized version of Hebrew—helped confirm the prejudice that there was indeed a form of "standard" language that was somehow natural.[126] The "realist language" claim of being representational strengthened the modernist idea of a standardized national language. By differentiating itself from "colloquial" types of speech, the national language was seen as something natural that existed, rather than just the product of the imagination. In Hebrew one needed to imagine a spoken language, in effect a language that relied on Yiddish for its syntax and expressions, since modern spoken Hebrew was barely taking its first steps at the time, mostly in Palestine.[127] On the other hand, Peretz was aware of the need to create a standard literary Yiddish language and permitted himself to write in colloquial Yiddish only when he wrote in a dialogue format. He avoided colloquialisms, and his Yiddish was thus comprehensible to speakers in all geographical regions. Shmuel Werses claims that this strategy contributed to an intensified sense of alienation in Peretz's Yiddish texts between the modern storyteller's voice and the common people.[128] But Werses forgets the dialectical relationship between Hebrew and Yiddish literatures, namely the New Wave's effort—which included Peretz's participation with stories like "The Mute" and "In a Summer House"—to create a spoken Hebrew literary language from scratch.[129]

The language of another Hebrew story by Peretz, "Bime'on kayitz" (In a summer house; 1893)[130] deserves discussion as well. The language and the tone of "In a Summer House" are utterly different from those prescribed by Ben-Avigdor, and when they do come close to conforming to his conventions, they do so in order to put them under a critical eye. The story is written mostly in a rich poetic language and features three full-blown romantic poems: one is an original by Peretz;[131] another is a translation of a German romantic poem by Chamisso; and finally, a "merry folksong," similar to many others of its kind written in Yiddish by various writers and in other languages. This story's main theme is the meaning of love and the different expressions it finds among people of different social classes. It ends humorously with the beloved expressing fear of pregnancy to her suitor:

I was afraid, my beloved, I was afraid	יראתי, דוד חונף, יראתי,
Our secret love would be revealed...	תגלה אהבה נסתרה...
And then my mother would ask, ha,	ואמי כי תשאל:"הה,
My daughter,	בתי,
Why is your gown so narrow?[132]	שׁלמה כתנתך כה צרה?"

Thus, as Peretz acknowledged in his writing, he is "by his nature a hopeless romantic"[133] who reduced the New Wave's call for realism in Hebrew literature to "Oys romantik! Oys poezye!" (No more romance! No more poetry!),[134] so this story can be viewed as a romantic response to the realist and naturalist demands of the New Wave. And, in that sense, it is unclear why Peretz placed this story in the category of "angry" stories.[135] This story was published in the first volume of the Hebrew yearly almanac *Luakh akhiasaf* (1893–1904[136]), one of Ben-Avigdor's endeavors. It was a Zionist publication and the only stage of expression for the New Wave writers since the decline of his penny library in 1894.[137] Because of its unique place for the New Wave writers, their literary conventions were clearly reflected in this almanac, most prominently by showcasing the works of Reuven Braynin (1862–1939), Ezra Goldin (1868–1915), Ben-Avigdor himself, and other New Wave writers. It was founded after the relative financial success of the "penny-library," and the first three volumes under Ben-Avigdor were rich with literary content.[138] "In a Summer House" was published not long before Peretz published his critical essays (two in 1894) challenging the literary norms set forth by Ben-Avigdor in his manifesto. The main question to ask, then, is whether this critique was reflected in the story, or rather, did it conform to the aesthetic conventions of the New Wave, as in "The Mute"? And if "In a Summer House" does differ from the New Wave in its aesthetic structuring, does the story also differ from the New Wave in its political-ideological stance?

The narrator here is once again a modern urban Jew touring the provinces. But unlike *Bilder fun a provints rayze*, where the province meant the backward and depressing shtetl, alien to the modern character, in this Hebrew story the province is a refuge. Here, the modern Jew, like any good bourgeois European, was going to the country to relax in accordance with his doctor's advice. He rented a room in the home of a Jewish merchant named Reb Avraham, whose son Shmuel was about to be married. The plot begins with humoristic commotion around the petty financial disputes between the two matchmakers and between the fathers of the bride and groom, which almost results in the cancellation of the wedding. The protagonist feels he needs to escape this anti-romantic "realist" atmosphere of "olam ha-kheshbon" (the world of arithmetic),[139] signaling a shift to a different, more genuine, authentic, and heartfelt meaning of love. In the second part of the story, the romantic yearnings of the protagonist surface through his communion with nature. He expresses these yearnings in the first part of the story in his sensual depiction of the bride going for a short outdoor stroll with the groom in order to escape the commotion: "The bride is a very pretty girl; she is a rose flower that had not yet bloomed . . . one kiss is enough in order to awaken the sleeping woman inside this young gentle body! One kiss is enough in order to create a gust in her chest, to light candles in the apples of her eyes, to give a breath of paradise to her nose and burning lips to her mouth."[140] This style is a clear diversion from the ugly realistic physicality of "The Mute." Peretz's transitional passage paints an exhilarating impressionistic sketch of the modern man's encounter with nature:

> The day's place was taken over by the evening . . . and I'm still sitting on the bank of the river without knowing what is going on inside the house.
>
> The sun is disappearing into the depths of blood and fire while the moon is rising out of the mist to wander like a hen among her chicks, the stars. I sit within the protection of the woods . . . the pure sky from above and the image of the woods are reflected in the crystal water below. The sound of the little waves chasing each other like playful children, the foam on the azure of the water, the shiver of the leaves of the woods, together with the soul of the grass and the flowers overlaid with the

drops of dew, night flakes, the voice of the nightingale between the branches—all of these carried me on the wings of spring to the world of nobility [*olam ha-atsilut*]. . . . My heart expanded and became as big as the gate of a world and it filled with the sorrow of all creatures and the love of the whole world, and my soul became weary within me from yearning and dreaming.[141]

Peretz uses this transformative journey from "olam ha-kheshbon" to "olam ha-atsilut" to redirect his readers away from the strangling aesthetics demanded by the New Wave to what he sees as liberating ones: a modernist, neoromantic, impressionist literature.[142] In this dreamy associative literature, prose, poetry, and drama intertwine as much as dreams and reality mingle. The Hebrew may not be heavily referential, and the story does take place in the present time, but it does not deal in any way with desperate living conditions or with the struggle for survival. One's impression of the beauty of nature replaces the observation of the ugliness of the downtrodden.

In the dreamy second part of the story, the protagonist hears a simple young sailor singing to his beloved. The country people's love is of an honest and noble manner; they speak in elevated Hebrew poetry between themselves, not the language of numbers and finance. In this idyll, "nature is the matchmaker."[143] While analyzing Schiller's hermeneutic system, Jameson notes that "the notion of a realization of freedom in art becomes concrete only when . . . Schiller descends into the detail of the work of art itself," where Schiller asks us "to see the very technical construction of the work as a *figure* of the struggle for psychic integration in general, to see in images, quality of language, type of plot construction the very figures (in an imaginary mode) of freedom itself."[144] If we arrive at political freedom through beauty,[145] then the idyll genre, writes Jameson, is the third logical possibility (after the elegiac and the satiric modes).[146]

The idyll genre imagines the possibility of the "genuinely free and harmonious personality"[147] becoming real someday when different and liberating social conditions should arise. In Peretz's "In a Summer House," this personality is embodied in the figures of the young singing sailor and his beloved country girl; their oneness with nature means they achieved what the modern protagonist is yearning for. The sailor's genuine love, poetic language, and images represented for Peretz the beauty that would make it possible for people to arrive at true political freedom. Stanzas such as these detail the all-encompassing totality of such love, creating within the reader an elevation of the soul:

Your pure forehead is my sky,	מצחך הזך לי רקיע,
The stars of your eyes will make it their tent;	יהלו שם כוכבי עיניך
	בלעדך צלמות כל חלדי,
Without you shadow of death is all my life,	כי שמשי—הצחוק על
For my sun—is the laughter on your lips.	שפתיך.
You are my light, you are my life!	את אורי, את חיי!
Without	בלעדיך
you I'm a clod among clods of earth!	אני רגב בין רגבי אדמה!
Because only from the light in your eyes	יען אך מנגהות עיניך
My soul was secretly woven[148]	נפשי בסתר נרקמה

In these verses, the speaker's voice is that of a passionate and soulful individual; six singular possessives ("my") appear in just two short stanzas. Simultaneously, the narrator universalizes the facial features of the female subject (forehead, eyes, lips), associating them with their fundamental qualities (sky, sun, earth). In turn, he is filling the universe with his genuine sense of love. For the sailor, the lack of love equals death. The sailor's emotional totality becomes a source of inspiration for the urban alienated subject who hears it and starts to open up emotionally. He hears how the voice of the sailor mingles with the waves and how one wave calls to the other: "Love! And the silver foam on the water's blueness utters: Love! And the nightingale between the tree branches gushes in his pleasant voice: Love! Love! And also my soul is gushing inside me, for it is too lovesick."[149] The transformation of the protagonist's soul in this passage is the transformative vision that Peretz sees as the true role of art, as opposed to pretending to reflect the world as it is.

If the rape scene in "The Mute" allegedly reflected reality in all its crudeness and cruelty, the discussion regarding the meaning of love in "In a Summer House" provided an alternative aesthetic vision. If, in "The Mute," "neshef-kheshek" (a ball) meant a corrupted scene of the decadent upper classes abandoning the simple folks, in "In a Summer House" it is the sailor's singing voice that causes the leaves in the wood to start shaking in their own organic "neshef-kheshek."[150] The mixture of literary genres that Peretz contrasted in this story creates the modernist fragmented feeling that Peretz wished to infuse in his text.

The modernizing role that Peretz took upon himself in Hebrew literature in the 1890s should be examined also through the story "A Night of Horror: A Research in Mental Disease" (1893), which was published in Sokolow's almanac *Ha-asif*.[151] Sokolow was the editor of the Warsaw

Hebrew daily *Ha-tsfirah*, where Peretz published much of his Hebrew work. Sokolow also shared Peretz's critical view of the New Wave in Hebrew literature and Ben-Avigdor's realistic-naturalist pretensions. In the same volume of *Ha-asif*, Sokolow published two reviews of Ben-Avigdor's stories ("Menahem the Writer" and "R' Shifra"), in which he expressed his critical views toward the New Wave's aesthetics. Sokolow mocked Ben-Avigdor's attempts to make impossible and intangible cultural-political synthesis, creating "realism-idealist-nationalist-cosmopolitan."[152] It is unsurprising, then, that Peretz found a home publishing such a gothic, macabre, psychological, modernist story as "A Night of Horror" in a publication by someone who shared a great deal of his aesthetic views. Peretz also published a poem and a feuilleton in the same volume of *Ha-asif*. The feuilleton wittily referred to a proposition to fund a financial support society for Hebrew writers.[153] Certainly this was not a case of biting the hand that feeds, as Peretz arguably did when he published his romantic, anti–New Wave story "In a Summer House" in the most important publication of the New Wave.

"A night of horror" consists of the inner thoughts—in the novel form in Hebrew and Yiddish literature of an internal monologue—of one character, Mr. Finkelman, during one sleepless, nightmarish night. His thoughts are torn schematically between his masculine side and his feminine, between a psychological identification with his father and with his mother (and wife), and between a heartless and crude capitalist mindset (he is a rich and ruthless businessman) and a compassionate socialist one.[154] Like other Hebrew stories by Peretz from the period including "The Thought," "The Harp," and "In a Summer House," the story "A Night of Horror" relies heavily on storytelling that centers around a series of contrasts and oppositions. If in "In a Summer House" the thematic contrast that Peretz puts forth between "olam ha-kheshbon" and "olam ha-atsilut" reflects contrast of genre between the bourgeois comedy and the idyll, in "A Night of Horror," like in "The Thought," "The Harp," and "The Teaching of Hasidim" (both in *The Arrow*), the central contrast is reflected thematically, but not in its genre.[155] Thus, in order to create a modernist fragmented feeling in "A Night of Horror," Peretz had to use other literary methods (like the use of internal monologue) besides the mixture of literary genres.

There are two other significant contrasts that are presented. The first is between forgetting and remembering: the protagonist struggles to remember the terrible thing that happened earlier that day, and while doing so he looks back at events from the past and from his childhood.

The second contrast is between life and death, and the living and the dead, using the *danse macabre* motif, a motif that Peretz would later develop in his large-scale symbolist drama *At Night in the Old Marketplace* and in "The Harp." A morbid, gothic sense throughout the story indicates a morbid solution to the plot, as the protagonist discovers at the end of the story that his wife has passed away. The protagonist, Mr. Finkleman, expresses inherent existential ambivalence as both a bourgeois and an anti-bourgeois figure;[156] it is a specifically gothic kind of ambivalence.[157] Finkleman's mental disorder and the set of binary oppositions within him are explicitly mentioned in the text as Finkleman's conflicted inner thoughts, for example this one:

> If his wife would turn her eyes away he would turn himself over and change as ink does; then the spirit of his father would revive him, then the spirit of true business would wrap him in his wings. . . . Then depression would befall him, his room would become a dark room, hell, he and the businessmen—nightmarish demons who wrestle one against the other with their hands, with shrewdness, with cheating, with deceit . . . then an attack war for life or death!
>
> But silence! . . . All of a sudden . . . there is no shrewdness and no power, justice—justice you shall pursue, love dominates, brotherhood and comradeship! . . . Now he realized his status is in constant change: one time he is his father's incarnation, and another time he is his mother's.[158]

Peretz's "scientific experiment" of exploring psychiatric illness might seem overly simplistic and schematic to many readers.[159] Examining the subject of psychological abnormality was not a total novelty in Hebrew literature.[160] There were a significant number of stories in Hebrew literature, starting from the late 1870s—notably, with Smolanskin's "Torat Ha-no'ar" (1878) and Abramovitsh's *Susati* (1886)—that dealt with insanity. Hebrew writers absorbed the late-nineteenth-century, pre-Freudian psychopathological contemporary thought.[161] Nineteenth-century European literature was full of madman diaries, most famously Gogol's "Diary of a Madman" (1835), which influenced all the Eastern European Jewish writers. As previously mentioned, Peretz himself had experimented with the insanity theme in his Yiddish writings, as in *Bilder fun a provints rayze* and "The Crazy Idler" (1890), and even in his earliest Hebrew prose with his story "The Dybbuk and the Crazy Person" (1886).[162] Bar-Yosef also sees traces in Peretz's Hebrew article "Mental Sickness among Writers" (*The Arrow*, 1894) of Max Nordau's idea that the European literature of the end of the nineteenth century was written by people who were mentally ill. Peretz wrote in this article that "the psychology of this time smashed the human's soul, which before then was perceived by the wise men as total unity, to little shreds . . . when the person is healthy, then all the spiritual visions unify to be one spirit, and if the person becomes sick, then many souls would split up in him and different characteristics would alternate one after the other."[163] But beyond the false attribution of novelty to Peretz, what does matter is what he achieved with this motif, and how he did it.

The psychological abnormality of the protagonist is surrounded by a deep gothic sense and reasoned to be caused by the influence of gothic literature on the protagonist himself. Finkelman remembers that his father was tough with him as a child so that he wouldn't grow up to be a coward (in his words, "a woman"), but

> even more so, his father got mad over his mother's nighttime stories, which were always woven out of fear: fear of souls of the dead, of moonlight and grave shadows. . . .
>
> And once, he was locked in a dark room for an entire night, in order to drive away any false fears from him. In the morning, when they unlocked the door of his cell, he was found foundering between life and death. . . .
>
> During that night—he told her—I suffered all the torments of hell, all the dead rose up from their graves and surrounded me . . . demons, gremlins, and dark spirits harassed me, until I fainted. . . .
>
> And in his heart he imagined that then he had indeed lost his sanity and he became an empty dummy to alternately receive the soul of his father or the soul of his mother.[164]

The gothic elements here are grounded in psychological-realist reasoning. Andrew Smith points out in his analysis of *Dr. Jekyll and Mr. Hyde*—perhaps the most famous gothic story to highlight a multiple personality disorder—that Hyde is separated from Jekyll along a social scale as well as a moral one: "Hyde becomes associated with a specific fear of the working class . . . his very existence suggests that the class hierarchy can be collapsed because it is reversible."[165] Here, the mother's stories filled the child with fear of the violence of the lower classes. However, her intent was to rally support for welfare policies that could ease and defuse social tensions. Conversely, his father insisted that his son needed to overcome these fears, disregard the pain caused by rising social gaps, and thus gain an even stronger dominance over the lower classes. I believe Jameson's analysis of gothic films is useful here for deciphering the social significance of gothic literature: "Gothics are indeed ultimately a class fantasy (or nightmare) in which the dialectic of privilege and shelter is exercised: your privileges seal you off from other people, but by the same token they constitute a protective wall through which you cannot see, and behind which therefore all kinds of envious forces may be imagined in the process of assembling, plotting, preparing to give assault; it is if you like, the shower-curtain syndrome (alluding to Hitchcock's *Psycho*)."[166] Applying this definition to Peretz's story "A Night of Horror," the text indeed wishes to uncover the dialectic of privilege and shelter. Mr. Finkelman constantly fears the elements that he sees as holding him back from increasing his fortune without restraint. He is constantly moving between a strong sense of admiration for the female figures in his life—his wife and mother, who both died young—and a sense of anger toward those same female figures because they functioned (according to the formulaic logic of the story) as barriers preventing him from accumulating more wealth: "if it weren't for Miriam, he now would have had four times as much wealth from what he owns now."[167] Jameson further writes that perhaps the only particular political significance of such gothic texts consists "in a coming to self-consciousness of the disadvantages of privilege in the first place."[168] Does Peretz's Mr. Finkelman become self-conscious of the disadvantages of privilege by the end of the story?

 Toward the end, the tension between his love for his wife Miriam and the value of accumulating wealth reaches its fatal climax. Endless numbers and calculations are running around in Finkelman's head—exactly how much money is he losing for her sake? He is trying to calculate the sums of money he could have possessed if it were not for his desire to please his wife. He sees numbers and digits in growing amounts, "and the bills were flying all around like birds in his brain." The image on the bills is of the demon Azazel laughing and of his father's rotten corpse, around which "worms and snakes are tangled," eating his flesh "with their many mouths," trying to seduce him to take the money. From all that pressure, Finkelman's "brain was about to pop!," and after he decided at the end not to take the money, "he dropped down to the ground and fainted."[169] After Finkelman woke up, he realized that his wife has died, and so the story ends. It seems that Finkelman did achieve awareness: he refused to take the money against the pressure to do so, and instead he chose his wife's love. Unfortunately, he made this choice too late. Becoming self-conscious of the disadvantages of privilege reflected in his recognition that his authentic feelings of love toward his wife were being systematically crushed by a socioeconomic system that sanctifies the pursuit of narrow self-interests and values the accumulation of wealth above all other social ideals.

Peretz would move on from this story to experiment with writing radical literature in Hebrew, mirroring his attempts in Yiddish. "The Wife Mrs. Hanna" (1896) and the humorous "Tmunot me-olam ha-tohu" (translated as "Scenes from Limbo"[170]), in which Peretz portrayed the negative mirror image of the "organic intellectual," serve as prime examples of this trend. In "Scenes from Limbo," Peretz rejected both Hebrew literatures: that of the *Haskalah* and that of the proto-Zionists (for its empty admiration for the Land of Israel and for its cooperation with the Jewish plutocracy). "Scenes from Limbo" hints at how Peretz would no longer ideologically be able to find his place in Hebrew literature. The voice he sought, a non-*maskilic*, non-Zionist, Jewish socialist and folkist voice, was found increasingly in Yiddish.

Tmunot is the Hebrew parallel for the Yiddish *Bilder*, and indeed Peretz created in this story a series of dramatic scenes and images set in a provincial shtetl like in *Bilder fun a provints rayze*. But here, he alternated the reportage style for a more dramatic one and eliminated the Peretzian writer-protagonist in favor of a mini-panoramic view of the town. Here you can see the influence of Abramovitsh's Hebrew work on Peretz, though Peretz's was a more dramatic style. It almost seems that this text was Peretz's early attempt to write a drama, an achievement he only accomplished during the following decade in Yiddish in two major plays (one of which had an early Hebrew version), and to a lesser degree in Hebrew.[171]

The negative mirror image of the "organic intellectual" portrayed in "Married" is embodied in several characters who are modernized to various degrees. First and foremost is the character of the twenty-four-year-old rabbi's son ("the rabbi's son" is the only way he is referred to in the story; his father is a government-appointed rabbi to the shtetl, meaning a reformist rabbi, not one from the Orthodox rabbinic establishment), who lives in Warsaw and appears modern by his dress and his lack of facial hair. There is some fear by people in the shtetl that the rabbi's son will corrupt things in the small town, be he actually came for business. He closed a deal with a man called Rafael to marry his daughter for a sum of money based on her looks and her taste in clothes. The father and the designated son-in-law also fabricated an interview scene for the sake of the "mesakelet" (modernizing) daughter, to make it seem as if she has a say in this process and it is up to her to choose her romantic partner. The exchange between the daughter, an enthusiastic reader of Schiller's poetry ("he is the comfort of my life, and the only unique pleasure"), and the rabbi's son seems like a series of romantic clichés (he speaks to her in poetry), while the comedic theatrical element is intensified by the fact that her parents are eavesdropping behind the door. When the rabbi's son tries to lure her to come with him to Warsaw and leave this town of "backward savages," the father barges in, claiming he did not agree to this and thus revealing the prearranged deal to the daughter. The deal is almost off (the rabbi's son has to tell the father he said what he said only for the sake of the interview), but the daughter, who feels betrayed at first, nevertheless decides at the end she wants to marry him.

In this farcical sketch, somewhat reminiscent of the first part of "In a Summer House," Peretz mocks the supposed social progressions of the *Haskalah*, which took the critique of arranged marriages as one of its major foci in its literature. The way the *maskil* (the proponent of the *Haskalah*) is introduced is highly ironic:

> The son of the rabbi . . . doesn't have pretty eyes, but rather dim and tired ones; he is twenty-four years of age, and already his cheeks lost their youthfulness, and he had a small bald spot on his head. But he is also not as ugly as Mikhaelko imagined him to be. . . . Maybe his eyes are tired and dim out of working too hard, and his forehead was trespassing on his scalp out of thinking too much,—who knows? But when he comes dressed in a suit and a necktie, to be seen and to see the daughter of Rafael from Kotsk, he was elegantly dressed, and so he was in her eyes.[172]

Peretz shows here that not only were the *Haskalah* reforms not achieved, but the true face of the *maskil* was rather pale, and his appearance and actions showed him to be not that sophisticated either. His "threat" to change the norms in traditional Jewish society (a long segment in the story is devoted to the townspeople discussing his arrival out of anticipation and fear) does not hold. He does not have any progressive social plan, besides arranging for himself a comfortable material status through marriage, acting as nothing more than a greedy bourgeois. His greediness is further revealed through his father, who tells the clockmaker that the only reason his son came into town was to collect his mother's inheritance, not caring to ask about her illness; that he sent a soapy poem called "Love of Zion" to the Baron de Rothschild, the financier of the early Jewish colonists in Palestine, and a romantic love poem to another maiden; and when asked if he liked the daughter of Refael he raised six fingers to show the six thousand that he received as endowment for the match. The progressive Jewish bourgeois figure of past generations, so potent in *Haskalah* literature, had now become degenerated and the beholder of reaction.

Among the other semimodern figures striving to hop on the "*Haskalah* wagon in the town of Limbo,"[173] whom Peretz parodied in this story, was Mikhael the Hebrew-Zionist poet. Mikhail writes about "all four seasons and about the Jewish people and its redemption"[174] and vehemently rejects the plan to settle Jews in Argentina. There is also Gavriel, who attacks Jewish education (another *maskilic* cliché), to some extent a self-parody by Peretz, the writer of "Bildung"; and Shmuel the Blond who aspires to become a Hebrew-prose writer. Peretz surveys here an array of tired, worn out, and ridiculed figures. The ridiculed shtetl-*maskil* from *Bilder fun a provints rayze* (chapter 6) has now become a *chovev tsiyon*, a proto-Zionist, who sings irrelevant lyrics using his elite yeshiva education, reserved only for males.[175] Jewish women's status did not improve with these new ideologies, the *Haskalah* and proto-Zionism. Both movements are depicted in the story as failed forms of Jewish modernization.

While Jewish socialism was not explicitly presented in the story as an alternative, it was still Peretz's point of departure, looking from a distance at these "failed" others. Explicitly in the text, those who "look" at the *maskilim* and who get the last word are eccentric figures in the town—the government-appointed rabbi (who "only seldom leaves his doorstep"[176]) and the clockmaker (who lives alone for years, never telling why). They bemoan the education they gave their sons—a *Haskalah* package of natural sciences, geography, music, Hebrew, and Jewish education—"but the heart, the moral, the pillars of man—we all forgot . . . yes, we are the guilty ones."[177] This lament at the end of the story is reminiscent of the way the Enlightenment project was criticized decades later by Adorno and Horkheimer for failing to properly consider questions of morality, something we will encounter in Peretz's Hasidic stories and his use of the radical conservative eye. By ending with these two characters, Peretz made the following statements: The clockmaker, a character who appreciates the concept of time, with his concern for the old watchtower, was the one who was ill-satisfied with the existing models of progress. The well-intentioned government-appointed rabbi represents the failure of the integrationist model of the *Haskalah* both by the way he is ostracized in Jewish society and by his failure with his son. The rabbi is too old himself to join the ranks of Jewish socialism, but the yearning for more morality in the *maskilic* educational model represents some primal sentiment in favor of social justice, and his mode of operation is in some way another form of favoring *doikayt* (repairing society where it resides) over Zionism. As opposed to the rabbi's biological son (and in this light one can see the irony of referring to him only as "the rabbi's son"), the reformist rabbi's spiritual son would be Jewish socialism.

"Scenes from Limbo" signified a poetic and ideological departure from past and present Hebrew literature. Stylistically and thematically, Peretz here not only does *not* follow the demands of the New Wave (by favoring ironic humor and farce over openly confronting the harsh socioeconomic reality of lower-class Jews and writing in a nonreferential Hebrew) but also doesn't directly reject them as he did in "In a Summer House" (using neoromantic impressionist literature). Though this was not Peretz's last literary text that was originally written in Hebrew, one can see in "Scenes from Limbo" how, on the ideological level, Peretz would soon be unable to find his proper place in Hebrew literature (hence the lack of presenting an explicit ideological alternative as he did in "Married"). The voice he was targeting, that of the non-*maskilic*, non-Zionist Jewish socialist and folkist, he was increasingly able to find only in Yiddish.

Coda

While Peretz never reached the same stature in Hebrew as he did in Yiddish, he did play a greater role in the modernization of Hebrew literature than Yiddish critics typically acknowledge.[178] Many Hebrew critics tended downplay the radical and non-Zionist Peretz and failed to give enough credit to Peretz's attempts to introduce a radical mindset into Hebrew literature.[179] Such omissions failed to include sufficient explanations of the context of Peretz's publications and creations in Yiddish from the period. The Hebrew critic who first acknowledged Peretz's unique contribution to Hebrew literature was Gershon Shaked, who wrote, "Peretz's stories mark an important evolution of Hebrew literature because of their clear socialist sympathies."[180] And although Peretz wrote less and less in

Hebrew in the twentieth century, he should always be examined as an important bilingual Hebrew and Yiddish writer.

This chapter focused on Peretz's Hebrew prose in the context of Peretz's evolving socialist tendencies and negative stance toward Zionism. The next chapter will take the discussion further and critically examine Peretz's poetry of the 1890s, both in Hebrew and in Yiddish, and its relation to his politics. Poetry was Peretz's dominant form of creative expression in his first decades as a writer and thus could serve as the most effective and fascinating tool for assessing his radicalization during the 1890s.

Chapter 4

On Love and Class War
Peretz's 1890s Hebrew and Yiddish Poetry

The Socialist Prophet

The previous chapters established the ways Peretz's radicalization manifested itself in his fresh Yiddish prose, acerbic articles, and attempts to duplicate the same edgy spirit in his Hebrew writings. In both languages he also expressed his resentment toward the rise of the Zionist movement and wish to dismantle its ideological foundations. However, for decades before the mid-1890s, Peretz was an established Hebrew poet. Socialism and political-left activism were still far from being widespread or vastly influential back then in the Jewish streets, and it was in this climate that Peretz matured as a creative writer. Therefore, it is all the more interesting to delve in this chapter into Peretz through the lens of his poetic productions, which I believe can give us the strongest indication of his political-creative transformation. On the surface, one would assume that some sort of clash between his decades-long measured maturation as a Hebrew poet and his newly found political convictions was bound to occur. But was that really the case?

In 1894, at the very height of his radical period, Peretz published a small collection of Hebrew love poems entitled *Ha'ugav* (The harp).[1] The poems were short, compact, and personal, and they dealt overwhelmingly with the longing of a "he" for a lost, idealized "she." To many, this collection echoed the lyrical style of the great German poet Henrich Heine in his *Buch der Lieder* (1827); it received great critical acclaim when it came out, and it was part of a wider trend at the time in Hebrew literature of interest in Heine.[2] Yosef Klausner, a literary critic who would later become a leading figure in Hebrew literary criticism, hailed the collection for its innovative deployment of sensual lyricism in Hebrew and for bringing new styles into Hebrew poetry. Klausner especially noted the personal "subjective poetry," which, he claimed, the readers of Hebrew literature were looking forward to.[3] Klausner was exaggerating. Sensual and erotic lyricism could already be found in Hebrew as early as the first half of the nineteenth century. Nevertheless, the fact that these poems stirred up a debate regarding the possibility of writing Hebrew romantic-love poetry means that Peretz did in some way challenge the commonly held understandings of Hebrew poetry at the time.[4]

When speaking to a crowd of Jewish labor activists in the mid-1890s, Peretz had to defend his poetry. The activists argued that if a writer wished to help the working class, he should focus on literary portrayals of class struggle: "This is what he has to write and the way he has to talk. The worker also understands a hint, but the hint should be aimed at what the worker understands."[5] Peretz responded to these populist arguments by saying that even in principle he could not bend to such programmatic demands from a writer. Around the same time that he wrote stories like "Bontshe the Silent" and addressed the worker-activists at the meeting, he also wrote a love ballad. The class struggle was for him only one single issue among a whole world of others. According to Peretz, what one should demand from a writer is justice, compassion, and morality. In those three foundations lie the writer's potential to find the truth.[6]

The activists' rhetoric reflected a deep misunderstanding of Marx's view of class struggle as "the history of all hitherto existing society"[7] in relation to questions of aesthetics. The Marxist reader needs to look for how the perception of love is determined by the socioeconomic base. He needs to examine whether the concept of love is represented in the work as an abstract bourgeois ideal or as a genuine emotion. Peretz's Hebrew story "In a summer house" (discussed in the previous chapter) addressed this very theme of the different meanings of love among people of different social classes. These claims also ignored obvious facts such as Marx and Engels's deep affection for the lyrical style of Heine and that the young Marx himself wrote Heine-inspired love poetry.[8] Meeting social activists certainly stimulated Peretz to be even more militant on the pages of the *Yontef bletlekh* and elsewhere, including in the creation of edgy Yiddish poetry. In the previous chapter, I discussed Peretz's sole radical Hebrew publication, *The Arrow*, mainly regarding its works of fiction and essays. But one can also find there the following Hebrew poem:

In vain, my Lord, you came down from the heavens to Mount Sinai	שוא, אלי, משחקים על סיני ירדת באש דתך;
With the fire of your law;	לחנם השמעת בקולות וברקים
For nothing you voiced with thunder and lightning	תורתך.
Your teaching, your Torah.	
If in a person's heart you planted exploitation,	אם בלב אדם העשק נטעת,
The root of poverty,	שרש הרוש,
Then golden calves would share the kingdom	ועגלי זהב יחלקו מלוכה
With Moloch and Chemosh!	עם מולך וכמוש!
O the depths of a person's heart, send from your teaching	אל נבכי לב אדם שלחמתורתך
At least beam of light!	אך קרן אור!
Without thunder and lightning on Sinai, in secret	ובלי קולות וברקים על סיני בסתר
Bury the evil!	את הרע קבור![9]

Here we read a prophet-speaker addressing the biblical God, accusing his "Lord" of creating evil, meaning exploitation (*oshek*), "the root of poverty" (*shoresh ha-rosh*). The poem shifts between personal experiences ("my Lord," "your Torah," "depths of a person's heart") and social ones ("Mount Sinai," "poverty," "exploitation"). Looking into the "depths of a person's heart" is how Peretz, even while demanding to put an end to social ills such as poverty and exploitation, emphasized the individual's perspective. The poem does not speak from a conscious class perspective but from the point of view of an individual prophet asking *his God* to work for social justice. In Peretz's Yiddish poem "Dos gebet" (The plea; also 1894), the poetic speaker addresses God informally, asking him to take responsibility for the unjust world he has created:

When will you, Master of the Universe,	ווען וועסט דו, רבונו של עולם,
Cover the deep pit,	פערשיטטען דען אבגרונד, דען טיעפען,
Which divides your children	וואס טהיילט דיינע קינדער
Between strong and weak,	אויף שטארקע און שוואכע
Between lambs and oppressors?	אויף לעמער און שינדער?[10]

The call for a deus ex machina to fix society's problems, starting with the elimination of the oppressive class system, is not an articulate political program, but neither is it a simple love poem. These harangue poems against God Almighty employ the literary device of the poet-prophet, as Peretz envisioned the true poet, as opposed to the mere rhetorician he viewed many of the Hebrew *Haskalah* poets to be.[11] Peretz's pseudoprophetic poems followed the conventions of the time in Slavic literature. In 1892, in his Yiddish poetry book *Poezye*, Peretz published several translations of poems by a Russian poet of Jewish descent, S. I. Nadson (1862–87), including a pseudoprophetic poem.[12]

Peretz's longing for prophecy was written in a language that aspired to emulate that of the biblical prophets. Morris Vintshevski was the one who introduced the genre of the prophetic speaker into modern Hebrew poetry with his socialist poem "Masa duma" (The burden of duma; 1877). In so doing, he gave rise to an array of Hebrew pseudoprophetic poems.[13] Written as a pseudobiblical chapter, Vintshevski's work was divided into biblical-style verses (*psukim*). It used common biblical phrases ("ko amar adonay tsva'ot"; so the Lord Almighty has spoken) and made God its speaker. God has come to speak because "the blood of thee who starved to death has spoken to me from the earth" ("Dmey ḥalaley ra'av tsa'aku elay min ha-adama"; דמי חללי רעב צעקו אלי מן האדמה), an allusion to the biblical story of murder among siblings. God warns the kingdoms that "because you degraded the labor, and against the working class you raided as locust" ("Ekev ki bzitem et ha-avoda, ve-al ḥel ha-oved pshetatem ka-yelek," עקב כי בזיתם את העבודה, ועל חיל העובד פשטתם כילק), He would punish them seven times for their sins. "You will not rise above the meager and poor, through the fruit of their labor you have fattened and thickened" ("lo titnas'u al ani va-rash, mipri yedehem shumantem avitem"; לא תתנשאו על עני ורש מפרי ידיהם שמנתם עביתם).[14]

One can find this sense of longing in Peretz's poem "The Date Palm," from *The Harp*, and, as we saw, in his Yiddish poems as well (following a long tradition of Yiddish translations of the Hebrew Bible).[15] By evoking a traditional, authoritative voice as his vehicle for communicating radical social ideas to his traditional readership, Peretz sought to bestow on his message—and, by extension, on socialism as a secular movement in general—a theological authority. In other words, he wanted to make the case that capitalism is fundamentally opposed to God's will.

In Hebrew Zionist poetry, Bialik is considered to be the greatest example of the prophetic poet.[16] Bialik employed a prophetic speaker in his famous poem "In the City of Slaughter" (1903–4), which Peretz translated into Yiddish under the title "Mase Nemirov."[17] Hannan Hever showed how Bialik used the authoritative "truthful and just" voice of the prophet in order to attack the "weak Jews" (victims of the pogrom who didn't fight back enough, according to Bialik), thus combating the enemies of Zionism within the Jewish people. While Bialik's poem can be seen as a secular rebellion against God, Hever shows how past scholarship neglected the role of the poem in establishing a national theology. Bialik's prophet persona, as well as Aḥad Ha'am's articles that influenced Bialik (such as "A Priest and a Prophet"; 1894), wished to give the ultimate authority to Zionism. In their voices, the establishment of a Jewish-national community represents the holiest goal of the Jewish people.[18]

The Russian poet Pushkin also used figurative biblical speech in his influential poem "The Prophet" (1826), but his manner was different from Peretz's. Unlike Pushkin and Bialik in "In the City of Slaughter," Peretz did not quote God speaking to his prophet. God's silence in Peretz's prophetic poetry gives it a more secular quality than Pushkin's and Bialik's work. Despite Peretz's evocation of "God's law," by omitting God's words, he strengthened the notion of God's existence as a mere metaphor. While it is true that romantic poets tended to humanize God, and that Bialik's God resided mainly within his own psyche and was not a transcendental being,[19] Peretz's poetry was more firmly secular. As opposed to Bialik and Aḥad Ha'am's subordination of the universal to the service of the Jewish nation,[20] Peretz successfully constructed the moral-universal ideal of the prophet as a representative of universal social justice. This assessment applies equally to Peretz's "nationalist" Yiddish poems that were published in the *Bletlekh*, taken in the particular context in which they were written.

One of Peretz's most powerful poems, the Yiddish "Meyn nisht" (1906), also used a prophetic voice to call for a radical progressive social change. But in Hebrew there are only a few examples of poems that call for social justice (the poem from *The Arrow* stands out in this regard). Radical political poems by Peretz are more readily available in Yiddish, as we have seen in previous chapters regarding his overall body of work. In Hebrew, Peretz's critical literary productions were focused less on the radical social concerns that he expressed in Yiddish. In the scholarship, his Hebrew writings are notable for the ways in which they helped drive the modernization of the compositional and stylistic elements of the art form. Many contemporary readers consider his book of poetry *The Harp* to be one of the first true modernist works in Hebrew literature, a view that I will examine in this chapter, while rejecting the false dichotomy between political poetry and aesthetics.

Writing Hebrew Poetry: Early Years as a Poet

As previously stated, during the 1870s and 1880s, Peretz was mostly known in the literary scene as a Hebrew poet. He also wrote a few poems in Polish during these early years: translations from German of poems by Goethe and erotic poetry. But these early efforts were never published.[21] In Hebrew, he wrote some medium-length and long narrative poetry, generally following the pre-modernist structural conventions of European poetry. His first big attempt at writing Hebrew poetry was the long narrative poem "Life of a Hebrew poet" ("Hayey meshorer ivri," 1877), which he was alleged to have co-written with his father-in-law, Gabriel Judah Lichtenfeld (1811–77), but in fact he was the sole writer. "Life of a Hebrew poet" is an unfinished rhymed novel, divided into ten chapters, that was published as part of the poem collection *Stories in Verses* (*Sipurim beshir veshirim shonim*).[22]

"Life of a Hebrew poet" was one of the most salient examples out of a series of similar attempts in Hebrew poetry of the time of incorporating structures borrowed from the novel. This incorporation was the way poetry responded to and tried to compete with the prose genre and with the rise of the Hebrew novel in particular. It was Peretz's attempt to take on the prose-structured narrative poems created by the aforementioned Hebrew poet Yalag, whose "Tip of a Yud" is considered to be its pioneering effort. In contrast to Yalag's more focused plot development, "Life of a Hebrew poet" encompassed a broad novel structure, and unsurprisingly, Peretz's was much longer than Yalag's (close to twelve thousand lines!).[23]

In "Life of a Hebrew poet," Peretz dealt with themes he would later explored in depth, such as the status of women in Jewish society, the Jewish bourgeoisie, socialism, sibling rivalries, poetic norms, and others.[24] One of the interesting ways these themes come into play is when one of the poem's protagonists, Daniel, who used to believe equally in traditional Jewish piety and in the financial market, loses his fortune in the stock market in the big economic crisis of 1873 (known as the Panic of 1873, or "krakh" in the poem, following the German *Gründerkrach*). The 1873 crisis brought in a wave of economic antisemitism, which particularly affected the Jews who had migrated to Germany from Russian-occupied Poland.[25] Peretz reacted to this crisis by giving voice to a rising nationalist sentiment. He did so by contrasting the character of Daniel with two characters who supposedly devoted their lives to "the people." First, to his brother Reuven, who was an artisan and educator who founded modern Jewish schools, thus embodying the agenda of the *Haskalah* (of Jewish productivization and worldly education). And second, Daniel is contrasted with the poverty-stricken young Hebrew poet Yaakov (also one of the names for the Jewish people), who fled to the big city of Warsaw earlier in his life, and whom Daniel's daughter Sarah falls in love with. Yaakov had fallen ill due to the meager conditions he was living in, and Sarah was now taking care of him:

Why are the roads of Vienna in mourning, and its street trembling? [. . .]	מדוע דרכי ויען אבלות, ובחוצות רתת? [. . .]
Because the stock market fell in the big storm,	כי נפלה הבערזע בסופה וסערה,
From its foundation to its roof it crumbled,	ממסד עד הטפחות פור התפוררה,
The temple of the businessmen has fallen; its priests became miserable [. . .]	מקדש הסוחרים נפל, כהניו אמללו, [. . .]
It has fallen, the stock market has fallen [. . .]	נפלה, נפלה הבערזע [. . .]
Canaanites in the rest of the lands, who trade with stocks,	כנענים בשאר המדינות בשטרות סחרו,
Their fortune was lost,	הונם הלך לתהו, המכו, נגערו,
Amongst them also Reb Daniel—	בתוכם רב דניאל—
Months have passed, and Yaakov rose up from his bed.	ירחים חלפו, ויעקב קם ממטתו.[26]

We see how the rise of nationalism (the rise of "Yaakov," i.e., the Jewish people) is directly bound in this poem with the capitalist crisis, in a direct cause-and-effect relationship. Meanwhile, the issue of antisemitism, because of the crisis, comes up only in an implicit manner if at all. This subtle treatment of antisemitism is not the case with Peretz's narrative poem "Kidush ha-shem" (Sanctification of the name of God; 1877), which dealt with the persecution of Jews as its main theme. "Sanctification of the name of God" innovated by introducing the martyrological theme into the Eastern European Jewish landscape (the plot takes place during the Khmelnytsky period, i.e., mid-seventeenth century). Peretz's poem directly corresponds with Yalag's poem "Bimtsulot yam" (Depths of the sea; 1868), which dealt with the martyrological theme but took place in medieval Spain. Peretz's poem is shorter than Yalag's (seventy-five lines as opposed to over one hundred fifty), and it focuses exclusively on the dramatic development of the plot (Yalag's poem contains a long, contemplative introductory section, according to *maskilic* convention). In both poems, a young Jewish female protagonist refuses the courting of a non-Jewish military leader. In each case, the Jewish heroine ultimately chooses to take her own life rather than submit to a man who devastated her people.

In Yalag's "Depths of the sea," the personal-sacrifice narrative received a unique agnostic interpretation. There, after the protagonist already saved her people from being sold off as slaves, she decides to take her own life out of "sanctification of her honor" and not sanctification of God.[27] In "Sanctification of the name of God," as its title suggests, Peretz actually returned to the more conventional religious-nationalist interpretation that dominated before Yalag. The protagonist utters in a prayer to the heavens, "Forgive me God for I shall take my own life, / I shall not give myself to the enemy—who butchered my parents" (סלח לי אל כי אטרוף).[28] נפשי בחפי,\ לא אהיה לצר – הורי לטבח הכריע Here Peretz partially shared the early nationalist spirit of the very first incarnations of the Lovers of Zion movement, which began to rise in Eastern Europe as early as the 1870s.

A solid example of a pre-1890s Hebrew poem that conveyed a radical message is "Li omrim" (I am told; 1876), which Peretz considered to be his first poem (though more in terms of its significance than being his actual first, which came out one or two years prior). It stands out as not being a narrative poem, as being short in length, and as more optimistic than some of Peretz's other poems of the period. It features this stanza:

I am told, the masses will be oppressed forever	לי אומרים, לנצח תהי עקת המונים
From privilege and money as in ancient times;	מיחש וכסף כבימים קדומים
Forever there will be masters and slaves,	לעד לא ישבתו—עבדים ואדונים,
And dictators will crush nations with their steps	ועריצים ימדו בשעלם לאמים[29]

Rozentsvayg correctly viewed this poem as being influenced by socialist ideas connected with ideas of national liberation.[30] Interestingly, this poem, with all its pathos and biblical-prophetic Hebrew, still had in its title and as an anaphoric base a phrase that was influenced by everyday Yiddish. *Hoben zey gezogt* (so they said) is used in Yiddish to dismiss an opinion that came from a third party rather than from the conversation at hand. The Hebrew *Li omrim* is a present-tense version of the Yiddish expression, and it functions in exactly the same way in this poem.[31] Peretz's 1880s Hebrew poetry presented new features in the Hebrew narrative poem, particularly in its shorter lines and choppier, edgier rhythm compared to Yalag's poems. This rhythm would later appear in Peretz's prose work, signified by its short lines and the frequent usage of ellipsis. Peretz's poetry employed features of a lyrical cycle, which was a structural and thematic innovation in Hebrew poetry at the time. The cycle structure made it possible for Peretz to write *ars poetica* and to tell a story with changes in attitude, tone, and rhythm—lessons he surely learned from Heine.

There are two major representatives of the cycles trend. The first is the rather nationalistic "Manginot ha-zman" (The melodies of the time; 1887), characterized by its changing tone, rhyme scheme, and rhythm throughout. Peretz wrote "The melodies of the time" in the years of disappointment with the liberal promise of emancipation for the Jews and the resulting rise of Jewish nationalism. The cycle focused on a polemic with the *Haskalah* regarding the fate of the Jewish people, though for the most part it is done in the form of a rationalist poetic debate in the spirit of *Haskalah* Hebrew poetry.[32] As a precursor to his Yiddish narrative poem "Monish" that came out a year later, Peretz deviated from the strict rationalist mode and moved into telling a legend. The poem's long tenth chapter tells the story of a witch who creates a monstrous figure: the Pharaoh who "did not know Joseph." She adds the last ingredients to the mix:

"Add a seven-eyed suspicion,	"הוסיפו חשד בעל שבע עינים,
The cunning of a fox, and the wickedness of Haman". . .	ערמת של שועל, ורשעת כל המן". . .
And out came Pharaoh king of Egypt	ויצא פרעה מלך מצרים
With a golden crown and purple cloth.	בעטרת זהב ולבוש ארגמן.[33]

The second half of the chapter is an adaptation of a midrash legend (*Tanhuma*) about the Hebrew children buried by Pharaoh who rose from the earth when they heard Moses singing. This incorporation of legendary material represents a more advanced stage in the development of the relation in Hebrew poetry to the supernatural legendary material.[34] The short eleventh chapter supposedly expresses reservations about using the legendary "pearls," in favor of returning to the rationalist mode of debate.[35] But the poet uses a great deal of irony in this transitional chapter. The poetic speaker doesn't simply surrender himself to the *maskilic* contempt toward legendary material; he says, "I will seek knowledge, for knowledge is in fashion."[36] The ironic use of "fashion" suggests that Peretz would continue to seek ways to challenge the literary conventions of his time. "The Melodies of the Time" included the aforementioned *ars poetica* deviation, praising the language of the common Jews, Yiddish, referring to it as "the language of Beril and Shmeril" (*sfat beril ve-shmeril*) or, with irony, as the "language of the Hebrews":

Not the holy tongue,	לא שפת הקדש.
Not the Language of the prophets,	לא לשון הנביאים,
But the language of the exiled,	אך שפת הגולים.
The language of the "Hebrews"!	לשון ה"עברײם"![37]

The second major example of Peretz's 1880s Hebrew poetry is the long poem "Ha-ir ha-ktana" (The little town; 1887), characterized by its short lines of two to three words and the edgy tempo throughout its sixty-five quadrilateral stanzas. In "The Little Town," one reads some conventional dismay about the hectic modern industrial city alongside the attempt of a modern man to find some refuge in the pre-modern Jewish shtetl, thus presenting the supreme romantic antithesis between city and country:

Here the air is pure	פה טהור האויר
From the smell of plague, free	מריח מגפה,
From steam and vapor	מקיטור ואדים
And signs of fire.	וסממני שרפה.[38]

This passage prepares the reader for an ironic antithesis: unlike nineteenth-century European Romantic poetry, the poetic speaker does not find refuge in country life or in nature. Instead—predating the alienated modern figure going back to the shtetl of Peretz's Yiddish masterpiece *Bilder fun a provints rayze*—there is a fundamental failure of communication between the poetic speaker and the local Jews. The scene of his visit resembles literary or cinematic depictions of a modern Westerner visiting a third-world village:

I came out—	—יצאתי החוצה
They surrounded me as bees,	כדבורים סבוני,
For they mistook my outfit	כי התעום שמלותי
And thought I was a lord.	ולאדון דימוני.
They surrounded me as bees,	סבוני כדבורים,
Pressed, pushed;	נלחצו, נדחקו
A circle of them around me,	כדור עלי חנו,
Begged, yelled.	יתחננו, יצעקו.
Ha, their voice	הה, קולם את לבי
Tore up my heart!	איך יקרע קרוע!
—What will the lord sell,	מה ימכור האדון,—
What will the wealthy man buy?	מה יקנה השׂע?[39]

Later in the poem, the modern Westerner encounters the exotic Eastern marketplace, with its various spices and perfumes. The Eastern European Jewish shtetl could easily be replaced by a village in Palestine in nineteenth-century French or English literature and one would hardly know the difference.[40] The depiction of the shtetl Jews as one loud and uncivilized crowd in the eyes of the modern Jew made his attempt to convince that same crowd that they belonged to the same community pathetic and futile. This is why, unlike the Romantic poets who found refuge in nature, the poem seriously questions whether Jews possess such a place: "Is this the resting place / For a troubled soul?" (הזאת המרגעה\ לנפשׁ אמללה?),[41] he asks at the end. The nationalist yearning is prominent in "The Little Town," especially in presenting its challenges. If the "The Melodies of the Time" dealt with the mythical past of the people, then "The Little Town" is more focused on the present reality of the community.[42]

The Hebrew narrative poems "The melodies of the time" and "The little town" signified the last stage in Peretz's writing career as a predominantly Hebrew poet.[43] Although we saw traces of awareness to sociopolitical issues in that early stage, dominant then were late *Haskalah* and early nationalist sentiments, devoid of calls for a working-class-centered political revolution. Peretz's major debut in Yiddish was followed by those two Hebrew poems: the narrative pseudoballadic poem "Monish" (1888) is considered to be the first time that folk narrative was seriously employed in modern Yiddish literature.⁴⁴ "Monish" has a style and plot heavily influenced by Goethe's *Faust*;⁴⁵ Peretz's protagonist is a promising yeshiva student who is seduced by the devil in the form of the daughter of a German merchant,⁴⁶ a newcomer to the shtetl. As in the inner story in "Weaver-Love," the invasion of capitalism into the shtetl means that now "everything is a commodity" (אַלעס איז סחורה), and "Everything becomes measured / With golden coins" (אַלץ ווערט מיט גאָלדענע \ רענדלעך געוווויגן).⁴⁷ The invasion of a particular German capitalist devil is also how Peretz shifted the discourse from the economic base into a cultural-ethnic discourse (or, in other words, to the cultural-symbolic realm): the invasion of the "German" economy into the Yiddish-speaking world (a distinction that does not exist in *Faust*). The diversion becomes a sexual one, through the voice and body of the daughter, especially her singing of "Maria," which marks the consummation of the seduction. Peretz uses here a common motif in modern Jewish literature: the temptation of non-Jewish culture for Jews as embodied by the non-Jewish woman (with typically "Aryan" features).⁴⁸ Peretz's usage of the temptation motif stands out through his use of music as a vehicle of seduction.⁴⁹

The poem's speaker intended to warn his readers away from this devil by elevating the symbolic value of Yiddish, the language of his readers. In a kind of an independence hymn of Jewish cultural autonomy, Peretz continued here the metalinguistic discussion of Yiddish as the language of "the people" that he began in "The Melodies of the Time." There, Yiddish was "the language of Beril and Shmeril," meaning of the common, "everyday Jews." It was a "confession" made by a member of the Hebrew intelligentsia about his fondness for Yiddish. In "Monish," he contrasted Yiddish (referred to as "zhargon," or jargon) with other European languages—in particular, German:

Differently would my poem have sounded,	אַנדערש וואָלט מײַן ליד געקלונגען,
If I were to sing it for non-Jews in their tongue,	כ'זאָל פֿאַר גויים גוייִש זינגען,
Not for Jews, not *zhargon*!—	נישט פֿאַר ייִדן, נישט "זשאַרגאָן"!
No proper sound, not proper tone!	קיין רעכטן קלאַנג, קיין רעכטן טאָן!
Neither for love, nor for emotion	ס'האָט פֿאַר ליבע, פֿאַר געפֿיל

It has the suitable vocabulary or style . . .	נישט קיין פּאַסנד װאָרט קיין סטיל...
Our Yiddish has only jokes, [. . .]	אונדזער ייִדיש האָט נאָר װיצן, [...]
Not one word is gentle and smooth,	קיין איינציק װאָרט איז צאַרט און גלאַט,
For love, it's dead and dull	עס איז פֿאַר ליבע טויט און מאַט[50]

Aware of the "low symbolic value" of Yiddish, Peretz had to conduct his humorous metalinguistic discussion in Yiddish to overcome its perceived status. The question of whether the Yiddish language can serve as a suitable tool for love poetry is one that Peretz repeatedly confronted in the decades that followed. While he did write Yiddish love poetry, he preferred to write poetry with such themes in Hebrew. In Yiddish he focused his attention on social-protest themes, on collecting Yiddish folk poetry, and on writing in a folk style himself—themes he perceived would be welcomed by his targeted readership of working-class Jews and labor activists.

As mentioned earlier, in Hebrew poetry, Peretz's most significant pretension of the 1890s was the collection of poetry *The Harp*: a cycle of twenty-seven short poems, divided into four chapters. The cycle structure allowed Peretz to express in short poems different opinions toward his beloved and the concept of love.[51] Very different than lengthy epic poetry, these poems also lacked narrative. They emphasized the "troubled soul" of the individual (who previously sought refuge in "The Little Town"), acting as the only source of poetic creation and perspective. Early on, interpreters and scholars related to this collection. David Frishman led the opposing camp, accusing it of lacking originality, of using improper and vulgar language, and of plagiarizing Heine.[52] In the introductory stanza to *The Harp*, we read Peretz's declaration of the kind of poetry he wants to create in this collection. It is a poetry influenced by the sophisticated oscillation between copresence and absence of the first-person speaker that characterized Heine's *Buch der Lieder*.[53] But it doesn't go all the way with this kind of poetics and instead allows its first-person speaker to dominate. Frishman was partially correct in observing that these lines lack a dialectical relationship between their components (there is a contradiction between muted lips and his "gush and lament" poetics, but they are complementary, not antithetical). Regardless of Frishman's allegations, Peretz has, as did many other Jewish writers, attempted in *The*

Harp to emulate Heine's unique style and the spirit of *Buch der Lieder* and *Romanzero* (1851) of short and highly ironic poems that contradicted one another, poems that seem naive and tragic, like the famous "Lorelei." Peretz had done so since his early attempts at writing Hebrew poetry starting in the mid-1870s, which were preserved as manuscripts and never published.[54] In contrast to Frishman's overall negative view, Klausner saw in these poems the passionate personal poetry that Hebrew literature needed to be recognized as "European literature." Klausner was also responding to the writer and essayist M. L. Lilienblum (1843–1910), who argued that Hebrew poetry lacked the foundations of European love poetry (the medieval tradition of chivalrous poetry) and that in fact love poetry originates from the Hebrew Bible.[55] As shown, it was Peretz who doubted a decade earlier, for other reasons, that love poems could be written in the language of the commoners—Yiddish.

Contemporary scholars tend to agree with Klausner about the novelty that the *Harp* poems possess. Bar-Yosef crowned Peretz as the writer who introduced modernist trends in Hebrew literature with *The Harp* and *The Arrow*. Peretz himself surely had such ambitions. But ambitions aside, at least as a poet (it was easier for him to be innovative in his prose work since he started writing prose in a much later period), he matured during the *Haskalah* period of Hebrew poetry. Younger poets, like Bialik and Tchernichovsky, would take the center stage and easily integrate modernist writing styles in their work. According to Miron, the focal shift from the social, historic, and conceptual outer spheres to the individual's inner human psychology typical of modernist literature did not achieve the same full and organic level of incorporation in Peretz's Hebrew poetry as Bialik and Berdichevsky achieved in their work.[56] Examining examples from *The Harp* would help determine to what degree Peretz succeeded in venturing away from traditional poetic structures. Shlomo Harel claims that the *Harp* poem "I Won't Come to Your House" was innovative in its poetic structure, for it provided its readers with a dynamic sort of reading, and its lines are rich with ambiguity and oxymoronic expressions. It can almost be called a "reverse poem," meaning a poem whose ending changes the meaning of the poem up until that point:[57]

I won't come to your house, my pretty one,	לא אבוא אל ביתך, יפתי,
For there are my moments of terrible bliss,	כי שם רגעי אשרי נוראים,

For it is not the light of your face and your grace	כי לא אור פניך וחסדך
You are bestowing to those who come;	מפלסת את בין הבאים;
There you tear up my heart,	את שם את לבבי קורעת,
And distribute to all the shreds;	ומחלקה לכל את הגזרים;
And why should I drown in my own blood	ולמה זה אטבע בדמי
And still pass between its pieces?	ואעבור עוד בין הבתרים?[58]

We see the emphasis on the invented subject and his relationship to a woman. The male poetic speaker won't come to "her" home because there he experiences moments of "terrible bliss"—an oxymoron expressing an intense level of emotion. Harel suggests that the adjective "nora" (terrible), particularly in rereading the poem after its full meaning has sunk in, means "very, great,"[59] but this was in fact a common feature in nineteenth-century poetry and does not necessarily indicate that this is a reverse poem. A key word in the poem for determining whether it is a reverse poem is the word "betarim" (pieces, parts) at the end. *Betarim* was used in the Hebrew Bible to signify the covenant between God and Abraham ("brit ben ha-btarim," an agreement between the parts consecrated through the dissection of animals into pieces). Its connotation strengthens the interpretation of both the beloved's home as being parallel to the Promised Land—God's promise to Abraham of his seed in a "land other than their own" (Genesis 15:13)—and the promise of romantic favors of the beloved to the poetic speaker, a promise to his own private seed. The speaker likens himself to the fire that went between God and the "betarim"—that is, the fire of passion. However, the word *betarim* does not change the overall meaning of the poem. The line it appears in does not contradict the meaning of the poem thus far but rather continues the same argument from the first line, which warned of the danger of sexual passion. This argument might seem to be an inner contradiction, but it is one that is put forth clearly in the first reading of the poem.

One aspect of the *Harp* collection has been largely ignored by scholars of Hebrew poetry, namely its relation to Peretz's Yiddish poetry and to his interest in the ballad form and in folklore in general. In the gushing introduction to this volume, its publisher, Shvartsberg, puts the nationalist values of the *Harp* collection front and center. Shvartsberg included these poems as part of Hebrew poetry as a whole, which he characterized as "the poetry of Zion in the Diaspora." Peretz's cycle, wrote the publisher, can bring back "the lost sons to their mother, that is Hebrew poetry."[60] But these Hebrew poems were not detached from Peretz's creativity in Yiddish. During the first half of the 1890s Peretz published a series of ballads in Yiddish that in many ways paralleled the Hebrew poems of *The Harp* in form and style. One striking similarity is between the Hebrew "Kadru shamaym ka-ḥeres" and the Yiddish "A volkn hot fardekt dem himl." The poem in Hebrew (on the right) and in Yiddish (left) reads,

א װאָלקן האָט פֿאַרדעקט דעם הימל,	קדרו שמים כחרס ונפשי נפעמה;
װי אַ שװאַרצער שאַרבן:	כי חיש גם את עיני יכסו
עס איז פֿינצטער װי אין קבֿר,	חרסי אדמה.
דאַכט זיך מיר, כ'װעל שטאַרבן.	ובטפות קרות יבכיו
. . . .	עתה העבים על שברי;
אױף מײַן קרענקלעך־הײסן שטערן	ובדמעות קרות תבכינה
פֿאַלט אַ טראָפּן שװער;	אז עיני היפה על קברי.[62]
צי װעט דעמאָלט, אױף מײַן קבר	
פֿאַלן אירס אַ טרער?[61]	

A cloud covered the sky,	The sky darkened as a broken earthen pot
As a black broken earthen pot:	And my soul was thrilled;
It is dark as in the grave,	For soon my eyes would also be covered
It seems to me, I will die.	By clods of earth.
. . . .	And with cold drops would weep
On my hot-feverish forehead	Now the clouds on my crisis;
Drops heavily a drop;	And with cold tears then will cry
Will then, on my grave,	The eyes of the pretty one over my grave.
Fall her tear?	

Peretz's achievement in both these poems is clearer when it is understood that he based them on a folk ballad from a collection of Yiddish folk songs that he was collecting at the time.[63] This ballad opens with the lyrics "Black clouds covered the sky, / It became dark in the world; / And a thousand people went on a walk, / Everybody walked as one."[64] Then, a young man's cry for help came from the river. The people pulled out his body, but they were too late; he was dead, and his feet were bitten in several places. His young fiancée shed her tears next to his corpse, and the poem ends with the verse "While he was brought to the cemetery, / His fiancée shed so many tears; / Master-of-the-Universe, show your wonders, / Allow me to lay by his feet!"[65] Modernizing the folk ballad expressed itself in several ways. First, it meant the elimination of the clear narrated balladic structure and the replacement of its multiple voices (voices of the narrator, the fiancée, and people by the river) with the single individual voice. In the Yiddish version, Peretz replaced the weeping fiancée at the grave and the exclamation mark at the end with the question in first person from the male speaker, "Will then, on my grave, / Fall her tear?"

In the ballad, the young fiancée is not only accompanied by one thousand people who "walked as one" but also sheds "so many tears," while the poetic speaker in the Yiddish version craves a single tear from his loved one. In both languages, the female figure is transformed from being a fiancée in the ballad (a woman with a defined role in traditional society), to a mere adjective, "the pretty one" in the Hebrew. In Yiddish she is even further reduced to just the pronoun "her" (from "her tear"). The last two examples show that in certain elements, Peretz took this poem in Yiddish into an even more modern direction than he did in Hebrew. In addition, in Peretz's poems all the Jewish folkloristic pre-modernist elements in the ballad concerning a Jewish wedding and burial were left out in favor of a sheer neutral setting both ethnically and religiously: the board on which dead people are laid before cleansing (*ta'are-bret*), the engagement contract (*di tnoim*), the invocation of the Master of the Universe (*riboyne-shel-oylem*), and so on. One element that was preserved in all three versions of this poem was its rhyme scheme—in all of them, it is the standard ABCB (two broken long lines make each stanza).

Modernizing folk ballads was common in European poetry during the eighteenth century. Poets such Blake, Wordsworth, and Scott were often referred to as belonging to the "ballad revival." It was at times associated with democratization and progressive currents, marking a breaching of the boundaries between elite and popular culture, creating a place where utopia could surface.[66] The opposite view, stemming from postcolonial theory, sees this movement as nothing more than an attempt by elite circles to appropriate popular culture. Accordingly, the modernization of folk ballads was an act of borrowing of "low art" by producers of "high art," at times used in the cause of imperialism.[67] But Steve Newman correctly points out that "popular song is not intrinsically progressive," and one needs to pay attention to the mediations that structure our culture in divisions between "high" and "low" and to questions of accessibility. "To erase those mediations courts a facile notion of the relationship between culture and politics."[68] This observation means that one must consider the ballads in their own right, viewing in each case whether Peretz's modernization of ballads resulted in a progressive poem or was merely an appropriation of popular culture. These distinctions will emerge again when analyzing Peretz's socialist Yiddish poetry, as well as when we explore how deeply Peretz's practice of collecting Jewish folklore informed his work. Regarding the economies of production, especially concerning the *Bletlekh*, where much of this material was published, I have already shown the progressive nature of this publication outlet.

The significance of adopting a bilingual view when speaking of Peretz's poetry cannot be overstated. However, beginning with "Monish," continuing with his positivist long poem *Der balegole* (The coachman; 1891[69]), and through the 1890s and onward, Peretz produced more and more of his poetry in Yiddish, which was the proper poetic medium for addressing the Jewish working class,[70] even while he continued to publish Hebrew poems until close to his death.[71] While both languages informed his writing, Yiddish was the primary vehicle for his ethno-class faction. His Yiddish poetry from the 1890s was dominated by a radical Jewish-socialist tone.

Yiddish Socialist Poetry and Political Poetry

The cover of most issues of the groundbreaking journal *Yontef bletlekh* featured an original poem by Peretz, but poetry was rarely published in the inner pages of the journal. These Yiddish "cover poems" were meant to serve as a poetic companion to the articles and short stories that constituted the main content of the journal. According to Hever, political poetry needs to successfully result in the "disruption of the rules of discourse" and have a "political effect on readers."[72] Following these two requirements, I will ask, To what degree did these cover poems, and Peretz's other poems from the period, meet the basic requirements of political poetry?

One of the poems often pointed to as representative of Peretz's socialist convictions is "Dray neytorins" (Three knitters).[73] Peretz used here the popular form of the ballad, and it became a very popular song that was frequently included in anthologies of Yiddish folk songs and workers' poems.[74] According to one testimony from Łódź, a Polish city formerly known for its textile industry and for being a stronghold of

Figure 4.1. Cover page of the Hanukah volume of the *Yontef bletlekh* showing the poem "The Hanukah Candle." Steven Spielberg Digital Yiddish Library.

Jewish socialism, "this poem quickly became very popular and people started to sing it next to every weaving loom."[75] "Dray neytorins" was included in the collection *Arbeter lider* (Worker's poems; 1906), for

example, which also included a Yiddish translation of the Thomas Hood poem that influenced it.⁷⁶ Here it is in Yiddish alongside my English translation:

The eyes are red, the lips are blue	די אויגן רויט, די ליפּן בלאָ,
No drop of blood in the cheek,	קיין טראָפּן בלוט אין באַק נישטאָ,
The forehead pale, covered with sweat!	דער שטערן בלאַס, באַדעקט מיט שווייס!
The breath panting and hot—	דער אָטעם אָפּגעהאַקט און הייס—
Sit three maidens and sew!	עס זיצן דרײַ מיידלעך און נייען!
The needle—shiny, the linen—snow	די נאָדל—בלאַנק, די לײַוונט—שניי
And one of them thinks, "I knit and knit.	און איינע טראַכט איך ניי און ניי.
I knit by day, I knit by night,	איך ניי בײַטאָג, איך ניי בײַנאַכט,
No wedding dress I made for myself!	קיין חופּה-קלייד זיך נישט געמאַכט!
What comes out of it, I knit?	וואָס קומט אַרויס, איך ניי?
I don't sleep and I don't eat . . .	נישט איך שלאָף און נישט איך עס . . .
I would have gone to ask for a miracle,	איך וואָלט געגאַנ׳ען אויף מאיר-בעל-הנס,
Maybe that would have benefited me:	אפֿשר וואָלט ער זיך געמיט:
At least a widower, an old Jew.	אַן אַלמן כאָטש, אַן אַלטן ייִד.
With small children, a shock!"	מיט קינדערלעך אַ שאָק!
The second thinks, "I knit and stitch,	די צווייטע טראַכט, איך ניי און שטעפּ,
And stitch myself a gray solitude!	און שטעפּ מיר אויס נאָר גראָע צעפּ!
The head—it burns, the shoulder—it breaks,	דער קאָפּ—דער ברענט, די שלייף—די האַקט
And the machine knocks to the rhythm:	און די מאַשין קלאַפּט-צו צום טאַקט:
Ta-ta, ta-ta, ta-ta!	טאַ-טאַ, טאַ-טאַ, טאַ-טאַ!

On Love and Class War | 137

I understand as you know that guy's wink! Without a canopy, without a ring, It would have been a game, a dance, A love for a whole year! But afterwards, afterwards?"	איך פֿאַרשטײ דאָך יענעמס װינק! אָן אַ חופּה, אָן אַ רינג, וואָלט געווען אַ שפּיל, אַ טאַנץ, אַ ליבע אויף – אַ יאָר אַ גאַנץ! נאָר דערנאָך, דערנאָך?
The third spits blood and sings: "I'm knitting myself sick, I'm knitting myself blind. The breast breaks with every stitch . . . And he—is getting married this week! I don't wish him any harm!	די דריטע שפּײַט מיט בלוט און זינגט: איך נײ מיך קראַנק, איך נײ מיך בלינד. עס צווײקט די ברוסט בײַ יעדן שטאָך . . . און ער—האָט חתונה די װאָך! איך ווינטש אים נישט קיין שלעכטס!
Eh, to forget what was! . . . Shrouds the community will give me, And also a tiny piece of land, I will rest undisturbed, Sleep, sleep, sleep!"	עט, פֿאַרגעסן וואָס אַמאָל! . . . תּכריכים וועט מיר געבן קהל, אויך אַ קליינטשיק פּיצל ערד, איך וועל רוען אומגעשטערט, שלאָפֿן, שלאָפֿן, שלאָפֿן!

The poem consists of seven stanzas of five short lines each and has an AABBC rhyme scheme. Its content is built on monologues by three different seamstresses, working under difficult conditions and with poor chances of establishing a happy family life or economic stability. Introducing them is a stanza by a poetic narrator, probably male. The dramatic progression from the first seamstress (who hopes to match with "At least a widower, an old Jew / With small children") to the second seamstress (who is only offered a short-term romance "Without a canopy, without a ring," thus a life of "gray solitude!") and the third ("shrouds" and "a tiny piece of land" to bury herself while her man "is getting married") signifies a process of decay. The poem goes through the following stations: (1) pathetic hopes, (2) living with the realization of a lack of options, and (3) quitting with life altogether.

As in "Weaver-Love," the thread that thematically connects the components is the inability to fulfill the hope for marriage. Here, the bourgeois ideal of marriage is shattered among the members of the new urban working class. The labor of lower-class women prevents them from fulfilling their dreams of family life, exhausts them, and leads them in some cases to prefer to end their meager existence. As in our times, when low-wage workers cannot afford the products they make, so too in Peretz's poem, the seamstresses cannot afford to purchase their own work. "No wedding dress I made for myself!" says the first woman, expressing her sense of alienation from the product of her labor, as Marx described. By focusing on the inability to marry (at best, they can have an affair) as the key disaster of the modern enslavement of the seamstresses, Peretz tied personal and familial suffering to the economic contradictions of the emerging capitalist society. Peretz disrupted the rules of discourse—he was breaking the artificial walls separating the socioeconomic sphere from the sphere of familial love. He was by no means the first writer to connect economic and romantic relations. However, here he achieved a successful artistic exploration of this theme. But another reality is exposed in Peretz's poem, namely that the institution of marriage itself constitutes a form of oppression for women. In Engels's view, the institution of marriage is for women not fundamentally different from that of prostitution: "marriage is determined by the class position of the participants, and to that extent always remains marriage of convenience . . . this marriage of convenience often enough turns into the crassest prostitution—sometime on both sides, but much more generally on the part of the wife, who differs from the ordinary courtesan only in that she does not hire out her body, like a wage-worker, on piecework, but sells it into slavery once and for all."[77] Peretz used the format of unreliable speakers who speak directly to stress the falseness of their ideology: the ideology of marriage. His knitters see their only possible redemption in the fulfillment of marriage, and they mourn the impossibility of achieving it. In contrast, the speaker of the introductory stanza does not mention marriage at all but just stresses the body marks and the physical symptoms of the female knitters caused by the toll of their labor. He thus underlies the unreliability of the three female speakers, and, in this manner, Peretz exposes their false view of marriage as redemption as opposed to a social struggle. But another way of looking at this "neutral" narrator is that he occupies the role of an anti-*shadkhan* (an anti-matchmaker). Such a character of an anti-*shadkhan* serves as the one who depicts the biophysical unworthiness of the three young women in the modern-day marital industry. According to this interpretation, Peretz affirms rather than disrupts the rules of discourse, because the conclusion for the community in the poem is to better the working conditions of female laborers mainly so they would be more suitable for marriage.[78] Thus remains the question, Has Peretz succeeded here in creating revolutionary art and a political poem? Is there a call in the poem to better the working conditions of women workers—the obvious political effect such a poem is supposed to have on its readers? Helpful in this regard would be to first contextualize Peretz within the framework of leftist Yiddish poetry.

Peretz's Poetry in the Context of Socialist Yiddish Poetry

Before Peretz, others have introduced radical socialist sentiments into the repertoire of Yiddish poetry. Poets like Morris Rosenfeld (1862–1923), Joseph Bovshover (1873–1915), Dovid Edelstadt (1866–92), and other "sweatshop poets" who operated in America dominated the Yiddish poetic scene of the time and influenced the development of Yiddish poetry in Eastern Europe.[79] These poets were not a monolithic group. While Rosenfeld was depicting the lives of the exploited workers and tended to be less ideological, Bovshover and Edelstadt wrote anarchistic hymns and raised different motives than Rosenfeld did. These poets created the proletarian base in Yiddish literature, while the three classics—Abramovitsh, Peretz, and Sholem Aleichem—were preparing the field for Yiddish literature in general.[80]

Another important pioneer of socialist Yiddish poetry was the aforementioned Vintshevski. He started off as a Hebrew poet who was in fact continuing the tradition Yahalal and others started in the 1870s of socialist Hebrew poetry. As shown in this chapter, Vintshevski pioneered the pseudoprophetic poem style in Hebrew literature. His poetry called for social justice, and it influenced Peretz deeply. Since the 1890s, Vintshevski had published Yiddish poetry that was dominated by social themes and expressed enthusiastic support for the socialist movement and its leaders. His poetry was at times sentimental, thus different from the rhetorical agitation poetry created by the American Yiddish poets such as Bovshover and Edelstadt. Like many others, Peretz was influenced by Vintshevski's poetry and essays, and he even invited him to contribute to the *Bletlekh*. Scholars have shown the similarity between Peretz's most famous Yiddish poetry and earlier poems by Vintshevski. Many agree that the poems "Dray neytorins" and "Baym fremdn khupe kleyd" were heavily influenced by Vintshevski's adaptation to Yiddish of the very popular English poem

"The Song of the Shirt" (1843) by Thomas Hood, entitled "Dos lid fun hemd" (1884).[81] Its opening lines read,

With meager fingers, skinny and crooked,	מיט מאָגערע פֿינגער, דאַר און אויסגעדרייט,
With eyes, which are already blind from work—	מיט אויגן, וואָס זיינען פֿון אַרבעט שוין בלינד—
A young woman sits down, dressed in rags,	אַ וויַיבעלע זיצט זיך, אין לומפּן געקלייַדט,
And works quickly with the needle and thread,	און וואַרפֿט מיטן נאָדל און פֿאָדעם געשווינד,
Stitch—stitch—stitch!	שטעך—שטעך—שטעך!
In hunger, in dirt, alien from the whole world,	אין הונגער, אין שמוץ, פֿאַר דער גאַנצער וועלט פֿרעמד,
I knit with a double thread: for myself	ניי איך מיט אַ דאָפּלטן פֿאָדעם: פֿאַר זיך
Shrouds—for other people a shirt	תּכריכים—פֿאַר אַנדערע מענטשן אַ העמד[82]

Compare the opening lines to the original English by Hood. Vintshevski combined Hood's first stanza and its refrain with the ending of Hood's fourth stanza. Hood's first stanza reads as follows: "With fingers weary and worn, / With eyelids heavy and red, / A woman sat, in unwomanly rags, / Plying her needle and thread— / Stitch! stitch! stitch! / In poverty, hunger, and dirt, / And still with a voice of dolorous pitch / She sang the 'Song of the Shirt!" The ending of Hood's fourth stanza matches with Vintshevksi's ending of his first; Hood's reads, "Stitch—stitch—stitch, / In poverty, hunger, and dirt, / Sewing at once, with a double thread, / A Shroud as well as a Shirt."[83] The similarity to Peretz's *Dray neytorins* is striking and undeniable: the female speaker, the similar profession, and the poor conditions that lead the speaker believe she is knitting both a shirt for another and shroud for herself. Vintshevski and Peretz were both following a tradition in English poetry and culture of the 1840s that began with Hood's poem and introduced the pitiable figure of the solitary seamstress. Peretz in his poem portrayed three such characters. As Patricia Zakreski shows, in English culture this figure became the embodiment of the passive victim of the economic forces of capitalism. And like Peretz's portrayal of the knitters' longing for matrimony in "Dray neytorins," this is a figure of the vulnerable and helpless women in the public domain, "a perfect example of a modest and reluctant worker who can be unproblematically pitied." Furthermore, "her qualities of moral purity and feminine modesty made her a safe and convenient figure throughout the 1840s for charitable appeals to the middle class."[84] Evocation of pity as opposed to social struggle is present in the poem not only as an expression of the characters but also by the poem's narrative structure. By portraying a process of decay and degeneration rather than an element of opposition as the poem progresses from one seamstress to the second, and to the third, Peretz neatly reinforced this message. Thus, the charitable pithiness and the centrality of the institution of marriage make Peretz's poem "Dray neytorins" in the last analysis an apolitical poem. It is doubtful that this poem would have had a political effect on its readers. Peretz has not succeeded here in sending a rousing socialist message, as he aspired to do. Zakreski touches on this point, writing, "Middle-class audiences could feel sorry for the seamstress or might contribute to a philanthropic organization . . . but in the course of such objectification she was reduced to a symbol of working-class vulnerability that was convenient for reformers who thought women and the working classes unable to help themselves. The middle classes could help if they chose, but the difficulties of the seamstress did not appear in the end to affect them directly."[85]

Thus, as much it genuinely strived to align itself with the working class, the poem "Dray neytorins" was written from a middle-class perspective. It is not the only example in which the poetry of Peretz's radical years fails to fully acknowledge the revolutionary potential of the poor. Peretz's poem "Oysgeshtorbn" (Extinct; 1894), published in the New York paper *Arbeter-tsaytung*, laid forth the notion of the decline of generations over time.[86] The speaker in the poem yearns for heroes he could use as models in his art but argues that today they are all extinct. A devout and well-formed socialist such as Vintshevski felt he had to counter what he viewed as Peretz's sentimentality in "Extinct" and instead offer up the working class as the obvious heroic subject of the era: "You will find masses / Of heroes amongst the working people, / Who serenely sacrifice themselves / In this battle."[87]

This simplistic poem by Vintshevski may have influenced Peretz. Most of Peretz's truly socialist poetry, such as "Baym fremdn khupe kleyd: A stsene fun varshever lebn" (By a foreign wedding dress: A scene from life in Warsaw), appeared during the second year of the *Bletlekh*. "Baym fremdn khupe kleyd" appeared in two consecutive volumes of the *Bletlekh*[88] and was described as "the most perfect social thing by Peretz,"[89] a statement worth examining closely. Its title suggests the central role that the institution of marriage plays in the poem, but its actual plot surrounds the manufacturing of a fancy wedding dress, the object of fetish throughout its course. The poem is over eighty stanzas long and contains various rhyme schemes and tempos. Many of the stanzas are structured as a folk song: two long lines broken into four (quatrains) and an ABCB rhyme scheme, but occasionally the lines are rhymed using couplets, and these lines tend to be longer. The story is set in a sweatshop that produces high fashion. It is a dramatic poem, featuring several characters, who are supposedly speaking to one another: a matron, two female hatmakers, and a choir of young seamstresses. The collective voice of the choir takes the class-oriented voice of the three seamstresses one step forward, joining their individualistic voices and expressing collective class interests, spoken in a tight folk-song style. The collective voice of the workers changes one-quarter of the way into the poem, when a young female laborer, who calls herself "lustik-lebn" (cheerful-life), steps out of the group and starts to argue with the others. She claims she wants to enjoy her young years without any excessive material gains like the diamonds and pearls that are placed on the wedding dress they are working on. But the poor, depressed choir mocks her cheery "modesty-vanity" as the product of her youth and naivete.

This long poem unfolds as a discussion among the have-nots held during the manufacturing of an item for the haves. After two ballads by the choir, the theme focuses on an inner story, structured as a folk story, told by one of the hatmakers. This inner story, which the narrator heard from her grandmother, expresses what Minkov termed "symbolism-out-of-realism," in which, like in Hood's poem, "the realistic character and the atmosphere around it turn into a symbol."[90] This inner story is reminiscent of the inner story in "Weaver-Love" where the "capitalist" sorcerer enters into the pious shtetl.[91] In both cases, a pseudo folk legend serves the dual purpose of making an anti-capitalist statement and a statement regarding the potential power of literature in promoting social change. By shedding light on their situation, the inner stories in Peretz's work help his working-class characters become aware of their exploitation and of the social dynamic that defines it.[92]

The story recounts the tale of two brothers who live together in a modest little house in the valley. Though their house is modest, it is a happy one, with a tiny little window, which lets just the right amount of golden sunshine inside. The brothers work hard and live a modest life of brotherly affection. However, as in "Weaver-Love," this idyll is disrupted when a rich, seductive snake enters their relationship and promises the older brother wealth beyond his imagination. The intimate relationship between the brothers ("two faithful hearts together"; Peretz, *Ale verk*, 1:224) is replaced by a brother-snake relationship when the snake reveals the secrets of gaining wealth to the older brother. The snake tells the older brother that the key to his happiness rests upon the exploitation of his younger brother's labor: his blood, sweat, and tears are literally worth diamonds and riches to the older brother.[93] The older brother is advised to produce blood by stabbing his brother with a needle and sweat by making him work in high temperatures. Now, the seductive, biblical-like snake tells him, "You have a factory, / And make your fortune, / You're stronger and already know the secret!" (1:226). The outcome of this story is of course capitalism. Technically, the hatmaker never heard the end from her grandmother, but after she heard parts of it, the gloom of the story penetrated her reality. When the older brother returns home, we read the following:

The moon still hears the only night,	עס הערט די לבֿנה נאָך ד'איינציקע נאַכט,
How in the shack it cried and laughed,	ווי ס'האָט אינעם שטיבל געוויינט און געלאַכט.
The stars are looking inside the windows:	עס קוקן די שטערן אין פֿענצטער אַריַין: ווי לאַכט עס אַ ברודער בײַם ברודערס געוויַין?!
How come a brother laughs at his brother's cry?!	די זון האָט צומאָרגנס געוווּנדערט זיך שטאַרק: ווי שלאָגט עס אַ ברודער דעם צווייטן אין קאַרק?
The sun was wondering:	עס ווונדערט צוגלײַכדעם וואַלד און דעם טײַך:
How come one smacks his brother in the neck?	וואָס איז עס אין שטיבל געשען?
The forest and the river are wondering as well:	
What happened in the shack? (1:226–27)	

In the original *Bletlekh* version, another stanza appears after this one in which we learn that both brothers suffer. One cannot sleep due to physical pain, while the other can't sleep out of fear of losing his property (the "disadvantages of privilege" we saw in Peretz's gothic story "A Night of Horror"). The ending of the inner story tells us how within the dominance of capitalism, exploitation of labor creates animosity between people, causing them to selfishly compete for empty promises of wealth, to the point that they are willing to suck the blood, sweat, and tears from a brother. This provocative story and the series of rhetorical questions at its end stir anger in its readers, making "Baym fremdn khupe kleyd" a bona fide political poem. In addition to its clear critique of capitalism, the poem is also critical of the institution of marriage. It exposes the exploitative process that goes into producing the wedding dress, which becomes the fetish of the narrative of marriage. Peretz also

Figure 4.2 The cover of most issues of the groundbreaking journal *Yontef bletlekh* featured an original poem by Peretz. These poems were meant to serve as a poetic companion to the articles and short stories that constituted the main content of the journal. The second volume for Lag Ba-Omer was the first to have a poem on its cover. Steven Spielberg Digital Yiddish Library.

subverts the *Haskalah* literature and drama that preceded him, which promoted the Romantic version of marriage as superior to matchmaking and, unlike Peretz's self-published *Bletlekh*, had the Jewish bourgeoisie as its main patron.[94]

When Peretz wrote genuine socialist poetry, he also modernized the means of artistic creation, introducing new forms and styles into Yiddish literature. The mixture of styles, the usage of symbolist techniques, the polyphonies—all are examples that show that although Peretz's poetry still cannot be categorized as modernist, he did incorporate modernist elements in his poetry. This is in contrast to a convention held by some scholars, such as the three editors of *The Penguin Book of Modern Yiddish Verse*—Irving Howe, the Israeli Khone Shmeruk, and the neoconservative Ruth Wisse—who omitted almost any trace of leftist Yiddish poetry from their volume. The one meager exception is the sweatshop poet Rosenfeld, who is represented by a single poem ("The Sweatshop"). This case of underrepresentation is a result of the false contradiction these scholars made between politically committed art and aesthetics.[95] The incorporation of modernist elements in his socialist poetry proves that Peretz innovated stylistically and aesthetically while being committed ideologically to the cause of the Jewish working class, pushing the envelope simultaneously on both fronts.

Collecting "Jewish Folklore"

Besides the purely socialist poems, many poems in the *Bletlekh* consisted of motifs of "national rejuvenation" and the struggle for national freedom. Poems like "Treyst mayn folk" (Take comfort my people) and "Friling" (Spring) describe the "sleepy people" that need to be woken up ("my people are lazy and still, / Have not awoken yet, no!"[96]). Despite their past popularity, in which they were set to music and were widely sung,[97] today these works have lost their relevance. At the time when these poems were written, despite their nationalist tone, they did not necessarily contradict the ideal of universal social justice. Given the progressive outlet in which they were published, these Yiddish poems had the potential of serving as a tool of empowerment for the Jewish working class in Eastern Europe (the ethno-class faction), which was represented politically by the Bund. In other words, these works were progressive in the sense that they fostered a sense of imagined community among an underprivileged, marginalized group. *Folk*, in this case, as in *folks-bildung*, meant the common Jewish people, the populace, as opposed to the Jewish people as a whole.

Starting in the mid-1890s, Peretz was busy collecting folk songs, acting as a pioneer in this field of Jewish folklore.[98] He gathered the material during the years 1894–95, and by 1896 he had a collection of Yiddish folk songs that he intended to publish as a supplement to the *Yontef bletlekh*. Some of the poems, though it is not clear which, were actually Peretz's adaptations of songs he heard or read.[99] Many of these songs dealt with issues of love, themes whose ability to be adequately expressed in Yiddish Peretz had previously questioned. A handful of these poems were variations on similar themes: some tell the story of an innocent young woman who is drowned in the river by her seducer; others are about the life of a Jewish soldier in the Russian army; others represent a selection of stories of failed love. Some of these poems have known writers (Peretz was not a professional folklorist, and he did not strictly follow the conventional understanding of folk songs as being composed by anonymous writers and belonging to a group of people), and some poems Peretz reworked and incorporated in his Yiddish cycle of love poems entitled *Romantsero*.[100]

The combination of folk songs and socialism, so typical of the *Bletlekh*, perfectly illustrates Peretz's attraction to the Jewish labor movement at the time and the role he played as the cultural agent of the Jewish working class. One can learn from this collection about Peretz's desire to find inspiration for his own work in this material, which he believed embodied a "Jewish life" to be cherished.[101] Starting from "Monish," he employed folkloristic elements in his work, viewing folklore as "a deep well of symbolic truth, to be interpreted by the modern artist and adapted to the spiritual needs of the modern Jew."[102] As Jameson points out, folktales tend to voice a silenced, counterhegemonic sentiment, which is by definition missing from the cultural monuments that have survived,[103] and which would be lost if not for the work of the collectors. An assembler like Peretz plays a crucial role in this process, because without his praxis of "restoration or artificial reconstruction" of these marginalized Yiddish voices, they would be absent from the dialogue of the class system.[104] Discredited by many *maskilim* as superstitions to be forgotten,[105] the meaning of his Yiddish folklore works increased the symbolic capital of Yiddish, mostly vis-à-vis Hebrew literature.

The long Yiddish poem "Reb Yosl" (Mr. Yossel; 1895), published in the third volume of *Di yidishe bibliyotek*, is, like "Monish," infused with larger doses of Jewish folklore. Both poems incorporate various rhyme schemes and rhythms and center on a traditional protagonist who is well versed in the *sforim* (traditional Jewish literature) but who is less in touch with earthly affairs. Peretz criticizes this character for his lack of worldliness, just as he criticized the Jewish intelligentsia for being detached from the common people. In "Reb Yosl," the traditional character is a *melamed* who is immersed in his studies and "sitting from afar . . . this shtetl is not his, he wants to know of nothing / And study constantly his traditional book" (*Ale verk*, 1:156). Together with a pupil of his, Khaymel, the orphan whom he shelters, Reb Yosel lives in the attic of Reb Gavriel and his wife, Tsipe. Reb Gavriel is a shoemaker by day and security guard by night.

Peretz expanded the "demonic" motif in this poem relative to "Monish"; it includes the *danse macabre* motif that Peretz will go back to in his later works, and we find here an open declaration that this poem is a kind of archival assembly of Jewish folklore. Toward the end of the first section, the *melamed* Reb Yosl gives his students a vivid and detailed description of the wrath of hell to keep them on the right path. In *Haskalah* literature, the *melamed* was always described as an ignorant and coarse man;[106] Peretz stretched this literary type to its extreme up to the point of creating a parody of that figure. This authority figure, with all his cruelty, was an essential literary type of the newly termed "Jewish folklore"; he is a carrier who passes on a slice of Jewish culture through the generations. The last stanza of this section clearly states, in Reb Yosl's frightening voice, the significance of folklore (*Ale verk*, 1:159):

And fire, and flames, and autos-da-fé,	און פֿײַער, און פֿלאַמען, און אויטאָ־דע־פֿעען,
And everything, which a Jew saw in exile	און אַלץ וואָס אַ ייִד אין גלות געזען
And has laid in the hell-archive,	און אָפּגעלייגט אין גיהנום אַרכיוו,
Everything he distributes, the awful things	דאָס אַלצדינג פֿאַרטיילט ער, די שרעקלעכע זאַכן
For improper touch, for speaking, for naughtiness, for laughing,	פֿאַר מוקצה, פֿאַר רעדן, פֿאַר שטיפֿן, פֿאַר לאַכן,
And according to the most severe tariff!	און לויט דעם שטרענגסטן טאַריף!

This "hell-archive" is a kind of a self-parody of what Diaspora folkists like Peretz tried to establish: the business of accumulating documentation of all aspects of Jewish life in the Diaspora, thus creating a people's library. Peretz terms assembling the documented history of Jews—meaning humorously here the history of the persecution of Jews—a kind of devil's work. In this way, Peretz parodies an imagined utopian space in which such an archive does exist, a safe place for his poems and folk songs to be kept. Establishing such an institution will ultimately enable the inclusion of Eastern European Jews in the modern European national project.

The orphan Khaymel receives private lessons in misogyny from Reb Yosl, who tells him that women are seductive witches, devils in disguise. This lecture is overheard by Tsipe, who tells her husband Reb Gavriel what a terrible man Reb Yosl is: "he frightens the children . . . [Reb Yosl] is a terrible-creature, / I would have torn him into pieces out of anger!" (*Ale verk*, 1:167). And, indeed, Tsipe will get her revenge. She first tries to convince her husband (who tends at first to take Reb Yosl's side in patriarchal solidarity) that she means business and that her "Torah-words" are of no less symbolic worth than Reb Yosl's and those of men in general. Her education is based on the *Tsene-Rene* book (1:169), the popular compilation of adaptations in Yiddish of weekly Torah portions, mainly for women who generally were not taught to read Hebrew.[107] "Toyre iz toyre, tsi di, tsi yene" (Torah is Torah, whether this one or that one; 1:169), she tells him. She acquired her skills, she declares, not by reading popular Yiddish novels (1:176), but from traditional texts.

Tsipe uses her knowledge to lecture her husband about her view of the famous Torah stories:[108] from the Garden of Eden plot of seduction up until the tale of Samson—the ultimate story of the hero who falls at the hand of a woman. In Eastern European Jewish folklore, there was the common expression *shimshn der nebekhdiker* (the lame Samson), which best describes the protagonist Reb Yosl. His nebbish authority relies on his symbolic capital of knowing Hebrew and being versed in traditional texts rather than on his monumental physique. The multiple allusions to Samson foreshadow Tsipe's plot to get even with Reb Yosl—not because of tribal wars, as in the Bible, but as part of the social wars between men and women, of the young and orphaned against the patriarchal order embodied by Reb Yosl's cruelty and misogyny as well as the passive cooperation he received from Reb Gavriel. What angered Tsipe so much was the way Reb Yosl concluded his "hate-lecture" to the orphaned boy. In his conclusion, he uttered lines (on the right) that are a variation of the opening stanzas of "Monish" (left):

איר ווייסט—מן-הסתּם—
די וועלט איז אַ ים,
מיר זענען פֿיש;
(טייל זענען העכט,
שלינגען נישט שלעכט . . .
זאָגט, אפֿשר נישט?)
די וועלט איז אַ ים,
ברייט אָן אַ שיער;
די פֿיש זענען מיר,
די פֿישער איז ס״מ

"אָ, חיימל הער, איך זאָג דיר נישט מער,
די וועלט—צו וואָס איז זי גלײַך?
די מענטשן—וואָס נישט?—זײַ זענען נאָך פֿיש,
זײַ שווימען אַרום אין אַ טײַך . . .
פֿאַרשטייסט מן-הסתּם, דער פֿישער איז ס״ם,
ער שטייט זיך בײַם ים טײַכל, בײַם ברעג,
און לאָזט אָפּ דעם ל״ץ, די אישה—זײַן נעץ . . .
רחמנא-ליצלן, איז אַן עק!"[109]

"You probably know—	"Oh, Khaymel hear, I will tell you no more,

"You probably know—
The world is an ocean, we are fish;
(Some are pikes,
They swallow not bad . . .
Say, maybe not?)
The world is an ocean,
Endlessly wide;
We are the fish,
The fisherman's the devil."
(*Ale verk*, 1:3)

"Oh, Khaymel hear, I will tell you no more,
The world—to what is it similar?
The people—what else?—They are still fish,
They are swimming around in a river. . .
You probably know, the fisherman's the devil,
He stands by the riverbank,
And releases the demon, the woman—his net. . .
Good God, it's the end of it!"

This direct reference to "Monish" inside this later poem begs for comparison between the two. "Reb Yosl" has never been seriously analyzed, in striking contrast to "Monish." Rozentsvayg made one short remark that "in essence it is a radical variant of 'Monish'"[110] but gave no further explanation of how it functions as such. What is striking in comparing the two poems is the radically different roles Peretz assigned to his women figures. In "Monish," the central female figure is a seductive, *shikse*-like character who is ultimately a nameless and passive tool sent by the devil to seduce the pious yeshiva student and who (like the ideal bourgeois woman) sings at home as a hobby. But in "Reb Yosl," the female figure has a name: Tsipe, the name of the dark-skinned wife of the greatest biblical prophet, Moses—Zipporah (Numbers 12:1). Moreover, she belongs to the lower classes—"I am a tailor's daughter, go on laugh, / My mindset will always be that of a tailor" (*Ale verk*,1:169), and she is anything but passive, gentile, and unsophisticated as she plots her Delilah-like payback.

In a kind of a parody of Peretz's own "Monish," Reb Yosl becomes convinced that Tsipe wants to seduce him (she promises him hot soup as her husband is about to leave the house). He prays to God that he won't succumb to his sexual desire; "I don't want any temptation" (*nisoyen*), he utters, and claims that he prefers to die rather than have a sexual encounter with her. To strengthen his efforts, he also prays to the Almighty to make her ugly and foul, to make it easier for him to resist. He hallucinates that she comes to him as Shulamis, the female protagonist of the Song of Songs, trying to sweet talk him into bed: "Ikh bin dokh di shenste, a royz tsvishn derner! . . . / Mikh meynt ir, nisht kneses-yisro'el!" (I am the prettiest of them all, a rose among thorns! . . . / You mean me, not the Jewish people!;[111] 1:174). In fact, Tsipe uses her sharp senses to scheme and to execute her own plan against Reb Yosl. Her plot involves seduction, drugging, and cutting of his "Jewish hair" (his *shpitsn* and *peyes*, meaning the tips of his beard and his side curls). "Tsipe executes the gag with mercy, / She smiles and—is holding the shears" (1:177).

Tsipe embodies the revolutionary potential of the lower classes, and particularly of the female lower-class Jew. She demonstrates the capacity for anger as well as the capability of using her anger to motivate her to act for change. The ability to express anger recalls "Anger of a Jewish woman," but here Peretz takes that theme a step further. Though Tsipe supposedly holds a "demonic" power over men, this is ultimately a very positive force. It is noteworthy that "Anger of a Jewish woman" was itself a radical variant of a humoristic poem by Peretz, "Reb Khanine ben Dosa (a talmudishe zage)" (1891). It features the character of the idle, only studying husband and his complaining wife: "what's it worth for me your Torah . . . / I wonder idle with the kids, / Khanine ben Dosa, give food!" (*Ale verk*, 1:38); their kids are hungry and crying. But the poem conveys a sense of cynical humor toward the exploiting husband ("should all my loved ones die here out of hunger, / And there your chair should not even crack"; 1:42) rather than the anger and protest of the later story.[112]

In "Reb Yosl," Peretz echoes, besides his own "Monish," an early long Hebrew poem called "Bruria" (1825) by Samuel I. Mulder from Amsterdam, which represented a significant milestone in Hebrew narrative poetry. Unlike the epic poetry of *Haskalah* masters such as N. H. Wessely (1725–1805), who told the life story of a biblical character, Mulder's poem was based on various postbiblical sources (from the Talmud to Rashi), and it was not a biographical poem. Instead, Mulder focused on the battle of the sexes through the debate and intrigue between its three protagonists.[113] In "Bruria" it is the husband, the Mishna-sage Rabbi Meir, who plots against his opinionated and educated wife, Bruria, following their debate as to whether women are "light-minded." Rabbi Meir sends his beloved pupil Uriah to seduce Bruria and thus to prove his point regarding the nature of women. The plot centers on this story of seduction, revenge, and sexual desire. Both Mulder and Peretz centered their poems on an educated woman who is debating with her husband while reinterpreting traditional Jewish literature's message about the role of women in society. In "Reb Yosl," Peretz took the strong woman who was plotted against in Mulder's poem and made her into the one who herself plots against the male figures. Besides writing in Yiddish, Peretz also transferred the plot to a contemporary Eastern European setting. In addition, he made the male figures unimpressive, reducing them to parodies of the legendary sage Rabbi Meir and his pupil of Mulder's poem.

By the end of "Reb Yosl," Peretz loses a great deal of the subversive momentum he built through the poem by making Tsipe totally remorseful over her actions. He thus transforms the poem into a moral play, in which the actual sinner is Tsipe and not Reb Yosl. "I've sinned . . . I know it myself!" she tells her husband in shame. Reb Gavriel does not accept what she has done and makes her feel awful for it. In the final account, she accepts the social norms set by men, and totally backs down from the anarchistic impulse she had shown before. Her action made her into a miserable creature, suffering on the psychological level for her attempt to correct society in an "impulsive and irrational" (i.e., feminine) manner. The poem ends with the sadness of the female protagonist, who, even though years have passed since the incident, regrets that she ever launched her war to begin with: "Tsipe? Who knows? / Sometimes she pauses to stare, / And her eyes shed a tear!" (1:179).

At the end of "Bruria," both Bruria and Rabbi Meir lose their minds because of their deeds, and the speaker ends by giving thanks to the Lord. Miron claims that the big questions raised in "Bruria" regarding the depth of passion and revenge are not disrupted even by the final, God-praising words at the end, which are mostly formal. Peretz's poem does not conclude with reference to any transcendental being, though in his poem Reb Gavriel also remains sad for years after the event. Peretz's ending, despite its similarities to "Bruria," does not avoid the class-gender war, but it does blunt its edginess. While "Reb Yosl" is, as Rozentsvayg commented, something of a "radical 'Monish,'" it avoids making an overt call for gender revolt. "Reb Yosl" does disrupt the rules of discourse, mostly through Tsipe's voice and actions. However, the total regret expressed at the story's end causes it to fall short of meeting the second requirement for political poetry, as defined by Hever, of having a political effect on its readers.

Among Marx, Heine, and Peretz

> The Hebrew prophets seriously influenced me; for a long time I was as you know under the influence of Heine and Börne—my first Jewish poetry.
>
> —Peretz, in a letter to Y. Tsinberg, 1911

Eigenthum! Recht des Besitzes!	אָ, דאָס אייגנטום! חזקה
O des Diebstahls! O der Lüge!	אויף אַ ליגן, אַ גנבֿה!
Solch Gemisch von List und Unsinn	אַזאַ שקר, אַזאַ שווינדל
Konnte nur der Mensch erfinden.	קאָן אויסטראַכטן נאָר אַ מענטש!

Property! Possessors' rights!	Oh, property! Claiming a right
O such thievery—saucy lies!	To a lie, a theft!
Mingling such of cunning, nonsense,	Such a lie, such a deceit
As only man could have invented.	Only a human being can come up with!

—Heine, Atta Troll, 1841–43   —Peretz's Yiddish translation of Atta Troll, 1894

According to his own account, the cultural heritage Peretz carried included the German poet of Jewish descent Heinrich Heine (1797–1856). Heine not only heavily influenced Peretz as a poet, as frequently noted by his readers and interpreters, but also bequeathed to him his view of Marx and the socialist movement and as a writer of edgy feuilletons. The great influence of Heine on Peretz's poetry is widely acknowledged, especially that of Heine's love poetry.[114] In fact, it was Peretz's *Harp* that sparked the debate in the second half of the 1890s over Heine's place in Hebrew literature.¹¹⁵ Peretz borrowed from Heine the title "Romanzero" for his own Yiddish poem cycle. He translated Heine's poem "An Edom" into Yiddish for his second volume of *Di yidishe bibliyotek*, which sarcastically deals with Jewish-Christian relations from the point of view of a Jew. He borrowed an epigraph from Heine—"Es ist eine alte Geschichte, / Doch bleibt sie immer neu"¹¹⁶—for another of his Yiddish poems from the same period, "Er un zi" (1891), which was added in a Rashi-like script in order to give it extra respectability and authority (it's also used in his one-act Yiddish play by the same title, *Er un zi*, 1904). In the same almanac in which he published his translation of *Atta Troll*, Peretz also published a dramatic-poetic Yiddish text entitled "A Scene (from Heine)." Even his early poetry in Polish showed a few signs of Heine's influence.¹¹⁷ Leah Garrett has shown how Peretz adapted Wagner's musical version of the Germanic myth Tannhäuser into a Yiddish short story entitled "Self-Sacrifice" ("Mesires-nefesh," 1904). Peretz Judaized the plot, turning it into a story about Jewish learning and Jewish life. Heine's poem "Der Tannhäuser" (1836) predated the adaptations by Wagner and Peretz. While Heine used the myth to politically satirize Germany, Peretz emphasized the redemptive elements of the story, transforming it from a Catholic redemption into a story of Jewish redemption.¹¹⁸

Heine's political influence on Peretz is not often discussed. This omission is strange given the fact that both authors were very involved in the sociopolitical currents and issues of their time. Heine knew the young Marx personally when they were both in Paris and was exposed directly to his evolving mindset. Heine also extensively discussed various socialist platforms and thinkers in his journalistic writings. In Germany, Heine was a radical poet and a dissident because of his frequent criticism of what he viewed as the militaristic nationalist culture that was sweeping away his beloved homeland. He was a cultural hero not only to Peretz but to many Europeans of Jewish descent, including Theodor Herzl, Peretz's parallel in the Zionist movement,¹¹⁹ as more and more Jews were included in the European middle and upper classes. Heine made numerous comments about his Jewish background and wrote the famous "Hebrew Melodies" cycle and an unfinished Jewish novel, *The Rabbi from Bacharach*. To what extent was Heine himself a radical writer?

One of Heine's most celebrated satirical political poems was *Germany: A Winter's Tale (Deutschland: Ein Wintermärchen*, 1844). It was written in a four-stanza style of folk poetry, and it subversively used (Germanic) folkloric material to promote progressive ideas. Heine was poking fun at German nationalism while calling for an end to poverty: "Es wächst hienieden Brot genug. Für alle Menschenkinder" ("Bread grows on the earth for every one / Enough, and e'en in redundance").[120] The poem's speaker remembers the comment made by the French revolutionary Saint-Just that the sickness of society demands a stronger medicine than rose water. Like Peretz's *Bletlekh*, it was the most radical text Heine was able to release under restrictions imposed by censorship.[121] *Germany: A Winter's Tale* was a sequel to his former *Atta Troll: A Midsummer Night's Dream*. The stanza above borrows the title of a book by the French "utopian socialist" Pierre-Joseph Proudhon (1809–56), *What is Property? Theft!* (1840; 1844 in German). Proudhon's book put forth the argument that property is gained only through exploitation. Exploitation can only be eliminated by giving each worker the means of production and through organizing the trades (not by the state, as was Marx's platform, thus placing Proudhon's philosophy squarely in the anarchistic tradition).[122] These stanzas are read in the voice of Atta Troll, the bear protagonist of the poem (on the right is Peretz's translation):

Keine Eigentümer schuf	קיין שום קנין האָט באַשאַפֿן
Die Natur, denn taschenlos,	די נאַטור, װײל אָן טאַשן
Ohne Taschen in den Pelzen,	אין די פּעלצן קומען אַלע
Kommen wir zur Welt, wir alle.	אַלע ברואים אויף דער װעלט!

A pocket! Unnatural	No property was created
As the property,	By nature, for without pockets
As the rights of possession—	In the fur, come all
People are born pocketless!	All the creatures of the world!

Peretz translated this part, making it very Yiddish, with no fewer than six Yiddish words of Hebrew origin: *khazoke* (claim), *gneyve* (theft), *sheker* (lie), *shum* (none), *kinyen* (property), *bruim* (creatures), and several others from *Atta Troll*, to include them in his essay "Dos eygentum" (Property; 1894[124]). This essay was mostly devoted to arguing with Atta Troll, who speaks Proudhon's words, saying that property is not a human invention; that property exists in nature as well, as in the case of marsupials and camels. He ends the essay with a promise to tell the history of property among people.[125] Unfortunately that promise, which would have helped us better understand Peretz's views, never was fulfilled.

In several of his writings over the years, Heine expressed an ambiguous stance toward a proletarian revolution. On the one hand, he was seriously contemplating the revolutionary option. Marx's influence on Heine is clearly seen, for example, in the poem "Die schlesischen Weber" (The Silesian weavers), which was published in Marx's journal *Vorwaerts!* (1844), portraying the first German workers' uprising.[126] Such a poem surely influenced Peretz thematically, as we saw in his poems and stories concerning weavers and knitters, as well as by its radical spirit.[127] On the other hand, at the same time Heine expressed fear in his writings regarding the possibility of full realization of the communist platform in the future. In the French edition of "Lutetia" (1855), he wrote,

> This confession, that the future belongs to the Communists, I made with an undertone of the greatest fear and anxiety and, oh!, this tone by no means is a mask! Indeed, with fear and terror I imagine the time, when those dark iconoclasts come to power: with their raw fists they will batter all marble images of my beloved world of art, they will ruin all those fantastic anecdotes that the poets loved so much, they will chop down my laurel forests and plant potatoes and, oh!, the herbs chandler will use my *Buch der Lieder* to make bags for coffee and snuff for the old women of the future—oh!, I can foresee all this and I feel deeply sorry thinking of this decline threatening my poetry and the old world order—And yet, I freely confess, the same thoughts have a magical appeal upon my soul that I cannot resist . . . I cannot object to the premise "that all people have the right to eat."[128]

Heine called in this text for justice, for the destruction of the old world based on egoism, where one man exploits the other.[129] But he also expressed here fears of radical change that would completely abolish the world as he knew it, including the things he cared deeply about, like culture and aesthetics. Heine's fear of a socialist revolution also influenced Nietzsche, though the latter was far from any ambiguous stand on the matter (i.e., he was in strict opposition to the socialist utopia and viewed it as complete mediocrity). Nietzsche wrote about the great influence Heine's language had on him, and some critics see Heine as anticipating Nietzsche in certain ways.[130] Nietzsche was also starting to influence Peretz and other modern Jewish thinkers by the 1890s; in particular, he was heavily influential on Peretz's folk stories and Hasidic tales, as I will discuss in the next chapter.

Peretz's writings include very similar ponderings to Heine's, especially in light of the 1905 revolution. Peretz wrote an article in 1906 in Yiddish entitled "Hofenung un shrek" (Hope and fear), in which he put forth an ambiguous stance toward the vision of social revolution that strongly echoed that of Heine. Wisse writes that in "Hope and fear" Peretz was rejecting socialism altogether.[131] But in fact Peretz wrote clearly that his heart was with the socialists. He addresses them, saying, "I want, I hope for your victory, but I fear and I tremble from your victory" and also "cruelly will you defend the entitlement of your herd to equal shares of grass under its feet and to roof over its head, while your enemies will be free individuals, overmen (*Übermenschn*), genius inventors, prophets, redeemers, poets and artists" (*Ale verk*, 8:226–29).

Not without reason, Heine and Peretz were linked in a 1943 article by the pro-Soviet Yiddish essayist Alexander Pomerantz (1901–65). In his apologetic piece, the essay's title, "Heine and Peretz Feared and Doubted for Nothing,"[132] is repeated after each time Pomerantz makes an argument disproving the pair's predictions concerning the dismal fate of art and the individual spirit under a socialist regime. Pomerantz first identified the similarity between the two authors by stating that "both were contradictory poets because of the contradictory situation of the petit bourgeois between the proletariat and the bourgeoisie."[133] He then goes on to prove how in the socialist Soviet Union art and artists were aligned with the masses and thus enjoyed an unprecedented cultural renaissance. In this state, Heine and Peretz receive the highest honors; the Olympic Games are played, including an orchestra that plays the Tannhäuser march. And the bottom line remains at the end: "Heine and Peretz feared and doubted for nothing" ("הײַנע און פּרץ האָבן זיך אומזיסט געהאַט און געצווייפֿלט").[134]

Pomerantz's essay was published in the United States as part of a book commemorating twenty-five years of the Soviet Union with the express goal of improving the understanding between American Jews and Soviet Jews. Boasting an impressive photo of Stalin on page 6, it aimed to prove to progressive Jews in the West that their cultural heroes, had they lived to see the Soviet state, would have become huge fans of that state and widely celebrated within it. In retrospect, of course, it is very hard to imagine such a scenario. The yearning of Peretz and Heine for socialism in the true sense, one that deeply enhances freedom rather than restricts it, remains unfulfilled. Neither of them ever doubted the deep moral-value basis of communism.

Despite all his doubts regarding the implementation of revolution and the socialist platform that became apparent in his later years, Peretz published one of his most radical poems during his so-called reactionary period,[135] namely the Yiddish poem "Meyn nisht" (Do not think). The poem speaks in an authoritative, prophetic language and warns the "haves" that their time is up and that they will have to face the wrath of the "have-nots." This is the original poem alongside my English translation:

Do not think the world is a tavern—	—מיין נישט, די וועלט איז א קרעטשמע
Created so you can make a way for yourself with your fists and your nails	באשאפֿן צו מאַכן א וועג מיט פֿויסטן און נעגל
To the tavern-barrel, and gorge and booze, when others	צום שענקפֿאַס, און פֿרעסן און זויפֿן, ווען א נדערע
Are looking from afar with glassy eyes,	קוקן פֿון ווײַטן מיט גלעזערנע אויגן
Fainting, and swallowing their spit and pulling together their bellies, quivering with cramps!	פֿאַרחלשט, און שלינגען דאָס שפּײַעכץ און ציען
Oh, do not think the world is a tavern!	צוזאַמען דעם מאָגן, וואָס וואַרפֿט זיך אין קרעמפֿן!
	אָ, מיין נישט די וועלט איז א קרעטשמע!
Do not think the world is a stock market—created	מיין נישט די וועלט איז א בערזע—באשאפֿן
So the stronger could deal with the tired and weak,	דער שטאַרקער זאָל האַנדלען מיט מידע און שוואַכע,
Could buy from poor girls their shame	זאָל קויפֿן בײַ אָרעמע מיידלעך די בושה,
From women the milk from their breasts, from men	בײַ פֿרויען די מילך פֿון די בריסטן, בײַ מענער
Their bone marrow, from children their smiles, that rare guest on their growing faces—Oh, do not think, the world is a stock market!	דעם מאַרך פֿון די ביינער, בײַ קינדער דעם שמייכל, דעם זעלטענעם גאַסט אויפֿן וואַקסענעם פּנים
	—אָ, מיין נישט די וועלט איז א בערזע!

Do not think the world is lawlessness—created	מיין נישט די וועלט איז אַ הפֿקר—באַשאַפֿן פֿאַר וועלף און פֿאַר פֿוקסן, פֿאַר רויב און פֿאַר שווינדל;
For wolves and for foxes, for theft and for deceit;	
Its sky—a curtain so God should not see;	דער הימל—אַפּאָרהאַנג אַז גאָט זאָל נישט זען;
Its fog—so people cannot look at your hands;	דער נעפּל—מען זאָל אויף די הענט דיר נישט קוקן;
Its wind—to smother the wild cries;	דער ווינט—צו פֿאַרשטיקן די ווילדע געשרייען;
Its land is to absorb the blood of victims—	די ערד – אײַנצוזאַפֿן דאָס בלוט פֿון קרבֿנות—
Oh, do not think the world is lawlessness!	אָ, מיין נישט די וועלט איז אַ הפֿקר!
The world is neither a tavern, nor a stock market, nor lawlessness!	די וועלט איז קיין קרעטשמע, קיין בערזע, קיין הפֿקר!
Everything measured, everything weighed!	געמאָסטן ווערט אַלעס, געוויגן ווערט אַלעס!
No tear and no blood drop are fading.	קיין טרער און קיין בלוטיקער טראָפּן פֿאַרגייען.
No spark in an eye is extinguished for nothing!	אומזיסט ווערט קיין פֿונק אין קיין אויג נישט פֿאַרלאָשן!
Tears become rivers, rivers become oceans,	פֿון טרערן ווערט טײַכן, פֿון טײַכן ווערט ימען,
From oceans a flood, from sparks—thunder—	פֿון ימים – אַ מבול, פֿון פֿונקען—אַ דונער—
Oh, do not think there is neither law nor judge!	אָ, מיין נישט, לית דין ולית דיין!
	(*Perl fun der yidisher poezye*, 71–72)

This poem was Peretz's strongest response to the failed 1905 revolution. Clearly, it conveys the message that the fight isn't over yet. The tavern, stock market, and lawlessness parallel one another, collectively representing the social foundations of this world. They are accompanied by the anaphoric warning ("Do not think the world is. . .") that relates to the temporality of the current social order. The use of exclamation points and the lack of rhyming intensify the severity of the message. The poem anticipates the unity of people and the great force this unity possesses, a force strong enough to create a flood of biblical dimensions.

This unity of revolutionary sparks is a force that no power in the world can withstand. Peretz expresses here the longing for a sense of morality that he believes has been lost in modernity.

In poetry Peretz made his point far more firmly than he did with any essay raising questions, problems, or grievances. These words were sung through the years by Jewish socialists, and they express the desire of the modern person to live in a world based on morals, on social equality, and on equal justice for all. With these very words, writes the Bundist Shlomo Mendelson,

> Peretz attacked the world, its order, its culture, its justice, its spiritual dejection, its non-sincerity. The Jewish worker felt that through Peretz's mouth he could storm the world. This very contest added wings to his mutiny, his rebellion, which the Jewish revolutionary movement, the "Bund," arose in him.
> פרץ האָט געשטורעמט די וועלט, איר סדר, איר קולטור, איר יושר, איר גייסטיקע געפֿאַלנקייט, איר נישט-אויפֿריכטיקייט. דער ייִדישער אַרבעטער האָט דערפֿילט, אַז דורך פּרצעס מויל שטורעמט ער די וועלט. דער דאָזיקער פֿאַרמעסט האָט צוגעגעבן פֿליגלען זיין בונט, זיין רעבעליע, וואָס עס האָט אין אים אויפֿגעוועקט די ייִדישע רעוואָלוציאָנערע באַוועגונג, דער "בונד".[136]

I have shown in this chapter how Peretz's inspirational political poetry was also some of his finest poetry overall. The false contrast between those two elements, politics and aesthetics, was at times shared by leftist activists, pro-Soviets, and conservative scholars alike. In a similar vein, the Soviets and the conservatives, each for their own purpose, also misinterpreted Peretz's Hasidic stories in prose. I will show in the next chapter how the prophetic-biblical sense Peretz injected in his political poetry is not dissimilar to the way he used Hasidic motifs in his prose to call for a social revolution.

Chapter 5

Between Liberal Satire and Socialist Roots

Peretz's Hasidic Creations of the 1890s

[A proletarian writer] is in fact not limited to descriptions "of working people's lives": his field is much broader; it is in fact unlimited.

—M. Olgin, 1939

In any case, those who think that Peretz simply rewrote the homey Hasidic tales are mistaken; that in accepting its content he intended no more than to celebrate its forms. In any case, Peretz's impersonators and followers, who imitated or reiterated the Hasidic story and thus had the naive intention to become through it "sorts of Peretz" were mistaken. On the contrary, Peretz rebuilt the old Hasidic imagery and secularized it, in order to bury it under its own content and issue a call for rebellion.

במילא האָבן שוין אַ טעות יענע, וואָס מיינען, אַז פּרץ איז געווען פּשוט אַן
איבערדיקטער פֿון דער חסידיש־היימלשער היימישקייט, אַז אַננעמענדיק איר
אינהאַלט איז ער אויסן געווען נישט מער, ווי צו באַזינגען אירע פֿאָרמען. במילא
האָבן שוין אַ טעות געהאַט פּרצעס פּלומרשטע נאָכמאַכער און נאָכפֿאָלגער, וואָס
האָבן אימיטירט אָדער איבערגעזעצט די חסידישע מעשׂה און געהאַט דערבײַ
די תּמימותדיקע כּוונה צו ווערן דורך דעם "שטיקלעך פּרץ". אַדרבא, פּרץ האָט
דורך זײַן אינהאַלט איבערגעבויט די אַלטע חסידישע בילדערלעכקייט און האָט זי
סעקולאַריזירט, כּדי אונטערצעגראָבן מיט דעם איר אייגענעם אינהאַלט און רופֿן
צו מרידה.

—Dovid Bergelson, 1925[1]

The militant early Eastern European *Haskalah* literature, produced by masters such as the Galician Joseph Perl (1773–1839), frequently attacked the Hasidic movement. At the time, Hasidism was the most widespread Jewish religious movement in Europe.[2] The early *maskilim* scorned the Hasidim (Hasidic people) for adhering to irrational mystical beliefs, for being tied to the dying feudal social structure, and for numerous other reasons.[3]

An-ski testified in his memoirs to how far the real Peretz was removed from the Hasidic world, thus emphasizing its use by him as a symbol, not as a modern ideology. His view was also shared by Soviet interpreters before Rozentsvayg, like Nusinov.[4] An-ski wrote that Peretz, "the highest poet of the Hasidic legend, did not like, almost hated, Hasidic Rebbes, seeing most of them as con men."[5] Peretz also showed negative feelings toward Hasidim in response to their protests against his story "Shamya gibor," which they prevented from being published. In a letter to Dinezon, he stated that the Hebrew readers were worse than the Yiddish ones and that the worst among them were the Hasidim, whom he portrays as an old hag who can't take a joke: "kebogeret zkeyna asher lo . . . takhpots bemahatalot."[6]

In the initial stages of his career, Peretz continued this *maskilic* tradition of satirizing the Hasidic world. One can see it in his very first published work: the poem "Ha-shutafut" (The partnership; 1875) took aim at the Hasidic rebbe. He continued to write critiques of the Hasidic movement throughout the 1880s. At this time, the Hasidic movement was still the dominant religious group in Poland, over half a century since the *maskilim* began to take shots at it. But Peretz's closeness to the labor movement and his attraction to socialism during the mid-1890s led him to develop a more nuanced critique of the popular Hasidic movement and even an appreciation for some of its strengths as he perceived them. This process occurred also under other influences.

The very first spurts of a revision of the early *maskilic* negativity toward the Hasidic movement can be found in Eliezer Zweifel's work "Shalom al Yisrael" (Peace upon Israel; late 1860s–early 1870s), which was influential even to later figures such as Berdichevsky.[7] While classic *Haskalah* literature criticized Hasidism for its reliance on superstition and its abuse of divine authority for financial gain, some of Peretz's treatments of the Hasidim can be viewed as a stylized critique of capitalism itself—stylizing the radical socialist ideas expressed in his urban social-realist stories. His writings during this time were also an attempt to synthesize folkist, nationalist, and socialist ideas to create a particular modern Jewish group identity. Peretz's broad political treatment of social movements goes far beyond the traditional perspective of the *Haskalah*, which was defined by its close ties to the up-and-coming Jewish bourgeoisie in Europe. In fact, Peretz took an antithetical perspective to that of the *Haskalah*. He was developing the insight that every social group, class, or force has its progressive and reactionary period and its corresponding progressive or reactionary potential. This insight led him to try to locate the revolutionary core embedded within the Hasidic movement.[8]

Peretz perceived Hasidism as a folksy mass movement that swept Eastern European Jewry with an agenda of democratizing Jewish traditional knowledge and attending to the needs and concerns of everyday people. His interest in the movement inspired him to create Hasidic stories over a period of years, a project that many scholars associate with the later neoromantic or so-called reactionary Peretz, or one who "became disillusioned by his socialist involvements," as Ken Frieden argued.[9] In fact, I argue that the roots of his Hasidic themes were already apparent in his 1890s work at the very height of his radical period. Ross wrote extensively about the nationalist, neoromantic trends that marked the turn-of-the-century neo-Hasidic literature as produced by Peretz, Berdichevsky, Buber, An-ski, and others.[10] My analysis does not necessarily dispute this view. Rather, it elaborates on the breed of Diaspora Jewish nationalism that was manifested in Peretz's Hasidic stories, and it highlights their radical and class-oriented elements. In particular, I argue that this kind of nationalism is bounded within a particular ethnic class—meaning in this case, the Jewish working class—and I show, while engaging with Marxist criticism and its various historical manifestations, how these stories combined neo-Hasidism with radical political thought.

I examine in this chapter Peretz's Hasidic stories that danced between satirical mockery, with their different targets and forms, and fascination with the traces of revolutionary inspiration Peretz found within the movement. I do so by closely reading Peretz's texts set in the Hasidic world, which deal with questions of atheism, faith, and social change. The first segment will examine Peretz's early prose efforts, in both Yiddish and Hebrew, and address his usage of religion and pious figures as themes in his work.

Peretz and Religious Figures: The Beginning

Peretz's first-ever publication was the Hebrew poem "Ha-shutafut," an anti-Hasidic *maskilic* satire.[11] His early long poem "Life of a Hebrew Poet" (1877) also included a negative portrayal of a Hasidic figure in its ninth chapter. Peretz's first dealings with a Hasidic figure in prose occurred in his Hebrew story "The Kaddish" (1886), which also marks his prose debut in Hebrew.[12]

"The Kaddish" is a simplistic text. The narrative is structured with a frame story that takes place thirty years after the inner story in which an old man tells a young listener about a man who has just recited the prayer for the dead in his honor. In the inner story, the business-oriented wife Esther, who may have been punished for her commercial wisdom, cannot fulfill her maternal role. Her role as businesswoman is inconsistent with the role that European bourgeois society would assign to women. Her sorrow over her barrenness leads to her gradual self-destruction. She starves herself, fearing that her husband, Reb Yitskhak, will leave her because she is barren, as he is allowed to do according to Jewish law. Reb Yitskhak, who actually never had plans of leaving, soon follows her to the next world, but not before he issues his will and gives instructions to the then-young storyteller about how to carry it out. He turns his house into an institution for the sick and needy (where he dies "among his people"), and he orders money to be sent to the Land of Israel.

The story talks about the ability of the "good plutocrat" to trickle his wealth down to the poor sods of his own ethnic group and be a responsible member of his group. It also imbues the Jewish economy with gender characteristics, assigning the woman, Esther, a prominent level of practical business acumen. The man, Esther's husband, Reb Yitskhak, speaks with the Jewish ethical voice and oversees distributing the wealth his wife accumulated after her death.

What is most interesting in this story, for this discussion, is the text's depiction of Hasidim. They are first mentioned as the old storyteller is retelling the story of a pre-Hasidic Jewish-Polish (Austro-Hungarian) past, a time that corresponds to the period when the inner story is taking place. In that time and place, Reb Yitskhak and Esther couldn't easily resolve their infertility problem, for "then there weren't any Hasidim and people of action to pay barren women a visit (laughter of contempt was spotted on the old man's lips) the habit of amulets and therapeutic oil was not yet widespread."[13] Peretz here was repeating the quite common Jewish Enlightenment stereotype of the hypersexual Hasidic rebbe, who works the miracle of "helping" infertile women become fertile. And if the cynicism wasn't clear enough, the text makes sure the mockery is understood by making the kind of laughter ("shok la'ag") explicit as the old storyteller recounts this line. Also, working within a clear historical timeline makes the present (i.e., mid-1880s) dominance of Hasidim in Jewish life undeniable.

Toward the end of the story, we are told that it is impossible to rebuild the institution for the needy in the present time because "the rich people of the city are great Hasidim but not people of action!" If in the first quotation the Hasidim are grouped together with the "people of action" (or "practical men"), in the second quotation they are just the opposite. But in any case, there is a clear recognition regarding the dominance of Hasidim in the Jewish community: the Hasidic movement managed to mobilize wealthy Jews into its ranks.[14] This observation should not be mistaken as an example of Peretz's affiliation with Jewish socialism, as Shaked asserts,[15] since Jewish socialism barely existed at the time the story was published and Peretz was not then a socialist. But Shaked is correct in assessing the achievement of Peretz's (pseudo) Hasidic tales "in which he dealt in a different way with many of the same subjects he had already tackled in his sentimental fictions of the ordinary and every day. Insofar as these works express the author's commitment to the common people, as opposed to people of privilege, and to those of warm of heart and feeling (the Hasidim), as opposed to the legalistic and cerebral *mitnagdim* [their opponents]."[16]

While in his early effort in Hebrew "The Kaddish" Peretz expressed contempt toward Hasidim as holding power over the Jewish community but lacking in social consciousness and practical sense, this attitude would shift slightly in his next literary depiction of pious figures. The story "Ha-mekubalim"[17] (Kabbalists) debuted in Hebrew in 1891, and its Yiddish version, "Mekubolim" (*Yontef bletlekh*, 1894), was the earliest of his tales that were included in the 1901 selection called "Hassidic."[18] The central motif here is death by purposeful starvation, which appeared in "The Kaddish" with the death of Esther. While in both stories mystical beliefs possess no healing power for the protagonists, the later story, "Kabbalists," is not a simple negation of the power of mysticism. Moreover, the Hasidim in the story (Chabad Hasidim, according to the Hebrew version) hold little if any real power over the community (especially in the later Yiddish version). The power of the Hasidim is crumbling alongside the whole social and economic basis of the shtetl. By connecting it to the socioeconomic reality, Peretz differs from the early *maskilic* critics who viewed Hasidism as merely a swindle. Still, for Peretz, the power that a charismatic spiritual leader holds over the individual follower can be deadlier than any opium.

The story tells of a young yeshiva student, the last student of his yeshiva in a small shtetl, not so different from the ones Peretz depicted in his Yiddish fiction such as *Bilder fun a provints rayze*, which came out at the same year. This student, who receives a name only in the Hebrew version (the satirical Lemekh[19]), under the guidance of this spiritual leader, Rebbe Yaakov/Yekl (his name in Hebrew and Yiddish, respectively), abstains from eating in order to reach the highest spiritual level, until eventually he drops dead in the middle of the night. Both Hasidic characters in the story—the rebbe and his pupil—suffer from hunger, but they treat it as "religious fasting." Only in the more satiric Hebrew version does the fasting also become "a source of blessing" for them. Although Peretz pokes fun at the beliefs of the pious in "Kabbalists," he goes much deeper in exploring the mystical journey and the irrational psyche than he did in "Kaddish." He explores the erroneous sense of idealism that there is in the act of starving oneself, and he does so by grounding it in a *materialist interpretation*. He notes that hallucinations can come because of extreme hunger, lack of sleep, and poor material conditions in general.[20] Mystical experiences do not just come through miracle working but rather from a particular physical condition. Peretz spells out this rationale clearly and concisely in the Yiddish version:

> And they both [the rebbe and his pupil] suffer from hunger from time to time. From little food comes little sleep, of whole nights of no sleep and no food—a desire for Kabbalah!
>
> In either case—if one must be awake whole nights and fast whole days—one should at least make some use of it, it should at least be: fasts with mortifications, it should at least open all the gates of this world with secrets, spirits, and angels! And they are studying Kabbalah for a while now!

און זיי ביידע לײַדן אױך אַמאָל הונגער. פֿון װײניק עסן קומט װײניק שלאָפֿן, פֿון גאַנצע נעכט נישט שלאָפֿן און נישט עסן—אַ חשק צו קבלה!

ממה נפֿשך—דאַרף מען זײַן אױף גאַנצע נעכט און הונגערן גאַנצע טעג,—לאָז מען כאָטש דערפֿון אַ נוצן האָבן, זאָל כאָטש זײַן: תּעניתים מיט סיגופֿים, זאָלן זיך כאָטש עפֿענען אַלע טױערן פֿון דער וועלט מיט סודות, רוחות און מלאכים! און זיי לערנען שױן קבלה אַ צײַט!

(*Ale verk*, 8:20)

These "rationalist" lines were criticized by the Yiddish and Hebrew writer H. D. Nomberg as not befitting the elevated style of the rest of the story.[21] The Hebrew version not only elaborates this part but also includes some more kabbalistic technical terms, such as the differentiation between *kabala iyunit* (notional or theoretical kabbalah) and *kabala ma'asit* (practical kabbalah). This is due to its Hebrew language medium,[22] which is closer to the language of genuine kabbalistic texts. If the Yiddish version clearly belongs to Peretz's radical period of the *Bletlekh* years, it is interesting to compare the interpretive passage quoted above to its first Hebrew version. The latter version came out around the same time that Peretz wrote "Bildung" (1891), before he developed a more socialist point of view. This is how the hunger is dealt with in the Hebrew version:

> The rebbe and his student discussed: what should they do against the bitter and annoying hunger, and they examined the matter and decided: to immerse themselves in theoretical and practical kabbalah, and so they did, and the fasting became a source of blessing for them!
>
> Through the gates of practical kabbalah they have not yet passed, but the theoretical came to them as water that was filled by the respect they received from the entire shtetl, and to their dry bones it was as oil. Both kabbalists, the rebbe and the student, acquired a name for themselves across the town and its nearby towns and all the people who arrived at the gates of the town waited eagerly until the end would come! Not the end of messiah, when the son of David himself will come, tomorrow, and for that nobody in town would lift a finger, but the end of theoretical kabbalah is the beginning of the practical, and then great wonders and extraordinary things.[23]

> נועצו הרבי ותלמידו: כדת מה לעשות לרעב המר והנמהר והמציק, ויחקרו וידרשו ויחליטו: לעסוק בקבלה העיונית והמעשית. ויעשו כן, ויהיו להם הצומות למקור ברכה!

> אל שערי הקבלה המעשית לא באו עוד, אך העיונית באה בקרבם כמים, שמלוא כל טשאכנובקה כבודם, ולעצמומיתיהם היבשות כשמן היתה. שני המקובלים, הרב והתלמיד, כבר נחלו שם בכל העיר ובנותיה, וכל באי שעריה של טשאכנובקה חכו בכליון עינים עד בוא הקץ! לא קצו של משיח, בן דוד יבוא מעצמו, מחר, ובשביל זה לא ירים איש בטשכנובקה יד או רגל,—אך קצה של הקבלה העיונית שהיא התחלת המעשית, ואז יהיו נפלאות ונצורות וגדולות.

As expected, this passage from the early version is more *maskilic* in its tone than that from the later Yiddish version, a fact underscored by the high style and festive Hebrew in which it is written, in contrast to the worldly Yiddish of the later version. It shows less compassion toward the poor people of the shtetl and seeks more to unify them into a stereotypical, stupid group that passively expects miracles to happen. Making the poor seem dumb (also regarding the student's name in the Hebrew version) goes against the radical grain of seeing the revolutionary potential of the poor. Hence this kind of passage needed to be severely changed (if not almost entirely omitted) to fit the more socially oriented leftist point of view that Peretz held by the mid-1890s.

As Ken Frieden points out, "Kabbalists" contains both "irony and satire at the expense of the Rebbe," and he uses the term "hostile parody" to describe it. But Frieden also writes that the story "points the way to a more balanced portrayal" of pious figures, paving the way for Peretz's later Hasidic stories.[24] This duality is also reflected in the various reader responses to this story. Rozentsvayg divides these responses between those of the "radical readers," who emphasized the satirical aspect of the story, and "the Yiddishists in the reactionary period," who focused on the romantic tendencies in it.[25] As an example of a radical reader's response, the following interpretation is one the Bundist A. Litvak heard from the socialist Yiddish activist Avraham Amsterdam while they were serving time together in neighboring cells in a political prison in Vilnius. Amsterdam said these words to Litvak through a mouse hole in the floor of the prison cell:

> Only here in prison, where there is so much time to think, I understood the deep meaning of Peretz's "Kabbalists." The hunger brings individuals and peoples to hallucinations, to visions, to prophecy. Out of suffering one becomes a kabbalist mystic. When there isn't this world, one creates for himself a beautiful world to come.[26]

נאר דא אין טורמע, וואו עס איז פאראנען אזוי פיל צייט אויף טראכטן, האב איך
געכאפט דעם טיפן זינען פון פרצעס "מקובלים". דער הונגער ברענגט מענטשן
און פעלקער צו האלוצינאציעס, צו חזיונות, צו נבואה. פון יסורים ווערט מען א
מקובל. אז עס איז ניטא די וועלט, שאפט מען זיך א שיינע יענע וועלט.

This testimony, based on a reading of the story's Yiddish version, supports the argument that Peretz sharpened the materialist analysis of the mystical journey in the Yiddish version. This move made it more appealing to the radical reader's taste and expectations. It also shows how Peretz successfully depicted the world of the pious as *sheyn* (beautiful, lovely), marking a sharp turn away from the *maskilic* contempt for all things Hasidic. Particularly in the last segment of the story, we see, as Amsterdam observed, Peretz's early fascination with the prophetic power of the idealist individual figure. The last segment focuses on the student's mystical journey, the one that was materialistically grounded earlier in the text. In both the Hebrew and the Yiddish version, there is a desire to portray the student's experience in an emotionally honest way. As much as the rebbe's teachings are put into question, there is no doubt that the young student is an idealist who is eager to learn and to practice what he learns. The student continued his fast after breaking (in his view) the "Thou shall not covet" commandment when he stared at his teacher's food before receiving his own portion when both men were receiving charity meals from the community.

In Peretz's mind, given the right guidance and influence, young Jews like the student would be able to devote themselves to a progressive agenda. This last notion is comforting in a story that is essentially about hunger and death, and it provides satisfaction for the radical reader seeking to mobilize the young poor Jews out of the shtetl into their urban ranks. This notion also allowed Peretz to discuss the responsibilities of the individual leader over those young Jews. In the story, the rebbe instructs his students about the different spiritual levels of *nigunim* (melodic chants). The highest of all is the one without words or humming or moving of the lips—the one that exists purely in the heart. After a few days with no food, the student wakes his rebbe up in the middle of the night and tells him, in the Yiddish version, that he is now in the highest spiritual level:

> Rebbe—the student answered with even a weaker voice, I couldn't sleep, so I steeped myself in what you said . . . I really wanted to know this *nign* [melody], I began to cry . . . everything in me wept; all of my organs wept for the Master of the Universe!
>
> I made the combinations, which you entrusted in me . . . a wonderful thing: not with my mouth, but something inside . . . of its own self! Suddenly it lit for me . . . I held my eyes shut, and it was lighted for me, very lighted, very strongly lighted! . . .
>
> There! The head of the yeshiva tilts himself closer.
>
> Afterwards I felt so good from the light, so light . . . I felt that I was weightless, as if my body lost its weight, that I . . . could fly . . .
>
> There! There!
>
> Afterwards I became happy, vital, laughing . . . my face hadn't moved, nor my lips, but I was laughing . . . and so good, so good, so heartedly, so pleasurably!
>
> There! There! There!—Out of happiness!

Afterwards something was roaring inside of me, as if a beginning of a *nign* was roaring [. . .] Afterwards I heard how it began to sing inside of me! [. . .]

I felt that all of my senses were clogged and shut in me, and something inside was singing. . . and the way it should be—with no words at all, like this . . .

How? How?

No, I can't . . . earlier I knew . . . afterwards from the singing became . . . became . . .

What became—what? . . .

A kind of game . . . like, to make a distinction, I would have inside of me a fiddle, or like Yoyne Klezmer was sitting in me and played Sabbath songs, as by the Rebbe's table! Only that it was playing even better, even nobler, with even more spirit! And everything without a voice, without any voice—the most spiritual! . . .

You are blessed! You are blessed! You are blessed!

Now everything is gone!—The student says sadly,—my senses reopened in me, and I am so tired, so tired, so—tir—ed . . . ! That I . . .

Rebbe—he suddenly gave a scream, grasping on to his heart,—Rebbe! Say the confession with me! They came after me!—The ministering angels had no melody! An angel with white wings! . . . Rebbe! Rebbe! Shma Yisroel; Shmaa . . . Yis . . .

רבי—האָט דער תּלמיד מיט נאָך אַ שוואַכערן קול געענטפֿערט, איך האָב נישט געקאָנט שלאָפֿן, האָב איך מיר פֿאַרטיפֿט אין אַמער שמועס . . . איך האָב געוואָלט דווקא קענען דעם ניגון . . . און איך האָב . . . אָנגעהויבן וויינען . . . עס האָט אין מיר אַלץ געוויינט; אַלע אברים האָבן געוויינט פֿאַרן רבונו של עולם!

דערבײַ האָב איך געמאַכט די צרופֿים, וואָס איר האָט מיר איבערגעגעבן . . . אַ וווּנדערלעכע זאַך: נישט מיטן מויל, נאָר עפּעס אינעווייניק . . . פֿון זיך אליין! ראפּטום איז מיר ליכטיק געוואָרן . . . איך האָב געהאַלטן צו די אויגן, און עס איז מיר געווען ליכטיק, זייער ליכטיק, זייער שטאַרק ליכטיק! . . .

אָט! בייגט זיך צו דער ראָש-ישיבֿה.

דערנאָך איז מיר געוואָרן פֿון דעם ליכט אַזוי גוט, אַזוי לויכט... עס האָט זיך מיר געדאַכט אַז איך וועג גאָרנישט, אַז מײַן גוף האָט די וואָג פֿאַרלאָרן, אַז איך קען פֿליִען . . .

Between Liberal Satire and Socialist Roots | 171

אָט! אָט!

דערנאָך בין איך געוואָרן לוסטיק, לעבעדיק, לאַבנדיק . . . דאָס האָט זיך מיר
נישט גערירט, די ליפּן אויך נישט, און איך האָב דאָך געלאַכט . . . און אַזוי גוט,
אַזוי גוט, אַזוי האַרציק, אַזוי נחתדיק געלאַכט!

אָט! אָט! אָט!—מתּוך שׂמחה!

דערנאָך האָט עפּעס אין מיר געברומט, ווי אַן אָנהייב פֿון אַ ניגון געברומט [. . .]
דערנאָך האָב איך געהערט, ווי עס האָט אין מיר אָנגעהויבן זינגען! [. . .]

איך האָב געפֿילט אַז אַלע חושים זענען מיר פֿאַרשטאָפֿט און פֿאַרמאַכט, און
עפּעס אינעווייניק זינגט . . . און אַזוי ווי מען דאַרף—גאָר אָן ווערטער,
אָט אַזוי . . .

ווי אַזוי?! ווי אַזוי?!

נייַן, איך קען נישט . . . פֿריִער האָב איך געוווּסט . . . דערנאָך איז פֿונעם זינגען
געוואָרן . . . געוואָרן . . .

וואָס איז מיר געוואָרן—וואָס? . . .

אַ מין שפּילן . . . גלײַבּר, להבדיל, איך וואָלט אינעווייניק אין מיר אַ פֿידל געהאַט,
אָדער גלײַבּר יונה קלעזמער זאָל אין מיר זיצן און שפּילן זמירות, ווי בײַם רבין צום
טיש! נאָר עס האָט געשפּילט נאָך בעסער, נאָך איידעלער, מיט נאָך מער רוחניות!
און אַלץ אָן אַ קול, אָן אַ שום קול—סאַמע רוחניות! . . .

ווייל איז דיר! ווייל איז דיר! ווייל איז דיר!

אַצינד איז אַלץ אַוועק!—מאַכט טרויעריק דער תּלמיד, - עס האָבן זיך מיר
צוריקגעעפֿנט די חושים, און איך בין אַזוי מיד, אַזוי מיד, אַזוי—מי-ד . . . ! אַז
איך . . .

רבי—האָט ער ראַפּטום אַ געשריי געטאָן, זיך אָנבאַפֿנדיק בײַם האַרץ,—רבי!
זאָגט מיט מיר ווידוי! מען איז געקומען נאָך מיר!—עס האָט דאָרט אין פּמליא
של מעלה אַ זינגערל פֿאַרפֿעלט! אַ מלאך מיט ווײַסע פֿליגל! . . . רבי! רבי! שמע
ישראל; שמעע . . . יש . . .

Peretz touches here on the experience of death in a way atypical for the secular modern. The young idealist protagonist goes through his fatal mystical journey without a shred of doubt or disbelief in his mission to live an utterly moral life. Peretz is dealing here with the notion that the thought of death declines with modernity; as Benjamin argued, death becomes a metaphor for alienation and for the death of the spirit under capitalism.[27] Peretz presented a romantic textual alternative to this feeling of decline. The yeshiva, the spirit of the Jewish precapitalist era, is diminishing. Idealism, the willingness to face death to reach a higher cause, and the whole discussion of the meaning of mortality—all diminish in the face of capitalist development. If Peretz tried to give the story a satirical framework, he only partially succeeded. The intensity of the student's kabbalistic experience is strong enough in the first Hebrew version and perhaps even slightly stronger in the Yiddish version (due to its dramatic character being now in a spoken language, and due to the larger space it received). This intensity represents the longing for a spiritual-philosophical quest outside the norm. The Yiddish and Hebrew writer Hersh Dovid Nomberg described the strong impression the reader gets from this story as follows:

> You play ball or tennis on an open meadow, and it laughs and is lively. Now you are in a deep old forest. Quiet! Listen! You are alone with your soul, and your soul will unravel to you. A soft sound passes above the mountain tops, and the everlasting secret, which both scares and delights, assaults you. This is the impression from "The Kabbalists."[28]

> איר האָט אויף אַ פֿרײַער לאָנקע באַלעם אָדער טעניס געשפּילט, און עס איז געוועון לאַכנדיק און רירעוודיק. איצט זענט איר אין אַ טיפֿן אַלטן וואַלד אַרײַן. שאַ, שטיל, און האָרך אויף! דו ביסט אַליין מיט דײַן נשמה, און זי וועט זיך דיר אַנטפּלעקן. אַ שטיל געוויש ציט אין דער הויך איבער די שפּיצן, און דער אייביקער סוד, וואָס שרעקט און אַנטציקט צוזאַמען, איז אַזוי באַפֿאַלן. דאָס איז דער אײַנדרוק פֿון "די מקובלים".

What Nomberg was describing is the way the story evolves from being more lighthearted and satirical at first to sweeping away the reader into the student's mystical journey. The reader does not mock the student at these moments, as he might do before and after this scene, but instead the reader joins him through an emotional experience. The possibility of a gate or a bridge to some sort of a different dimension or sensation or knowledge appeals to the modern individual, who now lives with an intensified sense of loss over the previous world that vanished with modernity. The element of "hostile parody" gets minimized, and its arrows go only against the source of power that impacts the student—that is, only against the rebbe. But even the rebbe, although he was misguided in his direction of the student, did nevertheless succeed in producing a human being who was deeply committed to a higher cause. The idea of the charismatic figure appealed to Peretz, who himself aspired to be a modern leader. He would only do so by substituting the merits of starvation and silent *nigunim* with favoring action to better socioeconomic conditions for everybody, not by keeping silent.

The death motif appears also in Peretz's short story "Mishnat ḥasidim" (The teaching of Hasidim) that was published both in Hebrew (1894) and in Yiddish ("Mishnes khsidim," 1902). In Hebrew it was published in *The Arrow*, Peretz's sole attempt at publishing radical material in Hebrew.[29] Peretz wrote this story under the pen name "The Orphan of Nemirov," an allusion to Nathan (Nosn) Sternhartz (1780–1884). Born in Nemirov, Ukraine, Sternhartz was a close student of the founder of the Breslov Hasidic group, Nachman of Breslov (1772–1810) and is credited with having written down the teachings of his rebbe in order to make them public.[30] And indeed, in "The teaching of Hasidim," Nosn Sternhartz appears as the narrator for a tale that borrows and expands parts of Nachman of Breslov's biography.

"The teaching of Hasidim" is a monological story that uses as its first-person narrator a simple Hasidic follower of the rebbe. But, as Pinsker points out, this narrator unwittingly reveals ironies and uncertainties and thus complicates what seems at first to be a traditional hagiographic tale.[31] The Hasidic narrator tells the story of the rebbe's daughter's wedding to none other than a "dry" *Litvak*. The young Hasid (whose own affection toward the rebbe's daughter is more potent in the early Hebrew version) worries that the Hasidic dynasty is in danger, since no direct Hasidic heir to the rebbe would be produced from this "mixed" match (between a Hasid and a *Litvak*). The language of the Hasid is passionate and enthusiastic when he talks about his rebbe and his teachings, in contrast to his unbridled negativity toward the *Litvak* groom. The language of symbols becomes intensified in the later Yiddish version, when the Hasid transmits the rebbe's teachings, celebrating individuality through the figure of music:

> Every person is also a musical instrument, and a person's life is a melody, a happy or a sad melody, and when the melody is over, the soul flies out of the body and the melody, meaning the soul, unites itself again with the great melody before God's throne . . . and unhappy is he, the Rebbe said, who lives without his melody.[32]

יעדער מענטש איז אויך אַ כּלי-נגינה, און דאָס לעבן פֿון אַ מענטש איז אַ ניגון, אַ פֿרײלעכער, צי אַ טרויעריקער ניגון, און אַז מע ענדיקט דעם ניגון, פֿליט אַרויס די נשמה פֿון גוף און דער ניגון, די נשמה הייסט עס, באַהעפֿט זיך צוריק מיט דער גרויסער נגינה פֿאַרן כּסא הכּבֿוד. . . און ווײ, האָט ער געזאָגט, איז דעם מענטש, וואָס לעבט אָן זײַן ניגון.

The ideals of music and dance are realized during the rebbe's daughter's wedding. The band plays, and the rebbe stands at the center of the room, chanting and dancing with his feet, swaying with the rest of the guests around him. But the *Litvak* does not dance, which greatly angers the narrator. In Nachman of Breslov's biography, there is a segment about the wedding of Nachman's daughter and the celebration during the Sabbath before the wedding. In it, Nosn recounts how Nachman danced as he never had before, throughout almost the entire day. "And the amount of happiness there one cannot tell, happy is he who saw it."[33] Peretz clearly was influenced by these passages, given the setting of the plot and the language of the story.[34] Toward the end of Peretz's story, the Hasid is amazed to discover that people begin to gather around the *Litvak* to hear his *dvar-toyre* (words of Torah), the same way they gathered around the rebbe while he was dancing and chanting.

In "The teaching of Hasidim," writes Nicham Ross, Peretz shows clear symbolist tendencies in his writing, tendencies that would intensify in his later Hasidic stories. The mystical "feet dance," which is a nonverbal, experiential, and symbolic gesture, is preferred by the Hasidic tzaddik over the *Litvak*'s intellectual words of Torah. According to this story, the main Hasidic innovation is shifting the focus to emotions or to insights that are impossible to accurately define in words.[35] Classic Marxist literary criticism has traditionally disfavored symbolist writing, instead overwhelmingly preferring realist writing. The use of symbolism was viewed as the writer's inability "to grasp the meaning of that particular reality. . . . He resorts to symbols when he cannot solve difficult, sometimes insoluble problems."[36] However, this orthodoxy in the scholarship was challenged when Yiddish critics were faced with certain trends in modern Yiddish literature. For instance, when Soviet critic Moyshe Litvakov confronted the discrepancy between Der Nister's "non-communist" symbolist art and his ideological commitment to communism, Litvakov was forced to acknowledge "that ideologically defective creative methods can bring with them technical improvements, as already shown by [the Marxist theoretician] Plekhanov, talking, for example, about Impressionism."[37] Soviet critic Yitskhok Nusinov, who wrote about the influence of Peretz's symbolist art on Der Nister, went even further in contesting the negative attitudes toward modernist forms, viewing such critiques as essentialist and ahistorical.[38] Benjamin, writing about the French symbolist poet Charles Baudelaire, noted "it is an illusion of vulgar Marxism that one can determine the social function of a material or intellectual product without reference to the circumstances and the bearers of its tradition."[39]

This debate surrounding the political function of symbolism also pertains to any discussion of Peretz's literary choices, which included both realist and symbolist (and other modernist) tendencies, the circumstances of their production, and the kind of historical lessons they provide. What was the basis for Peretz's aesthetic choices? And how do these choices relate to his ideological wanderings? The one who dealt most with this issue in relation to Peretz was Nomberg, a member of Peretz's young writers' circle in Warsaw (alongside Yiddish writers Avrom Reyzn and Asch, one of several Hebrew writers whom Peretz encouraged to switch to writing in Yiddish). Nomberg wrote about the different influences Peretz absorbed during his writing years, defining him as someone who was constantly searching for ideas. As real as his affiliation with the rising Jewish labor movements was, so too was Peretz's affection toward less socially oriented philosophies, among them Nietzschean philosophy. According to Nomberg, "Nietzsche was the protest against the materialism of the previous generation, against vulgar democracy, against the demand that the individual submit to society and the environment. Here individualism had its greatest prophet. . . . Of course, this current didn't pass over Peretz. He fell down under its influence, as everybody then did."[40] Contemporary critics often avoid Marxist readings of Peretz's Hasidic stories. Regarding "The teaching of Hasidim," Roskies comments on how the faith of the simple Hasid in his rebbe "becomes for Peretz a Nietzschean search for a leader who can bear the world's suffering."[41] According to this view, which is compatible with Peretz's interest in Nietzschean philosophy, the same movement that Peretz and other modern Jewish writers viewed as democratizing Jewish knowledge and life is also a movement that demands a charismatic leader and emphasizes individual redemption. Peretz published the Hebrew version of this story at the height of his radical years. Could it be that Peretz was expressing doubts over socialist ideas even as early as the mid-1890s and instead advocating a focus on the merits of the individual charismatic leader?

"The teaching of Hasidim" does seem anomalous for the work Peretz was publishing at the time. It is hard to detect an obvious radical political sentiment in the text beyond a focus on social tension. However, it can be argued that Peretz chooses here to present the class conflict in scholarly rather than in economic terms, by contrasting the simple, unlearned Jew's attraction to the "soulful" Jewish practice he finds in Hasidism with the intellectual elitism and rigid commitment to Jewish law as represented by the *Litvak*.[42]

As previously shown, one of the major thinkers who Peretz challenged at the time and also in the pages of *The Arrow*, where this story was published, was the rationalist Zionist thinker Aḥad Ha'am. Aḥad Ha'am became interested in Nietzsche following his discussions and polemics with the Hebrew writer M. Y. Berdichevsky (1865–1921), who first introduced Nietzschean philosophical concepts to Jewish intelligentsia circles. The polemics between these two influential figures in Hebrew-Zionist culture during the 1890s impacted Peretz a great deal, who influenced and in turn was influenced by Berdichevsky's interests in Nietzsche and in Hasidism.[43] Together with Nietzsche and Berdichevsky, Aḥad Ha'am is a silent participant in this text. The story challenges the rationalist method of thinking, paving the path for a revolutionary mode of thought by emphasizing the superiority of Hasidism over the *mitnagdim*.[44] It presents the rationalist view as elitist and overly intellectual, one that the narrator has trouble following, and as lacking the same charisma and mobilizing potential that the teachings of Hasidism possess. Contrary to Aḥad Ha'am, it is also non-Zionist in its Eastern European focus.

The first thinker to make the connection between Hasidism and Nietzscheanism was in fact Aḥad Ha'am, in his polemical article "Shinuy ha-arakhin" (Change of values; 1898). He coined there the term "Jewish Nietzscheanism" ("*nietzscheanismus yehudi*") for those "abandoning their Jewishness in favor of Nietzsche" (like Berdichevsky). It became a common phrase for those who meshed their interests in Nietzsche and Judaism.[45] Aḥad Ha'am wrote that Judaism "never made its own **Übermensch** as subsidiary for the great masses, as if his whole being is to work in favor of the masses. . . . The tzaddik was not created for the sake of others, but the opposite: 'the whole world was created only for this purpose,' and he is an end to itself."[46]

In "The teaching of Hasidim," and even more so in "Between two mountains," Peretz gave voice to debates that were going on at the time, in which Aḥad Ha'am was one of the first to participate.[47] Peretz added a grounding in class analysis to these debates: both between the elitist *Litvak* and the simple Hasid, as Ross points out, and between the rebbe and the Hasid himself. The idea of Hasidism's superiority over *misnagdim* seems to miss the fact that the story "The teaching of Hasidim" presents an image of Jewish national unity through the sayings and the death of the rebbe. While Hasidim are presented in the story as more attractive to the simple, unlearned Jew, their rebbe belongs to both worlds. The rebbe, capable of mesmerizing people through his physical gestures and dances, still shows appreciation for the intellectual accomplishment of his new son-in-law. The whole story revolves around a wedding of the rebbe's daughter to a pupil of the leader of the *mitnagdim* and promotes understanding between the different Jewish factions involved. In this sense, the premise is reminiscent of Zweifel's apologetic view toward Hasidism in "Peace upon Israel," promoting peace between the different factions of the Jewish people. Furthermore, the rebbe (the spirit) eventually dies because of the death of his son-in-law (the body). The two opposites that make together the imagined whole are thus as one. The story's more expansive Yiddish version strengthened the line of national unity, appearing at the same time as Peretz's major Hasidic stories, such as "If Not Even Higher," "Between two mountains," "The metamorphosis of a melody," and others.

Peretz's main artistic achievement with "The teaching of Hasidim" was the introduction of symbolist tendencies into modern Hebrew literature. In addition, this story is a precursor to many of Peretz's future Hasidic creations, one of his first nonsatirical stories that was couched in the Hasidic world. In his neo-Hasidic literature, Peretz did not simply abandon radical thinking, as he was accused of doing by progressive literary critics.[48] In fact, his use of Hasidic symbolism reflected his search for the spirit of revolution. Peretz saw Hasidic literature as the true pioneering work of modern Yiddish literature,[49] trying in this way to ground his modern secular project in archaic Jewish symbolism. Marx famously wrote of the reliance of French revolutionaries on Roman symbolism to stir up feelings of heroism to glorify their struggles and confer upon them some higher cultural meaning:

> Unheroic though bourgeois society is, it nevertheless needed heroism, sacrifice, terror, civil war, and national wars to bring it into being. And in the austere classical traditions of the Roman Republic the bourgeois gladiators found the ideals and the art forms, the self-deceptions, that they needed to conceal from themselves the bourgeois-limited content of their struggles and to keep their passion on the high plane of great historic tragedy. . . .
>
> Thus the awakening of the dead in those revolutions served the purpose of glorifying the new struggles, not of parodying

the old; of magnifying the given task in the imagination, not recoiling from its solution in reality; of finding once more the spirit of revolution, not making its ghost walk again.[50]

Aber unheroisch, wie die bürgerliche Gesellschaft ist, hatte es jedoch des Heroismus bedurft, der Aufopferung, des Schreckens, des Bürgerkriegs und der Völkerschlachten, um sie auf die Welt zu setzen. Und ihre Gladiatoren fanden in den klassisch strengen Überlieferungen der römischen Republik die Ideale und die Kunstformen, die Selbsttäuschungen, deren sie bedurfte, um den bürgerlich beschränkten Inhalt ihrer Kämpfe sich selbst zu verbergen und ihre Leidenschaft auf der Höhe der großen geschichtlichen Tragödie zu halten. . . .

Die Totenerweckung in jenen Revolutionen diente also dazu, die neuen Kämpfe zu verherrlichen, nicht die alten zu parodieren, die gegebene Aufgabe in der Phantasie zu übertreiben, nicht vor ihrer Lösung in der Wirklichkeit zurückzuflüchten, den Geist der Revolution wiederzufinden, nicht ihr Gespenst wieder umgehen zu machen.

Finding once more "the spirit of revolution" was indeed the task Peretz took upon himself while creating his Hasidic stories. However, the story of Peretz and of Diaspora Jewish nationalism in general, particularly in its Bundist form, was not one of "limited bourgeois struggle," as Marx said, for it represented the interests of working-class people without aspirations of founding a nation-state. The development of an ethno-class consciousness in Eastern European Jews of the turn of the twentieth century required some ancient ethnic symbolism for its cultural platform.[51] The Hasidic world, which came out of Eastern European Jewish life, provided a rich bank of symbols for the proponents of Diaspora Jewish nationalism in Eastern Europe, including the Jewish socialists. As the Jewish labor movement moved from revolutionary internationalism to revolutionary Jewish socialism during the 1890s,[52] it drew inspiration from the Hasidic world to glorify its own struggle, not to parody that world.[53]

Before confronting Peretz's major Hasidic texts, I will turn now to examine further the intertwinement of religion and radical thought in relation to Peretz, using Terry Eagleton's work as a backdrop. For I believe that although the influence of Nietzschean thought over Peretz in these stories is clear and indeed needs to be properly deciphered, still the social interpretation of Peretz's Hasidic stories has been neglected in recent years and deserves a reassessment.

Figure 5.1. Bundist demonstration in Dvinsk (now Daugavpils, Latvia) in 1905, a year of anti-czarist revolutionary activity throughout the Russian Empire. Archives of the YIVO Institute for Jewish Research.

Faith and Revolution, Secularism, and Imperialism

In his book *Reason, Faith and Revolution*, Terry Eagleton explored the benefits that radicals can receive by exploring Jewish and Christian scriptures. "Radicals," he writes, "might discover there some valuable insights into human emancipation, in an era where the political left stands in dire need of good ideas."[54] Speaking for our own time, Eagleton's words are equally applicable to Peretz's time. The rise of a Jewish labor movement at the end of the nineteenth century in Eastern Europe required some agency to mediate radical social ideas to semitraditional readers. This tendency to write stories couched in a Hasidic milieu intensified toward the turn of the century. One reason might be Peretz's internalization of the fact that he was no longer writing exclusively for a readership of "Jewish intelligentsia." In the late 1890s he began lecturing to Jewish workers, a wider audience than in the gatherings at his literary salon, which consisted of narrow circles of intellectuals.[55]

The politicization of the Jewish masses in Eastern Europe, which the Bund and other movements were aiming for, required a kind of modern literature that would be critical of the bourgeois mindset and yet include some specific Jewish symbolism. The Hasidic movement, a modern movement in itself, was a perfect cultural tool to serve this purpose. In a way, Jewish Marxists, while incorporating some form of national agenda into their radical platform (i.e., forming the Bund), needed to reflect this national agenda on the cultural front. Peretz, while himself not a Hasid, produced cultural material that would meet these needs.[56] Hasidism can be *reinvented* for this purpose as a socially democratizing movement (historical accuracy aside)—the sort of Judaic tradition to which Marx owes a great deal,[57] a movement that promotes a communal life based on morality and that, very importantly, is built on the linguistic symbolic capital of Yiddish rather than Hebrew.[58]

Eagleton shows the similarities between socialist revolutionary thinking and the scriptures of various religions as they relate to the establishment of a utopian society based on moral vision. He analyzes the way modern Western atheism can serve to distinguish "us" from "them." For pro-war liberal atheists, the concept of the peacemakers and the meek inheriting the earth is distasteful.[59] For both socialist and religious belief systems, "no middle ground" is permitted: "the choice between justice and the powers of this world is stark and absolute, a matter of fundamental conflict and antithesis. What is at issue is a slashing sword, not peace, consensus, and negotiation. Jesus does not seem to be any sort of liberal."[60]

In Peretz's mid-decade *Bletlekh* articles, he related sarcastically to Jewish religious traditions and gave a socioeconomic-class-oriented interpretation of Jewish religion. The belief that "charity would save from death," Peretz wrote, is not a lucrative business since "one does not get any money from it! When you give, you have less, and the poor man has barely enough for his immediate needs."[61] This sarcasm is reflective of a few changes Peretz had gone through since the late 1880s and early 1890s. In his article "What Do I Want?" (1895), he viewed religion as an instrument of control of public opinion in the hands of the rich and powerful, perpetuating (rather than subverting) the current unequal power relations. In this article, Peretz was very cynical toward the custom of praying:

> From praying one doesn't get any money . . . and the proof—our plutocrats, who strain their lives and very often with compassion, with integrity and with humanism together, all to become richer, do not themselves pray at all, and are only

pleased, when poor people don't put their prayer books out of their hands.

If the prayer book was to have the power as a three-ruble bill . . .—the *Yontef-bletlekh* would have been distributed to the poor and all of the loan sharks and bankers would have held prayer books and prayed.⁶²

פון דאוונען האט מען אויך קיין געלט נישט . . . א והא ראיה—אונזערע
גבירים, וואס שטערקן דאס לעבן און גאנץ אפט מיט רחמנות, מיטן יושר און
מיט דער מענטשלעכקייט צוזאמען, אבי רייכער צו ווערן, דאוונען אליין גאר
נישט, און זענען נאר צופרידן דערפון, וואס אריגעלייט לאזן דאס סידורל נישט
ארויס פון דער האנט . . .

עס זאל אין סידורל שטעקן א כוח פאר א דרייער . . . וואלט מען די אריגעלייט
געטיילט יום-טוב-בלעטלעך און אלע פראצענטניקעס און באנקירן וואלטן
געהאלטן סידורים און געדאוונט . . .

This passage ridicules capitalist society. It resonates with Marx's view on religion both as an "opium" and as a "soul in a soulless world." It offers the *Bletlekh* as the opposite of the daily prayer book—the *sider*. The interest of the higher classes today maintains that the latter (the *sider*), which literally means "arrangement" or "order," would arrange the lives of the poor. However, this "arrangement" would change in a heartbeat if the rich could find a way to make their own practice of religion profitable. Peretz's conclusion in the years that followed regarding the usage of religious codes, language, and characters in his modern literature took things a step further. He understood that this religious "arrangement"—which was being fed from the top down to the poor—could be reversed and become a mobilizing tool of the poor in their struggle to inherit the earth.

Through Hasidic figures, Peretz reached a much higher level of artistic and political sophistication, aiming to break beyond the narrow circles of the intelligentsia, his customary readership. Radical ideas could not be communicated to masses of traditional Jews simply through a simplistic attack on the "religious," as members of the Jewish Enlightenment typically proposed. "Religion needs to be patiently deciphered," Eagleton paraphrased Marx, "not arrogantly repudiated."⁶³ Even more so, the "religious," as much as it is a valid category in the first place,⁶⁴ contains some socializing traits that the so-called modern can learn from. The power of "faith" is needed in order to keep on believing that "against all appearances to the contrary, the powerless can come to power."⁶⁵ So these texts by Peretz, set in the Hasidic world, cannot be ideologically dismissed by progressives, as they were by critics in the Soviet Union, who saw them as a mere reflection of Peretz's return to a petit bourgeois nationalist agenda.[66] Instead, they should be viewed as his attempt to communicate radical ideas to a semitraditional readership. For Peretz, progressives must succeed at winning the traditional readers' hearts for the struggle for true emancipation to succeed. This attempt allowed him to explore new aesthetic forms and discursive means and put him in a natural position to criticize liberal-positivist principals. The following quotation from Eagleton accurately describes Peretz's view of religion:

> Karl Marx described religion as "the sigh of the oppressed creature," as well as the soul of the soulless conditions . . . it [religion] does not understand that we could live spiritually in any authentic sense of the word only if we were to change materially. Like Romanticism, it is a reaction to a heartless world which stays confined to the sphere of feelings and values. It therefore represents a protest against a spiritual bankruptcy with which it remains thoroughly complicit. Yet such religion is a symptom of discontent even so, however warped, and repugnant. Phrases like "the sigh of the oppressed creature," the heart of a heartless world," and "the soul of the soulless conditions" are not for Marx purely pejorative. Religious illusions stand in for more practical forms of protest. They signpost a problem to which they themselves are not the solution.[67]

Peretz altered his viewpoint on religion. He went from seeing it as a problem in itself to seeing it as merely the signpost indicating a deeper social problem. But his split attitude toward it can be traced back, as previously shown, even to his early prose set in the Hasidic world. I will now examine the last argument by looking further at Peretz's Hasidic stories from the height of his radical years and by elaborating the discussion concerning the intersection between radical thought and religion.

Making Sense of the Ridiculous, Confronting Materialist Faith

The Yiddish story "Dem rebns tsibek" (The rebbe's pipe) was first published in the second year of the *Bletlekh* (*Der omer*, 1895). It tells the tale of how a poor and childless Jewish couple finds financial prosperity and gains children through entrepreneurship with a "holy artifact" that belonged to the rebbe. The couple's new source of income comes from selling the right to touch the rebbe's pipe, which the couple received from the rebbe himself. This magic phallic object solves their infertility problem as well. More often than not, this story was viewed by critics as a mere satire of Hasidism.

Klausner criticized this story's inclusion in Peretz's first set of collected works, to which Klausner himself wrote the introduction: "in my opinion there wasn't any need to include the story 'The Rebbe's Pipe' in the *Collected Works*, [the story] is a weak satire of Hasidism in the spirit of the writers of *Hashaḥar*."[68] Ken Frieden, a contemporary interpreter, holds a similar view that "The rebbe's pipe" is a satire of Hasidim, as is the short story "Dos shtrayml" (The fur hat; 1894).[69] An earlier example that includes satirical elements against Hasidim is the rather weak Hebrew short story "Shmaya gibor."[70] It has some elements from "Kabbalists" (a Hasid dies during a night of hallucinations, also a variation in "A Night of Horror"), and it presents an early version of the Hasid-versus-traditional rabbi confrontation ("Teaching of Hasidim," "Between two mountains")—but both these elements are poorly executed in relation to those other stories. However, this soft satire created a commotion in the editorial office of Ha-tzfira, which received protest letters from Hasidic people for the way they were portrayed (a group of Chabad Hasidim is presented in the story as violent zealots). The old editor of the paper, Slonimski, did not allow Peretz to publish any additional material in the paper as a result and blamed his associate editor, Sokolow, for publishing the story. Peretz told this story in a letter to Dinezon and referred to Slonimski as "that old, stupid dog."[71]

"The fur hat," through an ironic monologue by a traditional Jewish hatmaker who worships the traditional Hasidic fur hat, utilizes this piece of garment synecdochally to target and subvert religious authority and the community that empowers it.[72] At first, the two stories seem to be similar in their anti-religious satire through the exaggerated importance given to religious leaders, embodied by artifacts they either smoke or wear on their heads. The targets of criticism in "The fur hat" are made clear through simple ironic inversions of the panoramic view of the Jewish shtetl society and its beliefs, provided by the speaker. I agree with Ken Frieden's characterization of "The fur hat" as "so-called Hasidic." Frieden terms thusly a number of similar stories by Peretz from that period, which generate a "serious parody."[73] This term "serious parody" was coined by Linda Hutcheon to mean "a form of imitation, but imitation characterized by ironic inversion, not always at the expense of the parodied text. . . [it is] repetition with critical distance."[74] But one must differentiate, when it comes to modern forms of parody (a suitable framework for Peretz's work), between the use of the parodied text as a target versus the use of the parodied text as a weapon.[75]

I argue here that this definition of modernist parody that uses the parodied text as a weapon is applicable in the case of "The rebbe's pipe." The Hasidic background and motifs are used, at least in this story, not in order to satirize Hasidim but rather as a weapon against a much broader range of targets, namely features of the modern economy, such as entrepreneurship, the concept of fetish, and the social ladder itself. Unlike "If Not Even Higher" and other Hasidic stories by Peretz, in which the story is told through the eyes of the *Litvak* "other," or outsider, Hasidic people are at the center of "The rebbe's pipe." When the story opens, the main protagonists, the couple Sore-Rivke and Khaim-Borekh, lack both children and bread. The husband is a typical pious Jew who sits and learns traditional books and does not earn an income. Khaim-Borekh, Peretz tells us with great irony, used to sit for long hours with the rebbe, "and they didn't utter even one word between themselves, but rather communicated through eye contact, with a wink! Well, would you speak with such a figure about business?" (*Ale verk*, 4:36).

His wife, Sore-Rivke, works to provide for the family. She deals in beans and yeast, eking out just enough to earn her husband the title "Khaim-Borekh Sore-Rivke's," or "Sore-Rivke's husband." Their depiction is consistent with the common portrayal of traditional Eastern European Jews living in severe poverty. Their wedding money is gone; their small house had to be sold; they nourish themselves on potatoes with water for breakfast and soup with an old bagel for supper; the mythical number seven signifies the number of years it took until the wife could afford to make her husband a new coat (*a kapote*). This banal description of Jewish poverty bears some similarity to the description in Peretz's realist short story "The anger of a Jewish woman." But in this story, the husband decides to act: he will have a word with the Hasidic rebbe about the matter.

And what "wise advice" does the rebbe have for Khaim-Borekh? The rebbe advises him that he should rid himself of the small tobacco pipe he's been using (*dos pipkele*, only fit for a common coachman, according to the rebbe) and take the rebbe's own festive tobacco pipe with a shaft instead. Thus far, the story is like many other *maskilic* satires against the backwardness of Hasidim and their adherence to the silly authoritative voice of the rebbe. But further developments in the plot alter the targets of critique, and the Hasidic backdrop becomes a weapon in a greater battle, as in this passage from the ending of the story, when Khaim-Borekh returns to his shtetl with the rebbe's pipe:

> Even before Khaim-Borekh was off the cart, a hundred people had already asked him to lend them his pipe, for a month, a week, a day, an hour, a minute, a second . . .
>
> People wanted to cover him with gold!
>
> And to all of them he answered:
>
> "What do I know? Ask Sore-Rivke . . ."
>
> A prophecy came out of his mouth
>
> Sore-Rivke has a nice business . . .
>
> Eighteen big coins for a blow from the pipe! Eighteen big coins, not a cent less!
>
> And the pipe helps!
>
> And people paid. Now Sore-Rivke had her own little house, a nice shop, lots of yeast in the shop, and many other kinds of merchandise besides.
>
> She herself became rounder, healthier, filled out! She made her husband new underwear, put away his glasses . . .
>
> For a few weeks the nobleman's people came asking about the pipe! Three silver rubles were put down, you bet!
>
> And kids? You want to know.
>
> Sure! Three or four already . . . he completely settled down as well . . .
>
> In the study house there is constant chatter.

> Some say that Sore-Rivke is not willing to return the pipe and that she refuses to give it back to the Rebbe!
>
> Others say that she already returned it to him a while back! And that the one she has now is a different one . . .
>
> He himself, Khaim-Borekh, is silent.
>
> And what's the difference? As long as it helps! (*Ale verk*, 4:41–42)

The passion to consume the pipe, its surrounding fetish, the redeemed manhood of Khaim-Borekh, and the thriving entrepreneurship of his wife—all get mixed up in this libidinal-financial extravaganza. Could this really be summed up as a simple satire against Hasidim? In fact, Peretz's creation can easily be equated to celebrity fetishism in our time: consider athletes' logos, rock-and-roll museums, or celebrity brands like that famous singer's "unique" fragrance. The business of profiting from people's irrationality has only increased with the progress of the famously termed "cultural industry." This development comes hand in hand with a liberating effect as well—the protagonist's sexual potency and his ability to reproduce are dependent on this "nice business," which is based on deceit. This deceit becomes the source of life and livelihood for the couple. They have mastered the rules of the modern economy, exactly what Peretz is targeting in this "modernist parody."[76]

The story "He who gives life, provides shelter" (1897), from the series "Yokhanan the Melamed's stories," presents a unique pious character.[77] The fact that it was published so close in time to the clearly socialist "Weaver-Love" confused Peretz's interpreters, who pointed to them as contrasts, an example of Peretz's duality and ambivalence toward radical politics.[78] But that is a false conclusion that stems from a misinterpretation of the story and of Peretz's usage of pious figures. The story did not achieve canonical status among Peretz's radical readers, nor among his romantic followers. It showed the sociopolitical, theological, and cultural-literary problems and concerns that Peretz was addressing at the time. Like "Weaver-Love," it related to social struggles, class politics, and class relations.

"Weaver-Love" was written in an epistolary form and discussed the idea of social struggle and its merits, exploring the possibility of a working-class revolt. "He who gives life" is narrated by a Hasid who is a traditional *melamed*, a teacher of children in a *kheyder*. He tells a story of the failed marriage of his late brother's daughter, Brokhe-Leah, who married a modern man. In the eyes of the narrator, this groom is a nihilist and a crude man who spends his time playing cards and shouting at his wife. The narrator's criticism is warranted; his niece's husband physically abuses his pregnant wife, causing harm to her and their baby. He abandons his wife and baby, fleeing alone to America to find his fortune.

Here Peretz reveals the dark side of the American dream, exposing the viciousness inherent in the selfish pursuit of wealth. The husband had demanded his wife have an abortion, "as the rich women do," with the ironic justification that he cannot afford to support the child. The traditional narrator-character of Yokhanan the Melamed is in no way glorified. Although Yokhanan confronts the abusing husband, he does so only after learning that the young husband had cursed his late brother, not because of the violence he committed against the young wife. We understand indirectly that Yokhanan himself is not opposed to violence. He admits that he himself was violent toward his young pupils, believing in the merit of "educational violence," especially toward a student who is on a "bad path," meaning secularized. Moreover, he has inner thoughts of wanting Brokhe-Leah's son to die, for he fears that he is not capable of supporting the child and the rest of his family.

The fact that both the traditional narrator and the secularized husband are violent people illustrates the point Peretz was trying to make by employing a traditional figure as his storyteller. In the rather long introduction by Yokhanan, Peretz lays out the cultural conflict between "religious Jews" and "enlightened Jews." According to him, each side possesses a form of faith: enlightened Jews believe in abstract scientific concepts; traditional Jews believe in a divine being: "Everybody has his Rebbe, his faith, almost—his little idol worshiping! . . . one kisses the curtain that covers the Torah, although he doesn't know what's written inside; and a second one kisses his copy of *The Revealer of Secrets*. [. . .] How are our people worse than the enlightened Jews, who do nothing more than tell and tell old wives' tales and sing the praises of their great men?" (*Ale verk*, 4:46–47).[79] It is interesting that both "Weaver-Love" and this story relate to Josef Perl's *maskilic* novel *The revealer of secrets* (1819). Perl's book employed a Hasidic protagonist, but he used the epistolary form to satirize the Hasidic world, similar but not parallel to Montesquieu's *Persian Letters* (the latter targeted his own French society, not Persian society). "Weaver-Love" used the epistolary form as well, but not satirically—rather, in the sense of portraying the struggle for the creation of the self-consciousness of the individual subject, like Dostoyevsky's *Poor Folk*. As for the sociopolitical context, while Perl's novel is related to the rise of the modern state and of the bourgeoisie, Peretz's stories discuss broader social struggles and the role of the working class.

Peretz here, through his religious character, evens out the cultural playing field between modern realistic cultural productions (the popular nineteenth-century Hebrew translation of *Les mystères de Paris* is also mentioned) and hagiographic literature. It stressed, perhaps unintentionally, the fact that modern Jewish literature did not seamlessly take the place of religious literature. In fact, religious literature continues to exist and flourish today. Peretz himself tried to create a modern Jewish literature, in Yiddish and in Hebrew, that would build upon traditional Jewish sources like the Bible and Rabbi Nachman of Breslov's writings, and, unlike other writers such as Berdichevsky, Peretz had no real intention to "rescue" genuine Hasidic teachings or stories for his own modern era.[80]

Peretz tells us how subjective and contingent the concept of "the real" is. In the realm of art, it is uncertain what is closer to reality or what functions as a more useful cultural tool. Both the pious and the modernizing character suffer from economic hardships. The secular husband does not have better and more moral ways to deal with them. He chose to beat his pregnant wife and flee to America, believing he was just. *Bildung*—self-improvement through education—is something that is highly valued by the pious character in the story. Yokhanan, a teacher himself,[81] glorifies the value of learning for learning's sake—for him, it serves as an escape from his troubles:

> I open the Talmud and I feel that the sky has opened for me! That the Master of the Universe with his great grace gave me wings; he gave me big, wide wings! And I fly with them; I'm an eagle! And I fly far, far away! Not across the ocean; I fly out of this world!
>
> Out of this world of deceit, of flattery, of evil torments!
>
> And I fly inside a completely different world! To a new world, to a world of plenty of good things, of only good things; to a world without the authority of bellied bosses, of aristocrats—ignorant; a world without the shape of a coin, without being worried about making a living. There isn't any woman who is having hard labor, aren't any hungry children, aren't any feminine voices!
>
> And there is me, me the poor, sick, beaten, famished and parched teacher,—me crushed by poverty, who is silent here as a fish, people are stepping on me like a worm,—there I am

the man, the aristocrat, the person in charge! And I'm free and free is my will, and I can create! Worlds I create and worlds I demolish! And I build new ones in their place! New, better and prettier worlds! And I live in them, fly around in them, I'm in paradise . . . in true paradise! (*Ale verk*, 4:57)

מיש איך אויף די גמרא, פֿיל איך, אַז דער הימל האָט זיך מיר געעפֿענט! אַז דער רבונו של עולם האָט מיר מיט זײַן גרויס חסד געגעבן פֿליגל; גרויסע, ברייטע פֿליגל האָט ער מיר געגעבן! און איך פֿלי מיט זיי; אַן אָדלער בין איך! און פֿליען—פֿלי איך וויַט, ווײַט! נישט מעבֿר־לים; פֿון דער וועלט אַרויס פֿלי איך! פֿון דער וועלט מיט שקר, מיט חנופֿה, מיט יסורים רעים!

און איך פֿלי גאָר אין אַן אַנדערער וועלט אַרײַן! אין אַ נײַער וועלט, אין אַ וועלט פֿון כּל־טובֿ, פֿון רק־טובֿ; אין אַ וועלט אָן אַ דעה פֿון בײַיִקע באַלעבאַטים, פֿון מיוחסים – עמי־הארצים; אַ וועלט אָן צורת מטבע, אָן אַ דאגת־פּרנסה. דאָרט איז נישטאָ קיין מקשה לילד, קיין הונגעריקע קינדער, קיין ווײַבערישע קולות!

און דאָרטן בין איך, איך דער אָרעמער, קראַנקער, דערשלאַגענער, אויסגעהונגערטער און אויסגעדאַרטער מלמד,—איך עני מדוכא, וואָס שטומט דאָ ווי אַ פֿיש, וואָס מען טרעט דאָ ווי אַ וואָרעם,—איך בין עס דאָרט דער מענטש, דער מיוחס, דער בעל־דעה! און פֿרײַ בין איך און פֿרײַ איז מײַן רצון, און צו שאַפֿן האָב איך! וועלטן בוי איך אויף און וועלטן צעוואַרף איך! און איך בוי מיר נײַע אויף זייער אָרט! נײַע, שענערע און בעסערע וועלטן! און איך לעב אין זיי, פֿלי אַרום אין זיי, אין גן־עדן בין איך . . . אין אמתן גן־עדן!

There are some variations in comparison with the Hebrew version. For example, Yokhanan describes the strength he feels in the study room as opposed to his weakness in the outside world in a more violent tone in Hebrew:

I am there a man among men, a violent man, a ruler and a governor, and my hand is in everything and everything is in my hand; and I build 310 worlds and destroy them . . .[82]

אני שם גבר בגוברין, גבר אלים, שליט ומושל, וידי בכול והכול בידי; ואני בונה ש״י עולמות ומחריבם . . .

Peretz portrays here the reactionary mindset—the one who criticizes bourgeois values for their materialism and instead offers a romantic return to some ancient wisdom. As Eagleton pointed out, "in the absence of genuinely revolutionary art, only a radical conservatism, hostile like Marxism to the withered values of liberal bourgeois society, could produce the most significant literature."[83] That and the conceptualization of the Enlightenment as a belief system allow both the reactionary and the progressive to join forces, at least on the cultural front, in challenging the bourgeois dominance. Peretz's literature, in speaking in the people's languages, is capable of addressing "the losers" in the modern rat race, giving them refuge in a made-up traditional past and incorporating them in his progressive agenda.

The second story of the "Yokhanan the Melamed's stories" series portrays the modern working environment. One of Yokhanan's students, Itsikl, takes Yokhanan on a visit to his father's factory. There, the workers are reduced to simple accessories of the machine; as Yokhanan observes, "the working man and his workshop seem as one body, as one who is suffering from epilepsy who throws himself, shakes and sits" (*Ale verk*, 4:74). As Yokhanan's ears become deaf from the "sea of sounds" he hears in the plant, this thought comes into his head, and later he asks Itsikl,

> And if the greatest prophets were to come here, in this hell, . . . Isaiah, Jerimiah . . . and if it were Moshe Rabeynu himself,—when they want to open their mouths, and wish to speak—would they have outshouted this hell? Would one of these tormented souls hear them?
>
> No, absolutely not! I'm thinking and running out, covered with cold sweat from fear!
>
> And we're going further through a narrow anterior room, and Yitskhok and I can't go through together . . .
>
> Why is it so narrow here? I ask.
>
> Here the workers get searched,—answers little Yitskhok—one after the other they get searched . . .
>
> Why?
>
> People steal from the plant . . . tools . . . merchandise . . .
>
> Thieves they are, thieves? Are they thieves? Thieves?
>
> Not everybody, God forbid! Only some are being suspected! . . .
>
> And when some are being suspected, all of them get searched?
>
> My father says that you can't disgrace just one, so even the managers get searched . . . (*Ale verk*, 4:75)

און ווען עס קומען אַהער, אין דעם גיהנום, די גרעסטע נביאים ... ישעיה,
ירמיה ... און ווען משה רבינו אַליין,—ווען זיי עפֿענען די מײַלער, און—זיי ווילן
רעדן—צי וואָלטן זיי איבערגעשריִען דאָס גיהנום? צי וואָלט זיי עמעצער פֿון די
געפּײַניקטע נשמות געהערט?

ניין, זיכער נישט! טראַכט איך און לויף אַרויס, באַגאָסן מיט קאַלטן שווייס פֿאַר
שרעק!

און מיר גייען ווײַטער דורכן שמאָל פֿעדערצימער, און איך מיט יצחקן קאָנען
צוזאַמען נישט דורכגיין ...

נאָך וואָס איז דאָ אַזוי ענג? פֿרעג איך.

דאָ רעווידירט מען די אַרבעטער,—ענטפֿערט יצחקל—איינעם נאָכן צווייטן
רעווידירט מען ...

נאָך וואָס?

מען גנבֿעט פֿון פֿאַבריק ... כּלים ... סחורה ...

גנבֿים זענען זיי, גנבֿים?

נישט אַלע, חס-ושלום! נאָר אויף אַ טייל פֿאַלט אַ חשד! ...

און אַז אויף טייל פֿאַלט אַ חשד, רעווידירט מען אַלע?

דער טאַטע זאָגט, אַז מע קאָן נישט מבֿייש זײַן, רעווידירט מען אַפֿילו די מײַסטער
אַליין ...

The great irony of this passage lies in the observation that the oppression of the workers is something that the reactionary protagonist can sense and be sensitive about, while the capitalist, portrayed by Itsikl, is totally blind to the suffering and humiliation he inflicts upon his labor force. The modern workplace is no less than a hell on earth that is louder than the voice of any prophet, and the radical conservative is the one who points this out. In 1897, modern Jewish politics were on the verge of establishing an identity; both political Zionism and the Bund were established that same year. Each movement offered a different yet equally modern solution to the plight of the Jewish working class. And each of them,

Peretz tells us, will have a challenging time competing for the hearts of the Yokhanan Melameds of the world. Further examining Peretz's most popular Hasidic works, written at the beginning of the twentieth century, would reveal a great deal about his evolving approach toward literature and its ability to both inspire and challenge progressive activists and working-class Jews.

Keep Lifting Me Higher and Higher

The Yiddish writer Avrom Reyzn explained in his memoirs why those who "call for rebellion" were attracted to Peretz's short Yiddish story "If Not Even Higher: A Hasidic Story" (1900):[84] "The radical reader looked for social and universal content in the story, especially since Peretz—the creator of 'Bontshe Shvayg'—wrote it, and thus it was certainly kosher."[85] "If Not Even Higher" became one of the most famous Yiddish stories of all time.[86] It was written by Peretz during the three months in 1899 that he served in prison for appearing at an illegal workers' gathering (together with fellow writer Mordkhe Spektor). Some argue, like Reyzn, that this experience changed his political perception and with it his writing style.[87]

Rozentsvayg, writing in Stalin's era in the Soviet Union, argued that this romantic-nationalist material fit the nationalist-reactionary tone of the Yiddish-Zionist journal in which it was first published, *Der yud*. In his view, it signified Peretz's distancing himself from the workers, their interests, and the ideal of class war in general. He writes, "Peretz had thus stepped in at the time in his sad mission—to be the literary-artistic agent of the bourgeois-nationalist as *if above* class ideas in the petit bourgeois and proletarian environment."[88]

So, which is it? Did Peretz use the Hasidic motives in a subversive and sophisticated way to call for revolt? Or does he suddenly "become" a romantic nationalist who abandons his radicalism and progressive undertones of the *Yontef bletlekh* years? Is he writing quasi-Hasidic stories? Peretz's subheading for the story "If Not Even Higher" is "A khsidishe dertseylung," a Hasidic story. Again, was he parodying Hasidism or glorifying it?

I argue that "If Not Even Higher" is indeed progressive in its humanistic message, even though it does not contain any explicit socialist content such as class war. As previously shown, Peretz has some stories that were more *maskilic* in tone, but gradually he realized the mobilizing

פרץ אלס ארעסטאנט אין צענטן פאווילאן, 1899
(פון צענטראלן היסטארישן ארביוו אין מאסקווע)

Figure 5.2. Peretz's mugshot, 1899. Peretz wrote "If Not Even Higher: A Hasidic Story" during the three months he served in prison in 1899 for appearing at an illegal workers' gathering. Some argue that this experience changed his political perception and with it his writing style. Archives of the YIVO Institute for Jewish Research.

potential of the social construct that is religion. This social construct was defined by Marx in a very humanist yet critical fashion as "an expression of and a protest against real wretchedness. Religion is the sigh of the oppressed creature, the heart of a heartless world and the soul of soulless conditions. It is the opium of the people."[89]

"If Not Even Higher" was based on an older Hasidic tale in Hebrew.[90] Unlike typical Hasidic hagiography, where the narrator is a passionate Hasid telling a story that glorifies his tzaddik (in which he himself plays the small role of an observer), Peretz used a Hasid as a storyteller, but he recast the tale by using a doubtful *Litvak* as his observer and making that observer the central figure. During this very short story (4.5 pages), the skeptical protagonist undergoes a transformation in his attitude toward the Hasidic religious leader, becoming a believer in the tzaddik's moral virtues and leadership strengths.

The story revolves around the Rebbe of Nemirov,⁹¹ who disappears every year during the penitential prayers preceding Yom Kippur. His followers believe he rises up to the heavens to plead on behalf of his congregants in the holy courts. The *Litvak* doesn't believe this theory and wants to see with his own eyes what's really going on. He hides under the rebbe's bed and then watches as the rebbe disguises himself as a poor, non-Jewish peasant. The *Litvak* follows the rebbe as he goes to chop wood in the forest and then takes the wood to an elderly Jewish woman. Without accepting payment, the rebbe sets up the wood and lights a cozy fire for her in her fireplace. While the rebbe is working around the fireplace, he hums the Jewish ritual tunes of the penitential prayers (*di slikhes*). This humanist gesture by the rebbe turns the doubtful *Litvak* into a Hasid, a devoted follower of the rebbe. And thus, the story ends:

> The *Litvak*, who saw everything, remained a follower of the Rebbe of Nemirov. And later, if a Hasid said that the Rebbe of Nemirov rises up at the time of the penitential prayers every morning, and flies up into the sky, the *Litvak* stopped laughing, and would add quietly: If not even higher! (*Ale verk*, 4:102)

דער ליטוואק, וואס האט דאס אלץ געזען, איז שוין געבליבן א נעמיראווער חסיד. און שפעטער, אויב א חסיד האט אמאל דערציילט, אז דער נעמיראווער הייבט זיך אויף, סליחות-צייט, יעדן פרימארגן, און פליט ארויף אין הימל אריין, פלעגט שוין דער ליטוואק נישט לאכן, נאר צוגעבן שטילערהייט: אויב נישט נאך העכער!

In this story, Peretz offered a humanist interpretation of religion. He showed an understanding of the social function of Hasidism, which promises some sense of communal life in an age of increasing social atomization and alienation. Comparing his story with the original Hasidic version would clarify how Peretz reworked it and what he wanted to achieve by creating his version. The original story appeared in Hebrew in the book *Ma'ase tsadikim* (Story of tzaddiks; 1864) by Menakhem Mendl Bodek.⁹² Peretz split the role of the Hasidic narrator and observer into two (the Hasidic narrator and a doubtful *Litvak* as an observer-protagonist). He also changed the setting of the story with respect to the observance of the Jewish calendar: in the original, the story takes place during the nightly ritual of Tikkun Chatzot (an after-midnight prayer to mourn the destruction of the temple); in Peretz's version, during the yearly High Holiday prayers, the penitential prayers that are recited communally between Rosh Hashanah and Yom Kippur. By changing to the less frequently occurring but better-known Jewish ritual, Peretz was adapting the story to his modern readers, who were not as likely as Hasidic Jews to be frequent synagogue visitors.

Peretz also added an introduction to get the reader into the Hasidic world and mindset as he imagined it. This setup was not necessary for the original Hasidic story, which would have been orally transmitted by Hasidim to Hasidim and would not have had need for such a bridge. Interestingly, there is no trace in the original story that the Hasidim believe the rebbe is traveling to the heavens. Instead, it is sufficiently awesome to the reader to observe that the rebbe chants a *nign* (wordless song of prayer) in a very elevated manner.

Moreover, Peretz changed the identity of the woman whom the rebbe visits. In the original it is a poor Jewish woman ("bat yisrael") who is giving birth at the time of the visit to a baby boy. Perez changed this character to be an old and sick Jewish widow who is left alone because her son is at work. In this way, Peretz eliminates any suspicion of a sexual connotation, which a modern reader might have suspected in the original—a younger woman, giving birth alone (something the rebbe was involved in?), which might have given the story an unintended quality of an anti-Hasidic *maskilic* satire.[93]

In the original, a young male Hasid is about to be born, a sign of continuity and vitality—in Peretz's shtetl people are older (birth would be an anomaly in a "dead town"), with little future ahead of them. Peretz's characters are also needier (the temporality of giving birth versus the constant bad state of the old, sick woman). The coldness in the woman's house is emphasized in the original: "in her house it was freezing cold, because it was one of those winter nights when it was very, very cold. And the woman in childbirth, her bones were shaken because of the coldness and the chill."[94] Thus, the importance of the rebbe heating up her place becomes greater, and his action in such a short story even more glorified. In Peretz's story the woman is "farviklt in shmates" (wrapped in rags)—almost the sole indication of the low temperature. The elaborate description of the cold temperature that appears in the original version stands out as a rarity. In general, the original story, which is much shorter than Peretz's, focuses tightly on the actions of the characters rather than on descriptive details. Peretz's version significantly expands certain features.

In the original, after the woman says she doesn't have the money to pay for the wood, the rebbe answers that he will come back tomorrow to collect, and they move on to something else. In Peretz's version, the woman tells him twice she doesn't have the money to pay (can't buy and can't loan). When the rebbe answers the second time, he starts off with a whole monologue on the subject: "Silly person—scolds her the Rebbe,—look, you are a poor sick Jewish woman and I trust you, I have faith that you will pay; and you have such a mighty strong God, and you don't believe him . . . and for a measly six coins for a small pack of wood you have no faith in him!" (*Ale verk*, 4:101). The "scolding" (*musern*), calling her "silly person" (*narish mentsh*), could be interpreted as a patronizing attitude by the rebbe or just as a friendly tease. But, more importantly, Peretz's addition of this moral lecture concerning the importance of faith is a point he wants to emphasize for his modern readers. Peretz wants his readers, who had lost (or who were in the process of losing) their faith in a transcendental being, to retain faith in the moral values of helping and of being able to trust other people. It is also meant to teach his modern readership about the social role of faith and religion among the lower classes.

As previously mentioned, in Peretz's version the role of the observer dramatically increases. In the original, the peeking Hasidic narrator appears only at the beginning and at the end of the story. Peretz makes the peeking character, the *Litvak*, a central character in his version. The readers follow the story through the *Litvak*'s eyes and ears. We follow his reactions, his senses (he "sees" and "hears" the actions that take place), his feelings, his thoughts. We follow the way he starts to shriek when he stays alone with the rebbe and is under the bed ("eyme," "shrek") and when he is "shaking" from fear when following the rebbe to the forest at night. There the *Litvak* is "startled and amazed" ("nivl venishtoymem") seeing the rebbe chop wood before he visits the woman. In the original, the rebbe chops the wood in the woman's house, after the woman asks him to do so. Peretz adds the nightly visit to the forest, a literary convention that signifies the unknown, the uninhibited, and lawless surroundings (a place where miraculous transitions might occur), in order to intensify the drama and to signify for the modern reader a transition to a different reality. In this case it is a transition from the modern world to a world based on morality and the scales of justice.

The moaning ("krekhtsn") of the old woman and the rebbe, and vocals in general, play a significant part in Peretz's version and are absent in the original. The *Litvak* listens to the rebbe moaning in the beginning, when his "cold heart" is not affected by it, in contrast to the Hasidic narrator who imagines it expresses the "sorrow for all the Jewish people." The *Litvak* hears the rebbe moan when he is putting the wood into the fireplace; he has then already transformed to a Hasid who "hears" the rebbe's *nign*. He is also

Figure 5.3. "If Not Even Higher" became one of the most famous Yiddish stories of all time. Here it is shown in a children's book version published in the United States in 2010. Amazon.

the one who recognized the voice of the person the rebbe is visiting as the sounds of a "poor Jewish woman." This extensive use of vocals is how Peretz emphasizes the eavesdropping, "spying" position of the *Litvak*. His spying actions are expressed in the language as well. The *Litvak* "sneaks himself in" (*ganvet zikh arayn*)—first inside the rebbe's house, crawling under the rebbe's bed, and later inside the woman's little house, following the rebbe. Peretz elaborates the role of the observer as a meaningful literary device; he plays the role of the outside spectator, the spy, observing the actions of "those" Hasidic Jews, who here play a performative, metaphoric role for the modern reader—who, like Peretz, is the "enlightened" person looking from the outside at this imagined pious community.

By casting the stereotypically extreme-rationalist, skeptical *Litvak* figure as the transformed character, Peretz throws the Enlightenment's version of rationalism and science into doubt. Adorno and Horkheimer famously criticized the Enlightenment for failing to consider moral questions adequately.[95] Peretz injects this direct concern for morality into the story when he shows that the mystical journey to heaven (believed only by his literary

Hasidim) is actually achieved by a moral and earthly act of kindness for another person, performed without recompense or recognition by others.

It is also important that Peretz chose here to adapt a Hasidic story in which the rebbe reaches out to the poor person, a poor Jewish woman, and assists her while disguised as a goyish peasant. The act of disguising oneself, which Peretz dramatizes using dialogue in Polish, is something he and his modernizing readers can relate to. Like the rebbe, they too operate in both worlds, knowing both Yiddish and the "state language." The act of performance operates here in both ways: if the rebbe can play the common "goy" (which is also the way shtetl Jews would relate to the modern Jew in Peretz's writing), then the modern reader can certainly play the common "Jew" and become an organic intellectual aligned with working-class Jews.

One can also compare the relations between Jews and Gentiles in this story concerning pious people with the secular nationalist characters in "In the Mail Coach" (1890), discussed in the first chapter. The latter story portrayed the tense relationship between the Jew and the Gentile, both middle class, and exposed some Jewish-chauvinist sentiments. In "If Not Even Higher," the highest Jewish ideal is to assist your fellow human being, and it takes place among the lower classes. This is the social and universal content the radical reader looked for in the story that Reyzn was referring to. Peretz here does not focus his critical arrows against Hasidism per se, not even against his Hasidic literary representations who believe in the rebbe's divinity.[96] Not necessarily at odds with the social significance of the story, Peretz is interested in exploring the power of the individual to be a charismatic and stimulating positive force for others. This interest reflects a Nietzschean influence.

In order to fully examine the thesis of the Jewish labor movement taking inspiration from the Hasidic world in order to glorify its own struggle, one has to look into what is considered by many scholars Peretz's highest achievement in writing Hasidic stories, the Yiddish story "Between two mountains" ("Tsvishn tsvey berg," 1900). In this story, the different powers at play reach epic proportions.

"Between Two Mountains": Dreaming of an Ethnic-Class Jewish Identity

The story "Between two mountains" revolves around the confrontation between two archetypes of Eastern European Jewish thought: a *misnaged* (opponent of Hasidism) rabbi (the rabbi of Brisk, or the *Brisker*) and a Hasidic rebbe (the rebbe of Biyale, or the *Bialer*). The story ostensibly takes place during the early days of the Hasidic movement. It has no real historical backing,[97] but the setting offers a way for Peretz to examine the spirit of the Hasidic revolution, with "Hasidism representing the proletariat."[98] As in "The teaching of Hasidim," "Between two mountains" uses a simple Hasid as the narrator. The narrator is a teacher in the home of a rich *misnaged*; his patron represents the capital over which the two archetypes and Jewish cultural capitalists fight to gain control. The rich *misnaged*'s daughter marries the son of the Brisker Rov (according to the late Yiddish version of the story), and the Hasidic narrator calls on the Bialer Rebbe for help when the Brisker's daughter has trouble giving birth. Moreover, the Bialer Rebbe is a former student of the rigid Brisker Rov; he had left the world of the "Litvish" yeshiva, which he viewed as dry and disconnected from people's lives following a dream he had.

In the introduction to Peretz's Hasidic stories in Hebrew, the Hebrew literary critic Reuven Braynin praised "Between two mountains" for its artistic achievement but criticized Peretz for acting in it as "the defense attorney of the Hasidic world"; he concluded by stating that "the artist would have achieved an even higher level if he had not put his head between those two mountains and been affable towards one side while showing an angry face towards the opposite side."[99] Braynin viewed this story as an apology for Hasidism and as Peretz's literary climax. He only criticized what he saw as Peretz's favoritism toward Hasidism against the *misnagdim*.

Like Braynin, Frieden views this story as "the masterpiece that best illustrates how Peretz recycled tradition in order to innovate."[100] But, contrary to Braynin, Frieden attributes the success of the story to the fact that Peretz *is* balanced and does *not* take any clear side. It is the unreliable narrator, "with his superstitious belief in his Rebbe's powers," who takes the side of the Bialer Rebbe, not Peretz himself. Even so, according to Frieden, the story is not "anti-Hasidic" and does not take "the perspective of a Hasidic disciple simply to undermine his credibility." And at the same time Peretz does permit "a powerful portrait of the Brisker Rov."[101] Thus, "Between two mountains" both shows favoritism toward the Hasidim (proletariat) and acknowledges the strength of their opponents, the *misnagdim*, similar to the way Marx was simultaneously in awe of and totally rebellious toward the bourgeoisie.[102]

In the first stages of the story, the prodigious young yeshiva student and future Hasidic Bialer Rebbe dreams about being led by the Brisker Rov through the halls of a great palace with shiny crystalline walls. It was the palace of the nether paradise, without windows and without doors other than the one they entered through. There was no sign of other people, just the Brisker and his student. The student became tired from walking, his eyes tired from the constant shine inside the isolated palace. And so, the dream continues, as told by the simple Hasid,

> A strong longing fell on him, a longing for Jews, for friends, for all-of-Israel! A trifle—one cannot see any Jew in front of him! . . .
>
> Do not long for anybody—said the Brisker Rov—this is a palace only for me and for you . . . you will also one day become the Brisker Rov!
>
> And the Rebbe became even more fearful and pushed himself against the wall, so as not to fall down. And the wall scalded him! But it did not scald him as fire does, but as ice scalds!
>
> Rabbi!—he gave a scream—the walls are ice, not crystal! Simply ice!
>
> The Brisker Rov was silent.
>
> And the Rebbe screamed more:
>
> Rabbi! Lead me out of here! I do not want to be alone with you! I want to be together with all-of-Israel!
>
> And barely had he uttered these words when the Brisker Rov disappeared and he remained all alone in the palace.
>
> He doesn't know any way, neither in nor out; from the walls, a cold fear struck him; and the longing, for a Jew, to spot a Jew, even a shoe-maker, or a tailor, became all the stronger in him. And he began to weep heavily . . .
>
> "Master of the Universe," he pleaded, "take me out from here! Better in hell with all-of-Israel together, than here all alone!" (*Ale verk*, 8:104–5)

און עס איז אים אָנגעפֿאַלן אַ שטאַרקע בענקשאַפֿט, אַ בענקשאַפֿט צו ייִדן, צו חבֿרים, צו כּל-ישׂראל! אַ קלייניקייט—מע זעט קיין ייִד נישט פֿאַר זיך! . . .

בענקט נישט צו קיינעם,—מאַכט דער בריסקער רבֿ—דאָס איז אַ פּאַלאַץ נאָר פֿאַר מיר און פֿאַר דיר . . . דו וועסט אויך אַמאָל זײַן בריסקער רבֿ!

און דער רבי האָט זיך נאָך מער דערשראָקן און אָנגעכאַפּט זיך אָן דער וואַנט, נישט אומצופֿאַלן. און די וואַנט האָט אים אָפּגעבריט! נאָר נישט ווי פֿײַער ברית, נאָר ווי אײַז ברית!

רבי!—האָט ער אַ געשרײַ געטאָן,—די וואָנט זענען אײַז, נישט קריסטאַל! פּשוט אײַז!

דער בריסקער רבֿ שווײַגט.

און דער רבי שרײַט ווײַטער:

רבי, פֿירט מיך אַרויס פֿון דאַנען! איך וויל נישט זײַן אַליין מיט אײַך! איך וויל זײַן צוזאַמען מיט כּל-ישׂראל!

און קוים האָט ער עס אַרויסגעזאָגט, איז דער בריסקער רבֿ נעלם געוואָרן און ער איז געבליבן איינער אַליין אין פּאַלאַץ.

קיין וועג, ווי אויס און ווי אײַן, ווייסט ער נישט; פֿון די וואַנט שלאָגט אויף אים אַ קאַלטער פּחד; און דאָס בענקשאַפֿט צו'ן אַ ייִד, צו דערזען אַ ייִד, באַדײַ אַ שוסטער, אַ שנײַדער, איז אַלץ בײַ אים שטאַרקער געוואָרן. האָט ער אָנגעהויבן שטאַרק צו וויינען . . .

"רבונו של עולם, האָט ער זיך געבעטן,—נעם מיך אַרויס פֿון דאַנען! בעסער אין גיהנום מיט כּל-ישׂראל צוזאַמען. איידער דאָ איינער אַליין!"

The dream portrays a clear dichotomy facing the prodigious student between the elitist ivory tower of the rationalist, cold "Litvish" yeshiva and the outer reality of connecting to simple Jews. Here Peretz is alluding to Dostoyevsky's negative portrayal and polemic against London's Crystal Palace (originally a huge iron-and-glass structure, built for the Great Exhibition of 1851). The palace became the symbol of rationalist utopia for Russian social reformers. Dostoyevsky visited the palace in the early 1860s and mentioned it in two of his writings: *Winter Notes on Summer Reflection* (1863) and his novella *Notes from the Underground* (1864). In the latter text, Dostoyevsky used the symbol of the Crystal Palace to counter the positivist-rationalists' ideal of a society based purely on rationalist foundations, a predictable society where people make their choices based solely on their interests. Dostoyevsky championed the notion of the individual's independent choice, even (and maybe especially) if the individual desires a "stupid choice." This because "it preserves for us what is most precious and most important—that is, our personality, our individuality."[103] Dostoyevsky wrote these words a few decades before Nietzsche, and his work had a significant impact on the Yiddish and Hebrew literary republic of the early twentieth century.[104] Peretz borrowed this metaphor from Dostoyevsky, creating a setting for his dream of a Jewish crystal palace, which turns out to be a shaky, cold palace made out of ice.

In constructing the Jewish setting, Peretz goes back in time—ostensibly around a hundred years, but really to a mythical Eastern European Jewish time that never existed—in order to portray a conflict between the nascent Hasidic movement and the leaders of the traditional "Litvish" yeshivas. Peretz wished to equate the dream of escaping one world and connecting to another with the dilemma of the modern intelligentsia between elitist ideologies and inclusive ones. He also explored the conflict between the individual's will, which consists of reason, versus his unpredictable impulses.[105] It was these more human, emotional impulses that led the yeshiva student to flee from his yeshiva and to become a Hasidic rebbe of the common Jews. Here Peretz depicted a process of radicalization reminiscent of the one he himself went through in the 1890s, eventually serving as the de facto literary agent of the Jewish working class, politically embodied by the Bund.

A simple Jew in the dream functions as the protagonist's savior: "This little Jew, while being silent, took him by his shoulder, led him out of the palace, and disappeared" (*Ale verk*, 8:105). Dressed as a coachman, this character alludes to a character in Peretz's late addition to the *Bilder* "The dead town." In that story, the modern Jewish intellectual goes on a ride and hears a monologue from a fellow passenger about the death of the Jewish shtetls. The speaker contemplates the possibility of an alignment with the Jewish lower classes.

"Between two mountains" recounts a revolutionary calling of going to the people[106] and then its realization the next day: Another "small Jew" like the one he encountered in his dream appears on his way to the yeshiva, where he goes to ask a learned man to help him decipher his dream. Instead, in true legendary fashion, the simple coachman helps him, using language that alludes to the biblical commandment that God gave to Abraham, "gey dir dayn veg!" ("lekh lekho!"; go forth!). And so the revolutionary journey of the Hasidic leader begins.

Against the world he left behind, the Bialer has a chance, years later, to lay out in person his arguments to his former teacher and leader of that world, the Brisker. He tells the great Brisker Rov,

> Your Torah, Rabbi, is just law, it's without compassion! Without a shred of charity is your Torah! And therefore, it is without happiness, without breathing space . . . just iron and copper, iron rules, copper laws . . . and just exalted Torah, for

learned people, for extraordinary individuals! ... [...] and tell me, Rabbi, what do you have for the Jewish people as a whole? For the lumberjack, for the butcher, for the craftsman, for the simple Jew? ... especially—for a sinful Jew? What, Rabbi, do you have for unlearned men? (*Ale verk*, 8:115)

אייער תורה, רבי, אז סאמע דין, אן רחמים איז זי! אן פונק חסד איז אייער תורה!
און דעריבער איז זי אן שמחה, אן פרייען אטעם ... סאמע ברזל ונחושת,
אייזערנע חוקים, קופערנע דינים ... און סאמע הויכע תורה, פאר לומדים, פאר
יחידי-סגולה! ... [...] ... און זאגט מיר רבי, וואס האט איר פארן כלל-ישראל?
פארן האלץ-העקער, פארן קצב, פארן בעל-מלאכה, פארן פראסטן ייד? ...
בפרט – פאר א זינדיקן ייד? וואס, רבי, האט איר פאר נישט לומדים?

The commitment to the law and the focus only on extraordinary individuals—a clear reference to Nietzschean philosophy—which the Hasidic rabbi attributes to the yeshiva world, can easily be attributed to the liberal legalistic mindset and its focus on the individual. Even though the Bialer isn't necessarily talking in class terms when he repeats the term "all of Israel," he then proceeds to mention only working-class Jews in relation to the broader Jewish public, hence an ethno-class approach. The rebbe calls for the democratization of the Torah (the scholarly level), which figuratively means a broader application of liberal values of equality, exactly what socialists demand.

What kind of revolutionary vision does the rebbe offer to counteract the rationalist world he denounces? At the end of the story, the Hasidic leader asks his former teacher, the Biyaler Rebbe, to gaze from his porch at the sight of dancing Hasidim. The euphoric vision they share represents the revelation of a utopian alternative to the current reality. The utopian philosopher Ernst Bloch distinguishes between "dreaming" and "daydreaming." A dream, in Bloch's view, is "a journey back into repressed experiences and their associations." This view corresponds to Peretz's use of the Bialer's dream at the beginning of the story, in which, as we saw, the long years that the Bialer spent as a student at the Brisker's yeshiva appear to him as a suffocating crystal palace, isolated from his imagined concept of society. In contrast, a daydream, in Bloch's terms, is an "unrestricted journey forward, through images of what is not-yet ... fantasized into life and into the world."[107] The Bialer is eager to show the Brisker Rov an image of his not-yet, to show the Brisker what could be the meaning of his *toyre* (his teaching) in practice. Thus, the narrator describes what he sees:

> In the meadows with the small flames, sects and sects of Hasidim were circling around . . . the silk and even the worsted wool kaftans were glittering like a mirror, the torn ones just as much as the whole ones . . . and the small flames that wrenched themselves between the small weeds threw themselves and leeched into the mirroring holiday garments, and it seemed that they were dancing around every Hasid, with enthusiasm, with love . . . [. . .] Every sect was singing its own melody, but in the air, all the melodies and all the voices were being mixed up; and to the Rebbe's porch one melody arrived. . . as if everybody was singing one tune. And everybody was singing—the sky was singing, the spheres were singing, and the earth was singing from its very base, and the soul of the world sang—everything was singing! (*Ale verk*, 8:116–17)

This passage resonates with Bloch's depiction of the daydream as a vision of a better future. It speaks of an "enthusiasm that soars out of love beyond the given means and situation," which Bloch observed "might create tension in us, trying to fill us full of life, and thus inspire us with an aspiration to move forward."[108] The Bialer's description also resonates with *Lebensphilosophie* and vitalism, the nineteenth-century theories that emphasize the value of experience over abstract thought and of the search for the spark that transfers from nature to every individual being. That spark was also interpreted as the soul, "the soul of the world." These nonmaterialist theories enriched Peretz's expressive art, but they do not undermine the materialist base of Peretz's revolutionary vision. One can detect here a trace of messianism, which is not necessarily incompatible with Marx's materialist conception of history; as Bloch commented, "messianism is the red secret of every revolutionary."[109]

Miron used the words "revolutionary idealism" to stress, correctly in my mind, that Peretz's legends and Hasidic stories are the opposite of escapist: "They confront reality with a revolutionary idealism, with a demanding humanist system of norms, which is in essence foreign to the authentic folks-mentality and to the historical reality of Hasidism."[110] But contrary to Miron's concept of "revolutionary idealism" in relation to Peretz's Hasidic stories, I argue that there was a materialist (rather than mere idealist) basis in Peretz's Hasidic stories.[111] Historically, Peretz's "daydreamy" Hasidic stories were misread by both nationalist-conservative and Soviet interpreters. The first group analyzed these stories in a narrow nationalist framework as embodying the soul of the Jewish people and romanticizing Hasidim. Conversely, Rozentsvayg and other Soviet interpreters failed to see the progressive-utopian vision of a harmonious world that Peretz presented. Rozentsvayg viewed this story as "an expression of the fundamental ideas" of Peretz's creative work and saw in Peretz's view of the united dancing of all Israel, with "'the whole kaftans joined together with the torn ones' surrounding the Rebbe's ostensibly democratic personality," as representing an ideal that "directly countered the ideal of class war" ("Di dozike ideye iz aroysgeshtelt gevorn direkt kegn der ideye fun klasnkamf").[112] To back his claim, Rozentsvayg references the view from the rebbe's porch, a description that he calls "a typical example of Peretz's reactionary-nationalist subjective-idealist art in this period."[113] Rozentsvayg failed to see how Peretz used the Hasidim as a literary device to showcase moral ideals that have little in common with the practice of actual Hasidim or with Peretz's view of them, as we saw previously in this chapter.

Embodying the secular ideal of the intellectual who "speaks truth to power"[114] and creating literature that challenges authority, Peretz painted us a picture at the end of "Between two mountains" of a world that is worth fighting for. He tells us that the social struggle for equality, with all the hardships and setbacks it contains, could eventually lead to the establishment of a new world, a world that overcomes the modern sense of social alienation and instead is governed by the reign of pure music.

Conclusion

The radical works of the Yiddish and Hebrew writer I. L. Peretz reflect artistic, ideological, and political choices. I have shown that, in a significant body of work during an intense period of time, Peretz made clear and obvious choices: he aligned himself with the needs of working-class Jews in Eastern Europe. In this book, I uncovered the neglected radical Peretz. I highlighted his role in the Jewish labor movement, and I contextualized his art within its apt mode of production. I contrasted the prevailing decontextualized framing of Peretz that is typically employed by neoconservative scholars to obscure his underlying radical-left-leaning foundation.

Through an in-depth look at Peretz's cultural productions, incorporating both his Yiddish and his Hebrew body of work, I illuminated the complex and inherently tenuous process of becoming an "organic intellectual." I applied Peled's political-economic analysis regarding the rise of an ethno-class consciousness among Jewish workers in Eastern Europe and showed that Peretz's instrumental role in the cultural sphere complemented what the Bund was doing in the political sphere. Rozentsvayg's comprehensive study of Peretz's radical period was a source of inspiration for my work, but I revised his orthodox Marxist viewpoint, applying tools from neo-Marxist critics, Anderson's study of the rise of nationalism, and postcolonial theory. I showed that Peretz's search for new artistic paths in his poetry, Hasidic tales, and short prose was not inherently contradictory to his radicalism; in fact, it often served to enhance the radical spirit, not to subvert it. His search for new aesthetics signified his desire to propel his revolutionary politics with revolutionary art. In the case of the *Yontef bletlekh*, his drive to create revolutionary art led to revolutionizing the means of artistic production.

The great leader of the Bund, Vladimir Medem, wrote an essay about Peretz and his relations with the Bund entitled "Us and Peretz" following Peretz's first *yortsayt* (the anniversary of his death) in 1916. Medem's essay testifies to the deep importance of Peretz to the Bund. Medem did not ignore Peretz's doubts in his later years over the validity of their struggle, nor his clear negative depiction of labor politics and labor activists in some of his later work.[1] Aware of these criticisms and doubts, Medem did not lose sight of the bigger picture, and he acknowledged Peretz for his overwhelming contributions. He writes,

> [Peretz] became a piece of our lives. Because our lives were also a part of him. He contained and absorbed in himself the broad, rich folk-life—possibly not all of it, but nonetheless it was our lives. Absorbed it, entwined it with beauty—and gave it back to us again. From us he took, from us he drew those priceless gifts, which he then lavished upon us. [. . .] Our souls were in him, and he became a part of our souls. And in that sense, he is "ours."
>
> He felt himself as a part of our lives. But he felt it not only as people's lives in general, and not only as Jews' lives, not only as folks-life. He felt it as workers' lives. He felt the worker's hardship and the worker's agony, and a thirst for justice and a cry for redemption come out of his works: our thirst and our cry.
>
> And if he used to turn back to the distant past and draw from it priceless stone for his artistic constructions, it wasn't a yearning for the past, but rather an outer form for his dreams about the future. And if the dream was weaved with mist, spun with clouds, it was nonetheless the dream of our future that we, awoken and secular, are preparing with a firm hand, with a clear eye. [. . .]
>
> The great poet gave us the treasures of his rich, warm, stormy heart. And we became richer, and prettier, and bigger. And all the higher our head rises, and stronger pounds our awakened heart, and the crooked, bent down back of "Bontshe" is becoming straight, firm, and proud. (April 21, 1916)[2]

According to Medem, Peretz was the one who defined the starting point of the workers' struggle, set its goals, and envisioned its future. By creating the silent Bontshe to represent the many real "Bontshes," the marginalized subjects of discrimination, Peretz encouraged them to fight back. By creating the revolutionary Bialer Rebbe (in what Medem termed "the distant past"), he empowered them to dream about the just future they were struggling to achieve. In these works and throughout his life as an author, Peretz chose full heartedly to be the organic intellectual that working-class Jews so desperately needed to build their movement. He firmly associated himself with the Bund later in life, as clearly exemplified in a 1906 letter to the editor: "I did not come out against the Bund and didn't say that it wants to extinguish the Jewish soul. Au contraire, in a private conversation with the new members of this new society, I said: I don't belong to any party, but the closest [party] to me is the Bund."[3]

During the interwar years, Peretz Societies, the majority of which were affiliated with the Bund, popped up en masse and served as a strong testament to relationship and importance Peretz had to the Bund. In Argentina, for example, the Bundist-affiliated Peretz School, founded in the early 1930s, also served as a Bundist meeting space.[4] Literary associations bearing Peretz's name were headed by the Bund.[5] And in postwar New York, Jewish labor groups, like Arbeter Ring (Workmen's Circle), were among who advocated for naming a square on the city's Lower East Side after Peretz, on the hundredth anniversary of his birth.[6] Bundist leader and educator Yankev Pat spoke at the square's unveiling event, equating it to the "Ohel Peretz" monument in Warsaw. "We, here in America," he asserted, "where five million Jews live and create as equals among equals, will hold high the flag of spiritual revival that I. L. Peretz had raised."[7]

During my work covering a rich body of material and focusing on its most revealing points, many questions arise from my research that are ripe for further inquiries beyond the scope of this book. For example, How did other left-leaning Yiddish writers like Avrom Reyzn and Kalman Marmor, inspired by Peretz like so many others, take on the position of organic intellectuals for the Yiddish-speaking working class? How did non-leftist Yiddish writers, like Nomberg, Aaron Zeitlin, and I. B. Singer, also inspired by Peretz's art but challenged by his politics, reconcile with his legacy?[8] How do Peretz's relations with the Bund stand in comparison with organic intellectuals of different languages, spaces, or periods?

Peretz's story has taught us that, taken out of context, a working-class champion can easily be reframed in ways that undermine the cultural and political beliefs at the heart of his creativity and at the center of his being. We have seen how the power dynamics Peretz stood up against in his lifetime resemble the ways scholarly evaluations of his works have been disseminated in contemporary circles of power. His story illustrates the relevance of the interpretations of past struggles for justice in the ongoing struggles of the present.

Figure 6.1. Collection of photographs from the opening of Peretz Square in New York, 1952. Jewish Historical Press.

Conclusion | 211

Figure 6.2. Illustration from the Yiddish daily *Forverts*: "Today Mayor Impellitteri Opens the Peretz Square near Second Avenue." The theater managers stand next to the mayor on a ladder, putting up the sign of the new square; one manager tells the other, "Well, if we have already an I. L. Peretz Street near Second Avenue, maybe we'll be permitted to speak Yiddish on the Yiddish stage?" Jewish Historical Press.

Figure 6.3. Peretz Square Park in lower Manhattan. Courtesy of Ahuva Yonit Mahalel.

Appendixes

Appendix to Chapter 1

Hints of I. L. Peretz's soon-to-be-proclaimed pro-labor direction, informed by the *Bilder* experience and his face-to-face encounter with the poverty among Jews, can also be found in a letter Peretz wrote to Dinezon in 1892. He wrote this letter when he was compiling his popular science booklet about the cholera epidemic, and when he was not prospering financially. In the booklet, Peretz hints that the epidemic has a social-class element by asking why the poor suffer more than others.[1] In the letter he links the oppression of non–Eastern Orthodox Christians within the czarist empire and the modern oppression of the poor under the rule of the bourgeoisie:

> Until today we said that God belongs to the Eastern Orthodox Church and that he protects only those who belong to the Eastern Orthodox Church as he protects the eye in his head. Now we sense that he is also a full-on member of the bourgeoisie, that he is the God of the rich. In Lublin there was a terrible epidemic, and even now, although it is weaker, it takes many victims each day. But only poor people die, and the chunky rich people are living and are healthy and strong. Until now the rich use to die out of fear, but now it is clear, that the epidemic is an epidemic for poor people, and the rich are happy and . . . give charity. . . .
>
> I was chosen to be the committee's writer to assist the poor at the time of the plague . . . from it I will have an addition to my salary; salt to add to the peanuts.[2]

Appendix to Chapter 2

This segment is taken from the story "Weaver-Love," from very close to its final conclusion. In it, the weaver-protagonist discusses his attempt to stir up a social struggle among the workers:

> Have you ever seen how sparks fly over a smithy? Millions of sparks, and they won't light even one straw on the thatched-roof! But take them together, they will burn everything! Society is the same! Barely did the crowd gather together, then it burned! Deaf people heard, the mute spoke, lame people were running everywhere, the paralyzed wanted to hit, only to hit others were screaming, so that as long as the bellies of two or three employers remained not torn apart in the middle of the marketplace, the troubles will not end!
>
> I hate violence: by my nature I can't hear bellies being torn up, and I want to sneak myself out of the crowd with its sharp tongues and blunted heads; unfortunately, people took notice of me and it suddenly became a clamor: he escapes! He's going to hand us in to the authorities! To hand us in! And these words were enough to make me want to go back, to jump up on the first table and begin to talk, as if also I had something missing in the head and my heart had also grown bigger in all directions.
>
> Should I tell you my stupid words? For what? I only wanted the weavers to understand their own place of work, to make them realize, that first they must hold together firmly, that the "Workers of Justice"[3] has to be refreshed and become stronger, that they must collect money, money for the sick, money for the old without strength, for the weaver without a job, money for everybody in a difficult period, when it doesn't pay to work . . . and the main thing is that the weavers never have to compete against one another, not with income, not with prolonging the hours of work . . . I told them, that somewhere else people work only twelve hours, abroad only ten hours, in a few places only eight. I told them, that a person is not a horse, and that as we know, horses work less than the laziest weaver . . . and more such things, that a sensible person keeps to himself and doesn't say out in the open. You might say differently darling Miriam? However, you always loved to refute me, to contradict me, but we'll talk about that at home! Meanwhile it troubled me.

The whole time that you didn't receive letters from me, I did time, and God knows why? Only when people finally found out for sure that I kept away from smacking and cutting bellies I was released. But I was told to go out of the city for a couple of years . . . a weaver, they say, needs to sit and work, not to jump on tables and speak . . .

Bad, but two things comfort me! I've planted a seed and I am certain that it will grow; from afar I see already how it grows! And it grows, as it should: in the dark, quiet and humble, like a rooster that doesn't need to crow! And second, that darling Miriam wish will be fulfilled and we will see each other . . . see each other very soon . . . Just prepare a bit of salt, to rub me on my shoulders; they were slightly chopped.

Yours . . . (Peretz, *Ale verk*, 2:513–15)

Appendix to Chapter 3

Peretz dramatized here a fictional satirical discussion of writers on the matters of the day—the New Wave in Hebrew literature, Hebrew-Yiddish relations, and Zionism—in which he asked,

> "Who amongst the writers would be accepted as a member of the support society?" To this question I received many answers: "Everybody—besides the critics who dance on the blood of their fellow writers! Everybody—besides the writers who write in the spoken language [i.e., Yiddish] on a regular or on a casual basis, because they humiliate the value of literature to the level of the mob. Everybody (I recognized the voice of Menahem the writer) besides he who is not an enthusiastic nationalist and a supporter of Choveve Tsiyon. The society should be idealist-realist, its members should be realists-idealists and indeed nationalism and Choveve Tsiyon are realism and idealism or idealism and realism which *hitmalgemu** and became one!
>
> *This word was recently renewed by Menahem the writer, and without a doubt will come out soon in print, may God be with him and may he rise to success!"[4]

Notes

Introduction

1. Take for example a sampling of the numerous book titles that include his name: Nachman Mayzel, *I. L. Peretz: Zayn lebn un shafn* [I. L. Peretz: His life and creations; in Yiddish] (New York: IKUF, 1945); H. D. Nomberg, *Y. L. Perets* (Buenos Aires: Tsentrale farband fun poylishe yidn in argentine, 1946); Shmuel Niger, *I. L. Peretz* (Buenos Aires: Yiddish Cultural Congress, 1952); Chone Shmeruk, *Peretses yiesh-vizye: Interpretatsye fun Y. L. Peretses "Bay nakht oyfn altn mark"* [Peretz's vision of despair: Interpretation of I. L. Peretz's *At Night in the Old Marketplace*; in Yiddish] (New York: YIVO, 1971); Ruth Wisse, *I. L. Peretz and the Making of Modern Jewish Culture* (Seattle: University of Washington Press, 1991).

2. Shoshana Anish Stiftel, *The Mediator: Nahum Sokolow's Leadership between Tradition and Zionism* [in Hebrew] (Jerusalem: Mosad Bialik, 2012), 88–89.

3. Nahum Sokolow, *Ishim* [Personalities; in Hebrew] (Tel Aviv: Stybl, 1935), 53, quoted in Anish Stiftel, *Mediator*, 102.

4. I. L. Peretz, *Briv un redes* [Letters and speeches; in Yiddish], compiled by Nakhman Mayzel (Vilnius: B. Kletskin, 1929), 17–18; see also pp. 11–45 (letters 1–6 and 8–10). Peretz's debut in Yiddish, the long poem "Monish," was published in 1888 in Sholem Aleichem's almanac *Di yudishe folks-bibliyotek*. All translations in this book from Yiddish or Hebrew were done by the author.

5. More about the positivist milieu in Warsaw can be found in Jacob Shatzky, "Perets-shtudyes" [Peretz studies; in Yiddish], *YIVO-bleter* 28 (1946): 40–80.

6. I. L. Peretz, *Kitvey Y. L. Perets* [Writings by I. L. Peretz; in Hebrew] (Tel Aviv: Dvir), 483–84.

7. Dan Miron, *A Traveler Disguised: The Rise of Modern Yiddish Fiction in the Nineteenth Century* (Syracuse, NY: Syracuse University Press, 1996), 12.

8. Peretz, *Briv un redes* (1929), 26. On the fact that Peretz held Sholem Aleichem in the highest esteem, contrary to the way he was looked down upon by intellectuals, see Y. Y. Trunk, *Poyln: Zilkhroynes un bilder* [Poland: Memories and scenes] (New York: "Unzer tsayt," 1949), 5:119–23.

9. Peretz, *Briv un redes* (1929), 38.

10. I. L. Peretz, *Ale verk*, 8:8. All quotations will be taken from *Ale verk fun Y. L. Perets* [Collected works of Y. L. Perets], 11 vols. (New York: CYCO, 1947–48).

11. Joseph Lang, "Foundation and Development of the Safa Brura"[in Hebrew], *Cathedra* 68 (June 1993): 67–79. Peretz mentions them in his article "Bildung," and he gave lectures in Hebrew (with a Polish accent) addressing topics such as Jewish education. But he became skeptical about Safa Brura in later years.

12. Ela Bauer, "From the Salons to the Street: The Development of the Jewish Salon in Warsaw at the End of the 19th Century," *Jahrbuch des Simon-Dubnow-Instituts / Simon Dubnow Institute Yearbook* 7 (2008): 155.

13. Yudl Mark, "An analiz fun Y. L. Peretses shprakh" [An analysis of I. L. Peretz's Language; in Yiddish], *YIVO-bleter* 28 (1946): 111.

14. Dan Miron, From Continuity to Contiguity: Toward A New Jewish Literary Thinking (Stanford, CA: Stanford University Press, 2010), 80. I disagree with Miron that Peretz's nationalism was "more civilizational in its character than political" (80). I believe it was both, particularly because it was a nationalism that propagated for Jewish cultural autonomy.

15. Peretz borrows from German the common nationalist lingua of *Volk* and *Bildung*. See, for example, Fritz Ringer, "Bildung: The Social and Ideological Context of the German Historical Tradition," *History of European Ideas* 10 (1989): 193–202; and Reinhart Koselleck, Fritz Gschnitzer, Karl Ferdinand Werner, and Bernd Schönemann, "Volk, Nation, Nationalismus, Masse," in *Geschichtliche Grundbegriffe: Historisches Lexikon zur politisch-sozialen Sprache in Deutschland*, ed. Reinhart Koselleck (Stuttgart: Klett-Cotta Verlag, 1992), 7:141–431.

16. "Individuals need not and cannot unite, nor—peoples!" (Peretz, *Ale verk*, 8:16).

17. Peretz, *Ale verk*, 8:16.

18. Peretz, 8:12.

19. However, Renner's model did not include diasporas of scattered minorities. See Bill Bowring, "Burial and Resurrection: Karl Renner's Controversial Influence on the 'National Question' in Russia," in *National Cultural Autonomy and Its Contemporary Critics*, ed. Ephraim Nimni (London: Routledge, 2005): 191–206; Ephraim Nimni, "National-Cultural Autonomy as an Alternative to Minority Territorial Nationalism," *Ethnopolitics* 6, no. 3 (2007): 345–64; and Ian Reifowitz, "Otto Bauer and Karl Renner on Nationalism, Ethnicity & Jews," *Journal of Jewish Identities* 2, no. 2 (2009): 1–19.

20. "Hebrew we have to know as Jews, but—as educated people, as living people, we must know the state language" (8:11).

21. For example, during the years 1874–97, the Jewish population of Warsaw grew by 130 percent, from 90,000 to 220,000. See Yoav Peled, *Class and Ethnicity in the Pale: The Political Economy of Jewish Workers' Nationalism in Late Imperial Russia* (New York: St. Martin's Press, 1989), 21–30; and Daniel Blatman, "Bund," trans. David Fachler, *YIVO Encyclopedia of Jews in Eastern Europe*, 2010,

http://www.yivoencyclopedia.org/article.aspx/Bund. Two known books on the subject are Jonathan Frankel, *Prophecy and Politics: Socialism, Nationalism, and the Russian Jews, 1862–1917* (Cambridge: Cambridge University Press, 1981); and Ezra Mendelsohn, *Class Struggle in the Pale: The Formative Years of the Jewish Workers' Movement in Tsarist Russia* (Cambridge: Cambridge University Press, 1970).

22. Peled, *Class and Ethnicity*, 25–27.

23. For the history of the Warsaw Jewish community during the nineteenth century, see Yankev Shatsky, *Di geshikhte fun yidn in Varshe* [The history of the Jews in Warsaw; in Yiddish], 3 vols. (New York: YIVO, 1947–53).

24. Peter van den Dungen, *The Making of Peace: Jean de Bloch and the First Hague Peace Conference* (Los Angeles: Center for the Study of Armament and Disarmament, California State University, 1983). Peretz mentions the pacifist movement several times in his articles.

25. Peled, *Class and Ethnicity*, 22–24.

26. Jacob Lestschinsky, The development of the Jewish people in the last one hundred years [in Yiddish] (Berlin, 1928), 1, quoted in Abram Leon, The Jewish Question: A Marxist Interpretation (New York: Pathfinder Press, 1971).

27. Peled, *Class and Ethnicity*, 22–24.

28. Wisse, *Modern Jewish Culture*, 18–19.

29. The discriminatory legislation against Jews was a reflection of the class struggle between the upper bourgeoisie and the old Polish aristocracy, in which the latter used antisemitism in its reactionary struggle against modernization at large. See Ayzik Rozentsvayg, *Der radikaler periyod fun Peretses shafn: "Di yontef bletlekh"* [The radical period of Peretz's creative work: *The Holiday Pages*] (Kyiv: Melukhe-farlag fun di natsyonale minderhaytn, 1934), 36–41.

30. The first socialist brochure in Yiddish printed in Warsaw was toward May Day 1893. An alter bakanter [Y. Pesakhzon], "In varshe erev 'bund'" [In Warsaw eve of the Bund], in *25 yor: Zamlbukh* (Warsaw: Di velt, 1922), 41–42.

31. He wrote in 1891 in a book review, "On konkurents hot zikh di melokhe nisht antvikelt, zi iz shtendik af eyn ort geshtanen . . . az ale shnayder fun der gantser velt zoln makhn shutfes, tsu der groyser fantazye iz er nokh nit gekumen" (Without competition, craftsmanship did not develop; it was always stuck . . . the author had not yet come to this great fantasy that all the tailors of the world should make a partnership). Peretz, "In vos iz ayer hilf" [In what is your help; in Yiddish], *Ale verk*, 7:20.

32. Sokolow, *Ishim*, 265–66. Sokolow prescribed similar aspirations for the Polish-Jewish intelligentsia (including the temporal use of Yiddish) through a series of articles in Polish that came out at the same time as "Bildung." See Ela Bauer, "Yaadey Ha-Intiligentsya Ha-Yehudit-Polanit" [The goals of the Jewish-Polish intelligentsia; in Hebrew], *Tsiyon*, vol. samekh"khet, no. 3, tasha"g: 335–58.

33. Daniel Gutwein, "Ha-diplomatia Ha-yehudit ba'me'a ha-tsha esre: Reshit ha-leumiyut ha-yehudit?" [Jewish diplomacy in the nineteenth century: The eve of Jewish nationalism?], in *Le'umiyut ve-politica yehudit: Perspectivot hadashot*

[Nationalism and Jewish politics: New perspectives; in Hebrew] (Jerusalem: Merkaz Zalman Shazar le-toldot Yisrael, 1996), 171.

34. Nahum Sokolow, "Yosl the Crazy (Sketches from my memory)" [in Hebrew], *Hatekufah* 26–27, 2nd ed. (1935): 61.

35. Peretz, *Kitvey Y. L. Perets*, 489–90.

36. Dan Miron, *The Image of the Shtetl, and Other Studies of Modern Jewish Literary Imagination* (New York: Syracuse University Press, 2000), 102–4.

37. Mayzel, *Peretz: Zayn lebn un shafn*, 110–11. Mayzel states that "in spite of some false starts, over time it was not difficult for Peretz to communicate with the shtetl residents." Quoted in Marc Caplan, "The Fragmentation of Narrative Perspective in Y. L. Peretz's *Bilder fun a Provints Rayze*," *Jewish Social Studies: History, Culture, Society*, n.s., 14, no. 1 (Fall 2007): 67–68.

38. Ruth R. Wisse, "Peretz, Yitskhok Leybush," *YIVO Encyclopedia of Jews in Eastern Europe*, December 15, 2010, http://www.yivoencyclopedia.org/article.aspx/Peretz_Yitskhok_Leybush.

39. Wisse, *Modern Jewish Culture*, 19.

40. Alon Altaras, "The islands of Antonio Gramsci: An introduction," in *About the hegemony* [in Hebrew], Antonio Gramsci, trans. Alon Altaras (Tel Aviv: Resling, 2009), 35.

41. Naturally, the very idea of politically committed intellectuals who align themselves with the underprivileged predates Gramsci. Numerous examples range from the poets Janet Hamilton and John Clare to Victor Hugo and Émile Zola; the list includes many active in the cultural-political world of Eastern European Jewry, such as Morris Vintshevsky.

42. Gramsci, *About the hegemony*, 59–60; Gramsci, *Prison Notebooks*, ed. and trans. Joseph A. Buttigieg (New York: Columbia University Press, 2011), 202.

43. An alter bakanter, "In varshe erev 'bund,'" 43–47.

44. Joshua Meyers, "The Bund by the Numbers: The Ebbs and Flows of a Jewish Radical Party," *In geveb*, May 6, 2020, https://ingeveb.org/blog/the-bund-by-the-numbers; Blatman, "Bund."

45. For a recent discussion of the term *do'ikayt*, see Madeleine Cohen, "*Do'ikayt* and the Spaces of Politics in An-sky's Novella *In shtrom*," *East European Jewish Affairs* 50, no. 1–2 (2020): 6–20.

46. Blatman, "Bund"; David Slucki, *The International Jewish Labor Bund after 1945: Toward a Global History* (New Brunswick, NJ: Rutgers University Press, 2012).

47. Peled, *Class and Ethnicity*, 1.

48. For recent brief surveys see Slucki, *International Jewish Labor Bund*, 46; and Jack Jacobs, introduction to *Jews and Leftist Politics: Judaism, Israel, Antisemitism, and Gender*, ed. Jack Jacobs (Cambridge: Cambridge University Press, 2017), 14n38.

49. Frank Wolff, *Yiddish Revolutionaries in Migration: The Transnational History of the Jewish Labour Bund*, trans. Loren Balhorn and Jan-Peter Herrmann (Leiden: Brill, 2021), 12.

50. Roni Gechtman, "Nationalising the Bund? Zionist Historiography and the Jewish Labour Movement," *East European Jewish Affairs* 43, no. 3 (2013): 249.

51. As Peled concludes in "The Concept of National Cultural Autonomy: The First One Hundred Years," in *Jewish Politics in Eastern Europe: The Bund at 100*, ed. Jack Jacobs (New York: New York University Press / Żydowski Instytut Historyczny—Instytut Naukowo-Badawczy, 2001), 268.

52. Gechtman later acknowledges Peled's criticism stems from an international perspective ("Nationalising the Bund?," 252). For an obvious illustration of Peled's nonnationalist scholarship, see Horit Herman Peled and Yoav Peled, "The Way Forward in the Middle East," in *Israel and Palestine: Alternative Perspectives on Statehood*, ed. John Ehrenberg and Yoav Peled (Lanham, MD: Rowman & Littlefield, 2016), 187–99.

53. Peled, *Class and Ethnicity*, 9.

54. Shakhne Epshteyn, *Y. L. Perets als sotsyaler dikhter* [Y. L. Peretz as a social poet] (New York: Max N. Maisel, 1916), 8.

55. Walter Benjamin, "The Author as Producer," trans. John Heckman, *New Left Review* I/62 (July/August 1970): 220–38.

56. A convention Rozentsvayg has articulated at the very opening of his work: "Peretz's contradiction is evident not only in various periods of creativity but also in every period taken separately . . . contradictory are also very often even distinct works" (*Der radikaler periyod*, 3).

57. See Nomberg, *Y. L. Perets*.

58. Shmuel Charney used the pen name Shmuel Niger. Recently it has been argued that scholarship should use his original name due to the negative connotations his pen name evokes in English. See Eli Bromberg, "We Need to Talk about Shmuel Charney," *In geveb*, October 2, 2019, https://ingeveb.org/articles/we-need-to-talk-about-shmuel-charney. To avoid confusion, when citing his works, I stuck to the name under which he authored his numerous books and articles.

59. Niger, *Peretz*, 226–27.

60. The Bund post-1905 enjoyed the easing up of government restrictions on free speech (Frankel, *Prophecy and Politics*, 156), but it only began operating legally as a party in 1917 (Blatman, "Bund"), after Peretz's death.

61. See Shmeruk, *Peretses yiesh-vizye*.

62. See Wisse, *Modern Jewish Culture*, 47. Wisse later gave a more nuanced take on Peretz's class and national politics in her essay "The Political Vision of I. L. Peretz," in *The Emergence of Modern Jewish Politics: Bundism and Zionism in Eastern Europe*, ed. Zvi Gitelman (Pittsburg: University of Pittsburg Press, 2003), 120–31.

63. In 1912, during their meeting in Vilnius, Peretz told the literary critic and Bundist activist Moyshe Olgin, "I declare openly that I am a tendentious writer . . . I create the scenes only in order to illustrate the particular idea." Moshe Olgin, "A Day with I. L. Peretz" [in Yiddish], in *Y. L. Perets* (New York: IKUF, 1955), 20–21.

64. Wisse, *Modern Jewish Culture*, 109. The tendency of blaming Jews for their own persecution has a history in Zionist thought that can be traced back to Hayim Nahman Bialik's influential poem "In the City of Slaughter" (1904). See Michael Gluzman, Hannan Hever, and Dan Miron, eds., *Be-ir ha-haregah: Bikur me'uchar* [In the city of slaughter: A visit at twilight; in Hebrew] (Tel Aviv: Resling, 2005).

65. Miron, *From Continuity to Contiguity*, 80, 505n39. Taken from Peretz's keynote speech at the 1908 Yiddish language conference in Czernowitz.

66. See Peretz's article "Nationalism and Zionism," in I. L. Peretz, *Ale verk*, 9:419; also quoted in Ze'ev Goldberg, "On Y.-L. Perets' relationship to Zionism" [in Hebrew], *Khulyot* 7 (2002): 77.

67. See Adi Mahalel, "Yiddish, Scholarship, and Neoconservatism," *AJS Review* 44, no. 1 (April 2020): 119–47. Several contemporary scholars adopt a nonmaterialist version of postcolonial theory, portray Peretz ahistorically as a postnationalist skeptic, and, similarly to their predecessors, blur his ideological commitments. Their lack of class analysis results in a tendency to essentialize Jewish difference. See Samuel J. Spinner, *Jewish Primitivism* (Stanford, CA: Stanford University Press, 2021), 21–40; and Caplan, "Fragmentation."

68. Rozentsvayg, *Der radikaler periyod*, 3–4.

69. Peretz himself divided his writing career into three periods: (1) stories of pity toward the poverty-stricken Jew, (2) stories of anger toward Jewish passivity, and (3) symbolist texts expressing the problems of Jewish life in Yiddish plays and late Hasidic stories (Olgin, "A Day with I. L. Peretz," 20–21). Although the radical Peretz is often the angry Peretz, I argue radical tendencies are also to be found in his symbolist texts in Yiddish and Hebrew.

70. Peretz never sold enough copies to justify more editions. After poor sales of the first *Bibliyotek*, he wrote to his close friend Yankev Dinezon, "It's been several months and I haven't sold one copy. I blame it on a lack of awareness and the cholera epidemic." Peretz, *Briv un redes* (1929), 75.

71. Cornel West, "Introduction: The Radical King We Don't Know," in *The Radical King*, Martin Luther King Jr., ed. Cornel West (Boston, MA: Beacon Press, 2015), xv.

Chapter 1

1. Peretz, *Di yudishe bibliyotek* (Warsaw, 1891), 2:7; Peretz, *Ale verk fun Y. L. Perets* (New York: CYCO, 1947–48), 8:37.

2. I. L. Peretz, Briv un redes fun Y. L. Perets [Letters and talks by I. L. Peretz], ed. Nachman Mayzel (New York: IKUF, 1944), 129, quoted in Shmuel Niger, I. L. Peretz (Buenos Aires: Yiddish Cultural Congress, 1952), 196.

3. See also Ruth R. Wisse, "The Political Vision of I. L. Peretz," in *The Emergence of Modern Jewish Politics: Bundism and Zionism in Eastern Europe*, ed. Zvi Gitelman (Pittsburg: University of Pittsburg Press, 2003), 124.

4. Peretz, *Di yudishe bibliyotek*, vol. 1. The second epigraph is from *Iber profesyonen*; its first edition came out as a supplement to the first volume of *Di yudishe bibliyotek*.

5. Scott Ury, "The Culture of Modern Jewish Politics," in *Insiders and Outsiders: Dilemmas of East European Jewry*, ed. Richard I. Cohen, Jonathan Frankel, and Stefani Hoffman (Oxford: Littman Library of Jewish Civilization, 2010).

6. See many examples for the centrality of education reform since the Haskalah's inception in Berlin in Shmuel Feiner, *The Jewish Enlightenment*, trans. Chaya Naor (Philadelphia: University of Pennsylvania Press, 2011).

7. Feiner, *Jewish Enlightenment*, 92.

8. Shin"yud Ben-Khaim Moshe [Sholem Yankev] Abramovitsh, "Mikhtav Al Dvar Ha-Khinukh," *Ha-Magid*, July 15, 1857.

9. Dovid Pinski, "Dray yor mit Perets" [Three years with Peretz], *Di Goldene Keyt* 8 (1951): 5–31. On the mixed reactions to "Bildung" amongst Yiddishists, see Niger, *Peretz*, 210–16.

10. The message of first fixing the economy and only later addressing other issues such as one's proper social behavior and conduct can be found all over Haskalah literature, especially since the 1860s—for example, in chapter 15 of Abramovitsh's novel *Susati* (My horse; *Di kliyatshe* in Yiddish).

11. See Yoav Peled, *Class and Ethnicity in the Pale: The Political Economy of Jewish Workers' Nationalism in Late Imperial Russia* (New York: St. Martin's Press, 1989), 21–30, for a discussion of Jewish and non-Jewish workers in the Pale of Settlement.

12. M. Khmelnitski, "Y. L. Perets' popular-meditsinishe broshur: Az me vil nisht, shtarbt nisht fun kholi-ra," *YIVO-bleter* 28 (Fall 1946): 146–52. Peretz's adviser on these issues was Josef Kirshrot (1843–1906), who worked for Jan Bloch and was an attorney in Warsaw. Kirshrot was the founder of the first Jewish workmen's association (Niger, *Peretz*, 210). For a reference point to compare their numbers with contemporary scholarship, see Bina Garncarska-Kadari, *The role of the Jews in the development of Warsaw industry in the years 1816/20–1914* [in Hebrew] (Tel Aviv, 1985).

13. Khmelnitski, "Y. L. Perets' popular-meditsinishe broshur: Az me vil nisht, shtarbt nisht fun kholi-ra" [I. L. Peretz's popular medicine brochure: Whoever doesn't want to doesn't die of cholera].

14. Curiously, Perez does not mention the Jewish day of rest, the Sabbath. He might be trying to hide such objective obstacles (the different day of rest) to the full incorporation of Jews in the workforce. Acknowledging this difference undercuts his message aimed at Jews correcting *their* ways and discussing *their* responsibilities toward self-improvement.

15. In the original it's either from *kheyder* (a traditional school for young Jewish males) or at least from a *talmetoyre* (a Jewish religious elementary school for the poor).

16. "The drunken *goyishe* peasants we [Jews] would never want to be like"—as quoted by the Yiddish writer Abraham Shulman. Dovid Katz, *Words on Fire: The Unfinished Story of Yiddish* (New York: Basic Books, 2004), 363.

17. *Shund* was the derogatory term that was used for popular Yiddish literature—literally, "trashy." Sholem Aleichem famously waged an open war against the popular Yiddish writer Shomer (1849–1905). In a pamphlet entitled *Shomer's mishpet* (Shomer's trial), he attacked Shomer's works. See Jeremy Dauber, "Shomer," *YIVO Encyclopedia of Jews in Eastern Europe*, accessed April 1, 2013, http://www.yivoencyclopedia.org/article.aspx/Shomer; and Sophie Grace-Pollack, "Shomer in the Light of *Shomer's mishpet*" [in Hebrew], *Khulyot* 5 (1998): 109–59. For an English translation of the pamphlet, see Justin Daniel Cammy, "The Judgment of Shomer, or The Jury Trial of All of Shomer's Novels," in *Arguing the Modern Jewish Canon: Essays on Literature and Culture in Honor of Ruth R. Wisse*, ed. Justin Daniel Cammy, Dara Horn, Alyssa Quint, and Rachel Rubinstein, 129–88 (Cambridge, MA: Center for Jewish Studies at Harvard University, 2008).

18. Sholem Aleichem was inventing his own version of a Yiddish canon in his almanac *Yudishe folks-bibliyotek* along with authors such as Joel Linetsky Abramovitsh (1839–1916) and Yankev Dinezon (1856–1919).

19. Iris Parush, *Reading Jewish Women: Marginality and Modernization in Nineteenth-Century Eastern European Jewish Society*, trans. Saadya Sternberg (Waltham, MA: Brandeis University Press, 2004), 169.

20. See Sholem Aleichem's introduction to his 1888 novel *Stempenyu* in the first volume of his almanac *Di yudishe folks-bibliyotek*.

21. More is in Dauber's biography of Sholem Aleichem: Jeremy Dauber, *The Worlds of Sholem Aleichem: The Remarkable Life and Afterlife of the Man Who Created Tevye* (New York: Schocken, 2013).

22. David G. Roskies, "The Small Talk of I. L. Peretz," *In geveb*, May 22, 2016, https://ingeveb.org/articles/the-small-talk-of-i-l-peretz.

23. See also Marc Caplan, "The Fragmentation of Narrative Perspective in Y. L. Peretz's *Bilder fun a Provints-Rayze*," *Jewish Social Studies: History, Culture, Society*, n.s., 14, no. 1 (Fall 2007): 71.

24. Peretz estimated the number of people predominantly speaking Yiddish in their daily lives to be three million ("Bildung," *Ale verk*, 8:11).

25. Taken from the second volume of Sholem Aleichem's almanac *Di yudishe folks-bibliyotek* (1889), which gives a list of all the Yiddish books that were printed that year.

26. Freud uses the joke about an encounter between two Jews at a train station in Galicia in his analysis of humor as an example of skeptical jokes: jokes that challenges our conception of truth and attack the certainty of our knowledge itself. Sigmund Freud, *Jokes and Their Relation to the Unconscious*, trans. and ed. James Strachey (New York: W. W. Norton, 1960), 115.

27. First published as Sholem Yankev Abramovitsh, "Shem ve-Yefet ba-'agala," in *Kaveret Kovetz Sifruti* [Kaveret literary compilation; in Hebrew] (Odessa, 1890), 45–59.

28. The seven laws in Jewish tradition that apply to non-Jews.

29. Peretz, *Ale verk*, 2:72. A full English translation is in I. L. Peretz, "In the Mail Coach," trans. Golda Werman, in *The I. L Peretz Reader*, ed. Ruth R. Wisse (New York: Schocken Books, 1990), 104–18.

30. Gisèle Sapiro, introduction to *La Domination Masculine* [in Hebrew], by Pierre Bourdieu, trans. Avner Lahav (Tel Aviv: Resling, 2007), 16.

31. Not by challenging the gendered division of labor at its base—for example, the inequality resulting from women being excluded from the modern labor force or, if they enter it, earning lower wages in comparison with men. See Irene Padavic and Barbara F. Reskin, *Women and Men at Work* (London: Sage Publications, 2002).

32. Parush, *Reading Jewish Women*, 145–46.

33. Take such Hebrew writers as Y. Ch. Brenner, Yosef Luidor, and Moshe Smilansky, who made the concept of "negation of exile" (i.e., negating any place that is not the Land of Israel, including a negation of Jews living in Poland) into a central theme in their writings, "portraying the Jews' exilic condition as a national pathology. . . . The negation of exile [is] the pinnacle of Zionist ideology." Michael Gluzman, *The Politics of Canonicity: Lines of Resistance in Modernist Hebrew Poetry* (Stanford, CA: Stanford University Press, 2003), 45.

34. A term famously coined by Anderson for modern nationalist communities; see Benedict Anderson, *Imagined Communities: Reflections on the Origin and Spread of Nationalism*, rev. ed. (London: Verso, 1991). I argue that there was already an emerging modern imagined Jewish community at the time, growing side by side with the Yiddish press in Eastern Europe and overseas (and an already established Hebrew press).

35. This is more than just a crisis of mediation between the modern and the traditional spheres, as suggested in Caplan, "Fragmentation," 68.

36. Anderson, *Imagined Communities*, 82.

37. *Dos pintele yid* refers to the most basic point of identity of a Jew. It is based on the mystical assumption that all Jews have an inherent common "Jewish quality," regardless of their degree of piety.

38. Parush, *Reading Jewish Women*, 126–32.

39. Sholem Aleichem, "A briv tsu a gutn fraynd" [A letter to a good friend; in Yiddish], in Aleichem, *Di yudishe folks-bibliotek*, 2:307–8.

40. Terry Eagleton, *Literary Theory: An Introduction*, 2nd ed. (Minneapolis: University of Minnesota Press, 1996), 16.

41. Brian Porter, *When Nationalism Began to Hate: Imagining Modern Politics in Nineteenth-Century Poland* (New York: Oxford University Press, 2000), 69.

42. Gershon Bacon, "Poland: Poland from 1795 to 1939," *YIVO Encyclopedia of Jews in Eastern Europe*, March 14, 2011, http://www.yivoencyclopedia.org/article.aspx/Poland/Poland_from_1795_to_1939.

43. Porter, *Nationalism*, 176–82.

44. Take for example Aaron Halle-Wolfssohn's play, in both Yiddish (*Laykhtzin un Fremelay* [Silliness and sanctimony, ca. 1794]) and Hebrew (*Kalut da'at u-tseviʻut*). In it, the enlightened Jewish character has to "save" the young, Jewish, bourgeois daughter from assimilation in the corrupt (meaning non-Jewish) environment of brothels and prostitution. See Joel Berkowitz and Jeremy Dauber, eds. and trans., *Landmark Yiddish Plays: A Critical Anthology* (Albany: State University of New York Press, 2006). For the Hebrew, see Aaron Wolfssohn, *Kalut da'at u-tseviʻut: Rav. Ḥanokh ve-Rabi Yosefkeh* (Tel Aviv: Mif'alim ʻUniversitayim Le-Hotsa'ah Le-'or, 1977). In Peretz's Hebrew story "Ha-nidakhat" (The deposed; 1900), the non-Jewish lover abandons the young Jewish protagonist, and she is left neither here (in the Jewish world) nor there (in the goyish one). See Ruth Shenfeld, "The family crisis: An integrated view on the decline of the Jewish family unit in late-nineteenth- and early-twentieth-century Poland as reflected in the works of Frischmann, Peretz, Barashm, and Zapolska" [in Hebrew], in *Studies in East European Jewish history and culture in honor of Professor Shmuel Werses*, ed. David Assaf et al. (Jerusalem: Hebrew University Magnes Press, 2002), 346.

45. Peretz, *Kitvey Y. L. Perets* (Tel Aviv: Dvir), 490.

46. Parush, *Reading Jewish Women*, 246.

47. "We're going from house to house, from number one and beyond. I know where Jews and where non-Jews live; I only need to look inside the windows. Windows that turned yellow are a sign for 'the chosen people,' especially shattered glass, trampled with pillows and pillowcases . . . while—window boxes full of flowers and drapes are obvious proof that somebody else already lives here, someone who doesn't have such a monopoly on poverty" (*Ale verk*, 2:125).

48. David-Hirsh Roskies, "Sifrut Yidish Be-Polin" [Yiddish Literature in Poland; in Hebrew], in *Kiyum Va-Shever*, ed. Israel Bartal and Israel Gutman, vol. 2 (Jerusalem: Merkaz Zalma Shazar Le-Toldot Israel, 2001), 209–10.

49. Dan Miron, *Der imazh fun shtetl: Dray literarishe shtudyes* [The image of the shtetl: Three literary studies] (Tel Aviv, 1981), 105.

50. In a letter to Dinezon, Peretz writes that "the intelligentsia of Warsaw, who stand at the same level as the Kyiv intelligentsia, hate me with passion, but their hatred is hidden for they fear my sharp tongue. I am very pleased by it; . . . I sell the bib' almanac one by one and eat up my money. . . . If there were publicity, then I would have sold many. But you are without me a zero, and I without you less than that, I am a minus. When you'll come, some number will come out from the minus and the zero." *Briv un redes* (1929), 80. The "bib'" refers to copies of Peretz's alamac *Di yudishe bibliyotek* that featured *Bilder fun a provints rayze*.

51. Caplan, "Fragmentation," 7.

52. Peretz, *Yudishe bibliyotek*, 2:117. In the *Ale verk* version, the quotation is "on their young faces appeared fear and bewilderment, as if they spotted somebody from a different world" (2:164). There are a few differences between the *Ale verk* version and the original version from *Di yudishe bibliyotek* (1891). I translated according to the original version.

53. Sholem Aleichem, "Der yidisher dales in di beste verke fun undzere folks-shrift-shteler" [Jewish poverty in the best work of our writers], supplement to *Yudishes folksblat* (1888): 1075–90, 1101–10, 1149–57, 1183–89, 1205–16.

54. Writers like the Yiddish playwright A. Goldfaden and the Hebrew poet Y. L. Gordon (a great influence on Peretz), who were also cited by Sholem Aleichem, were crowned as "the Yiddish Nekrasov" or "the Hebrew Nekrasov." Yankev Shatzky, "Paltiel zamoshtishens letters to Sholem Aleichem," *YIVO-bleter* 11 (1937): 23–24.

55. For example, in his poem "Taybele": "They are taking a walk in Grand Street / Taybele shines in her dress! / Though the poor man in 'prince Albert' / Is haggard, pale as death." Kalmen Marmor, *Dovid Edelstadt* [in Yiddish] (New York: IKUF, 1950), 62–63.

56. Sholem Aleichem, "Der yidisher dales," 1077–78. Abramovitsh's poor were divided into two categories: the wandering "gypsy beggars" and those who stay in one place.

57. Dan Miron, "'The sentimental education' of Mendele Moykher Sforim" [in Hebrew], afterword to *Sefer ha-kabtsanim*, by Mendele Moykher Sforim (Tel Aviv: Dvir, 1988), 201–68.

58. Sholem Aleichem, "Der yidisher dales," 1188–89.

59. Patrick Greaney, *Untimely Beggar: Poverty and Power from Baudelaire to Benjamin* (Minneapolis: University of Minnesota Press, 2008), x.

60. Peretz, *Yudishe bibliyotek*, 2:103–4; *Ale verk*, 2:148–49. The most significant change here between the original version and the *Ale verk* one appears in the inner thoughts of the protagonist, who, after he wants to tell the boy to forget about the moon, also adds "think about bread!"

61. Peretz, *Yudishe bibliyotek*, 2:104; *Ale verk*, 2:149. The *Ale verk* version reads, "He doesn't know that if everybody would have had eaten alike, then everybody would have been equal."

62. Interestingly, the English word *pale* was borrowed from the term applied to the area of English settlement in Northern Ireland, where the lands of the "wild Irish" were considered "beyond the pale." John Klier, "Pale of Settlement," *YIVO Encyclopedia of Jews in Eastern Europe*, September 14, 2010, https://yivoencyclopedia.org/article.aspx/Pale_of_Settlement.

63. The term *Jewish diplomacy* means western Jews using their financial and social power for the sake of their poor fellow Jews from Eastern Europe or elsewhere. This phenomenon goes back to the Damascus affair of 1840.

64. Daniel Gutwein, "Ha-diplomatia Ha-yehudit ba'me'a ha-tsha esre: Reshit ha-leumiyut ha-yehudit?," in *Le'umiyut ve-politica yehudit: Perspektivot hadashot*

(Jerusalem: Merkaz Zalman Shazar le-toldot Yisrael, 1996), 159–76. Such auspices could be "bringing Christian morals to Africans" or "liberating" Afghan women.

65. As a result, the Jewish middle classes learned the foundations of political organization and action, while a gradual politicization of their Jewish identity occurred (Gutwein, "Ha-diplomatia Ha-yehudit ba'me'a ha-tsha esre").

66. This acting out the part of a reporter by the narrator should not be taken at face value but rather as just one of the methods, according to Miron, that Peretz used to lay out his vision of the shtetl existence (Miron, *Der imazh fun shtetl*, 104).

67. Peretz added this phrase at a time of a more established Jewish nationalism and in retrospect saw *Bilder* as a nationalist composition, or at least those were the aspects he wanted to emphasize to his later readers. See also Niger, *Peretz*, 200.

68. Gutwein offers one explanation of unequal development in modern times: "As much as the integration of the world market deepened the division of labor and strengthened the dependency between the industrial and the developed economies during the nineteenth century, in this process the importance of the peripheral countries became greater in the general economic and strategic considerations of western countries" ("Ha-diplomatia Ha-yehudit ba'me'a ha-tsha esre," 170). That said, unequal development is a universal law relevant to all economic systems. As Samir Amin puts it, "universal history is always the history of unequal development." *Class and Nation: Historically and in the Current Crisis* (New York: Monthly Review Press, 1980), 2.

69. Caplan, "Fragmentation," 85.

70. Caplan, 67.

71. David Berry, "Max Horkheimer: Issues Concerning Liberalism and Culture," in *Revisiting the Frankfurt School: Essays on Culture, Media and Theory*, ed. David Berry (Farnham, UK: Ashgate, 2012), 76–77.

72. Caplan argues that Peretz never quite provides either psychological insight or objective reportage, as one might expect of first- or third-person narrators in realist fiction. Peretz follows Abramovitsh's *Di kliyatshe* (which he read in Polish translation) insofar as the narrative voice shifts perspective between third-person description and first-person introspection (Caplan, "Fragmentation," 76–77).

73. Literally "soul in the stomach," meaning here a dybbuk.

74. Miron, *Der imazh fun shtetl*, 16.

75. Miron, 107.

76. Literally "the burned one," in the sense of losing his property in a fire.

77. The text specifically mentions the name of Jan Jeleński (1845–1909), editor of the antisemitic magazine *Rola* (The fields), who wrote against the "unproductiveness" of the Jews. This journal appealed to a Polish-Christian petty bourgeoisie engaging in economic competition with Jewish merchants. Stanislaus A. Blejwas, "New Political Directions: A Transition toward Popular Participation

in Politics, 1863–90," in *The Origins of Modern Polish Democracy*, ed. M. B. B. Biskupski, James S. Pula, and Piotr J. Wróbel (Athens: Ohio University Press, 2010), 41.

78. Peretz, *Ale verk*, 3:75–86; it is dated there 1895–1900. If this date is correct, then it is the Hebrew version of the story "Ir ha-metim" that was published earlier (in *Ha-tzfira [Hazefirah]*, no. 164 [August 5, 1892]: 646 and no. 165 [August 7, 1892]: 651).

79. Lestschinsky, *The development of the Jewish people in the last one hundred years* [in Yiddish], (Berlin, 1928), 1.

Chapter 2

Parts of this chapter were adapted from Adi Mahalel, "Weaving the Revolution: Peretz the Social Protest Writer," *In geveb: A Journal of Yiddish Studies*, May 22, 2016, http://ingeveb.org/articles/weaving-the-revolution-i-l-peretz-the-social-protest-writer.

1. Daniel Blatman, "Bund," trans. David Fachler, *YIVO Encyclopedia of Jews in Eastern Europe*, 2010, http://www.yivoencyclopedia.org/article.aspx/Bund.

2. B. Gorin, *Gezamelte shriftn* [Collected writings; in Yiddish], vol. 1 (New York: Elizabeth Gorin, 1927), 37.

3. A word-for-word translation would be "Bontshe shut up." The origin and the meaning of the name Bontshe are unclear, as concluded by Dov Sadan, "Bontshe Shvayg un zayne gilgulim" [Bontshe Shvayg and its metamorphosis; in Yiddish], *Folk un Tsiyon* 24 (1978).

4. A slightly revised version of the story, probably edited by Peretz himself, came out in his collected works in 1901. For an elaborate comparison between the two versions, see Bruce Zuckerman, *Job the Silent: A Study in Historical Counterpoint* (New York: Oxford University Press, 1991), 233–36n201. Stories published in the Yiddish press (especially in the Yiddish *socialist* press) often debuted in the United States even if originally written in Eastern Europe, appearing in publications such as the journal *Tsukunft* and the newspaper *Forverts* (founded in 1892 and 1897, respectively). Passages cited are from I. L. Peretz, *Ale verk fun Y. L. Perets* (New York: CYCO, 1947–48), which is based on the 1901 version.

5. Peretz, *Ale verk*, 2:420. In the 1894 version, the prosecuting angel's voice is described as "a soft voice like butter," which sharpens the dramatic irony (Zuckerman, *Job the Silent*, 234–35).

6. Berl Katznelson, *Hartsaot Berl Katznelson (1928)* [Lectures by Berl Katznelson], ed. Anita Shapira and Naomi Abir (Tel Aviv: Am Oved, 1990), 35.

7. Yoav Peled, *Class and Ethnicity in the Pale: The Political Economy of Jewish Workers' Nationalism in Late Imperial Russia* (New York: St. Martin's Press, 1989), 31–70.

8. Dovid Pinski writes about one of the early meetings between Peretz, the PPS, and proto-Bund activists in "Dray yor mit Y. L. Perets," *Di Goldene Keyt* 8 (1951): 22–24.

9. Joshua D. Zimmerman, *Poles, Jews, and the Politics of Nationality: The Bund and the Polish Socialist Party in Late Tsarist Russia, 1892–1914* (Madison: University of Wisconsin Press, 2004).

10. I discuss this further in Adi Mahalel, "We Will Not Be Silent: I. L. Peretz's 'Bontshe the Silent' vs. 1950s McCarthyism in America and the Story of the Staging of *The World of Sholom Aleichem*," *Studies in American Jewish Literature* 34, no. 2 (2015): 204–30.

11. Nahum Sokolow, "Le-'Bontshe shvayg' yesh ra'ayon klali, aval yesh lo gavan mekomi," in *Ishim* (Tel Aviv: Stybl, 1935), 270.

12. Dan Miron, for example, sees Bontshe as a representation of the Jewish people and the story itself as "a bitter satire on Jewish passivity." *The Image of the Shtetl, and Other Studies of Modern Jewish Literary Imagination* (New York: Syracuse University Press, 2000), 340.

13. Yankev Dinezon, *Y. L. Peretz Tsum Yortsayt* [I. L. Peretz to the anniversary of his death] (Vilnius: Farlag fun Bes. Alef Kletskin, 1916), 19, quoted in Ayzik Rozentsvayg, *Der radikaler periyod fun Peretses shafn* (Kyiv: Melukhe-farlag fun di natsyonale minderhaytn, 1934), 75. Peretz was a Polish Jew, while *litvakes* refers to the characteristics and tendencies of Jews from the "north," meaning parts of Belarus and Lithuania.

14. Rozentsvayg, *Der radikaler periyod*, 75; and in G. Aronson and J. S. Hertz, eds., *Di geshikhte fun Bund* [The history of the Bund], vol. 1 (New York: Undzer tsayt farlag, 1960), 95.

15. The publication of "Bontshe" followed a similar course, also due to censorship in Russia. Shakhne Epshteyn, "Yitskhok Leybush Perets: Tsum finfuntsvanstikstn yortog nokh zayn toyt" [Isaac Leybush Peretz: Twenty-five years after his death], *Sovyetishe literatur* (October 1940): 108.

16. Peretz was invited to the meeting, which took place in 1898, by PPS agitators. And, as told by the person who invited him to the meeting, "since that Saturday evening the late author used to be a frequent guest at secret workers' gatherings. At one of such gathering, a year later, he was arrested." Leon Gottlieb, "Perets af a geheymer arbeyter ferzamlung" [Peretz at a secret workers' gathering], *Forverts*, April 9, 1915, p. 4.

17. Joshua D. Zimmerman, "Dickstein, Szymon," in *YIVO Encyclopedia of Jews in Eastern Europe*, 2010, http://www.yivoencyclopedia.org/article.aspx/Dickstein_Szymon. See also Epshteyn, "Yitskhok Leybush Perets," 108.

18. See An alter bakanter [Y. Pesakhzon], "In varshe erev 'bund,'" in *25 yor: Zamlbukh* (Warsaw: Di velt, 1922), 38 and 43–44.

19. "Zoln ale fabrikn in dem gantsn land, zoln zey gehern tsu ale arbeter, zoln zey zayn zeyergemeynshaftlikher eygentum." Szymon Dickstein, *Fun vos eyner lebt?* (Warsaw: Di velt, 1906), 29.

20. "With what means should the factories and the land be taken away and how to achieve it?" The writer answers: "That is your business, so you have to think for yourselves . . ." ("Mit vos far a mitlen zol men tsunemen di fabrikn un di erd un vi azoy es tsu dergreykhn? Dos iz shoyn ayer gesheft . . ."). Dickstein, *Fun vos eyner lebt?*, 34.

21. Terry Eagleton, *Sweet Violence: The Idea of the Tragic* (Oxford: Blackwell, 2009), 97.

22. Peled, *Class and Ethnicity*, 49.

23. Peled, 9; emphasis mine.

24. Ber Borochov, "The Jubilee of the Jewish Labor Movement (1916)," in *Class Struggle and the Jewish Nation: Selected Essays in Marxist Zionism*, ed. Mitchell Cohen (New Brunswick, NJ: Transaction Books, 1983), 107.

25. Both Leftist Socialists and Nationalist Socialists (Mussolini's party) were using the term *fascio* to describe themselves. Elizabeth Guerra and Janet Farrar, *Stewart Farrar: Writer on a Broomstick* (Arcata, CA: R. J. Stewart Books, 2008), 39–40.

26. John Osborne, *Gerhart Hauptmann and the Naturalist Drama* (Amsterdam: Harwood Academic Publishers, 1998), 136–37.

27. Joe Bray, *The Epistolary Novel: Representations of Consciousness* (London: Routledge, 2003), 2.

28. This sense of optimism goes against Rozentsvayg's interpretation, which sees this story as being full of pessimism and longing "for the good old days." *Der radikaler periyod*, 77–78.

29. Ruth Adler, "Peretz's Empathic Linkage to Woman," *Studies in American Jewish Literature* 3, no. 2 (Winter 1977–78): 50.

30. Miron views all of Peretz's creations as based on the poetics of sensibility, which is the main way Peretz diverged from Yalag's more emotionally restrained poetics. See Miron, "I. L. Peretz as the Poet of the Jewish Age of Sensibility: On the Century of His Death 1915–2015," in *The Trilingual Literature of Polish Jews from Different Perspectives: In Memory of I. L. Peretz*, ed. Alina Molisak and Shoshana Ronen, pp.1–21 (Newcastle upon Tyne, UK: Cambridge Scholars Publishing, 2017).

31. Miron, "Jewish Age of Sensibility," 16–17; and also Dan Miron, "The spiritual world of I. L. Peretz: Fourth chapter" [in Hebrew], *Haaretz*, May 11, 2015, http://www.haaretz.co.il/literature/study/.premium-1.2632136.

32. Letter to Helena Ringelheim, in *Briv un redes fun Y. L. Perets*, ed. Nachman Mayzel (New York: IKUF, 1944), 31.

33. Jewish law permits suicide only in three cases: to prevent idol worship, incest, or murder. One addition to these three categories was made by the famous medieval rabbi Ya'akov ben Me'ir Tam (Rabenu Tam). He argued in *Tosafot masekhet avoda zara* (p. 18) that in a case of expecting extreme suffering and torment, a person is obliged to take their own life in order to avoid the pain (he was writing at the time of the Crusades, when many Jews underwent extreme torture at the hands of the Crusaders).

34. The latter is used often in Yiddish and Hebrew literature. For instance, the Hebrew writer Agnon explains the insanity of his protagonist in genetic and private (failed love) terms in his story "Sipur pashut" (Simple story).

35. The title "Anger Is an Energy" is borrowed from a phrase in the song "Rise" by Public Image Ltd (1986), which was inspired by the anti-apartheid struggle in South Africa.

36. Paula E. Hyman, "Gender," *YIVO Encyclopedia of Jews in Eastern Europe*, August 9, 2010, http://www.yivoencyclopedia.org/article.aspx/Gender.

37. Peretz, "Eshet khaver," *Ha-tzfira* [Hazefirah], no. 226 (December 16, 1890): 2; also in *Kitvey Y. L. Perets*, 201–3.

38. In Hebrew it can be read also as "Eshet Khever" (The wife of Heber), alluding to the biblical heroine Yael, who became associated with heroism for her role in the wars of the ancient Israelites. Miron sees here Peretz's ironic play with the Mishnaic and Talmudic meaning of חבר (khaver) as study partner and one who keeps the laws of purity and impurity (Miron, "Spiritual world").

39. The mother, Serl, represents the old Jewish female reader also because of her habit of reading sacred literature communally (she reads to her daughter) and her belief in it. Iris Parush, *Reading Jewish Women*, trans. Saadya Sternberg (Waltham, MA: Brandeis University Press, 2004), 141–42.

40. Yitshok Niborski, "Yunge geshtaltn bay Y.L. Perets un Dovid Pinski" [Young characters by I. L. Peretz and David Pinski; in Yiddish], *Yugntruf* no. 7 (December 1966): 9.

41. Yehuda Friedlander, "Halachic issues as satirical elements in nineteenth-century Hebrew literature" [in Hebrew], in *Jewish Humor*, ed. Avner Ziv (Tel Aviv: Papyrus, 1986), 136–39.

42. Naftali Herz-Tucker correctly points out to the similarity between the character of Zaynvel in this story and another fictional Zaynvel that Peretz created in his 1892 Hebrew story "The Mute" (discussed in chapter 3). Both Zaynvels are physically ugly, and both marry the women protagonists against the latter's will. The Zaynvel in "The Mute," though, is not as old as the Zaynvel in "Married," and he is also not as nearly as rich. Herz-Tucker, "Matchmaking, mating, and love in the stories of I. L. Peretz" [in Hebrew], *Yeda-Am* 65–66 (2005): 81.

43. Leonard Prager, "Tnuat ha-avoda ha-yehudit ve-sifrut yidish biyemey ha-'Yontef Bletlekh' shel Peretz ve-Pinski" [The Jewish labor movement and Yiddish literature at the time of the *Holiday Pages* of Peretz and Pinski; in Hebrew], in *Kovets Kenes Ha-Yesod* (Haifa: Haifa University, 1991), 46.

44. Rozentsvayg, *Der radikaler periyod*, 75.

45. In the much-abridged Hebrew version of the story (*Betula Niset*), the young man (the pharmacist apprentice with the weak heart) doesn't sing secular Yiddish songs instead of traditional Hebrew hymns but just "a secular song" (Peretz, *Kitvey Y. L. Perets*, 152–59).

46. For example, it has been estimated that one-third of the membership of the Bundist circles consisted of women and that women accounted for close to 20 percent of the organization's leadership (Hyman, "Gender").

47. H. D. Nomberg, *Dos bukh felitonen* [The book of feuilletons; in Yiddish] (Warsaw: Rekord, 1924), 190–94. See also the fourth chapter in this book.

48. I. L. Peretz, "In Eyrope un bay undz Untern Oyvn" [In Europe and in our little corner], *Yontef bletlekh* 8: *Dos khanike likhtl* (1894); and *Ale verk*, 8:79–88. See also his letter to the Hebrew writer Yaakov Tsuzmer, in *Briv un redes fun Y. L. Perets* (1944), 192.

49. Benjamin, "The Author as Producer," trans. John Heckman, *New Left Review* I/62 (July/August 1970).

50. Terry Eagleton, *Marxism and Literary Criticism* (London: Routledge, 1989), 57–58.

51. David E. Fishman, *The Rise of Modern Yiddish Culture Pittsburgh* (Pittsburgh: University of Pittsburgh Press, 2005), 21–25.

52. Shmuel Niger, *I. L. Peretz* (Buenos Aires: Yiddish Cultural Congress, 1952), 229.

53. Mordkhe Spektor (1858–1925), a Yiddish writer and publisher, was also involved in putting out the *Bletlekh* in its early stages. He very soon (after three volumes) disassociated himself from the *Bletlekh* because it indeed became too radical for his taste. Pinski, "Dray yor mit Y. L. Perets," 21.

54. Niger, *Peretz*, 323.

55. Bitter herbs (*morer*) are eaten at the Passover feast as a reminder of Jewish suffering in ancient Egypt.

56. The original idiom that Peretz uses is the Hebrew "brakha le-batala," meaning literally "an unnecessary blessing."

57. An important Bundist activist called these publications "the first swallows of legal Yiddish socialist literature in Lithuania and Poland." A. Litvak, *Literatur un kamf: Literarishe eseyn* [Literature and struggle: Literary essays; in Yiddish] (New York: Veker, 1933), 122.

58. Dovid Pinski, "Geshikhte fun di *Yontef-bletlekh*" [History of the "Holiday pages"], *Di tsukunft* (May 1945): 322.

59. Such as Ashmyany, Smorgon, and Lida. All three are towns in Belorussia that had significant Jewish populations at the time. In Ashmyny there was a famous yeshiva; the Yiddish poet Avrom Sutzkever came from Smorgon.

60. Kalmen Marmor, *Mayn lebns geshikhte* [My life's story; in Yiddish], vol. 1 (New York: IKUF, 1959), 296–97. Marmor was born in Lithuania, immigrated to the United States in 1906, and was involved in socialist-Zionist circles. On his way to the US, he spent time in London, where he shared a flat with the Hebrew writer Y.H. Brenner. In the US he became an active member of the American Communist Party and wrote for various Yiddish papers (most notably for the communist *Morgn frayhayt*). He achieved prominence as a cultural historian.

61. Pinski, "Geshikhte fun di *Yontef-bletlekh*," *Di tsukunft* (June 1945), 385.
62. Pinski, 386.
63. Shmul Gozhansky, "A briv tsu agitatorn," in *Di yidishe sotsyalistishe bavegung biz der grindung fun "Bund,"* ed. Elye Tsherikover et al., pp. 626–48, vol. 3 of *Historishe shriftn* (Vilnius: YIVO, 1939); Arkadi Kremer, *Ob agitatsii* (Geneva, 1897); English translation: Arkadi Kremer and Julius Martov, *On Agitation (1896)*, in *Marxism in Russia: Key Documents 1879–1906*, ed. Neil Harding, trans. Richard Taylor, pp. 192–205 (Cambridge: Cambridge University Press, 1983); and Peled, *Class and Ethnicity*, 34–39.
64. Roni Gechtman, "Gozhansky, Shmul," *YIVO Encyclopedia of Jews in Eastern Europe*, August 10, 2010, http://www.yivoencyclopedia.org/article.aspx/Gozhansky_Shmul. See also Peled, *Class and Ethnicity*, 38–39. Arkadi Kremer tried to master Yiddish "as is spoken by the people," but he thought that meant mixing his speech with many curse words. A. Litvak, *Vos geven* [What was; in Yiddish] (Poyln: Vilner farlag fun B. Kletskin, 1925), 98.
65. David E. Fishman, "The Bund and Modern Yiddish Culture," in *The Emergence of Modern Jewish Politics: Bundism and Zionism in Eastern Europe*, ed. Zvi Gitelman (Pittsburgh: University of Pittsburg Press, 2003), 110.
66. Lyesin became the editor of *Tsukunft*, a pioneering Yiddish socialist journal that was published in New York. Tony Michels, *A Fire in Their Hearts: Yiddish Socialists in New York* (Cambridge, MA: Harvard University Press, 2005), 151–52.
67. A. Liessin, *Zikhroynes un bilder* [Memories and sketches; in Yiddish] (New York: Tsiko, 1954), 117–19.
68. Y. Sh. Hertz, ed., *Doyres bundistn* [Generations of Bundists], vol. 1 [in Yiddish] (New York: Farlag Unser Tsayt, 1956), 225–27.
69. Hertz, *Doyres bundistn*, 258–62; and Jonathan Frankel, *Crisis, Revolution, and Russian Jews* (Cambridge: Cambridge University Press, 2009), 173.
70. Joshua D. Zimmerman, "Litvak, A." *YIVO Encyclopedia of Jews in Eastern Europe*, August 26, 2010, http://www.yivoencyclopedia.org/article.aspx/Litvak_A.
71. Litvak, *Vos geven*, 97–98.
72. Litvak, 97–98.
73. Litvak, 80. Litvak noted what a powerful agitation tool the *Bletlekh* were for the jargon committees and commented on their deep admiration for Peretz and Pinski. Their names "were holy"; Peretz's address in Warsaw was their "spiritual center"; distributing the *Bletlekh* was their joy. "And this wasn't just in Vilnius," he writes (83–84).
74. Litvak, 79.
75. Litvak, 79. According to Pinski, "The Rose" was one of the stories Peretz did not write especially for the *Bletlekh* but awhile beforehand (Pinski, "Dray yor mit Y. L. Perets," 16).
76. Litvak, 100–101.
77. Peretz, *Briv un redes* (1929), 90–91.

78. Rozentsvayg, *Radikaler peryod*, 184.

79. Peretz was also known to be a very domineering editor, which meant that even the texts that were signed by other writers, including by such prominent writers such as Morris Vintshevsky and the young S. Ansky, carried a heavy Peretz touch. On Ansky's first encounter with Peretz and on his sole publication in the *Bletlekh*, see S. An-sky, *Gezamlte shriftn* [Collected works; in Yiddish], vol. 10 (Vilnius: Ferlag Ansky, 1922), 152–54.

80. Miron, *A Traveler Disguised: The Rise of Modern Yiddish Fiction in the Nineteenth Century* (Syracuse, NY: Syracuse University Press, 1996). This was despite the fact that according to some accounts, Peretz used about seventeen different pen names in his career (Miron, 243n42). He used some of these pen names in his Hebrew writing as well.

81. He also did name both the rising socialist party and the pacifist movement in the political feuilleton "Europe with its bow and arrow" in the second *Bletl*.

82. In other articles and especially in later periods, he would emphasize the biblical prophets as a basis for a moral-driven society.

83. The *Collected works* version ends a line before the text quoted here and goes on for another paragraph. See *Ale verk*, 8:102 (1947). The line was also omitted in earlier collected works, like the 1920 edition by the Idish publishing company. Probably it was omitted by Peretz himself.

84. Avrom Reyzn, *Epizodn fun mayn lebn: Literarishe erinerungen* [Episodes from my life: Literary memories; in Yiddish], vol. 1 (Vilnius: Vilner Farlag fun B. Kletskin, 1929), 246–47.

85. Reyzn, *Epizodn*, 248–49.

86. Litvak, *Vos geven*, 90.

87. "For England, as a commercial country, it's very useful that wars should cease; but it's only useful for others to disarm themselves, while it could in the meanwhile grab with its sword more and more countries in Asia, Africa, and Australia. It wants also to strengthen its hold in Egypt, Afghanistan, and other countries. England had not yet dressed everybody with its wool from Manchester and had not granted everybody its pocket knives from Birmingham" ("Europe with a bow and arrow," 1894). Although Peretz's former patron, Jan Bloch, was becoming one of the leading pacifists in Europe, Peretz himself went further to the left than Bloch's liberal pacifism.

88. Peretz, "Vos zol ikh veln?" [What should I want?], *Hoyshayne* [Osier branch], 1894, in *Ale verk*, 8:74–75.

89. Peretz, "Vos zol ikh veln?" in *Ale verk*, 8:76.

90. Litvak, *Vos geven*, 82.

91. Pinski writes that it was "a monthly journal almost without coworkers. Peretz himself could fill out the thin *Bletlekh*. He could take from his already written material, short stories and poems, which he wrote a long time ago, and add material he wrote overnight" ("Geshikhte" [May 1945]," 324).

92. Peretz, "Vos viln mir?," in *Literatur un leben: A zaml-bukh far literatur un gezelshaft*, ed. Peretz (Warsaw: Funk, 1894).

93. Ruth Wisse, *I. L. Peretz and the Making of Modern Jewish Culture* (Seattle: University of Washington Press, 1991), 42.

94. As Wisse argued in regard to Peretz's "ambivalence about dogmatic social theory and the world order that it championed" (*Modern Jewish Culture*, 42).

95. Peled, *Class and Ethnicity*, 121.

96. Benjamin, "The Author as Producer," 4.

97. Benjamin writes that, contrary to the bourgeois writer of popular stories, the progressive writer makes a choice "determined on the basis of the class struggle when he places himself on the side of the proletariat" ("The Author as Producer," 1–2).

98. Emanuel S. Goldsmith, "A Modern Judaism for the Yiddish World," in *The Enduring Legacy of Yitzchok Leybush Peretz: Proceedings of a Literary and Cultural Symposium*, ed. Benny Kraut, pp. 21–29 (New York: CUNY Center for Jewish Studies, 2005).

Chapter 3

1. Peretz's personal secretary at the time, Meir Jacob Fried (1871–1940), wrote in his memoirs that, being a Zionist loyal to the Hebrew language, it was hard for him to contribute to Peretz's Yiddish almanac *Literatur un lebn* (1894). "But at the same time," he wrote, "in the Hebrew collection *The Arrow* I contributed quite a few literary works, occupying almost a half of the entire booklet." Meir Yaakov Fried, *Yamim ve-shanim: Zikhronot ve-tziyurim mi-tekufah shel hamishim shanah* [Days and years: Memoirs and vignettes from a fifty-year period; in Hebrew] (Tel Aviv: Dvir, 1939), 2:74. Officially, Fried is credited in *The Arrow* only as the translator of a short story by Alexander Kielland, "A Peat Moor." In *Literatur un lebn* he contributed a captivating Yiddish story told from the point of view of a dog ("Murza"), and to the *Yontef bletlekh* he contributed "Liza," told from a point of view of a cow (*Der tones*, 1894).

2. Shmuel Binyamin Shvartsberg lived in Warsaw around the same time as Peretz did. In 1897 he migrated to the United States, where he continued to work as a publisher, a bookseller in the Lower East Side, and a bibliographer of several Hebrew writers. Jacob Kabakoff, *Shoharim V'ne'emanim* [in Hebrew] (Jerusalem: Rubin Mass, 1978), 138–147.

3. Pinski, "Dray yor mit Y. L. Perets," *Di Goldene Keyt* 8 (1951): 18.

4. Anonymous, "Nitabin Le-egel Ve-notnim" [in Hebrew], *Ha-melitz* 156 (1894). The writer used the pejorative term "jargon" for Yiddish. See also a two-part review article in the same year by Avraham Zinger, in *Ha-melitz* 179.

5. I. L. Peretz, "Denial" [in Hebrew], *Ha-melitz* 169 (1894).

6. A. Litvak, *Vos geven* (Poyln: Vilner farlag fun B. Kletskin, 1925), 85.

7. Miron, *From Continuity to Contiguity: Toward A New Jewish Literary Thinking* (Stanford, CA: Stanford University Press, 2010), 298–302. Miron points out that during the last decade of Peretz's life (1905-15), while creating more content in Yiddish, "Hebrew and Hebrew writing progressively became a burden to the master . . . most of the Hebrew versions of his stories published during those years were actually based on translations done by others (such as the minor Hebrew novelist Y. Shaf) and slightly edited by the author" (298).

8. A. Litvak, "Di 'zhargonishe komitetn'" [The Yiddish committees], in *Royter pinkes* [in Yiddish] (Warsaw: Kultur lige, 1921), 5–30, 14.

9. Litvak described the later Yiddish translations by Jewish anarchist Avraham Frumkin that appeared in London in the first decade of the twentieth century as "wooden" (*Vos geven*, 85).

10. In Yiddish, one can already detect proto-socialist tendencies in S. Y. Abramovitsh's drama *Di takse* (The tax; 1869). In it, Abramovitsh emphasized the common denominator of the middle class: the readiness of different representatives to cooperate as long as it was mutually profitable and the general desire to exploit the poor and powerless. Dan Miron, "Abramovitsh, Sholem Yankev," *YIVO Encyclopedia of Jews in Eastern Europe*, 2010, http://www.yivoencyclopedia.org/article.aspx/Abramovitsh_Sholem_Yankev.

11. Yehudah Levi Levin, "Kishron Ha-ma'ase" [The ability to act], in *Ketavim nivharim [me-et] Y. H. L. L.* [Yehudah Levi Levin selected writings; in Hebrew], vol. 2 (Warsaw: Tushiya, 1911), 7. .

12. Levin, "Kishron Ha-ma'ase," 12.

13. Levin, 18.

14. "ידי צוברת – אך היא לא עמלה . . . ופועלים לרבבות למעני יגעו\ ושכרם נתתי די צרך ולבד רק לי כל אלה נשארו" עבודה\ רק די תת כחם לה לבלי יגועו . . . (Levin, 39).

15. See also Einat Baram-Eshel, "Haskala, socialism, and nationalism in the poetry of Yahalal" [in Hebrew], in *Poetics and ideology in modern Hebrew literature: For Menachem Brinker*, ed. Irish Parush, Hamutal Tsamir, and Hanna Soker-Schwager, pp. 254–76 (Jerusalem: Karmel, 2011).

16. Dan Miron, *Bodedim bemoadam* [Singular in their time; in Hebrew] (Tel Aviv: Am Oved, 1987), 279–99. On Lieberman and Vintshevski, see Jonathan Frankel, *Prophecy and Politics: Socialism, Nationalism, and the Russian Jews, 1862-1917* (Cambridge: Cambridge University Press, 1981), 28–48.

17. Frankel, *Prophecy and Politics*, 43–44; and David E. Fishman, *The Rise of Modern Yiddish Culture* (Pittsburgh: University of Pittsburgh Press, 2005), 23.

18. Zalman Reyzen, *Leksikon fun der yidisher literatur, prese un filologye* [Lexicon of the Yiddish literature, press, and philology; in Yiddish] (Vilnius: B. Kletskin, 1926), 977–78. For a lengthy discussion regarding *Asefat khakhamin* by Vintshevski himself, see Moris Vintshevski, *Erinerungen* [Memories; in Yiddish] (Moscow: Shul un bukh, 1926), 32–84, 97–99, 103–6. For a lengthy discussion of early socialist writing in Hebrew, see Yosef Klausner, *Historiiah shel ha-sifrut ha-'ivrit*

ha-hadashah [History of modern Hebrew literature; in Hebrew], vol. 6 (Jerusalem: Hebrew University Magnes Press, 1950), 126–350.

19. A. Litvak, "B. Gorin: A bisl erinerungen" [B. Gorin: A few memories; in Yiddish], in Gorin, *Gezamelte shriften* (New York: Elizabeth Gorin, 1927), 1:18. Gorin also published a short Yiddish story in the first volume of the *Yontef bletlekh*.

20. Isaac Ben-Mordecai, "Mavo" [Introduction; in Hebrew], in *Nitsane ha-Realizm ha-Siporet ha-'Ivrit* [The buds of realism in Hebrew fiction], vol. 2, ed. Yosef Even and Yitshak Ben-Mordecai (Jerusalem: Mossad Bialik, 1993), 37–42.

21. I. L. Peretz, "Ha-machshavah ve-ha-kinor (hagadah 'aravit)," in *Ha-ḥetz: Yalkut sifruti*, ed. Peretz (Warsaw: Shvartzberg, 1894).

22. Peretz, "Ha-machshavah ve-ha-kinor," 19. The passage in Isaiah 30: 26 reads "the light of the moon shall be as the light of the sun, and the light of the sun shall be sevenfold, as the light of the seven days." In rabbinic literature this passage is used to prove the claim that the light of the first day of creation was different than the light of the fourth day. Reb Nachman of Bratslav, whose writings influenced Peretz, links the stories of the Torah to the spiritual light of the first day. That light was hidden by God in the stories of the Torah. Howard Schwartz, *Reimagining the Bible: The Storytelling of the Rabbis* (New York: Oxford University Press, 1998), 16–17.

23. In the Song of Songs 5:7, the female protagonist goes out looking for her beloved and finds herself wandering in Jerusalem: "The guards found me in the city, hit me and wounded me; stripped me of my veil, the city guards."

24. Aḥad Ha'am, "Emet me-Erets Yisra'el" [Truth from the Land of Israel; in Hebrew], *Ha-Melits* (Sivan 1891).

25. Ze'ev Goldberg, "On Y.-L. Perets's relationship to Zionism" [in Hebrew], *Khulyot* 7 (2002): 68–71. But it was a one-sided relationship, for Aḥad Ha'am never seriously debated with or referred to Peretz.

26. Here Peretz is using the well-known literary motif of the "dance of the dead." He will later put this motif at the center of his 1908 symbolist play *At Night in the Old Marketplace*.

27. Yosef Klausner, "Our literature" [in Hebrew], *Hashiloach* 7: 543.

28. Klausner continues to explain Peretz's affection toward the poor by inaccurately attributing a background of poverty to his biography ("Our literature," 543). Klausner even attributes a kind of Hebrew quality to Peretz's Yiddish work, rendering even Peretz's Yiddish as inaccessible to the masses—for in Peretz's Yiddish "[t]here are too many idioms and Hebrew expressions, too many descriptions of Hebrew teachers and rabbinic authorities; they are filled with too many allusions to what is written in our ancient literature" (543).

29. Klausner, "Our literature," 540–47.

30. As late as 1952, while admitting that when "there was in Warsaw once a debate about Zionism and Socialism—and Peretz, who participated in the

debate, represented the Bundist-Socialist position," Klausner still felt a need to emphasize that "Peretz was a Zionist." "Perets haya tsiyoni" [Peretz was a Zionist], *Maariv*, May 16, 1952, p. 4).

31. Rozentsvayg, *Der radikaler peryod fun Peretses shafn* (Kyiv: Melukhe-farlag fun di natsyonale minderhaytn, 1934), 59.

32. Hamutal Bar-Yosef, *Decadent trends in Hebrew literature: Bialik, Berdychevski, Brener* [in Hebrew] (Jerusalem: Mosad Bialik, 1997), 19.

33. Bar-Yosef, *Decadent trends*, 19.

34. I. L. Peretz, "Huledet Moshe," in Peretz, ed., *Ha-chetz: Yalkut sifruti* (Warsaw: Shvartzberg, 1894).

35. The name of the father of the biblical prophet Jonah.

36. See also Ela Bauer, *Between Poles and Jews: The Development of Nahum Sokolow's Political Thought* (Jerusalem: Hebrew University Magnes Press, 2005), 131. For Bauer, Sokolow in this article is mostly repeating his 1870s and 1880s opinions regarding nationalism. Only in 1897, after attending the first Zionist congress in Basel, did Sokolow become an ardent Zionist.

37. Amittai, "Yotsrei tohu" [The creators of chaos], in Peretz, *Ha-chetz: Yalkut sifruti*. In this article, Sokolow expresses views similar to those of Ernest Renan (1823–92) regarding nationalism and Jewish identity. Renan wrote that according to the race-based nationalism that German peoples adhere to, the right of German peoples to a certain piece of land overcomes the right of the inhabitants of this land to determine their fate. Shlomo Sand and Ernest Renan, *On the Nation and the "Jewish People"* (London: Verso, 2010), 54.

38. Amittai, "Yotsrei tohu."

39. Peretz was never, as Michael Waltzer claims, "both a Zionist and a socialist." Waltzer, "The Strangeness of Jewish Leftism," in *Jews and Leftist Politics: Judaism, Israel, Antisemitism, and Gender*, ed. Jack Jacobs (Cambridge: Cambridge University Press, 2017), 33.

40. Marmor, *Mayn lebns geshikhte* (New York: IKUF, 1959), 1:317–18.

41. Ben-Avigdor, "Misefer zikhronotay," *Hatsefira*, April 19, 1917, p. 6.

42. *Ale verk*, 8:89, quoted in Goldberg, "Perets's Relationship to Zionism," 60–61.

43. Y. L. Perets, "Eyns dos andere opgenart" [One fools the other], *Yontef bletlekh* 11: *Kol khamiro* (April 1895), reprinted in Rozentsvayg, *Radikaler peryod*, 165.

44. Quoted in Rozentsvayg, 167. "*Kamarinsky* dance" is a traditional Russian folk dance.

45. Peretz, *Kitvey Y. L. Perets*, 9:482.

46. Rozentsvayg, *Radikaler israe*, 169.

47. Perctz, "Even ve-even, eyfa ve-eyfa," *Hatsefira* 237 (November 1890): 2.

48. Goldberg, "Perets's Relationship to Zionism," 57–58.

49. Peretz, *Ha-ilemet, Manginat ha-zman* [The mute, The melody of is age] (Warsaw: Ben-Avigdor, 1892).

50. Shmuel Niger, *I. L. Peretz* (Buenos Aires: Yiddish Cultural Congress, 1952), 294; published in Ben-Avigdor's penny-library series.

51. Peretz, *Ha-ilemet, Manginat ha-zman*, 28–29.

52. Peretz, 30.

53. Peretz, 30–31.

54. Imber, *N. H. Imber's Collected Poetry*, ed. Dov Sadan (1950). See Ruth Carton-Blum's anthology of proto-Zionist Hebrew poetry: *Ha-Shirah ha-ivrit bi-Tekufat Hibbat Ziyyon* [Hebrew poetry in the *Hibbat Zion* period] (Jerusalem, 1969).

55. Litvak, *Vos geven*, 81.

56. Michael Stanislawski, "Ḥibat Tsiyon," *YIVO Encyclopedia of Jews in Eastern Europe*, 2010, http://www.yivoencyclopedia.org/article.aspx/Hibat_Tsiyon.

57. The same year, Peretz wrote, "With one word everything was done, so the rabbis would say: 'Bom!' so the Choveve Tsiyon would have 'Bim-Bom'! And the sheep would shear themselves without bleating." "Lets fun redaktsye," *Literatur un lebn*, ed. Peretz (Warsaw: Funk, 1894), 195–96; and *Ale verk*, 7:93.

58. See also Goldberg, "Perets's Relationship to Zionism," 58–65.

59. "Der vikuekh," *Ale verk*, 8:127–32.

60. For example, the Hebrew phrase "to throw the fortunes of the Jewish people down the drain" ("Lehorid mamon israel letimyon") in relation to the actions of Choveve Tsiyon is repeated several times in a review article of the pro-Zionist Hebrew almanac *Ha-pardes*, edited by Aḥad Ha'am (Peretz, "Book review: *Ha-pardes*" [in Hebrew], *Ha-cetz*, 41–49).

61. Peretz, *Ale verk*, 8:84–85. Originally published in the *Yontef bletlekh* Hanukah volume, *Dos khaneke-likhtl* (1894).

62. Peretz, "Book review: *Ha-pardes*," 45, quoted in Goldberg, "Perets's Relationship to Zionism," 69.

63. Peretz, *Kitvey*, 10:252, quoted in Dan Miron, "Literature as a Vehicle for National Renaissance: The Model of Peretz versus That of Bialik," in *The Enduring Legacy of Yitzchok Leybush Peretz: A Literary and Cultural Symposium*, ed. Benny Kraut (New York: CUNY Center for Jewish Studies, 2005), 34.

64. For example, Miron, "Literature," 46–47.

65. Miron, 34.

66. Aḥad Ha'am, "Divrei shalom" [Greetings], in *Kol kitvei Aḥad-Ha'am* [The collected works of Aḥad Ha'am] (Tel Aviv: 1947), 59–60, which appeared in *Ha-Melitz* 34, no. 228–29 (1894).

67. *Literature and life*, 1894, 197–200; and *Ale verk*, 7:94–96. See also Goldberg, "Perets's Relationship to Zionism," 62–64.

68. Peretz's personal secretary, Meir Jacob Fried, claimed that although he and Peretz were close, he was unable able to visit Peretz for many years because Peretz disliked Fried's Zionist activities (*Yamim ve-shanim*, 2:80). However, Peretz and the Zionist Hebrew poet Bialik were good friends (Miron, "Literature," 30–48).

69. Peretz, "In eyrope un bay undz hintern oyvn," in *Ale verk*, 8:82–84.

70. Peretz, 83.

71. Peretz, 84.

72. David Frishman authored two mock versions of the *Yontef bletlekh* under the pseudonym Avrom Goldberg; see Goldberg, *A floy fun tishe-be'ov, Lokshen* (Warsaw: Gebrider Shuldberg, 1894).

73. See Yalag's article "Bine le-to'ey ruakh," in Yehuda Friedlander, "The struggle of Y. L. Gordon against Lithuanian rabbis" [in Hebrew], in *Studies in East European Jewish history and culture in honor of Professor Shmuel Werses*, ed. David Assaf et al., pp. 285–314 (Jerusalem: Hebrew University Magnes Press, 2002).

74. Peretz, "Ma'ase be-gimel Kabtsanim" [A tale of three beggars], *Ha-tsofe* 47 (March 1903). Peretz borrows the model from Rabbi Nachman's story "A tale of seven beggars." In this satire, Peretz was trying to please the publisher of *Ha-tsofe* (in which Peretz had a column), Eliezer Eliahu Friedman, who had a financial dispute with Ben-Avigdor. A. R. Malakhi, "Y. L. Perets in *Ha-tsofe*," *YIVO-bleter* 36 (1952): 75. In the quotation in the title of this section, "The Audacity to Demand Realism," Peretz was complaining that on top of the hardship that comes from writing in a nonspoken language such as Hebrew, which is "hard labor with the Bible and ten dictionaries in hand," and for meager pay, they also raised aesthetic demands (*Literature and life*, 184; and *Ale verk*, 7:84).

75. Shachar Pinsker, *Literary Passports: The Making of Modernist Hebrew Fiction in Europe* (Stanford, CA: Stanford University Press, 2010), 49–50.

76. There are many exceptions, of course, like Ben-Avigdor's historical Hebrew novel *Four hundred years ago*, or *A brother and a sister at a time of need* (1892), and earlier works by Hebrew writers that were set in the present time.

77. More examples of the numerous direct translations (creating many calques) from Yiddish in the Hebrew prose of the New Wave are in Menuha Gilboa, *The Hebrew New Wave and outside of it* [in Hebrew] (Tel Aviv: Tel Aviv University, 1991), 20–21, 29n41. On the strong influence of Yiddish on spoken modern Hebrew, see Ghil'ad Zuckermann, *Israelit safa yafa* [Israeli a fine language; in Hebrew] (Tel Aviv: Am Oved, 2008).

78. Hayim Nahman Bialik, "Yotser ha-nusah" [Creator of the formula], in *Kol kitve H. N. Bialik* [Collected works of H. N. Bialik] (Tel Aviv, 1938), 240–241.

79. Dan Miron, "Abramovitsh, Sholem Yankev," *YIVO Encyclopedia of Jews in Eastern Europe*, August 19, 2010, http://www.yivoencyclopedia.org/article.asp x/Abramovitsh_Sholem_Yankev .

80. Ken Frieden, "'Nusah Mendele' be-mabat bikorti" [A critical perspective on "Mendele's Nusah"], *Dappim le-mehkar be-sifrut* [Research on literature, Haifa] 14–15 (2006): 89–103. In the case of his novel *Fishke der krumer* (Frieden's focus), Abramovitsh's Hebrew reworking from Yiddish was influenced by Bialik's own Hebrew translation of his work, which tended to heighten the folksy Yiddish original.

81. Sholem Yankev Abramovitsh, "Shem ve-Yefet ba-'agala," in *Kaveret: Kovetz Sifruti*, pp. 45–59 (Odessa: Aba Dukhno, 1890).

82. Gilboa, *New Wave*; Isaac Ben-Mordecai, "Mavo," 2:45–48.

83. Quoted in Ben-Mordecai, 2:202–6; and Dan Miron, "Tarbut Ivrit Hadasha Be-varsha" [Modern Hebrew culture in Warsaw; in Hebrew], in *Zman Yehudi Hadash* [New Jewish times: Jewish culture in a secular age—An encyclopedic view] (Jerusalem: Keter, 2007), 3:347–48.

84. Ken Frieden, "Psychological Depth in I. L. Peretz' *Familiar Scenes*," *Jewish Book Annual* 47 (1989–90): 145.

85. See Leon Peretz, *Bekante bilder* [Familiar scenes] (Warsaw: Yitshak Funk, 1890), and *Ale verk*, 2:18–53.

86. Frieden, "Psychological Depth," 149.

87. Ben-Avigdor, "Misefer zikhronotay," *Hatsefira*, May 3, 1917, p. 7.

88. Yankev Dinezon, introduction to Peretz, *Bekante bilder*.

89. The first actual attempt at creating a highbrow Yiddish literature was made by Sholem Aleichem in 1888–89 with his almanac *Di yudishe folks-bibliotek*. See Sholem Aleichem, "A briv tsu a gutn fraynd," in *Di yudishe folks-bibliotek*, 2:307–8.

90. Dinezon, introduction to *Bekante bilder*.

91. Fried commended Ben-Avigdor's successful marketing skills, commenting on how the pocketbook format of the *Sifre-agora* was issued with an external splendor that satisfies the reader "and stimulates the urge, the urge for consumption" (*Yamim ve-shanim*, 2:152).

92. Litvak, "B. Gorin," 18. More on Ben-Avigdor's early-twentieth-century Hebrew publishing endeavors, including founding the important publishing house Tushiya and the Bibliyoteka series (which were the first to publish Peretz's Hebrew collected works, starting in 1899) is in Zeev Gris, "Avraham Leyb Shalkovitz ('Ben Avigdor') and the revolution in the world of Hebrew books at the beginning of the twentieth century" [in Hebrew], in *Yosef Daat: Research in modern Jewish history*, ed. Yosi Goldshteyn, pp. 305–28 (Beersheba: Ben-Gurion University).

93. Ben-Avigdor was influenced by the Russian literary critics of the 1860s, notably Pisarev (1840–68), who called for a socially useful literature that reflects life as it really is, even in its lowest and most disgusting manifestations (Ben-Mordecai, "Mavo," in *Nitsane ha-Realizm*, vol. 1 [1972], 13–17). He was also influenced by Emil Zola's naturalism.

94. In a letter from August 1892, Peretz wrote to Dinezon that he promised to write to Ben-Avigdor but suffers from writing block. The letter is undated (Peretz, *Briv un redes* [1929], 61–64), but according to its content it was written on April 8, 1892 (the day his story "Ir hametim" was published).

95. Meaning a slow process of Jewish immigration in order to "prepare the hearts" for a Jewish national revival in the Land of Israel. Later, Ben-Avigdor would voice strong opposition to Aḥad Ha'am's ideas. For an elaborate discussion of the Bnei Moshe movement and of Aḥad Ha'am's pivotal role in it, see the second

chapter in Steven J. Zipperstein, *Elusive Prophet: Ahad Ha'am and the Origins of Zionism* (Berkeley: University of California Press, 1993).

96. Only years later, a similar criticism would be expressed by Y. H. Brenner, the Hebrew Zionist writer, who acted in the spirit of Peretz's advice and wrote about the actual Land of Israel from his own experience living there. New Wave literature tended to focus more on the "economic dramas" of Jews living in Eastern Europe and less on the fulfillment of Zionism per se, but that does not indicate that it was not Zionist.

97. *Ale verk*, 7:96.

98. Peretz, *Ver es vil—shtarbt nisht af kholi-ra* (Warsaw: Varshaver hilf-komitet, 1892), 17. In another segment, he calls the Persians "wild savages" who "transport dead people's bodies with merchandise and food in one cart"(35).

99. Robert J. C. Young, *Postcolonialism: A Very Short Introduction* (Oxford: Oxford University Press, 2003), 2.

100. See Daniel Boyarin's application of Homi Bhabha's concept of "colonial mimicry" to the case of Herzl, in *Unheroic Conduct: The Rise of Heterosexuality and the Invention of the Jewish Man* (Berkeley: University of California Press, 1997), especially chapter 7.

101. Ahad Ha'am famously wrote in 1891 from Palestine, "We are used to believing outside of the Land of Israel that this land is now almost entirely empty, an unsown desert, and anybody who wishes to purchase its land will come and purchase as much as his heart desires, but truly it is not so. It is hard to find in all of the land unsown seed fields" ("Emet me-Erets Yisra'el," 1; and *Kol kitvey Ahad-Ha'am*, 23).

102. Peretz, *Ale verk*, 8:13–14.

103. Peretz, *Literature and life*, 178–79; *Ale verk*, 7:80–81.

104. This interest was part of a general trend as the positivist movement in Polish society was gradually succeeded by Młoda Polska (Young Poland) starting from the 1890s and lasting for almost thirty years. It was a modernist movement, influenced by the likes of Friedrich Nietzsche and Arthur Schopenhauer, that embraced impressionism, symbolism, decadence, and neoromanticism. Michael J. Mikoś, ed. and trans., *Polish Literature from 1864 to 1918: Realism and Young Poland: An Anthology* (Bloomington, IN: Slavica Publishers, 2006).

105. Peretz, "Ha-sifrut Ve-hayim," in *Ha-chetz*, 15–17, quoted in Bar-Yosef, *Decadent trends*, 20.

106. Karl Beckson and Arthur Ganz, *Literary Terms: A Dictionary*, 3rd ed. (New York: Noonday Press, 1989), 56.

107. Notably, Bialik's poem "Rechov Ha-yehudim" (The Jewish street; 1894), which was deeply related to Ben-Avigdor's story "Leah, the Fish-Monger."

108. Jean-Paul Sartre, "Sartre: The Novel and Reality, from *Speech at a Conference of European Writers*," in *Marxism and Art: Essays Classic and Contemporary*, ed. Maynard Solomon (New York: Knopf, 1973), 256. Regarding the fictional character "even" of socialist realism, Sartre said, "we must not forget

that socialist novels are still novels, that is to say creation. . . . Every writer lies in order to tell the truth" (255).

109. Bar-Yosef, *Decadent trends*, 18–22. Bar-Yosef also detects pioneering decadent trends in Peretz's collection of Hebrew poetry *The Harp* (1894).

110. Bar-Yosef, 20–21.

111. Peretz, "Mikhtavim Al Odot Ha-sifrut," in *Ha-chetz*, 18.

112. Niger, *I. L. Peretz*, 129–31.

113. Ruth Adler, "Peretz's Empathic Linkage to Woman," *Studies in American Jewish Literature* 3, no. 2 (Winter 1977–78): 52.

114. Ben-Mordecai, "Mavo," 2:34.

115. Marc Caplan, "The Fragmentation of Narrative Perspective in Y. L. Peretz's *Bilder fun a Provints-Rayze*," *Jewish Social Studies: History, Culture, Society*, n.s., 14, no. 1 (Fall 2007). The fragmented structure of inner stories and complex narration style in "The mute" was correctly viewed by Charney as characteristic for Peretz (Niger, *I. L. Peretz*, 255).

116. Ben-Mordecai, "Mavo," 2:34–35. Ben-Mordecai sees the mixture of the pathetic (the life of Chana and of her two orphaned children) and the comic (the discursive exchange between the two *yidenes*) as the feature that stands out the most at first.

117. One could argue that both discourses are intertwined in that "all of the troubles of the mute stem from Yaakov's (her true beloved) class position being changed" (Ben-Mordecai, 2:36).

118. Ruth Shenfeld, "The family crisis: An integrated view on the decline of the Jewish family unit in late-nineteenth- and early-twentieth-century Poland as reflected in the works of Frischmann, Peretz, Barashm, and Zapolska" [in Hebrew], in *Studies in East European Jewish history and culture in honor of Professor Shmuel Werses*, ed. David Assaf et al. (Jerusalem: Hebrew University Magnes Press, 2002), 350.

119. Peretz, *Ha-ilemet, Manginat ha-zman*, 14–15.

120. In this sense, it is similar to Peretz's Hebrew story "A Maiden Marries." Gershon Shaked, *Ha-Siporet Ha-Ivrit, 1880–1970* [Hebrew narrative fiction] (Jerusalem: Keter, 1977), 1:151.

121. Shenfeld, "Family crisis," 349–50.

122. Peretz, *Ha-ilemet, Manginat ha-zman*, 16–17.

123. Susanne Scholz uses the stories about rape of enslaved women in nineteenth-century America as a point of departure for her discussion about the stories of rape in the Bible. Scholz, *Sacred Witness: Rape in the Hebrew Bible* (Minneapolis: Fortress, 2010), 54.

124. Scholz, *Sacred Witness*, 55.

125. The later version was published by Dvir in his Hebrew Collected Works. See the "wedding soup" example in Peretz, *Ha-ilemet, Manginat ha-zman*, 16. A few more examples out of many are *Lama takshi kushiya kazot?* (Yiddish: *Far vos fregstu aza min kasha?*), *ofel yikkhehu* (Yiddish: *der shvarts yor zol im*

nemen), *yasim eyno aleha* (Yiddish: *vet leygn an oyg af ir*), and *neshama kshera* (Yiddish: *a koshere neshome*).

126. Terry Eagleton, *Literary Theory: An Introduction*, 2nd ed. (Minneapolis: University of Minnesota Press, 1996), 117.

127. Benjamin Harshav, *Language in Time of Revolution* (Berkeley: University of California Press, 1993), 81–182.

128. Shmuel Werses, *Sipur ve-shorsho: 'Iyunim be-hitpatbut ha-prosa ha-'ivrit* [Story and source: Studies in the development of Hebrew prose] (Ramat Gan, Israel: Massada, 1971), 125.

129. Parts of this chapter were adapted from Adi Mahalel, "'To Be a Fighter with Both Fists!': Peretz as a Radical Hebrew Writer," in *The Trilingual Literature of Polish Jews from Different Perspectives: In Memory of I. L. Peretz*, ed. Alina Molisak and Shoshana Ronen, pp. 284–97 (Newcastle upon Tyne, UK: Cambridge Scholars Publishing, 2017).

130. I. L. Peretz, "Be-maon Kaits" [In a summer house; in Hebrew], in *Luah ahiasaf*, vol. 1, pp. 75–82 (Warsaw: Ahi'asaf, 1893); and *Kitvey*, 250–53. A Yiddish version of the story, "Af a zumer voynung," came out in 1901.

131. It would later appear in Peretz's Hebrew poetry collection *The Harp* (1894).

132. Peretz, "Be-maon Kaits" and *Kitvey*, quoted in Hillel Barzel, *Toldot ha-shirah ha-ʿivrit mi-ḥibat tziyon ʿad yameynu—kerekh alef: Shirat ḥibat tziyon* [A history of Hebrew poetry], vol. 1: *The Ḥibat Tziyon period* (Tel Aviv: Sifriyat Poʿalim, 1987), 279.

133. Peretz, *Literature and Life*, in *Ale verk*, 7:86.

134. Peretz, *Ale verk*, 7:75.

135. Moshe Olgin, "A Day with I. L. Peretz," in *Y. L. Peretz* (New York: IKUF, 1955), 21.

136. Ben-Avigdor left *Luakh akhiasaf* in 1895 after being the editor of three volumes and went on to form the publishing house Tushiya.

137. The publishing house for *Luakh akhiasaf* was the newly formed Akhiasaf. In his Yiddish feuilleton "Di karnake nervn" (The sick nerves; *Yontef bletlekh* 5), Peretz described how Akhiasaf tried to convince booksellers to take Peretz's radical publications in Hebrew and Yiddish, *The Arrow* and the *Yontef bletlekh*, off their bookshelves and declared a boycott against Pinski's works that Peretz published: the story "R' Shloyme" and the essay "The Monkeys" (*Di treyst*, 1894; and *Ale verk*, 8:60–62). But Peretz's harsh criticism against them did not stop him from publishing again in *Luakh akhiasaf* (his story "Iskey kahal" was published in its eighth volume).

138. Hagit Cohen, *At the bookseller's shop: The Jewish book trade in Eastern Europe at the end of the nineteenth century* [in Hebrew] (Jerusalem: Hebrew University Magnes Press, 2006), 74–75. See also Eli Levin, "Shana Tova to the New Wave: 118 years to the publication of 'Luakh Am Akhiasaf'—A central stage for modern Hebrew literature at the turn of the centuries" [in Hebrew], *Haaretz*,

September 28, 2011, accessed October 16, 2012, http://www.haaretz.co.il/1.14850
52. The official name of the almanac at first was *Luakh-Am Akhiasaf*, which was parallel to the name of a Yiddish almanac that came out in the same years: the *Yidish folks-kalander* (Jewish people's calendar).

139. Peretz, "Be-maon Kaits," 79; and *Kitvey*, 251. Also, in *Bilder fun a provints rayze* the modern protagonist is doubtful toward the world of numbers and statistics. At the end of this story, it is referred to as "emek ha-kheshbon," "the valley of arithmetic" ("Be-maon Kaits," 82; *Kitvey*, 253).

140. Peretz, "Be-maon Kaits," 77; *Kitvey*, 250.

141. Peretz, "Be-maon Kaits," 79; *Kitvey*, 251.

142. The term *olam ha-atsilut* also has kabbalistic meaning as "world of emanation," one of the four elementary spiritual worlds.

143. Y. L. Ben-David, "A conversation in the world of literature" [in Hebrew], *Hatzfira* 228 (November 1893): 3.

144. Fredric Jameson, *Marxism and Form: Twentieth-Century Dialectical Theories of Literature* (Princeton, NJ: Princeton University Press, 1971), 91.

145. Jameson, *Marxism and Form*, 86.

146. "Insofar as modern sensibility incapable of any genuine concrete reunification or at-one-ment with the world, still finds it in itself to dream of such a state of plenitude, attempts to project forth an impoverished vision of what such a state might be like, there is room for yet a third logical possibility, namely the idyll, whose irreality is inscribed in the very thinness of its poetic realization itself" (Jameson, 92–93).

147. Jameson, 115.

148. Peretz, "Be-maon Kaits," 80; *Kitvey*, 251.

149. Peretz, "Be-maon Kaits," 80; *Kitvey*, 251.

150. Peretz, "Be-maon Kaits," 82; *Kitvey*, 252.

151. I. L. Peretz, "A night of horror: A research in mental disease" [in Hebrew], *Ha-asif* 6 (1893): 136–45; *Kitvey*, 219–25.

152. Nahum Sokolow, "Menahem the Writer: A literary picture by Ben-Avigdor" and "Rabi Shifra: A story by Ben-Avigdor" [in Hebrew], *Ha-asif* 6 (1893): 213–24.

153. I. L. Peretz, "About the 'Shulkhan arukh'" [in Hebrew], *Ha-asif* 6 (1893): 205. See the appendix for a long translated quotation from the text.

154. These contradictions can be presented schematically and are parallel to one another: masculine/father/capitalist versus feminine/mother + wife/socialist. Or it can be read as a clash between two sets of merged gender-psychological-social elements.

155. See also Niger, *I. L. Peretz*, 261.

156. Or to be more clinically accurate, his bipolar disorder, like the protagonist in his Yiddish story "Der meshugener batln" (The crazy idler;1890).

157. Terry Eagleton, *Myths of Power: A Marxist Study of the Brontës* (London: Palgrave Macmillan, 2005), 104–5, quoted in Andrew Smith, *Gothic Literature* (Edinburg: Edinburg University Press, 2007), 70.

158. Peretz, "Night of Horror," 138–39; *Kitvey*, 221.

159. Werses points out how one of the characteristics of Peretz's art of storytelling is indeed organizing his texts schematically "as geometrical shapes." These symmetrical structures can be found, besides in "A Night of Horror," in such stories as "Four Generations—Four Wills," "Ghosts Are Telling," "What Is Soul," "The Fur Hat," and others (Werses, *Sipur ve-shorsho*, 130–32).

160. As Charney incorrectly claims in Niger, *I. L. Peretz*, 256.

161. Hamutal Bar-Yosef, *The Russian context of Hebrew literature* (Jerusalem: Mosad Byaliḳ, 2020), 111–42.

162. *Ha-asif* 3 (1893): 627–33.

163. Peretz, "Mental Sickness among Writers," *The Arrow*, 19, quoted in Bar-Yosef, *Russian context*, 121.

164. Peretz, "Night of Horror," 141; *Kitvey*, 222–23.

165. Andrew Smith, *Gothic Radicalism: Literature, Philosophy and Psychoanalysis in the Nineteenth Century* (New York: St. Martin's Press, 2000), 169.

166. Fredric Jameson, *Postmodernism; or, The Cultural Logic of Late Capitalism* (Durham, NC: Duke University Press, 1991), 289.

167. Peretz, "Night of Horror," 138; *Kitvey*, 221.

168. Jameson, *Postmodernism*, 289.

169. Peretz, "Night of Horror," 146; *Kitvey*, 225.

170. Originally, it was published (as was "The wife Mrs. Hanna") in *Ha-tzfira* [*Hazefirah*], nos. 17, 18, 24, 27, 35, 56 (January–March 1896); *Kitvey*, 168–74. The English translation appears in Robert Alter, ed., *Modern Hebrew Literature* (New York: Behrman House, 1975), 41–64. Alter translated the version that has appeared in Peretz's various editions of *Collected Hebrew works* since 1899 (Dvir, 1951); it has minor variations from the original *Ha-tzfira* publication. I translated from the original. I couldn't find a Yiddish parallel to this story.

171. In the first decade of the twentieth century, Bialik prompted Peretz to write several short plays in Hebrew. Seven plays are found in *Kitvey*, 296–308; four Yiddish parallels to those plays are in *Ale verk*, vol. 6. Some familiar themes are present here, like the status of women, sexuality among different social classes, and the impossibility of marriage under capitalism (in plays like *Beshefel/Shvester*[1904/1905] and *Banim/Kinder* [1906/1907]). See Niger, *I. L. Peretz*, 420–40; and Yehuda Friedlander, *Existence and experience in the Hebrew writings of I. L. Peretz* [in Hebrew] (Tel Aviv: Hotsaat Dvir, 1974), 54–76. Friedlander includes one more play: *Shufey Zerem / A mol iz geven a meylekh* (1912/1907; 191–201).

172. Peretz, "Scenes from Limbo," *Ha-tzfira*, no. 35 (1896); *Kitvey*, 172.

173. Peretz, *Kitvey*, 170.

174. Peretz, 170.

175. Abramovitsh, who devoted periods in his life to writing in Hebrew, had to overcome the pressures from the conservative Hebrew *maskilim* after he transitioned in the 1860s to writing in Yiddish. He wrote sarcastically about them: "our writers, those grammarians who said: let us strengthen our language, the holy tongue; what have we in common with the common people?" Quoted in Dan Miron, *A Traveler Disguised: The Rise of Modern Yiddish Fiction in the Nineteenth Century* (Syracuse, NY: Syracuse University Press, 1996), 19.

176. Peretz, *Kitvey*, 172.

177. Peretz, 174.

178. "Peretz's Hebrew writings," wrote Shmuel Werses in the mid-1960s, "remained inaccessible to Yiddish readers, for there is no trace of them in his Yiddish 'Collected works'" (*Sipur ve-shorsho*, 119).

179. See, for example, Friedlander, *Existence and Experience*, 49–50.

180. Shaked, *Modern Hebrew Fiction*, trans. Yael Lotan, ed. Emily Miller Budick (Bloomington: Indiana University Press, 2000), 27.Originally written in the late 1970s.

Chapter 4

1. I. L. Peretz, *ha-'Ugav: Shire ahavah I me'et Y. L. Perets* [The harp: Love poems by I. L. Peretz] (Warsaw: Hotsa'at Sh. B. Shvartsberg, 1894).

2. Bar-Yosef claims that Hebrew literature's interest in Heine at the end of the nineteenth century was one of Hebrew literature's "early signs of openness toward Western European Decadence." *The Russian context of Hebrew literature* (Jerusalem: Mosad Byalik, 2020), 155.

3. Joseph Klausner, "Zion li-Meshorer, 2d ed., 1894. Shire Ahabah," in *Ha-Eshkol*, i, 54–71.

4. For a thorough discussion of *The Harp* in the context of the Hebrew poetry of that period, see Avner Holtzman, "*The Harp* by I. L. Peretz and the Controversy over Hebrew Love Poetry," in *The Trilingual Literature of Polish Jews from Different Perspectives: In Memory of I. L. Peretz*, ed. Alina Molisak and Shoshana Ronen, pp. 22–43 (Newcastle upon Tyne, UK: Cambridge Scholars Publishing, 2017).

5. Dovid Pinski, "Dray yor mit Perets," *Di Goldene Keyt* 8 (1951): 23.

6. Pinski, "Dray yor," 23–24.

7. Karl Marx and Friedrich Engels, *The Communist Manifesto* (Harmondsworth, UK: Penguin Books, 1970), 2.

8. Margaret A. Rose, *Reading the Young Marx and Engels: Poetry, Parody, and the Censor* (London: Croom Helm, 1978), 21, 24; and Marx, *Love Poems of Karl Marx*, ed. and trans. Reinhard Lettau and Lawrence Ferlinghetti (San Francisco: City Lights Books, 1977).

9. Peretz, *Kitvey Y. L. Perets*, 496. All poetry translations from Yiddish and Hebrew are done by the author of this book.

10. Peretz, "The plea," *Yontef bletlekh* 10: *Homentash* (1894): 25–6; and *Ale verk*, 1:150–51.

11. See Peretz's essay in Hebrew on the *maskilic* poet Yehuda Leyb Gordon: "Ma haya Gordon—balshan o meshorer?" [What was Gordon—a philologist or a poet?], in *Kitvey*, 10:161–200. This long article was originally published in *Ha-tsefira* (1896).

12. Nadson's poem translated into English reads, "Come now, come, oh prophet! With all our strength / Of sorrow and of love we call upon you! / Look how weak we are, tired and limp, / How strong is the enemy, how helpless are we. / This is the last hour; oh, save us from disgrace, / Drowsy is our consciousness by now, the night is without any ray of light; / Drowsy is our shame by now, astray is our understanding, / And the mediocrity preaches everywhere!" Chone Shmeruk, "Harkeriyah lenavi: Schneour, Bialik, Peretz veNadson" [Call to the prophet in Shne'ur, Bialik, Peretz, and Nadson], *Hasifrut* 2 (1969): 241–44; and Victor Erlich, *The Double Image: Concepts of the Poet in Slavic Literatures* (Baltimore: Johns Hopkins University Press, 1964). The poem is taken from Peretz, *Poezye* (Warsaw, 1892), 27, quoted in Shmeruk, "Hqeri'ah lanavi," 281.

13. Dan Miron, *H. N. Bialik and the Prophetic Mode in Modern Hebrew Poetry* (Syracuse, NY: Syracuse University Press, 2000), 18–19. The poem was originally published in the eighth and final volume of *Asefat ḥaḥamin*.

14. Reprinted in Morris Vintshevsky, *Gezamelte verk*, vol. 9 (New York: Frayhayt, 1927), 318. To strengthen its "biblical originality," "Masa duma" even included at the bottom of its page a note from the publisher: "Because this affair relates to the ancient past, and it is not known who of the Hebrew prophets has said," he is asking those with the proper knowledge of ancient Hebrew books to look for its source. Vintshevski's Hebrew socialist prophetic poem was also a response to Yalag (*Gezamelte verk*, 9:317–19).

15. See, for example, Shlomo Berger, *The Bible in/and Yiddish* (Amsterdam: Menasseh ben Israel Institute, 2007). Peretz wrote a series of poetic adaptations of the biblical prophets in Yiddish: Jeremiah, Ezekiel, Isaiah, and more. This approach is not unlike his use of the Hasidic world in his stories.

16. Miron, *Bialik*.

17. According to Miron, Bialik's first "prophecy" poem was actually his long poem in Yiddish "Dos letste vort" (The last word; 1901), whose main theme was the story of a prophet's mission that ends in utter failure. Dan Miron, "Mi'be'ir Ha'hariga va'hal'ah" [From the city of slaughter and beyond], in *Be-ir ha-haregah:*

bikur me'uchar bi-melot me'ah shanah la-po'emah shel Bialik [In the city of slaughter: A late visit on the hundredth anniversary of Bialik's poema; in Hebrew], ed. Michael Gluzman, Hannan Hever, and Dan Miron, pp. 88–97 (Tel Aviv: Resling, 2005).

18. Hannan Hever, "The victims of Zionism: On 'In the city of slaughter' by H"N Bialik," in Gluzman, Hever, and Miron, *Be-ir ha-haregah*, 37–70.

19. Miron, *Bialik*, 12–13.

20. Hever, "Victims of Zionism," 47–54.

21. N. Weynig, "Poylishe lider fun Y. L. Perez fun yor 1874" [Polish poems by I. L. Peretz from the year 1874; in Yiddish], *YIVO-bleter* 12 (1937): 191–204.

22. About Peretz's relationship to Lichtenfeld and their collection of poems together, see Menashe Vakser, "Dos lebn fun a yidishn dikhter," *YIVO-bleter* 12 (1937): 205–60.

23. Judith Bar-El, *The Hebrew long poem from its emergence to the beginning of the twentieth century: A study of the history of a genre* [in Hebrew] (Jerusalem: Bialik Institute, 1995), 118–19. See also Hillel Barzel, *Toldot ha-shirah ha-ʿivrit mi-ḥibat tziyon ʿad yameynu—kerekh alef: Shirat ḥibat tziyon* [A history of Hebrew poetry, volume 1: The Ḥibat Tziyon period] (Tel Aviv: Sifriyat Poʿalim, 1987), 252–54. The discussion over poetic norms was the central theme of Peretz's narrative poem "Nagniel" (1876). Miron sees Peretz's early Hebrew efforts in poetry as attempts to imitate Yalag ("I. L. Peretz as the Poet of the Jewish Age of Sensibility: On the Century of His Death 1915–2015," in *The Trilingual Literature of Polish Jews from Different Perspectives: In Memory of I. L. Peretz*, ed. Alina Molisak and Shoshana Ronen, pp. 1–21 [Newcastle upon Tyne, UK: Cambridge Scholars Publishing, 2017]).

24. Bar-El, *Hebrew long poem*, 119.

25. Felicity Rash, *German Images of the Self and the Other: Nationalist, Colonialist and Anti-Semitic Discourse, 1871–1918* (Basingstoke, UK: Palgrave Macmillan, 2012), 44.

26. I. L. Peretz and Gabriel Judah Lichtenfeld, *Sippurim be-shir ve-shirim shonimme'et Shenei Ba'alei Asufot* [Stories in verse and sundry poems from two anthologists; in Hebrew] (Warsaw: 1877), 51–52, reprinted in Yehuda Friedlander, *Existence and experience in the Hebrew writings of I. L. Peretz* (Tel Aviv: Hotsaat Dvir, 1974), 127–28. These lines are from the beginning of the fifth chapter.

27. Bar-El, *Hebrew long poem*, 88–96; Dan Miron, "Bein takdim le-mikreh—shirato ha-'epit shel Y"L Gordon u-mekomah be-sifrut ha-haskalah ha-ivrit" [Between precedent and happening: Y. L. Gordon's epic poetry and its place in Hebrew *Haskalah* literature; in Hebrew], *Jerusalem Studies in Hebrew Literature* 2 (1983): 127–97; and Miron, "Jewish Age of Sensibility," 8–9.

28. Peretz, *Kitvey*, 477.

29. Peretz, 478.

30. Ayzik Rozentsvayg, *Der radikaler peryod fun Peretses shafn: Di yontef bletlekh* (Kyiv: Melukhe-farlag fun di natsyonale minderhaytn, 1934), 21.

31. When a Yiddish translation of that old Hebrew poem was published in 1892-93 (it is uncertain whether it was done by Peretz himself or by somebody else), the anaphoric expression became "Men zogt" (people say). Shmuel Niger, *I. L. Peretz* (Buenos Aires: Yiddish Cultural Congress, 1952), 87-88; and Barzel, *Toldot ha-shirah ha-ʿivrit mi-ḥibat tziyon ʿad yameynu*, 1:261-63.

32. Dan Miron, *Boʾah, laylah: Hasifrut haʾivrit bein higayyon leʾe-gayyon bemifneh hameʾah haʾesrim* [Come, night: Hebrew literature between the rational and irrational at the turn of the twentieth century; in Hebrew] (Tel Aviv: Dvir, 1987), 92.

33. Peretz, *Kitvey*, 480.

34. Miron, *Boʾah, laylah*, 92.

35. Miron, 92-93.

36. Peretz, *Kitvey*, 481.

37. Peretz, 483-84. Barzel sees the presence of Yiddish as an underlying pattern in "Manginot Ha-zman" (*Toldot ha-shirah ha-ʿivrit mi-ḥibat tziyon ʿad yameynu—kerekh alef*, 1:265).

38. Peretz, *Kitvey*, 486.

39. Peretz, 489.

40. See also Barzel, *Toldot ha-shirah ha-ʿivrit mi-ḥibat tziyon ʿad yameynu*, 1:266.

41. Peretz, *Kitvey*, 490; and Miron, *Der imazh fun shtetl: Dray literarishe shtudyes* (Tel Aviv, 1981), 103-4.

42. See also Barzel, *Toldot ha-shirah ha-ʿivrit mi-ḥibat tziyon ʿad yameynu*, 1:263-68.

43. Barzel, 1:267.

44. Miron, *The Image of the Shtetl and Other Studies of Modern Jewish Literary Imagination* (New York: Syracuse University Press, 2000), 80.

45. David Roskies points to this in relation to Peretz's influence on I. B. Singer's demon stories. Roskies, *A Bridge of Longing: The Lost Art of Yiddish Storytelling* (Cambridge, MA: Harvard University Press, 1996), 290.

46. He is described as a "daytsh" (a German), though he may very well be, as Charney points out, a Jew from Danzig who dresses as a German (meaning in modern European clothing; *I. L. Peretz*, 173). This was not an uncommon way in Eastern Europe to refer to *maskilim* and secularized Jews.

47. Peretz, *Ale verk*, 1:15.

48. A famous example is Shay Agnon's Hebrew short story "Ha-adonist Veha-roḥel" (The lady and the peddler). For more on "Monish" and its elaborate publication history, see Niger, *I. L. Peretz*, 170-79; and Ruth Wisse, *I. L. Peretz and the Making of Modern Jewish Culture* (Seattle: University of Washington Press, 1991), 12-16.

49. Wisse, *Modern Jewish Culture*, 14.

50. Peretz, *Ale verk*, 1:20–21. A few sound-words are hard to translate from this passage in which he humorlessly puts down the Yiddish language (1:21):

A young heart, a soul, treasure	"הערצל", "זעלע", "שאַץ", און "שעצל" –
It has a flavor as licorice pastille	ס'האָט אַ טעם ווי לאַקריץ-פּלעצל
It has no flavor, it has no salt	עס האָט קיין טעם, עס האָט קיין זאַלץ
And it still smells like pig-fat!	און עס שמעקט נאָך חזיר-שמאַלץ!

51. "Rising, cresting, and then breaking down." Miron, "Jewish Age of Sensibility," 12. See also Holtzman, "Controversy," 37–40.

52. Frishman, *Mikhtavim ʿal hasifrut: Sefer alef* [Dispatches on literature: Book *alef*; in Hebrew] (Jerusalem: M. Newman Publishing, 1968), 120–21.

53. Naʾama Rokem, *Prosaic Conditions: Heinrich Heine and the Spaces of Zionist Literature* (Evanston, IL: Northwestern University Press, 2013), 26–27.

54. Peretz's few Polish poems of the 1870s carried a similar Heinesque quality. Those early Hebrew poems were reprinted in Niger, *I. L. Peretz*, 82.

55. On the storm that *The Harp* created, see Lilienblum, "Divrei Zemer," in *Luah aḥiasaf*, vol. 5 (Warsaw: Shuldberg Brothers, 1897); Rokem, *Prosaic Conditions*, 61–64; Hamutal Bar-Yosef, *Decadent trends in Hebrew literature: Bialik, Berdychevski, Brener* (Jerusalem: Mosad Bialik, 1997), 18–19; Barzel, *Toldot ha-shirah ha-ʿivrit mi-ḥibat tziyon ʿad yameynu*, 1:271–72; and Shlomo Harel, "Iyun Meḥudash be Shirei HaUgav shel Y. L. Peretz" [A reconsideration of the "organ poems" of I. L. Peretz; in Hebrew], in *Studies in Hebrew Literature*, vol. 5 (Tel Aviv: Tel Aviv University, 1986), 118–20. Frishman added about the language of *The Harp* that Peretz "is writing Yiddish in Hebrew words" ("jargonit be-milim ivriyot"; *Mikhtavim ʿal hasifrut*, 116–17). But the examples he gives are meager and less convincing. About Frishman's critique, see Menuha Gilboa, *Ben reʾalizm le-romantikah* [Between realism and Romanticism: A study of the critical work of David Frishman] (Tel Aviv: Tel Aviv University, 1975), 64–66.

56. Miron, *Boʾah, laylah*, 14–15.

57. A complex form in which Bialik excelled (Harel, "Iyun Meḥudash be Shirei HaUgav," 121–24). The term "reverse poem" was introduced by Menaḥem Peri in his article analyzing Bialik's poetry, "Hitbonenuyot ba-Mivne ha-Tematì shel Shire Bialik: Ha-Shir Ha-Mithapekh Ve-Eḥav" [Looking at the thematic structure of Bialik's poems: The reverse poem and its siblings; in Hebrew], *Ha-Sifrut* 1, no. 2 (1969): 40–82.

58. Peretz, *Kitvey*, 491.

59. Harel, "Iyun Meḥudash be Shirei HaUgav," 124.

60. Quoted in Barzel, *Toldot ha-shirah ha-ʿivrit mi-ḥibat tziyon ʿad yameynu*, 1:271.

61. Peretz, *Ale verk*, 1:192.

62. Peretz, *Kitvey*, 493. In the first version of the poem (1893), the third line of the third stanza starts with the vocal expression "haa" instead of the word "ki" (for) that is in the *Harp* version ("Ankhot ahava" [Moans of love], *Ha-asif* 6 [1893]: 170).

63. Khane Gordon-Mlotek, "Y. L. Perets' zamlung yidishe folkslider" [I. L. Peretz's collection of Yiddish folk songs], *YIVO-bleter*, n.s., 4 (2003): 40–41, 66n24. [AU: Could you please confirm that these citations are correct as shown here, i.e. that they are pages 40–41 note 24 and page 66 note 24?]

64. Gordon-Mlotek, "Perets' zamlung yidishe folkslider," 40–41.

65. Gordon-Mlotek, 41.

66. Maynard Solomon, "Ernst Bloch: Introduction," in *Marxism and Art: Essays Classic and Contemporary*, ed. Solomon, 571.

67. There are numerous studies on the subject, such as Albert Friedman, *The Ballad Revival: Studies in the Influence of Popular on Sophisticated Poetry* (Chicago: University of Chicago Press, 1961); and Steve Newman, *Ballad Collection, Lyric, and the Canon: The Call of the Popular from the Restoration to the New Criticism* (Philadelphia: University of Pennsylvania Press, 2007).

68. Newman, *Ballad Collection*, 14.

69. A poem similar in structure to his previous style of long Hebrew poems (short four-line stanzas, rhymed ABCB), in which an old coachman bemoans the destruction of the shtetl.

70. See also Miron, *Bialik*, 18–19.

71. Such as the stories "The Source of Souls" and "In a Summer Home." More in Barzel, *Toldot ha-shirah ha-ʿivrit mi-ḥibat tziyon ʿad yameynu*, 278–81.

72. Hannan Hever, "Poetry," trans. Lisa Katz, *Political Concepts: A Critical Lexicon* 2 (February 15, 2013): 1, 7, http://www.politicalconcepts.org/poetry-hannan-hever/.

73. *Yontef bletlekh*, vol. 11: *Kol khamiro* (1895); *Ale verk*, 1:153–54.

74. Yoysef Mlotek and Khana Mlotek, *Perl fun der yidisher poezye* [Pearls of Yiddish poetry; in Yiddish] (Tel Aviv: Y.-L.-Perets-Farlag, 1974), 70.

75. Mlotek and Mlotek, *Perl*, 541.

76. Moishe Teitsh, ed., *Arbeter lider (Anthology)* (Warsaw: Progress, 1906).

77. Friedrich Engels, "The Origin of the Family, Private Property and the State," in *The Marx-Engels Reader*, 2nd ed., ed. Robert C. Tucker (New York: W. W. Norton, 1978), 742.

78. An alternative view is that it casts their fate so bleakly that even if they had better pay and working conditions, they would still face the oppression of marriage and would still lack any political power.

79. Benjamin Harshav and Barbara Harshav, eds., *American Yiddish Poetry: A Bilingual Anthology* (Berkeley: University of California Press, 1986), 32–33; Nokhem Borekh Minkov, *Pionern fun yidisher poeziye in amerike*, vol. 1 [in Yiddish] (New York: Grenich, 1956); Marc Miller, *Representing the Immigrant Experience: Morris Rosenfeld and the Emergence of Yiddish Literature in America* (Syracuse, NY: Syracuse University Press, 2007); and Ori Kritz, *The Poetics of Anarchy: David Edelshtat's Revolutionary Poetry* (Frankfurt am Main: P. Lang, 1997).

80. M. Olgin, "Di proletarishe rikhtung in der yidisher literatur" [The proletarian direction in Yiddish literature; in Yiddish], *Almanakh: Yubilee fun Internatsyonaler Arbeter Orden fun Yidishn Folks Ordn* (New York: Cooperativa Folks Farlag fun Internatzationaler Arber Ordn, 1940), 367. Olgin admits that out of the first generation of classic writers, only Peretz wrote about Jewish workers (366).

81. Rozentsvayg, *Radikaler peryod*, 76; Minkov, *Pionern*, 1:61–62. Yankev Shatzky wrote about the influence of folklorists on Peretz in his writing of these poems and about Peretz's acquaintance with young female knitters, students of a Jewish evening artisan school, whom he met going to dance halls in Warsaw ("Perets-shtudyes," *YIVO-bleter* 28 [1946]: 54–57).

82. Vintshevski, *Gezamlte verk*, 2:23.

83. Thomas Hood, "The Song of the Shirt," *Punch* 5 (December 16, 1843): 260.

84. Patricia Zakreski, *Representing Female Artistic Labour, 1848–1890: Refining Work for the Middle-Class Woman* (Burlington, VT: Ashgate, 2006), 26–27.

85. Zakreski, *Representing Female Artistic Labour*, 32. Already in 1891 Oscar Wilde had written that charity is a way of trying of solving "the problem of poverty . . . by keeping the poor alive . . . it is not a solution: it is an aggravation of the difficulty. The proper aim is to try and reconstruct society on such a basis that poverty will be impossible," while "charity degrades and demoralises." Wilde, "The Soul of Man under Socialism," *Fortnightly Review* 49 (February 1, 1891), quoted in Slavoj Žižek, *Living in the End Times* (London: Verso, 2011), 117–18.

86. This is also the central motif of his Yiddish short story "Four generations, four wills" (1901), which associated social upward mobility with assimilation, decline, and mental illness.

87. Rozentsvayg, *Radikaler peryod*, 169–71; and Niger, *I. L. Peretz*, 184–85.

88. In the volumes *Oyneg Shabes* (The pleasure of the Shabbat; 1896) and the following *Khamishoser* (Tu Bishvat).

89. Rozentsvayg, *Radikaler peryod*, 77. Shakhne Epshteyn commented that the female workers in "Baym fremdn khupe kleyd" were not as downtrodden and depressed as the knitters in "Dray neytorins." Epshteyn, "Yitskhok Leybush Perets: Tsum fnf-un-tsvanstikstn yortog nokh zayn toyt," *Sovetishe literature* (October 1940): 101.

90. Minkov, *Pionern*, 1:61–62.

91. The similar theme in "Monish" bore a dominant nationalist tone rather than a socialist one.

92. For literature, Terry Eagleton reminds us, in a sense like political theory, is supposed to guide people's actions in the world. Eagleton, *The Event of Literature* (New Haven, CT: Yale University Press, 2012), 54. The story of the two brothers was also set to music as a popular oratorio, by the Jewish American communist composer Jacob Schaeffer (1888–1936).

93. The phrase "blood, sweat, and tears," though made famous by Winston Churchill during the Second World War, was already circulating in several European languages from the early to mid nineteenth century. It is possible that Peretz was familiar with its French version, *lacrime é sangue*.

94. Dan Miron, "Sifrut Ha-haskala Be-ivrit" [*Haskalah* literature in Hebrew], in *Zman Yehudi Hadash* [New Jewish times: Jewish culture in a secular age—an encyclopedic view], vol. 3, ed. Yermiyahu Yovel (Jerusalem: Keter, 2007), 27–41; and Immanuel Etkes, "Haskalah," trans. Jeffrey Green, *YIVO Encyclopedia of Jews in Eastern Europe*, 2010, http://www.yivoencyclopedia.org/article.aspx/Haskalah.

95. See Irving Howe, Ruth R. Wisse, and Khone Shmeruk, eds., *The Penguin Book of Modern Yiddish Verse* (New York: Penguin, 1987).

96. *Yontef bletlekh*, vol. 11: *Der oymer; Ale verk*, 1:152.

97. Both poems were included in an anthology of Yiddish poetry released in 1974, a testament to their ongoing popularity in Yiddish secular circles (Mlotek and Mlotek, *Perl*, 65–79). "Treyst mayn folk" also became the title for a popular biography of Peretz in Yiddish by Mark Schweid, published in 1955.

98. For a recent study on Peretz's usage of folklore, see Spinner, *Jewish Primitivism*, 21–40.

99. These poems were published as a whole for the first time in 2003 by Khane Gordon-Mlotek ("Perets' zamlung yidishe folkslider," 9–70).

100. Gordon-Mlotek, 62–70.

101. See the long Yiddish article by Peretz called "Jewish life according to Yiddish folk songs" ("Dos yidishe lebn loyt di yidishe folkslider," 1901; reprinted in *YIVO-bleter* 12 [1937]: 291–99).

102. Miron, *Image of the Shtetl*, 80.

103. Quoted in José Limón, *Mexican Ballads, Chicano Poems: History and Influence in Mexican-American Social Poetry* (Berkeley: University of California Press, 1992), 156.

104. Limón, *Mexican Ballads*, 156.

105. Mikhail Krutikov, *From Kabbalah to Class Struggle: Expressionism, Marxism, and Yiddish Literature in the Life and Work of Meir Wiener* (Stanford, CA: Stanford University Press, 2011), 172–77; and Itzik Nakhmen Gottesman, *Defining the Yiddish Nation: The Jewish Folklorists of Poland* (Detroit: Wayne State University Press, 2003).

106. Etkes, "Haskalah."

107. *Tsene-Rene* played a very important role in disseminating knowledge of the Bible and its commentaries throughout Eastern Europe. Jacob Elbaum and Chava Turniansky, "Tsene-rene," trans. Deborah Weissman, *YIVO Encyclopedia of Jews in Eastern Europe*, 2010, http://www.yivoencyclopedia.org/article.aspx/Tsene-rene.

108. These stanzas and others predated Itsik Manger's famous adaptations of the Torah into Eastern European Jewish life through Yiddish verse in his book *Khumesh-lider* (Pentateuch poems; 1935).

109. *Ale verk*, 1:165.

110. Ronzentsvayg, *Radikaler peryod*, 33.

111. A traditional interpretation of the Song of Songs relates the female protagonist to symbolizing the Jewish people (Knesset Yisrael); here, the cheeky female protagonist rejects this interpretation in favor of the outright sexual one.

112. This poem is a *maskilic* parody of a known Talmudic legend about the miracle worker Knanina Ben Dosa and his wife, known to be living in poverty and expecting their reward in the afterlife. More is in D. Kurlyand, "Tsu der frage vegn legendare syuzhetn in Peretses verk" [About the question of legendary themes in Peretz's works], *Sovetishe literatur* (October 1940): 126-28; and David Roskies, "Rabbis, Rebbes, and Other Humanists: The Search for a Usable Past in Modern Yiddish Literature," *Studies in Contemporary Jewry* 12 (1996): 58, 73n13.

113. Miron, "Bein takdim le-mikreh," 172-73.

114. See, for example, Sol Liptzin, "Heine and the Yiddish Poets," in *The Jewish Reception of Heinrich Heine*, ed. Mark H. Gelber (Tübingen, Germany: Niemeyer, 1992), 71-72.

115. Rokem, *Prosaic Conditions*, 61-62.

116. "It is an old story, / But it remains always new," taken from the final lines of Heine's poem "Ein Jüngling liebt ein Mädchen." Peretz, *Di yudishe bibliyotek*, 2:170. This same stanza, including its last two sentences, "Und wem sie just passieret, / Dem bricht das Herz entzwei (And to whom it just happened, / His heart breaks in two), is quoted by Frishman in his battles against "plagiarism" in Hebrew literature, and also by Klausner and Lilienblum to argue whether love poetry has a place in Hebrew literature (Rokem, *Prosaic Conditions*, 62-64).

117. Weynig, "Poylishe lider," 192-93.

118. Leah Garrett, *A Knight at the Opera: Heine, Wagner, Herzl, Peretz, and the Legacy of Der Tannhäuser* (West Lafayette, IN: Purdue University Press, 2011).

119. Wisse, *Modern Jewish Culture*, xiii.

120. Heinrich Heine, *Germany, a Winter Tale*, trans. Edgar Alfred Bowring (New York: Mondial, 2007), 4. Translated version from Heine, *Complete Poetical Works of Heinrich Heine* (Hastings, UK: Delphi Classics, 2016), 686. Quoted in Shlomo Barer, "Heine and Marx: The relationship between the prophet of communism and the poet who foresaw its horrors" [in Hebrew], in *Marx and the future of socialism*, ed. Uri Zilbersheid (Tel Aviv: Resling, 2005), 168, 170. On

whether the poem expresses any definite commitment to revolution, there have been many debates. For the view that negates such a commitment, see Shlomo Barer, *The Doctors of Revolution* (London: Thames & Hudson, 2000), 899n14; for the opposite view, see Hans Kaufmann, *Politische Gedicht und klassische Dichtung: Heinrich Heine, "Deutschland. Ein Wintermärchen"* [in German] (Berlin: Aufbau Verlag, 1959), 120–22.

121. Barer, "Heine and Marx," 171–72.

122. Jochanan Trilse-Finkelstein, *Heinrich Heine: Gelebter Widerspruch: Eine Biographie* (Berlin: Aufbau, 2001), 223–24. Proudhon was in fact the first to declare himself an anarchist, in the sense of holding a defined sociopolitical theory; he rejected any form of centralism, and thus he criticized the national movements fighting to establish centralized nation states (Avraham Yassour, ed., *Anarkhizm: Antologyah* [in Hebrew; Tel Aviv: Resling, 2008], 33–56). In his speech at the Czernowitz Yiddish language conference in 1908, Peretz expressed the view that all states are coercive and culturally reductive (Dan Miron, *From Continuity to Contiguity* [Stanford, CA: Stanford University Press, 2010], 80).

123. *Atta Troll*, canto 10, quoted in Frederic Ewen, *A Half-Century of Greatness: The Creative Imagination of Europe, 1848–1883*, ed. Jeffrey Wollock (New York: New York University Press, 2008), 365.

124. Printed in his almanac *Literatur un lebn*. A shortened version was reprinted in Rozentsvayg, *Radikaler peryod*, 161–63.

125. Rozentsvayg, 163.

126. Barer, "Heine and Marx," 168–170.

127. It is very ironic that of all people it was Peretz's nemesis, the Hebrew and Yiddish writer David Frishman, who translated this socialist poem by Heine into Yiddish—the same Frishman who attacked Peretz vehemently in the mid-1890s for allegedly plagiarizing Heine's poetry (see his seventh letter in his *Mikhtavim 'al hasifrut*, 100–146). Frishman himself never flirted with radical politics—never delved into Jewish nationalism, either—and remained a European liberal to his last day (see his essay about the poetry of Rosa Luxemburg in David Frishman, *Shiv'ah mikhtavim hadashim 'al devar ha-sifrut* [In Hebrew] [Berlin: Dvir, 1922–23], 180–300).

128. Heinrich Heine, *Heinrich Heines Samtliche Werke: Herausgegeben von Prof. Dr. Ernst Elster. Kritisch durchgesehene und erlauterte Ausgabe*, 7 vols. (Leipzig: Bibliographisches Institut, 1887–90, reprinted with revisions 1893), 6:572–73. Available in the Marxists Internet Archive at https://www.marxists.org/reference/archive/heine/lutece/preface.htm.

129. Heine, *Samtliche Werke*, 6:572–73; also Barer, "Heine and Marx," 173.

130. George F. Peters, *The Poet as Provocateur: Heinrich Heine and His Critics* (Rochester, NY: Camden House, 2000), 101–2.

131. Wisse, *Modern Jewish Culture*, 55.

132. Pomerantz, *Kavkaz* [Caucasus; in Yiddish] (New York: 1943), 75–92.

133. Pomerantz, *Kavkaz*, 76.

134. Pomerantz, 92.
135. Rozentsvayg, *Radikaler peryod*, 97–103.
136. Shlomo Mendelson, *Zayn lebn un shafn* [His life and work; in Yiddish] (New York: Undzer tsayt, 1949), 155.

Chapter 5

1. Olgin (1878–1939) was a Bundist activist in Eastern Europe who in the United States became a communist editor of the Yiddish communist paper *Frayhat*. Bergelson (1884–1952) was a leftist Yiddish writer who became pro-Soviet in 1926.

2. The Hasidic movement became a mass movement through its ability to adapt to the various institutions and social relationships in the Eastern Europe of its day (e.g., to the great Polish landowners and ruling aristocracy, the *szlachta*, who played the role of a governing oligarchy). This adaptability was key to its phenomenal success in overcoming the challenge of Polish geography and growing throughout the country. Adam Teller, "Hasidism and the Challenge of Geography: The Polish Background to the Spread of the Hasidic Movement," *AJS Review* 30, no. 1 (2006).

3. For examples in Perl's writings, see Jeremy Dauber, **Antonio's Devils**: *Writers of the Jewish Enlightenment and the Birth of Modern Hebrew and Yiddish Literature* (Stanford, CA: Stanford University Press, **2004**), 278–80; and Perl's most famous satire, *Sefer Megale Temirin* [Revealer of secrets; in Hebrew], ed. Jonatan Meir (Jerusalem: Mossad Bialik, 2013).

4. Yitshok Nusinov, "Der Nister," in *Gedakht*, by Der Nister (Kyiv: Kulturlige, 1929), xi.

5. S. An-sky, *Gezamelte shriftn: Tsenter band* [Collected work: Volume ten] (Vilnius: Farlag An-sky, 1922), 161.

6. Peretz, *Briv un redes* (1929), 71–72.

7. Nicham Ross, *Masoret ahuva ve-snu'a: Zehut yehudit modernit ve-ktiva neo-khasidit be-fetakh hame'a ha-esrim* [A beloved despised tradition: Modern Jewish identity and neo-Hasidic writing at the beginning of the twentieth century; in Hebrew] (Beersheba: Ben-Gurion University Press, 2010), 44–50. For more on neo-Hasidism, see David Biale et al., *Hasidism: A New History* (Princeton, NJ: Princeton University Press, 2018).

8. Raphael Mahler analyzed the Hasidim-versus-*Haskalah* conflict in terms of class war in *Der kamf tsvishn khsides un haskole in Galitsye* [The struggle between Hasidism and *Haskalah* in Galicia; in Yiddish] (New York: YIVO, 1942); "The Social and Political Aspects of the Haskalah in Galicia," *YIVO Annual of Social Jewish Research* 1 (1946): 64–85; and *Hasidism and the Jewish Enlightenment: Their Confrontation in Galicia and Poland in the First Half of the Nineteenth Century*,

trans. Eugene Orenstein, Aaron Klein, and Jenny Machlowitz Klein (Philadelphia: Jewish Publication Society of America, 1985).

9. Ken Frieden, *Classic Yiddish Fiction: Abramovitsh, Sholem Aleichem, and Peretz* (Albany, NY: State University of New York Press, 1995), 282.

10. Ross, *Masoret ahuva ve-snu'a*.

11. Published in *Ha-shahar* 5 (1875). See Hillel Barzel, *Toldot ha-shirah ha-ʿivrit mi-ḥibat tziyon ʿad yameynu—kerekh alef* (Tel Aviv: Sifriyat Poʿalim, 1987), 251, 261.

12. Ken Frieden, "Tradition and Innovation: How Peretz Made Literary History," in *The Enduring Legacy of Yitzchok Leybush Peretz: Proceedings of a Literary and Cultural Symposium*, ed. Benny Kraut (New York: CUNY Center for Jewish Studies, 2005), 52–53; and Shmuel Niger, *I. L. Peretz* (Buenos Aires: Yiddish Cultural Congress, 1952), 130. The story "Ha-kadish" was published in *Ha-yom* 14 (1886): 2.

13. Peretz, "Ha-kadish," 2.

14. A process that later on received another Yiddish literary representation in Sholem Ash's breakthrough novella, *Dos shtetl* (1904).

15. Gershon Shaked, *Modern Hebrew Fiction*, trans. Yael Lotan, ed. Emily Miller Budick (Bloomington: Indiana University Press, 2000), 27.

16. Shaked, *Modern Hebrew Fiction*, 27.

17. "Hamekubalim," *Gan perahim* 3 (1891): 83–85, reprinted in Peretz, *Kitvey Y. L. Perets*, 2A:167–71. In Yiddish: "Mekubolim," *Der tones—shive oser betamuz bletl* (1894).

18. Frieden, *Classic Yiddish Fiction*, 288.

19. The name Lemekh appears in the Bible, but in the Ashkenazi Jewish context it came to mean "a man of weak character," a "good for nothing," or just to be synonymous with stupidity. In Stuchkov's *Treasure of the Yiddish Language*, one can find the following illustrative proverb: *gey ikh gikh, tserays ikh di shikh, gey ikh pamelekh, bin ikh a lemekh* (if I go fast, I tear my shoes, if I go slowly, I am a Lemekh), says a complaining son-in-law of his father-in-law's comments. Nokhem Stuchkov, *Der oyster fun der yiddisher sprakh* [Treasure of the Yiddish language] (New York: Yidisher Visnshaftlekher Institut, 1950), 170.

20. This point is also emphasized by Ruth Wisse, who writes, "The material component of spiritual behavior was for Peretz a given, and neither in this early story about Kabbalists nor in his later writings did Peretz waver in his humanistic convictions." *I. L. Peretz and the Making of Modern Jewish Culture* (Seattle: University of Washington Press, 1991), 33.

21. "The rationalist Peretz interprets and puts out on the plate where the desire for kabbalah stems from—these seven lines are befitting to the story exactly as . . . well, let's say, as a pair of suspenders to a symphony. The smart reader spills black ink over these seven lines, and he earns a mitzvah: cleaning up a holy place out of a bit of spider webs." Originally published in 1910, reprinted in Nomberg,

Y. L. Perets (Buenos Aires: Tsentrale farband fun poylishe yidn in argentine, 1946), 16.

22. Frieden, "Tradition and Innovation," 54–55.
23. Peretz, "Ha-mekubalim," 83.
24. Frieden, "Tradition and Innovation," 54–55.
25. Ayzik Rozentsvayg, *Der radikaler peryod fun Peretses shafn: Di yontef bletlekh* (Kyiv: Melukhe-farlag fun di natsyonale minderhaytn, 1934), 82.
26. Litvak, *Vos geven* (Poyln: Vilner farlag fun B. Kletskin, 1925), 81. Litvak also noted how little noticed Peretz's first Hasidic story—meaning here the second Yiddish version of "Kabbalists" which appeared in the fouth volume of the *Yontef bletlekh* "Der tones" (The fast)—was among the radical milieu. He writes that he himself actually liked it when it came out, "but it surprised me," he writes, "since what connection does it have with the rest [of the material in that *Bletl* volume]?" (80–81).
27. Quoted in Caroline Evans, *Fashion at the Edge: Spectacle, Modernity and Deathliness* (New Haven, CT: Yale University Press, 2003), 187.
28. Nomberg, *Y.L. Perets*, 15.
29. Peretz, "Mishnat ḥasidim," in **Ha-chetz**: *Yalkut sifruti* (Warsaw: Shvartzberg, 1894). In Yiddish: "Mishnes khsidim," *Der yud* 4, no. 19 (May 8, 1902): 11–14. *Der yud* was a Yiddish Zionist publication that became a platform for Yiddish literature during its short run at the turn of the century. Ruth R. Wisse, "Not the 'Pintele Yid' but the Full-Fledged Jew," *Prooftexts* 15, no. 1 (1995): 33–61. Nomberg considered this story to be "undoubtedly the prime story of the [*Khsidish*] book" (*Y. L. Perets*, 17).
30. Peretz also used the pen name "The Orphan from Nemirov" to sign the short story "The rebbe's pipe."
31. Shachar Pinsker, *Literary Passports: The Making of Modernist Hebrew Fiction in Europe* (Stanford, CA: Stanford University Press, 2010), 299.
32. Peretz, *Ale verk*, 4:180.
33. Nosn, "Ḥayey moharan" [in Hebrew], ch. 117, *Sifre Breselev*, accessed August 23, 2013, http://breslev.eip.co.il/?key=3901.
34. See also Frieden, "Tradition and Innovation," 57n22–23.
35. Ross, *Masoret ahuva ve-snu'a*, 500.
36. According to Georgi Plekhanov, as quoted in Fredric Jameson, *Marxism and Form: Twentieth-Century Dialectical Theories of Literature* (Princeton, NJ: Princeton University Press, 1971), 337.
37. Moyshe Litvakov, "Di Nister problem" [The Nister problem], in *Af tsvey frontn* [On two fronts], by Litvakov (Moscow: Tsentraler Felker Farlag fun F.S.S.R., 1931), 170; see also Delphine Bechtel, *Der Nister's Work, 1907-1929: A Study of a Yiddish Symbolist* (Berne: Peter Lang, 1990), 27–34.
38. Nusinov, "Der Nister," i–xviii. In regard to Soviet Yiddish critics' attitude toward symbolism, including Nusinov, see Bechtel's essay about Der Nister: "Entre tradition juive et modernité révolutionnaire: Le combat de Der Nister contre la

critique littéraire soviétique," in *Contes fantastiques et symboliques*, by Der Nister (Paris: Editions du Cerf, 1997), 75–78.

39. Walter Benjamin, "The Paris of the Second Empire in Baudelaire," in *The Writer of Modern Life: Essays on Charles Baudelaire*, ed. Michael Jennings (Cambridge, MA: Belknap Press, 2006), 130.

40. Nomberg, "A literarisher dor," in *Y. L. Perets*, 61–62.

41. David Roskies, *A Bridge of Longing: The Lost Art of Yiddish Storytelling* (Cambridge, MA: Harvard University Press, 1996), 118.

42. Peretz offered a similar bifurcation several years later in his famous Hasidic story "Between two mountains." Nicham Ross, "I. L. Peretz's 'Between Two Mountains': Neo-Hasidism and Jewish Literary Modernity," in *Modern Jewish Literatures: Intersections and Boundaries*, ed. Sheila E. Jelen, Michael P. Kramer, and L. Scott Lerner (Philadelphia: University of Pennsylvania Press, 2011), 114–15.

43. The polemics between Aḥad Ha'am and Berdichevsky have been dealt with extensively in the scholarship. About Berdichevsky's influence on Peretz and his circle in Warsaw, see Nomberg, "A literarisher dor," in *Y. L. Perets*, 68–69. As early as 1893, Berdichevsky referred to Nietzsche as "my Rebbe" in a postcard to Aḥad Ha'am. Yaakov Golomb, "Al hapolmus ha-'Nietzscheyani' ben Aḥad-Ha'am le-Micha Yosef Berditshevsky" [About the Nietzschean polemic between Aḥad Ha'am and Micha Yosef Berditshevsky; in Hebrew], in *Misaviv lanekuda* (2007), 69n3. Golomb's article is based on chapters 3–4 in his book *Nietzsche and Zion* (Ithaca, NY: Cornell University Press, 2004).

44. Ross, *Masoret ahuva ve-snu'a*, 117.

45. Friedrich Niewöhner, "Jüdischer Nietzscheanismus seit 1888—Ursprünge und Begriff," in *Jüdischer Nietzscheanismus*, ed. Werner Stegmaier and Daniel Krochmalnik (Berlin: Walter de Gruyter, 1997), 22.

46. Aḥad Ha'am, *Kol kitve* (Jerusalem: Dvir, 1953), 154–55.

47. On the opposition to Aḥad Ha'am's rationalist-positivist viewpoint among the Hebrew writers at the turn of the twentieth century, like Brenner, Gnessin, and Shneur, see Dan Miron, **Bodedim bemoadam** [in Hebrew] (Tel Aviv: Am Oved, 1987), 363–65.

48. For example, Moyshe Olgin, quoted in Ross, "Peretz's 'Between Two Mountains,'" 115; and Rozentsvayg, *Radikaler periyod*, 100.

49. In his address to the 1908 Yiddish language conference in Czernowitz (Peretz, *Briv un redes fun Y. L. Perets* [1944], 371).

50. Karl Marx, *The Eighteenth Brumaire of Louis Bonaparte*, trans. Saul K. Padover from the German edition of 1869, 5–6 (Marx-Engels Archive, 1999). German text from Karl Marx, "Der achtzehnte Brumaire des Louis Bonaparte," in *Werke*, vol. 8, §116 (Berlin: Dietz Verlag, Berlin, 1972), transcribed in the Marx-Engels Archive, 1999, http://www.mlwerke.de/me/me08/me08_115.htm.

51. Yoav Peled, *Class and Ethnicity in the Pale: The Political Economy of Jewish Workers' Nationalism in Late Imperial Russia* (New York: St. Martin's Press, 1989), 16–30.

52. Peled, *Class and Ethnicity*, 31–70.

53. Take for example the works of S. An-ski, best remembered as the author of *The Dybbuk* (a Yiddish symbolist drama set in the Hasidic world) but who also wrote the lyrics for what became the Bund's anthem, "Di shvue" (The oath)—both from the beginning of the twentieth century—and many other texts dedicated to the Bund. Gabriella Safran, *Wandering Soul: The Dybbuk's Creator, S. An-Sky* (Cambridge, MA: Harvard University Press, 2011).

54. Eagleton, *Reason, Faith and Revolution: Reflections on the God Debate* (New Haven, CT: Yale University Press, 2009), xi–xii.

55. Ela Bauer, "From the Salons to the Street: The Development of the Jewish Salon in Warsaw at the End of the 19th Century," *Jahrbuch des Simon-Dubnow-Instituts / Simon Dubnow Institute Yearbook* 7 (2008): 155.

56. And not, as Pinsker argues, that "Peretz developed his neo-Hasidic stories mainly for literary and stylistic reasons," though Pinsker does admit that some socialist ideology exists in these stories (*Literary Passports*, 298).

57. Eagleton, *Reason, Faith and Revolution*, 18.

58. The relation of Hasidism to Yiddish was more complex than was portrayed by secular *Yidishists*, who tended to romanticize the usage of Yiddish by the Hasidic movement. Traces of such a romantic-yidishist approach can be found in relatively recent works as well: "Hasidism appeared on the scene and took up the already prepared instrument of Yiddish, thus precipitating a fruitful union of the two . . . Hasidism became the standard bearer of the ordinary folk, making brilliant use of their Yiddish tongue to explain to them the great new concept"; Yitzhak Korn, *Jews at the Crossroads* (New York: Cornwall Books, 1983), 161–63. A critical approach to the Hasidic movement identifies within it several currents: an elitist strand, for which Hasidic Hebrew homiletic literature was written; wonder tales in both Yiddish and Hebrew, for both elites and literate nonelites; and oral folk culture, for the semiliterate and illiterate masses. "Praise of the disenfranchised at the expense of elites is notably lacking in Hasidic homiletic literature, and this should come as no surprise: such biting social criticism would not have earned a very enthusiastic response in . . . [this] elite Hebrew readership"; Glenn Dynner, *Men of Silk: The Hasidic Conquest of Polish Jewish Society* (New York: Oxford University Press, 2006), 198.

59. Eagleton, *Reason, Faith and Revolution*, 14–15.

60. Eagleton, 23–24.

61. Peretz, "Vos zol ikh veln?" [What should I want?], in *Ale verk*, 8:72–73.

62. Peretz, *Ale verk*, 8:72–73.

63. Eagleton, *Reason, Faith and Revolution*, 90.

64. Gil Anidjar, "Secularism," *Critical Inquiry* 33, no. 1 (Autumn 2006).

65. Eagleton, *Reason, Faith and Revolution*, 27.

66. Mikhail Krutikov, *From Kabbalah to Class Struggle: Expressionism, Marxism, and Yiddish Literature in the Life and Work of Meir Wiener* (Stanford, CA: Stanford University Press, 2011), 242–46.

67. Eagleton, *Reason, Faith and Revolution*, 42.

68. Yosef Klausner, "Sifrutenu hadasha bishnat tara"s" [Our new literature, 1899–1900; in Hebrew], in *Sefer ha-Shanah*, ed. N. Sokolow (Warsaw, 1900–1906), 2:240.

69. Ken Frieden, "Parodya ve-hegyogrfya: Sipurim khasidiim-kivyakhol shel Perets," [Parody and hagiography: Peretz's pseudo Hasidic stories; in Hebrew], *Khulyot* 7 (2002): 45.

70. Peretz, "Shmaya gibor," *Ha-tzfira*, no. 183 (August 1892; 1902 in Yiddish).

71. Peretz, *Briv un redes* (1929), 71–72. Peretz was dependent on **Ha-*tzfira***; in return for his contributions they published advertisements for his publications, which were vital for generating his sales. His status in the paper improved greatly after his friend Sokolow became its sole editor in 1894.

72. Frieden, *Classic Yiddish Fiction*, 266–71.

73. Frieden, "Parodya ve-hegyogrfya," 45–46.

74. Linda Hutcheon, *A Theory of Parody: Teachings of Twentieth-Century Art Forms* (New York: Methuen, 1985), 6.

75. Hutcheon, *Theory of Parody*, 52.

76. Another possible interpretation is that the wife's entrepreneurship was not selling the right to use the pipe but rather the right to enjoy her sexual favors. This would explain her sudden fertility as well as her husband's associated silence. In French, the expression *faire une pipe* means to perform fellatio. But this expression dates only as far back as the first half of the twentieth century.

77. In Hebrew: Peretz, "Mespure Yokhanan Melamed," *Ha-Zfira*, January 12, 13, 14, 16, and 17, 1897; and *Ha-dor* 3–5 (1900–1901). An extended Yiddish version, dated 1897, is in *Ale verk*, vol. 4.

78. Rozentsvayg, *Radikaler peryod*.

79. Translated from the Yiddish version of the story. The Hebrew version of this passage is rather similar to the Yiddish, but, similar to Perl's *The Revealer of Secrets*, the Hebrew version is linguistically subversive in that it immolates the pious Hebrew tone of sacred Jewish texts but turns its meaning around satirically.

80. Pinsker, *Literary Passports*, 297–98.

81. Yokhanan had been a teacher for seven years in Warsaw (*Ale verk*, 4:46), just like Peretz himself, who moved to Warsaw in 1890 and published the story in 1897.

82. Peretz, "Mespure Yokhanan Melamed," *Ha-Zfira*, January 15, 1897, p. 11.

83. Terry Eagleton, *Marxism and Literary Criticism* (London: Routledge, 2002), 8.

84. Peretz, "Oyb nisht nokh hekher," *Der yud* 2, no. 1 (1900): 12–13; and *Ale verk*, 4:98–102.

85. Avrom Reyzn, *Epizodn fun mayn lebn: Literarishe erinerungen* (Vilnius: Vilner Farlag fun B. Kletskin, 1929), 1:238.

86. The story is considered, together with "Between two mountains," to be the climax of Peretz's Hasidic stories (Frieden, "Parodya ve-hegyogrfya," 46). It is often retold in various popular publications of and about Yiddish literature.

87. Reyzn, *Epizodn fun mayn lebn*, 1:238. The czarist regime forbade the right of assembly.

88. Rozentsvayg, *Radikaler peryod*, 99–101. This contrasts with Bergelson, quoted at the opening of this chapter, who was pro-Soviet but wrote before Stalin's era.

89. Karl Marx, "A Contribution to the Critique of Hegel's 'Philosophy of Right': Introduction," in *Critique of Hegel's 'Philosophy of Right*,' ed. Joseph O'Malley, trans. Annette Jolin and O'Malley (Cambridge: Cambridge University Press, 1970), 131. Originally published in Deutsch–Französische Jahrbücher (February 1844). Rozentsvayg regarded Hasidism merely as "opium" (*Radikaler eriod*, 100), as did many Marxists, thus echoing only a part of Marx's famous quotation.

90. Dan Ben-Amos and Dov Noy, eds., *Folktales of the Jews: Tales from Eastern Europe* (Philadelphia: Jewish Publication Society, 2007), 61; Nicham Ross, "Hasipur haḥasidi keyetsira sifrutit: Dilema pedagogit u-fitrona" [The Hasidic tale as a literary creation: A pedagogical dilemma and its solution; in Hebrew], *Mayim medalav* 18 (2007): 305–8, 328–31; Ross, *Margalit ṭemunah ba-ḥol: Y. L. Perets u-maʿaśiyot Ḥasidim* [Gem concealed in sand: I. L. Peretz and Hasidic Tales] (Jerusalem: Hebrew University Magnes Press, 2013), 27–43.

91. Meaning the Hasidic leader (or the tzaddik) from Nemirov (Nemyriv), in Ukraine.

92. Bodek, *Maʾase tsadikim* [Story of tzaddiks] (Lviv, Ukraine: 1864), 40–41.

93. Ross, "Hasipur hakhasidi keyetsira sifrutit," 329–30.

94. Bodek, *Maʾase tsadikim*, 41.

95. Max Horkheimer and Theodor W. Adorno, *Dialectic of Enlightenment: Philosophical Fragments*, ed. Gunzelin Schmid Noerr, trans. Edmund Jephcott (Stanford, CA: Stanford University Press, 2002).

96. As Jordan D. Finkin argues in **A Rhetorical Conversation**: *Jewish Discourse in Modern Yiddish Literature* (University Park: Pennsylvania State University Press, 2010), 161n53.

97. Ross, "Peretz's 'Between Two Mountains,'" 107–9; Ross, *Margalit ṭemunah ba-ḥol*, 112–18.

98. Ross, *Margalit ṭemunah ba-ḥol*, 115.

99. Reuven Braynin, "Y. L. Perets betor meshorer ha-ḥasidut," in *Khasidut*, by I. L. Peretz (New York: Kadima, 1917), v.

100. Frieden, "Tradition and Innovation," 57.

101. Frieden, 58.

102. "[The bourgeoisie] has been the first to show what man's activity can bring about. It has accomplished wonders far surpassing Egyptian pyramids, Roman aqueducts, and Gothic cathedrals," but on the other hand, "for exploitation, veiled by religious and political illusions, [the bourgeoisie] has substituted

naked, shameless, direct, brutal exploitation." Karl Marx and Friedrich Engels, "Manifesto of the Communist Party," in *Karl Marx and Frederick Engels Selected Works*, vol. 1, trans. Samuel Moore (Moscow: Progress Publishers, 1969), chap. 1, transcribed in Marx/Engels Internet Archive, accessed September 19, 2013, http://www.marxists.org/archive/marx/works/1848/communist-manifesto/ch01.htm.

103. Fyodor Dostoyevsky, *Notes from the Underground*, trans. Constance Garnett, ed. Charles Guignon and Kevin Aho (Indianapolis, IN: Hackett Publishing, 2009), 22. About the Crystal Palace, see xix n16, 19n8, and chaps. 7–10.

104. Miron, *Bodedim bemoadam*, 365.

105. Dostoyevsky, *Notes from the Underground*, 21.

106. This phrase shows a Narodnik influence. The Narodniks were left-wing radicals in Russia, active during the second half of the nineteenth century, who were influenced by the anarchist writings of Bakunin. Since the 1870s, they had embraced of the platform of "going to the people" and went to preach their ideas among the Russian peasantry.

107. Ernst Bloch, "Mashma'ut hautopya" [Meaning of utopia], in *Utopiot—antologia*, ed. Avraham Yassour and Noga Wolff (Tel Aviv: Resling, 2011), 225. On Bloch's complex German-Jewish theological-messianic anarchism and his brand of utopian Marxism, see Anson Rabinbach, *In the Shadow of Catastrophe: German Intellectuals between Apocalypse and Enlightenment* (Berkeley: University of California Press, 1997), 27–65.

108. Bloch, "Mashma'ut hautopya," 226.

109. Warren S. Goldstein, "Messianism and Marxism: Walter Benjamin and Ernst Bloch's Dialectical Theories of Secularization," *Critical Sociology* 27, no. 2 (2001): 246–81.

110. Miron, *Der imazh fun shtetl* (Tel Aviv: 1981), 113–14.

111. Marx famously viewed idealism as antithetical to materialism and in general condemned humanist nonmaterialist philosophies. More in Etienne Balibar, *The Philosophy of Marx*, trans. Chris Turner (London: Verso Press, 2007).

112. Rozentsvayg, *Radikaler periyod*, 100.

113. Rozentsvayg, 100.

114. Bruce Robbins, "Secularism, Elitism, Progress, and Other Transgressions: On Edward Said's 'Voyage In,'" *Social Text*, no. 40 (Fall 1994): 26. The "power" in Peretz's story is embodied by the Brisker Rov, who Nomberg considers to be the more impressive character of the two (*Y. L. Perets*, 113–15).

Chapter 6

1. For example, the short drama "A mol iz geven a meylekh" (Once there was a king; 1907; in Hebrew: 1912).

2. Vladimir Medem, "Perets un mir" [Peretz and we], in *Valdimir Medem tsum tsvantsikstn yortsayt* [Valdimir Medem twenty-five years to his death; in

Yiddish] (New York: Ameriḳaner reprezenṭants fun Algemeynem Yidishn arbeṭer-bund in Poyln, 1943), 344–45.

3. "איך בין ניט ארויסגעטראָטען געגען 'בונד' און האָב ניט געזאָגט, אַז ער וויל פערלעשען די אידישע נשמה. פערקערהרט, אין פריוואט געשפרעך מיט די נייע מיטגלידער פון דער ניער געזעלשאפט, האָב איך געזאָגט: איך געהער צו קיין פארטיי, אמנעכסטען דאָך שטעהט מיר דער 'בונד'" ("Y. L. Perets vegen 'Bund'" [I. L. Peretz about the Bund], Forverts, December 13, 1906, p. 8).

4. Frank Wolff, *Yiddish Revolutionaries in Migration: The Transnational History of the Jewish Labour Bund*, trans. Loren Balhorn and Jan-Peter Herrmann (Leiden: Brill, 2021), 348.

5. Jack Jacobs, "Written Out of History: Bundists in Vienna and the Varieties of Jewish Experience in the Austrian First Republic," in *In Search of Jewish Community: Jewish Identities in Germany and Austria, 1918–1933*, ed. Michael Brenner and Derek J. Penslar (Bloomington, IN: Indiana University Press, 1998), 132, quoted in Claudie Weill, "Russian Bundists Abroad and in Exile, 1898–1925," in *Jewish Politics in Eastern Europe: The Bund at 100* (New York: New York University Press / Żydowski Instytut Historyczny—Instytut Naukowo-Badawczy, 2001), 53.

6. "Fayerlekhe tseremonye in sity hol ven mayor shraybt unter bil far perets skver" [Festive ceremony in city hall when mayor signs bill for Peretz Square], *Forverts*, June 4, 1952, p. 1.

7. Pat represented at the event the Yidishe kultur kongres (Jewish Culture Congress), which was the major initiator of the Peretz Square ("Di derefenung funem 'perets-skver'" [The opening of the Peretz Square], *Fraye arbeter shtime*, December 5, 1952). The square is located between Houston Street and First Avenue. "Peretz Square," NYC Parks (website), New York City Department of Parks & Recreation, accessed September 8, 2021, https://www.nycgovparks.org/parks/peretz-square/.

8. I discuss Singer's politics at length in Adi Mahalel, "Yiddish, Scholarship, and Neoconservatism," *AJS Review* 44, no. 1 (April 2020): 119–47.

Chapter 7

1. I. L. Peretz, *Ver es vil nisht—shtarbt nisht af kholi-ra* [Whoever doesn't want to—doesn't die of cholera; in Yiddish] (Warsaw: Varshaver hilf-komitet, 1892). In this booklet Peretz also expressed an early interest in Jewish folklore when he added Jewish popular beliefs concerning the plague. Yankev Shatzky, "Perets-shtudyes," *YIVO-bleter* 28 (1946): 56.

2. Peretz, *Briv un redes* (1929), 59; also quoted in M. Khmelnitski, "Y. L. Perets' popular-meditsinishe broshur: Az me vil nisht, shtarbt nisht fun kholi-ra," *YIVO-bleter* 28 (Fall 1946): 152.

3. Poaley-tsedek, an old Jewish society.

4. Peretz, "Al Shulchan aruch" [About the "Shulkhan arukh"; in Hebrew], *Ha-asif* 6 (1893), 205.

Bibliography

Works by I. L. Peretz

Peretz, I. L [Perets, Y. L.]. "About the 'Shulkhan Arukh.'" [In Hebrew.] *Ha-asif* 6 (1893): 199–206.

———. *Ale verk fun Y. L. Perets* [Collected works of Y. L. Perets]. 11 vols. New York: CYCO, 1947–48.

———. "Ankhot ahava" [Moans of love]. [In Hebrew.] *Ha-asif* 6 (1893): 170.

———. *Bekante bilder*. With an introduction by Yankev Dinzeon. Warsaw: Yitshak Funk, 1890. Second edition published 1894.

———. "Be-maon Kaits." [In Hebrew.] In *Luah ahiasaf*, vol. 1, pp. 75–82. Warsaw: Ahi'asaf, 1893.

———. *Briv un redes*. [In Yiddish.] Compiled by Nakhman Mayzel. Vilnius: B. Kletskin, 1929.

———. *Briv un redes fun Y. L. Perets*. Edited by Nachman Mayzel. New York: IKUF, 1944.

———. "Denial." [In Hebrew.] *Ha-melitz* 169 (1894).

———. *Di yudishe bibliyotek*. Edited by I. L. Peretz. [In Yiddish.] 3 vols. Warsaw, 1891, 1895.

———. "Dos yidishe lebn loyt di yidishe folkslider." *YIVO-bleter* 12 (1937): 291–99.

———. "Eshet khaver." *Ha-tzfira* [Hazefirah], no. 226 (December 16, 1890): 2.

———. "Even ve-even, eyfa ve-eyfa." *Ha-tsefira* 237 (November 1890): 2.

———, editor. *Ha-chetz: Yalkut sifruti*. Warsaw: Shvartzberg, 1894.

———. *Ha-ilemet, Manginat ha-zman*. Warsaw: Ben-Avigdor, 1892.

———. "Ha-kadish." *Ha-yom* 1 (1886): 2.

———. "Hamekubalim." *Gan perahim* 3 (1891): 83–85.

———. "Ha-shutafut." *Ha-shahar* 5 (1875).

———. *Ha-'Ugav: Shire ahavah I me'et Y. L. Perets*. Warsaw: Hotsa'at Sh. B. Shvartsberg, 1894.

———. *Iber profesyonen*. [In Yiddish.] 2nd ed. Warsaw: Halter and Eisenshtat, 1894.

———. *The I. L Peretz Reader*. Edited by Ruth R. Wisse. New York: Schocken Books, 1990.

———. "In the Mail Coach." Translated by Golda Werman. In *The I. L Peretz Reader*, edited by Ruth R. Wisse, pp. 104–18. New York: Schocken Books, 1990.

———. "Ir ha-metim." [In Hebrew.] *Ha-tzfira* [Hazefirah], nos. 164–65 (August 1892).

———. *Kitvey Y. L. Perets*. [In Hebrew.] Tel Aviv: Dvir, 1926–27.

———. *Literatur un lebn: A zaml-bukh far literatur un gezelshaft*. Edited by I. L. Peretz. Warsaw: Funk, 1894.

———. "Ma'ase be-gimel Kabtsanim" [A tale of three beggars]. *Ha-tsofe* 47 (March 1903).

———. "Ma haya Gordon—balshan o meshorer?" [What was Gordon—a philologist or a poet?]. *Ha-tsefira*, 1896.

———. "Mespure Yokhanan Melamed." *Ha-dor* 3–5 (1900–1901).

———. "Mespure Yokhanan Melamed." *Ha-Zfira*, January 12, 13, 14, 16, and 17, 1897.

———. "Mishnes khsidim." *Der yud* 4, no. 19 (May 8, 1902): 11–14.

———. "A night of horror: A research in mental disease." [In Hebrew.] *Ha-asif* 6 (1893): 136–45.

———. "Oyb nisht nokh hekher." *Der yud* 2, no. 1 (1900): 12–13.

———. *Perets's bletlekh: Zhurnal far literatur, gezelshaft, un ekonomiye*. Warsaw: Progress, 1913. Reprint of *Yontev bletlekh* (1894–96).

———. "The plea." *Yontef bletlekh* 10: *Homentash* (1894).

———. *Poezye*. Warsaw: Gebrider Shuldberg, 1892.

———. "Shmaya gibor." *Ha-tzfira*, no. 183 (August 1892).

———. *Ver es vil—shtarbt nisht af kholi-ra*. [In Yiddish.] Warsaw: Varshaver hilf-komitet, 1892.

Peretz, I. L., and Gabriel Judah Lichtenfeld. *Sipurim be-shir ve-shirim shonim me'et Shenei Ba'alei Asufot* [Stories in verse and sundry poems from two anthologists]. [In Hebrew.] Warsaw, 1877.

Books and Articles in English, French, German, and Polish

Adler, Ruth. "Peretz's Empathic Linkage to Woman." *Studies in American Jewish Literature* 3, no. 2 (Winter 1977–78): 50–55. http://www.jstor.org/stable/41203768.

Alter, Robert, editor. *Modern Hebrew Literature*. New York: Behrman House, 1975.

Amin, Samir. *Class and Nation, Historically and in the Current Crisis*. New York: Monthly Review Press, 1980.

Anderson, Benedict. *Imagined Communities: Reflections on the Origin and Spread of Nationalism*. Rev. ed. London: Verso, 2006.

Anidjar, Gil. "Secularism." *Critical Inquiry* 33, no. 1 (Autumn 2006).

Balibar, Etienne. *The Philosophy of Marx*. Translated by Chris Turner. London: Verso Press, 2007.

Barer, Shlomo. *The Doctors of Revolution: 19th-Century Thinkers Who Changed the World*. New York: Thames & Hudson, 2000.

———. "Heine and Marx: The relationship between the prophet of communism and the poet who foresaw its horrors." [In Hebrew.] In *Marx and the future of socialism*, edited by Uri Zilbersheid, pp. 163–80. Tel Aviv: Resling, 2005.

Bauer, Ela. *Between Poles and Jews: The Development of Nahum Sokolow's Political Thought*. Jerusalem: Hebrew University Magnes Press, 2005.

———. "From the Salons to the Street: The Development of the Jewish Salon in Warsaw at the End of the 19th Century."*Jahrbuch des Simon-Dubnow-Instituts / Simon Dubnow Institute Yearbook* 7 (2008).

Benjamin, Walter. "The Author as Producer." Translated by John Heckman. *New Left Review* I/62 (July/August 1970): 220–38.

———. "The Paris of the Second Empire in Baudelaire." In *The Writer of Modern Life: Essays on Charles Baudelaire*, edited by Michael Jennings, pp. 46–133. Cambridge, MA: Belknap Press, 2006.

Bechtel, Delphine. *Der Nister's Work, 1907–1929: A Study of a Yiddish Symbolist*. Berne: Peter Lang, 1990.

———. "Entre tradition juive et modernité révolutionnaire: Le combat de Der Nister contre la critique littéraire soviétique." In *Contes fantastiques et symboliques*, by Der Nister. Paris: Editions du Cerf, 1997.

Beckson, Karl, and Arthur Ganz. *Literary Terms: A Dictionary*. 3rd ed. New York: Noonday Press, 1989.

Ben-Amos, Dan, and Dov Noy, editors. *Folktales of the Jews: Tales from Eastern Europe*. Philadelphia: Jewish Publication Society, 2007.

Berger, Shlomo. *The Bible in/and Yiddish*. Amsterdam: Menasseh ben Israel Institute, 2007.

Berkowitz, Joel, and Jeremy Dauber, eds. and trans. *Landmark Yiddish Plays: A Critical Anthology*. Albany: State University of New York, 2006.

Berry, David. "Max Horkheimer: Issues Concerning Liberalism and Culture." In *Revisiting the Frankfurt School: Essays on Culture, Media and Theory*, edited by David Berry. Farnham, UK: Ashgate, 2012.

Biale, David, David Assaf, Benjamin Brown, Uriel Gellman, Samuel C. Heilman, Moshe Rosman, Gadi Sagiv, and Marcin Wodziński. *Hasidism: A New History*. Princeton, NJ: Princeton University Press, 2018.

Blejwas, Stanislaus A. "New Political Directions: A Transition toward Popular Participation in Politics, 1863–90." In *The Origins of Modern Polish Democracy*, edited by M. B. B. Biskupski, James S. Pula, and Piotr J. Wróbel, pp. 23–60. Athens: Ohio University Press, 2010.

Bloch, Ernst. "Mashma'ut hautopya" [The significance of utopia]. [In Hebrew.] In *Utopiot—antologia* [Utopia: An anthology], edited by Avraham Yassour and Noga Wolff. Tel Aviv: Resling, 2011.

Borochov, Ber. "The Jubilee of the Jewish Labor Movement (1916)." In *Class Struggle and the Jewish Nation: Selected Essays in Marxist Zionism*, edited by Mitchell Cohen, pp. 105–10. New Brunswick, NJ: Transaction Books, 1983.

Bourdieu, Pierre. *La domination masculine*. Translated into Hebrew by Avner Lahav with an introduction by Gisele Sapiro. Tel Aviv: Resling, 2007. First published in French by Editions du Seuil, 1998.

Bowring, Bill. "Burial and Resurrection: Karl Renner's Controversial Influence on the 'National Question' in Russia." In *National Cultural Autonomy and Its Contemporary Critics*, edited by Ephraim Nimni, pp. 191–206. London: Routledge, 2005.

Boyarin, Daniel. *Unheroic Conduct: The Rise of Heterosexuality and the Invention of the Jewish Man*. Berkeley: University of California Press, 1997.

Bray, Joe. *The Epistolary Novel: Representations of Consciousness*. London: Routledge, 2003.

Bromberg, Eli. "We Need to Talk about Shmuel Charney." *In geveb*, October 2, 2019. https://ingeveb.org/articles/we-need-to-talk-about-shmuel-charney.

Cammy, Justin Daniel, trans. "The Judgment of Shomer, or The Jury Trial of All of Shomer's Novels." By Sholem Aleichem. In *Arguing the Modern Jewish Canon: Essays on Literature and Culture in Honor of Ruth R. Wisse*, edited by Justin Daniel Cammy, Dara Horn, Alyssa Quint, and Rachel Rubinstein, pp. 129–88. Cambridge, MA: Center for Jewish Studies at Harvard University, 2008.

Caplan, Marc. "The Fragmentation of Narrative Perspective in Y. L. Peretz's *Bilder fun a Provints-Rayze*." *Jewish Social Studies: History, Culture, Society*, n.s., 14, no. 1 (Fall 2007): 63–88.

Cohen, Madeleine. "*Do'ikayt* and the Spaces of Politics in An-sky's Novella *In shtrom*." *East European Jewish Affairs* 50, no. 1–2 (2020): 6–20.

Dauber, Jeremy Asher. *Antonio's Devils: Writers of the Jewish Enlightenment and the Birth of Modern Hebrew and Yiddish Literature*. Stanford, CA: Stanford University Press, 2004.

———. *The Worlds of Sholem Aleichem: The Remarkable Life and Afterlife of the Man Who Created Tevye*. New York: Schocken, 2013.

Dostoyevsky, Fyodor. *Notes from the Underground*. Translated by Constance Garnett, edited by Charles Guignon and Kevin Aho. Indianapolis, IN: Hackett Publishing, 2009.

Dungen, Peter van den. *The Making of Peace: Jean de Bloch and the First Hague Peace Conference*. Los Angeles: Center for the Study of Armament and Disarmament, California State University, 1983.

Dynner, Glenn. *Men of Silk: The Hasidic Conquest of Polish Jewish Society*. New York: Oxford University Press, 2006.

Eagleton, Terry. *Literary Theory: An Introduction*. 2nd ed. Minneapolis: University of Minnesota Press, 1996.

———. *Marxism and Literary Criticism*. London: Routledge, 2002.

———. *Myths of Power: A Marxist Study of the Brontës*. London: Palgrave Macmillan, 2005.

———. *Reason, Faith and Revolution: Reflections on the God Debate*. New Haven, CT: Yale University Press, 2009.

———. *Sweet Violence: The Idea of the Tragic*. Oxford: Blackwell, 2009.
———. *The Event of Literature*. New Haven, CT: Yale University Press, 2012.
Engels, Friedrich. "The Origin of the Family, Private Property, and the State." In *The Marx-Engels Reader*, 2nd ed., edited by Robert C. Tucker, pp. 234–59. New York: W. W. Norton, 1978.
Erlich, Victor. *The Double Image: Concepts of the Poet in Slavic Literatures*. Baltimore: Johns Hopkins University Press, 1964.
Evans, Caroline. *Fashion at the Edge: Spectacle, Modernity and Deathliness*. New Haven, CT: Yale University Press, 2003.
Ewen, Frederic. *A Half-Century of Greatness: The Creative Imagination of Europe, 1848–1883*. Edited by Jeffrey Wollock. New York: New York University Press, 2008.
Feiner, Shmuel. *The Jewish Enlightenment*. Translated by Chaya Naor. Philadelphia: University of Pennsylvania Press, 2011.
Finkin, Jordan D. *A Rhetorical Conversation: Jewish Discourse in Modern Yiddish Literature*. University Park: Pennsylvania State University Press, 2010.
Fishman, David E. "The Bund and Modern Yiddish Culture." In *The Emergence of Modern Jewish Politics: Bundism and Zionism in Eastern Europe*, edited by Zvi Gitelman, pp. 107–19. Pittsburgh: University of Pittsburg Press, 2003.
———. *The Rise of Modern Yiddish Culture*. Pittsburgh: University of Pittsburgh Press, 2005.
Frankel, Jonathan. *Crisis, Revolution, and Russian Jews*. Cambridge: Cambridge University Press, 2009.
———. *Prophecy and Politics: Socialism, Nationalism, and the Russian Jews, 1862–1917*. Cambridge: Cambridge University Press, 1981.
Freud, Sigmund. *Jokes and Their Relation to the Unconscious*. Translated by James Strachey. New York: Norton, 1960. First published in 1905 in German.
Frieden, Ken. *Classic Yiddish Fiction: Abramovitsh, Sholem Aleichem, and Peretz*. Albany, NY: State University of New York Press, 1995.
———. "Psychological Depth in I. L. Peretz' *Familiar Scenes*: On the 75th Anniversary of His Death." *Jewish Book Annual* 47 (1989–90).
———. "Tradition and Innovation: How Peretz Made Literary History." In *The Enduring Legacy of Yitzchok Leybush Peretz: Proceedings of a Literary and Cultural Symposium*, edited by Benny Kraut, 49–61. New York: CUNY Center for Jewish Studies, 2005.
Friedman, Albert B. *The Ballad Revival: Studies in the Influence of Popular on Sophisticated Poetry*. Chicago: University of Chicago Press, 1961.
Garrett, Leah. *A Knight at the Opera: Heine, Wagner, Herzl, Peretz, and the Legacy of Der Tannhäuser*. West Lafayette, IN: Purdue University Press, 2011.
Gechtman, Roni. "Nationalising the Bund? Zionist Historiography and the Jewish Labour Movement." *East European Jewish Affairs* 43, no. 3 (2013): 249–64.
Goldsmith, Emanuel S. "A Modern Judaism for the Yiddish World." In *The Enduring Legacy of Yitzchok Leybush Peretz: Proceedings of a Literary and Cultural*

Symposium, edited by Benny Kraut, pp. 21–29. New York: CUNY Center for Jewish Studies, 2005.

Goldstein, Warren S. "Messianism and Marxism: Walter Benjamin and Ernst Bloch's Dialectical Theories of Secularization." *Critical Sociology* 27, no. 2 (2001): 246–81.

Gluzman, Michael. *The Politics of Canonicity: Lines of Resistance in Modernist Hebrew Poetry*. Stanford, CA: Stanford University Press, 2003.

Gluzman, Michael, Hannan Hever, and Dan Miron, editors. *Be-ir ha-haregah: Bikur me'uchar bi-melot me'ah shanah la-po'emah shel Bialik* [In the city of slaughter: A late visit on the hundredth anniversary of Bialik's poema]. [In Hebrew.] Tel Aviv: Resling, 2005.

Gottesman, Itzik Nakhmen. *Defining the Yiddish Nation: The Jewish Folklorists of Poland*. Detroit: Wayne State University Press, 2003.

Gramsci, Antonio. *Prison Notebooks*. Edited and translated by Joseph A. Buttigieg. New York: Columbia University Press, 2011. 3 vols.

Greaney, Patrick. *Untimely Beggar: Poverty and Power from Baudelaire to Benjamin*. Minneapolis: University of Minnesota Press, 2008.

Guerra, Elizabeth, and Janet Farrar. *Stewart Farrar: Writer on a Broomstick*. Arcata, CA: R. J. Stewart Books, 2008.

Harshav, Benjamin. *Language in Time of Revolution*. Berkeley: University of California Press, 1993.

Harshav, Benjamin, and Barbara Harshav, editors. *American Yiddish Poetry: A Bilingual Anthology*. Berkeley: University of California Press, 1986.

Heine, Heinrich. *Complete Poetical Works of Heinrich Heine*. Hastings, UK: Delphi Classics, 2016.

———. *Germany, a Winter Tale*. Translated by Edgar Alfred Bowring. New York: Mondial, 2007.

———. *Heinrich Heines Samtliche Werke: Herausgegeben von Prof. Dr. Ernst Elster: Kritisch durchgesehene und erlauterte Ausgabe*. 7 vols. Leipzig: Bibliographisches Institut, 1887–90. Reprinted with revisions 1893.

Hever, Hannan. "Poetry." Translated by Lisa Katz. *Political Concepts: A Critical Lexicon* 2 (2012): 1–7. http://www.politicalconcepts.org/poetry-hannan-hever/.

Holtzman, Avner. "*The Harp* by I. L. Peretz and the Controversy over Hebrew Love Poetry." In *The Trilingual Literature of Polish Jews from Different Perspectives: In Memory of I. L. Peretz*, edited by Alina Molisak and Shoshana Ronen, pp. 22–43. Newcastle upon Tyne, UK: Cambridge Scholars Publishing, 2017.

Hood, Thomas. "The Song of the Shirt." *Punch* 5 (December 16, 1843): 260.

Horkheimer, Max, and Theodor W. Adorno. *Dialectic of Enlightenment: Philosophical Fragments*. Edited by Gunzelin Schmid Noerr, translated by Edmund Jephcott. Stanford, CA: Stanford University Press, 2002.

Howe, Irving, Ruth R. Wisse, and Khone Shmeruk, editors. *The Penguin Book of Modern Yiddish Verse*. New York: Penguin, 1987.

Hutcheon, Linda. *A Theory of Parody: Teachings of Twentieth-Century Art Forms.* New York: Methuen, 1985.

Jacobs, Jack. Introduction to *Jews and Leftist Politics: Judaism, Israel, Antisemitism, and Gender*, edited by Jack Jacobs, pp. 1–25. Cambridge: Cambridge University Press, 2017.

Jameson, Fredric. *Marxism and Form: Twentieth-Century Dialectical Theories of Literature.* Princeton, NJ: Princeton University Press, 1971.

———. *Postmodernism; or, The Cultural Logic of Late Capitalism.* Durham, NC: Duke University Press, 1991.

Katz, Dovid. *Words on Fire: The Unfinished Story of Yiddish.* New York: Basic Books, 2004.

Kaufmann, Hans. *Politische Gedicht und klassische Dichtung: Heinrich Heine, "Deutschland. Ein Wintermärchen."* [In German.] Berlin: Aufbau Verlag, 1959.

Korn, Yitzhak. *Jews at the Crossroads.* New York: Cornwall Books, 1983.

Koselleck, Reinhart, Fritz Gschnitzer, Karl Ferdinand Werner, and Bernd Schönemann. "Volk, Nation, Nationalismus, Masse." In *Geschichtliche Grundbegriffe: Historisches Lexikon zur politisch-sozialen Sprache in Deutschland*, vol. 7., edited by Reinhart Koselleck. Stuttgart: Klett-Cotta Verlag, 1992.

Kritz, Ori. *The Poetics of Anarchy: David Edelshtat's Revolutionary Poetry.* Frankfurt am Main: P. Lang, 1997.

Krutikov, Mikhail. *From Kabbalah to Class Struggle: Expressionism, Marxism, and Yiddish Literature in the Life and Work of Meir Wiener.* Stanford, CA: Stanford University Press, 2011.

Leon, Abram. *The Jewish Question: A Marxist Interpretation.* New York: Pathfinder Press, 1971.

Limón, José. *Mexican Ballads, Chicano Poems: History and Influence in Mexican-American Social Poetry.* Berkeley: University of California Press, 1992.

Liptzin, Sol. "Heine and the Yiddish Poets." In *The Jewish Reception of Heinrich Heine*, edited by Mark H. Gelber, pp. 67–76. Tübingen, Germany: Niemeyer, 1992.

Mahalel, Adi. "'To Be a Fighter with Both Fists!': Peretz as a Radical Hebrew Writer." In *The Trilingual Literature of Polish Jews from Different Perspectives: In Memory of I. L. Peretz*, edited by Alina Molisak and Shoshana Ronen, pp. 284–97. Newcastle upon Tyne, UK: Cambridge Scholars Publishing, 2017.

———. "Weaving the Revolution: Peretz the Social Protest Writer." *In geveb: A Journal of Yiddish Studies*, May 22, 2016. http://ingeveb.org/articl es/weaving-the-revolution-i-l-peretz-the-social-protest-writer.

———. "We Will Not Be Silent: I. L. Peretz's 'Bontshe the Silent' vs. 1950s McCarthyism in America and the Story of the Staging of *The World of Sholom Aleichem*." *Studies in American Jewish Literature* 34, no. 2 (2015): 204–30.

———. "Yiddish, Scholarship, and Neoconservatism." *AJS Review* 44, no. 1 (April 2020): 119–47.

Mahler, Raphael. *Hasidism and the Jewish Enlightenment: Their Confrontation in Galicia and Poland in the First Half of the Nineteenth Century*. Translated by Eugene Orenstein, Aaron Klein, and Jenny Machlowitz Klein. Philadelphia: Jewish Publication Society of America, 1985.

———. "The Social and Political Aspects of the Haskalah in Galicia." *YIVO Annual of Jewish Social Science* 1 (1946): 64–85.

Marx, Karl. "A Contribution to the Critique of Hegel's 'Philosophy of Right': Introduction." In *Critique of Hegel's "Philosophy of Right,"* edited by Joseph O'Malley, translated by Annette Jolin and Joseph O'Malley, pp. 129–142. Cambridge: Cambridge University Press, 1970. Originally published in *Deutsch–Französische Jahrbücher* (February 1844).

———. "Der achtzehnte Brumaire des Louis Bonaparte." In *Werke*, vol. 8, pp. 115–23, §116. Berlin: Dietz Verlag, 1972. Transcribed in Marx-Engels Archive, 1999. http://www.mlwerke.de/me/me08/me08_115.htm.

———. *The Eighteenth Brumaire of Louis Bonaparte*. Translated by Saul K. Padover from the German edition of 1869. Transcribed in Marx-Engels Archive, 1999, https://www.marxists.org/archive/marx/works/1852/18th-brumaire/index.htm.

———. *Love Poems of Karl Marx*. Edited and translated by Reinhard Lettau and Lawrence Ferlinghetti. San Francisco: City Lights Books, 1977.

Marx, Karl, and Friedrich Engels. *The Communist Manifesto*. Harmondsworth, UK: Penguin Books, 1970.

———. "Manifesto of the Communist Party." In *Karl Marx and Frederick Engels Selected Works*, vol. 1, translated by Samuel Moore. Moscow: Progress Publishers, 1969. Transcribed in Marx-Engels Archive, accessed September 19, 2013, http://www.marxists.org/archive/marx/works/1848/communist-manifesto/ch01.htm.

Mendelsohn, Ezra. *Class Struggle in the Pale: The Formative Years of the Jewish Workers' Movement in Tsarist Russia*. Cambridge: Cambridge University Press, 1970.

Meyers, Joshua. "The Bund by the Numbers: The Ebbs and Flows of a Jewish Radical Party." *In geveb*, May 6, 2020. https://ingeveb.org/blog/the-bund-by-the-numbers.

Michels, Tony. *A Fire in Their Hearts: Yiddish Socialists in New York*. Cambridge, MA: Harvard University Press, 2005.

Miller, Marc. *Representing the Immigrant Experience: Morris Rosenfeld and the Emergence of Yiddish Literature in America*. Syracuse, NY: Syracuse University Press, 2007.

Mikoś, Michael J., editor and translator. *Polish Literature from 1864 to 1918: Realism and Young Poland: An Anthology*. Bloomington, IN: Slavica Publishers, 2006.

Miron, Dan. *From Continuity to Contiguity: Toward A New Jewish Literary Thinking.* Stanford, CA: Stanford University Press, 2010.

———. *H. N. Bialik and the Prophetic Mode in Modern Hebrew Poetry.* Syracuse, NY: Syracuse University Press, 2000.

———. "I. L. Peretz as the Poet of the Jewish Age of Sensibility: On the Century of His Death 1915–2015." In *The Trilingual Literature of Polish Jews from Different Perspectives: In Memory of I. L. Peretz,* edited by Alina Molisak and Shoshana Ronen, pp. 1–21. Newcastle upon Tyne, UK: Cambridge Scholars Publishing, 2017.

———. *The Image of the Shtetl and Other Studies of Modern Jewish Literary Imagination.* New York: Syracuse University Press, 2000.

———. "Literature as a Vehicle for National Renaissance: The Model of Peretz versus That of Bialik." In *The Enduring Legacy of Yitzchok Leybush Peretz: Proceedings of a Literary and Cultural Symposium,* edited by Benny Kraut, pp. 30–48. New York: CUNY Center for Jewish Studies, 2005.

———. *A Traveler Disguised: The Rise of Modern Yiddish Fiction in the Nineteenth Century.* Syracuse, NY: Syracuse University Press, 1996. First published in 1973.

Newman, Steve. *Ballad Collection, Lyric, and the Canon: The Call of the Popular from the Restoration to the New Criticism.* Philadelphia: University of Pennsylvania Press, 2007.

Niewöhner, Friedrich. "Jüdischer Nietzscheanismus seit 1888—Ursprünge und Begriff." In *Jüdischer Nietzscheanismus,* edited by Werner Stegmaier and Daniel Krochmalnik. Berlin: Walter de Gruyter, 1997.

Nimni, Ephraim. "National-Cultural Autonomy as an Alternative to Minority Territorial Nationalism." *Ethnopolitics* 6, no. 3 (2007): 345–64.

Osborne, John. *Gerhart Hauptmann and the Naturalist Drama.* Amsterdam: Harwood Academic Publishers, 1998.

Padavic, Irene, and Barbara F. Reskin. *Women and Men at Work.* London: Sage Publications, 2002.

Parush, Iris. *Reading Jewish Women: Marginality and Modernization in Nineteenth-Century Eastern European Jewish Society.* Translated by Saadya Sternberg. Waltham, MA: Brandeis University Press, 2004.

Peled, Horit Herman, and Yoav Peled. "The Way Forward in the Middle East." In *Israel and Palestine: Alternative Perspectives on Statehood,* edited by John Ehrenberg and Yoav Peled, pp. 187–99. Lanham, MD: Rowman & Littlefield, 2016.

Peled, Yoav. *Class and Ethnicity in the Pale: The Political Economy of Jewish Workers' Nationalism in Late Imperial Russia.* New York: St. Martin's Press, 1989.

———. "The Concept of National Cultural Autonomy: The First One Hundred Years." In *Jewish Politics in Eastern Europe: The Bund at 100,* edited by Jack Jacobs, pp. 255–70. New York: New York University Press / Żydowski Instytut Historyczny—Instytut Naukowo-Badawczy, 2001.

Peters, George F. *The Poet as Provocateur: Heinrich Heine and His Critics*. Rochester, NY: Camden House, 2000.

Pinsker, Shachar. *Literary Passports: The Making of Modernist Hebrew Fiction in Europe*. Stanford, CA: Stanford University Press, 2010.

Porter, Brian. *When Nationalism Began to Hate: Imagining Modern Politics in Nineteenth-Century Poland*. New York: Oxford University Press, 2000.

Rabinbach, Anson. *In the Shadow of Catastrophe: German Intellectuals between Apocalypse and Enlightenment*. Berkeley: University of California Press, 1997.

Rash, Felicity. *German Images of the Self and the Other: Nationalist, Colonialist and Anti-Semitic Discourse, 1871–1918*. Basingstoke, UK: Palgrave Macmillan, 2012.

Reifowitz, Ian. "Otto Bauer and Karl Renner on Nationalism, Ethnicity & Jews." *Journal of Jewish Identities* 2, no. 2 (2009): 1–19.

Ringer, Fritz. "Bildung: The Social and Ideological Context of the German Historical Tradition." *History of European Ideas* 10 (1989): 193–202.

Robbins, Bruce. "Secularism, Elitism, Progress, and Other Transgressions: On Edward Said's 'Voyage In.'" *Social Text*, no. 40 (Fall 1994): 25–37.

Rokem, Na'ama. *Prosaic Conditions: Heinrich Heine and the Spaces of Zionist Literature*. Evanston, IL: Northwestern University Press, 2013.

Rose, Margaret A. *Reading the Young Marx and Engels: Poetry, Parody, and the Censor*. London: Croom Helm, 1978.

Roskies, David-Hirsh. *A Bridge of Longing: The Lost Art of Yiddish Storytelling*. Cambridge, MA: Harvard University Press, 1996.

———. "Rabbis, Rebbes, and Other Humanists: The Search for a Usable Past in Modern Yiddish Literature." *Studies in Contemporary Jewry* 12 (1996): 55–77.

———. "The Small Talk of I. L. Peretz." *In geveb*, May 22, 2016. https://ingeveb.org/articles/the-small-talk-of-i-l-peretz.

Ross, Nicham. "I. L. Peretz's 'Between Two Mountains': Neo-Hasidism and Jewish Literary Modernity." In *Modern Jewish Literatures: Intersections and Boundaries*, edited by Sheila E. Jelen, Michael P. Kramer, and L. Scott Lerner, pp. 104–26. Philadelphia: University of Pennsylvania Press, 2011.

Safran, Gabriella. *Wandering Soul: The Dybbuk's Creator, S. An-Sky*. Cambridge, MA: Harvard University Press, 2011.

Sapiro, Gisèle. Introduction to *La domination masculine*, by Pierre Bourdieu. pp. 7–22. Translated into Hebrew by Avner Lahav. Tel Aviv: Resling, 2007. First published in French by Éditions du Seuil, 1998.

Sartre, Jean-Paul. "Sartre: The Novel and Reality, from *Speech at a Conference of European Writers*." In *Marxism and Art: Essays Classic and Contemporary*, edited by Maynard Solomon, pp. 255–57 (New York: Knopf, 1973).

Scholz, Susanne. *Sacred Witness: Rape in the Hebrew Bible*. Fortress, 2010, 53-55.

Schwartz, Howard. *Reimagining the Bible: The Storytelling of the Rabbis*. New York: Oxford University Press, 1998.

Shaked, Gershon. *Modern Hebrew Fiction*. Translated by Yael Lotan and edited by Emily Miller Budick. Bloomington: Indiana University Press, 2000.

Shenfeld, Ruth. "The family crisis: An integrated view on the decline of the Jewish family unit in late-nineteenth- and early-twentieth-century Poland as reflected in the works of Frischmann, Peretz, Barashm, and Zapolska." [In Hebrew.] In *Studies in East European Jewish history and culture, in honor of Professor Shmuel Werses*, edited by David Assaf et al., pp. 343–60. Jerusalem: Hebrew University Magnes Press, 2002.

Slucki, David. *The International Jewish Labor Bund after 1945: Toward a Global History*. New Brunswick, NJ: Rutgers University Press, 2012.

Smith, Andrew. *Gothic Literature*. Edinburg: Edinburg University Press, 2007.

———. *Gothic Radicalism: Literature, Philosophy and Psychoanalysis in the Nineteenth Century*. New York: St. Martin's Press, 2000.

Solomon, Maynard. "Ernst Bloch: Introduction." In *Marxism and Art: Essays Classic and Contemporary*, edited by Maynard Solomon, pp. 567–75. New York: Knopf, 1973.

Spinner, Samuel J. *Jewish Primitivism*. Stanford, CA: Stanford University Press, 2021.

Teitsh, Moishe, editor. *Arbeter lider (Anthology)*. Warsaw: Progress, 1906.

Trilse-Finkelstein, Jochanan. *Heinrich Heine: Gelebter Widerspruch: Eine Biographie*. Berlin: Aufbau, 2001.

Ury, Scott. "The Culture of Modern Jewish Politics." In *Insiders and Outsiders: Dilemmas of East European Jewry*, edited by Richard I. Cohen, Jonathan Frankel, and Stefani Hoffman, pp. 151–65. Oxford: Littman Library of Jewish Civilization, 2010.

Teller, Adam. "Hasidism and the Challenge of Geography: The Polish Background to the Spread of the Hasidic Movement." *AJS Review* 30, no. 1 (2006): 1–29.

Waltzer, Michael. "The Strangeness of Jewish Leftism." In *Jews and Leftist Politics: Judaism, Israel, Antisemitism, and Gender*, edited by Jack Jacobs. Cambridge: Cambridge University Press, 2017.

West, Cornel. "Introduction: The Radical King We Don't Know." In *The Radical King*, by Martin Luther King Jr., edited by Cornel West, pp. ix–xvi. Boston, MA: Beacon Press, 2015.

Wilde, Oscar. "The Soul of Man under Socialism." *Fortnightly Review* 49 (February 1, 1891).

Wisse, Ruth R. *I. L. Peretz and the Making of Modern Jewish Culture*. Seattle: University of Washington Press, 1991.

———. "Not the 'Pintele Yid' but the Full-Fledged Jew." *Prooftexts* 15, no. 1 (1995): 33–61.

———. "The Political Vision of I. L. Peretz." In *The Emergence of Modern Jewish Politics: Bundism and Zionism in Eastern Europe*, edited by Zvi Gitelman, pp. 120–31. Pittsburg: University of Pittsburg Press, 2003.

Wolff, Frank. *Yiddish Revolutionaries in Migration: The Transnational History of the Jewish Labour Bund.* Translated by Loren Balhorn and Jan-Peter Herrmann. Leiden: Brill, 2021.

Young, Robert J. C. *Postcolonialism: A Very Short Introduction.* Oxford: Oxford University Press, 2003.

Zakreski, Patricia. *Representing Female Artistic Labour, 1848–1890: Refining Work for the Middle-Class Woman.* Burlington, VT: Ashgate, 2006.

Zimmerman, Joshua D. *Poles, Jews, and the Politics of Nationality: The Bund and the Polish Socialist Party in Late Tsarist Russia, 1892–1914.* Madison: University of Wisconsin Press, 2004.

Zipperstein, Steven J. *Elusive Prophet: Ahad Ha'am and the Origins of Zionism.* Berkeley: University of California Press, 1993.

Žižek, Slavoj. *Living in the End Times.* London: Verso, 2011.

Zuckerman, Bruce. *Job the Silent: A Study in Historical Counterpoint.* New York: Oxford University Press, 1991.

Articles, Books, and Almanacs in Hebrew and Yiddish

Abramovitsh, Sholem Yankev. "Mikhtav Al Dvar Ha-Khinukh." *Ha-Magid,* July 15, 1857.

———. "Shem ve-Yefet ba-'agala" [Shem and Japheth on the train]. [In Hebrew.] In *Kaveret: Kovetz Sifruti,* pp. 45–59. Odessa: Aba Dukhno, 1890.

Ahad Ha'am. "Emet me-Erets Yisra'el" [Truth from the Land of Israel]. [In Hebrew.] *Ha-Melits* (Sivan 1891).

———. *Kol kitve.* Jerusalem: Dvir, 1953.

———. *Kol kitvei Ahad Ha'am.* Tel Aviv: Dvir, 1947.

Aleichem, Sholem. "A briv tsu a gutn fraynd" [A letter to a good friend]. [In Yiddish.] In Aleichem, *Di yudishe folks-bibliotek,* 2: 304–10.

———. "Der yidisher dales in di beste verke fun undzere folks-shrift-shteler." Supplement to *Yudishes folksblat* (1888): 1075–90, 1101–10, 1149–57, 1183–89, 1205–16.

———. *Di yudishe folks-bibliyotek.* Kyiv: Yankev Sheftil, 1889.

Altaras, Alon. "The islands of Antonio Gramsci: An introduction." [In Hebrew.] In *About the hegemony,* by Antonio Gramsci. Tel Aviv: Resling, 2009.

An alter bakanter [Y. Pesakhzon]. "In Varshe erev 'bund.'" In *25 yor: Zamlbukh.* Warsaw: Di velt, 1922.

Anish Stiftel, Shoshana. *The Mediator: Nahum Sokolow's Leadership between Tradition and Zionism.* [In Hebrew.] Jerusalem: Mosad Bialik, 2012.

Anonymous. "Nitabin Le-egel Ve-notnim." [In Hebrew.] *Ha-melitz* 156 (1894).

An-sky, S. *Gezamlte shriftn.* [In Yiddish.] Vol. 10. Vilnius: Farlag An-sky, 1922.

Aronson, G., and J. S. Hertz, editors. *Di geshikhte fun Bund.* Vol. 1. New York: Undzer tsayt farlag, 1960.

Baram-Eshel, Einat. "Haskala, socialism, and nationalism in the poetry of Yahalal." [In Hebrew.] In *Poetics and ideology in modern Hebrew literature: For Menachem Brinker*, edited by Irish Parush, Hamutal Tsamir, and Hanna Soker-Schwager, pp. 254–76. Jerusalem: Karmel, 2011.

Bar-El, Judith. *The Hebrew long poem from its emergence to the beginning of the twentieth century: A study of the history of a genre*. [In Hebrew.] Jerusalem: Bialik Institute, 1995.

Bar-Yosef, Hamutal. *Decadent trends in Hebrew literature: Bialik, Berdychevski, Brener*. [In Hebrew.] Jerusalem: Mosad Bialik, 1997.

———. *The Russian context of Hebrew literature*. [In Hebrew.] Jerusalem: Mosad Byalik, 2020.

Barzel, Hillel. *Toldot ha-shirah ha-ʿivrit mi-ḥibat tziyon ʿad yameynu—kerekh alef: Shirat ḥibat tziyon* [A history of Hebrew poetry, vol. 1: The Ḥibat Tziyon period]. Tel Aviv: Sifriyat Poʿalim, 1987.

Bauer, Ela. "Yaadey Ha-Intiligentsya Ha-Yehudit-Polanit." [In Hebrew.] *Tsiyon*, vol. samekh"khet, no. 3, tashsa"g: 335–58.

Ben-Avigdor. "Misefer zikhronotay." *Ha-tsefira*, April 19, 1917, and May 3, 1917.

Ben-David, Y. L. "A conversation in the world of literature." [In Hebrew.] *Hatzfira* 228 (November 1893): 3.

Ben-Mordecai, Isaac. "Mavo." [In Hebrew.] Introduction to *Nitsane ha-Realizm ha-Siporet ha-'Ivrit*, vol. 1, Ben-Mordecai and Even, 1972.

———. "Mavo." [In Hebrew.] Introduction to *Nitsane ha-Realizm ha-Siporet ha-'Ivrit*, vol. 2, Ben-Mordecai and Even, 1993.

Ben-Mordecai, Isaac, and Yosef Even, editors. *Nitsane ha-Realizm ha-Siporet ha-'Ivrit* [The buds of realism in Hebrew fiction]. 2 vols. Jerusalem: Mossad Bialik, 1972, 1993.

Bergelson, Dovid. "Y. L. Perets un di khsidishe ideologye." [In Yiddish.] *Literarishe bleter*, April 10, 1925, p. 3.

Bialik, Hayim Nahman. *Kol kitve Ḥ. N. Bialik*. Tel Aviv: Dvir, 1938.

Bodek, Menakhem Mendl. *Maʾase tsadikim*. [In Hebrew.] Lviv, Ukraine: Lemberg Druk, 1864.

Braynin, Reuven. "Y. L. Perets betor meshorer ha-hasidut." [In Hebrew.] In *Khasidut*, by I. L. Peretz. New York: Kadima, 1917.

Carton-Blum, Ruth. *Ha-Shirah ha-ivrit bi-Tekufat Hibbat Ziyyon*. Jerusalem: Mossad Bialik, 1969.

Cohen, Hagit. *At the bookseller's shop: The Jewish book trade in Eastern Europe at the end of the nineteenth century*. [In Hebrew.] Jerusalem: Hebrew University Magnes Press, 2006.

Dickstein, Szymon. "Kto z czego żyje?" [By what do we live?]. [In Yiddish.] Warsaw: Di velt, 1906.

Dinezon, Yankev. *Y. L. Peretz Tsum Yortsayt*. Vilnius: Farlag fun Bes. Alef Kletskin, 1916.

Epshteyn, Shakhne. "Yitskhok Leybush Perets: Tsum finf-un-tsvanstikstn yortog nokh zayn toyt." [In Yiddish.] *Sovetishe literature* (October 1940).

———. *Y. L. Perets als sotsyaler dikhter* [Y. L. Peretz as a social poet]. New York: Max N. Maisel, 1916.

Fried, Meir Yaakov. *Yamim ve-shanim: Zikhronot ve-tziyurim mi-tekufah shel hamishim shanah* [Days and years: Memoirs and vignettes from a fifty-year period]. [In Hebrew.] Vol. 2. Tel Aviv: Dvir, 1939.

Frieden, Ken. "'Nusah Mendele' be-mabat bikorti" [A critical perspective on "Mendele's Nusah"]. *Dappim le-mehkar be-sifrut* [Research on literature, Haifa] 14–15 (2006): 89–103.

———. "Parodya ve-hegyogrfya: Sipurim khasidiim-kivyakhol shel Perets." [In Hebrew.] *Khulyot* 7 (2002).

Friedlander, Yehuda. *Existence and experience in the Hebrew writings of I. L. Peretz.* [In Hebrew.] Tel Aviv: Hotsaat Dvir, 1974.

———. "Halachic issues as satirical elements in nineteenth century Hebrew literature." [In Hebrew.] In *Jewish Humor*, edited by Avner Ziv, 135–47. Tel Aviv: Papyrus, 1986.

———. "The struggle of Y. L. Gordon against Lithuanian rabbis." [In Hebrew.] In *Studies in East European Jewish history and culture in honor of Professor Shmuel Werses*, edited by David Assaf et al., pp. 285–314. Jerusalem: Hebrew University Magnes Press, 2002.

Frishman, David. *Mikhtavim ʿal hasifrut: Sefer alef.* [In Hebrew.] Jerusalem: M. Newman Publishing, 1968.

———. *Shivʾah mikhtavim hadashim ʿal devar ha-sifrut.* [In Hebrew.] Berlin: Dvir, 1922–23.

Garncarska-Kadari, Bina. *The role of the Jews in the development of Warsaw industry in the years 1816/20–1914.* [In Hebrew.] Tel Aviv: Center for the History of Polish Jewry, Diaspora Research Institute, Tel-Aviv University, 1985.

Gilboa, Menuha. *Ben reʾalizm le-romantikah* [Between realism and Romanticism: A study of the critical work of David Frishman]. Tel Aviv: Tel Aviv University, 1975.

———. *The Hebrew New Wave and outside of it.* [In Hebrew.] Tel Aviv: Tel Aviv University, 1991.

Goldberg, Avrom. *A floy fun tishe-beʾov, Lokshen.* Warsaw: Gebdrider Shuldberg, 1894.

Goldberg, Zeʾev. "On Y.-L. Perets' relationship to Zionism." [In Hebrew.] *Khulyot* 7 (2002).

Golomb, Yaakov. "Al hapolmus ha-'Nietzscheyani' ben Ahad-Haʾam le-Micha Yosef Berdichevsky." [In Hebrew.] In *Around the Dot: Studies on M. Y. Berdichevsky, Y.H. Brenner and A. D. Gordon*, pp. 69–93. Beersheba: Mekhon Ben-Guryon Le-ḥeker Yiśraʾel yeha-Tsiyonut, Universiṭat Ben Guryon Ba-Negev, 2008.

Gordon-Mlotek, Khane. "Y. L. Perets' zamlung yidishe folkslider." *YIVO-bleter*, n.s., 4 (2003).

Gorin, B. *Gezamelte shriftn*. [In Yiddish.] Vol. 1. New York: Elizabeth Gorin, 1927.
Gottlieb, Leon. "Perets af a geheymer arbeyter ferzamlung." *Forverts*, April 9, 1915, p. 4.
Gozshansky, Shmul. "A briv tsu agitatorn." In *Di yidishe sotsyalistishe bavegung biz der grindung fun "Bund."* Edited by Elye Tsherikover, Avrom Menes, Frants Kursky, and Avrom Rozin (Ben-Adir), pp. 626–648. Vol. 3 of *Historishe shriftn*. Vilnius: YIVO, 1939. Originally published in 1893.
Grace-Pollack, Sophie. "Shomer in the Light of *Shomer's mishpet*." [In Hebrew.] *Khulyot* 5 (1998): 109–59.
Gramsci, Antonio. *About the hegemony*. [In Hebrew.] Translated by Alon Altaras. Tel Aviv: Resling, 2009.
Gris, Zeev. "Avraham Leyb Shalkovitz ('Ben Avigdor') and the revolution in the world of Hebrew books at the beginning of the twentieth century." [In Hebrew.] In *Yosef Daat: Research in modern Jewish history*, edited by Yosi Goldshteyn, pp. 305–28. Beersheba: Ben-Gurion University.
Gutwein, Daniel. "Ha-diplomatia Ha-yehudit ba'me'a ha-tsha esre: Reshit ha-leumiyut ha-yehudit?" In *Le'umiyut ve-politica yehudit: Perspectivot hadashot*. [In Hebrew.] Jerusalem: Merkaz Zalman Shazar le-toldot Yisrael, 1996.
Harel, Shlomo. "Iyun Mehudash be Shirei HaUgav shel Y. L. Peretz" [A reconsideration of the "Organ poems" of Y. L. Peretz]. [In Hebrew.] In *Studies in Hebrew Literature: V*. Tel Aviv: Tel-Aviv University, 1986.
Hertz, Y. Sh., editor. *Doyres bundistn*. [In Yiddish.] Vol. 1. New York: Farlag Unser Tsayt, 1956.
Herz-Tucker, Naftali. "Matchmaking, mating, and love in the stories of I. L. Peretz." [In Hebrew.] *Yeda-Am* 65–66 (2005): 70–85.
Hever, Hannan. "The victims of Zionism: On 'In the city of slaughter' by H"N Bialik." In Gluzman, Hever, and Miron, *Be-ir ha-haregah*, 37–70.
Imber, N. H. *N. H. Imber's Collected Poetry*. Edited by Dov Sadan. Tel Aviv: Neuman, 1950.
Kabakoff, Jacob. *Shoharim V'ne'emanim*. [In Hebrew.] Jerusalem: Rubin Mass, 1978.
Katznelson, Berl. *Hartsaot Berl Katsanelson(1928)*. Edited by Anita Shapira and Naomi Abir. Tel Aviv: Am Oved, 1990.
Khmelnitski, M. "Y. L. Perets' popular-meditsinishe broshur: Az me vil nisht, shtarbt nisht fun kholi-ra." *YIVO-bleter* 28 (Fall 1946): 146–52.
Klausner, Yosef [Joseph]. *Historiiah shel ha-sifrut ha-'ivrit ha-hadashah*. [In Hebrew.] Vol. 6. Jerusalem: Hebrew University Magnes Press, 1950.
———. "Our literature." [In Hebrew.] *Hashiloach* 7 (1901): 540–47.
———. "Perets haya tsiyoni." *Maariv*, May 16, 1952.
———. "Sifrutenu hadasha bishnat tara"s" [Our new literature, 1899–1900]. [In Hebrew.] In *Sefer ha-Shanah*, edited by N. Sokolow, 2: 230–77. Warsaw, 1900–1906.
———. "Zion li-Meshorer, 2d ed., 1894. Shire Ahabah." *Ha-Eshkol* 1 (1897–98): 54–71.

Kremer, Arkadi. *Ob agitatsii*. Geneva: Union of Russian Social Democrats Abroad, 1894.

———. *On Agitation [1896]*. In *Marxism in Russia: Key Documents 1879–1906*, edited by Neil Harding with translations by Richard Taylor, pp. 192–205. Cambridge: Cambridge University Press, 1983.

Kurlyand, D. "Tsu der frage vegn legendare syuzhetn in Peretses verk." *Sovetishe literatur* (October 1940).

Lang, Joseph. "Foundation and Development of the Safa Brura."[In Hebrew.] *Cathedra* 68 (June 1993): 67–79.

Lestschinsky, Jacob. "The development of the Jewish people in the last one hundred years." [In Yiddish.] In *Shriften far Ekonomik un Statistik*, vol. 1, edited by Jacob Lestschinsky. Berlin: YIVO, 1928.

Levin, Eli. "Shana Tova to the New Wave: 118 years to the publication of 'Luakh Am Akhiasaf'—A central stage for modern Hebrew literature at the turn of the centuries." [In Hebrew.] *Haaretz*, September 28, 2011, accessed October 16, 2012. http://www.haaretz.co.il/1.1485052.

Levin, Yehudah Levi. "Kishron Ha-ma'ase." [In Hebrew.] In *Ketavim nivḥarim [me-et] Y.H.L.L.*, vol. 2. Warsaw: Tushiya, 1911.

Liessin, A. *Zikhroynes un bilder*. [In Yiddish.] New York: Tsiko, 1954.

Lilienblum, M. L. "Divrei Zemer." In *Luah ahiasaf*, vol. 5. Warsaw: Shuldberg Brothers, 1897.

Litvak, A. "B. Gorin: A bisl erinerungen." [In Yiddish.] In Gorin, *Gezamelte shriften*, vol. 1.

———. "Di 'zhargonishe komitetn.'" [In Yiddish.] In *Royter pinkes*, vol. 1, pp. 5–30. Warsaw: Kultur lige, 1921.

———. *Literature un kamf: Literarishe eseyn*. [In Yiddish.] New York: Veker, 1933.

———. *Vos geven*. [In Yiddish.] Poyln: Vilner farlag fun B. Kletskin, 1925.

Litvakov, Moyshe. "Di Nister problem." In *Af tsvey frontn*, by Litvakov. Moscow: Tsentraler Felker Farlag fun F.S.S.R., 1931.

Mahalel, Adi. "Revolutionizing the Means of Artistic Production and Radicalizing the Jewish Calendar in the *Yontef bletlekh*." [In Hebrew.] *Kesher: Journal of Media and Communications History in Israel and the Jewish World* 48 (Summer 2016): 59–64.

Mahler, Raphael. *Der kamf tsvishn khsides un haskole in Galitsye*. [In Yiddish.] New York: YIVO, 1942.

Malakhi, A. R. "Y. L. Perets in *Ha-tsofe*." *YIVO-bleter* 36 (1952).

Mark, Yudl. "An analiz fun Y. L. Peretses shprakh." [In Yiddish.] *YIVO-bleter* 28 (1946).

Marmor, Kalmen. *Dovid Edelstadt* (Yiddish) (New York: Ikuf, 1950).

———. *Mayn lebns geshikhte*. [In Yiddish.] Vol. 1. New York: IKUF, 1959.

Mayzel, Nachman. *I. L. Perets:Zayn lebn un shafn*. [In Yiddish.] New York: IKUF, 1945.

Medem, Vladimir. "Perets un mir." In *Valdimir Medem tsum tsvantsikstn yortsayt*, pp. 344–45. [In Yiddish.] New York: Amerikaner reprezentants fun Algemeynem Yidishn arbeter-bund in Poyln, 1943.

Mendelson, Shlomo. *Zayn lebn un shafn*. [In Yiddish.] New York: Undzer tsayt, 1949.

Minkov, Nokhem Borekh. *Pionern fun yidisher poeziye in amerike*. [In Yiddish.] Vol. 1. New York: Grenich, 1956.

Miron, Dan. "Bein takdim le-mikreh—shirato ha-'epit shel Y"L Gordon u-mekomah be-sifrut ha-haskalah ha-civrit" [Between precedent and happening: Y. L. Gordon's epic poetry and its place in Hebrew *Haskalah* literature]. [In Hebrew.] *Jerusalem Studies in Hebrew Literature* 2 (1983): 127–97.

———. *Bo'ah, laylah: Hasifrut ha'ivrit bein higayyon le'e-gayyon bemifneh hame'ah ha'esrim* [Come, night: Hebrew literature between the rational and irrational at the turn of the twentieth century]. [In Hebrew.] Tel Aviv: Dvir, 1987.

———. *Bodedim bemoadam*. [In Hebrew.] Tel Aviv: Am Oved, 1987.

———. *Der imazh fun shtetl: Dray literarishe shtudyes* [The image of the shtetl: Three literary studies]. [In Yiddish.] Tel Aviv: I. L. Peretz Publishing-House, 1981.

———. "Mi'be'ir Ha'hariga va'hal'ah." In Gluzman, Hever, and Miron, *Be-ir ha-haregah*, 88–97.

———. "'The sentimental education' of Mendele Moykher Sforim." [In Hebrew.] Afterword to *Sefer ka-kabtsanim*, by Mendele Moykher Sforim, pp. 201–68. Tel Aviv: Dvir, 1988.

———. "Sifrut Ha-haskala Be-ivrit." [In Hebrew.] In *Zman Yehudi Hadash* [New Jewish times: Jewish culture in a secular age—an encyclopedic view], vol. 3, edited by Yermiyahu Yovel, pp. 27–41. Jerusalem: Keter, 2007.

———. "The spiritual world of I. L. Peretz: Fourth chapter." [In Hebrew.] *Haaretz*, May 11, 2015. http://www.haaretz.co.il/literature/study/.premium-1.2632136.

———. "Tarbut Ivrit Hadasha Be-varsha." [In Hebrew.] In *Zman Yehudi Hadash* [New Jewish times: Jewish culture in a secular age—an encyclopedic view], vol. 3, edited by Yermiyahu Yovel. Jerusalem: Keter, 2007.

Mlotek, Yoysef, and Khana Mlotek. *Perl fun der yidisher poezye*. [In Yiddish.] Tel Aviv: Y.-L.-Perets-Farlag, 1974.

Niborski, Yitshok. "Yunge geshtaltn bay Y.L. Perets un Dovid Pinski." [In Yiddish.] *Yugntruf* no. 7 (December 1966).

Niger [Charney], Shmuel. *I. L. Peretz*. Buenos Aires: Yiddish Cultural Congress, 1952.

Nomberg, H. D. *Dos bukh felitonen*. [In Yiddish.] Warsaw: Rekord, 1924.

———. *Y. L. Perets*. Buenos Aires: Tsentrale farband fun poylishe yidn in argentine, 1946.

Nusinov, Yitshok. "Der Nister." In *Gedakht*, by Der Nister. Kyiv: Kulturlige, 1929.

Olgin, Moshe. "Di proletarishe rikhtung in der yidisher literatur." [In Yiddish.] *Almanakh: Yubilee fun Internatsyonaler Arbeter Orden fun Yidishn Folks*

Ordn. New York: Cooperativa Folks Farlag fun Internatzationaler Arber Ordn, 1940.

———. *Y. L. Peretz.* New York: IKUF, 1955.

Peri, Menakhem. "Hitbonenuyot ba-Mivne ha-Temati shel Shire Bialik: Ha-Shir Ha-Mithapekh Ve-Ekhav." [In Hebrew.] *Ha-Sifrut* 1, no. 2 (1969): 40–82.

Perl, Joseph. *Sefer Megale Temirin.* [In Hebrew.] Edited and with an introduction by Jonatan Meir. Jerusalem: Mossad Bialik, 2013.

Pinski, Dovid. "Dray yor mit Perets." *Di Goldene Keyt* 8 (1951).

———. "Geshikhte fun di *Yontef-bletlekh.*" *Di tsukunft* (May 1945).

———. "Geshikhte fun di *Yontef-bletlekh.*" *Di tsukunft* (June 1945).

Pomerantz, Alexander. *Kavkaz.* [In Yiddish.] New York: Morgn Freiheit, 1943.

Prager, Leonard. "Tnuat ha-avoda ha-yehudit ve-sifrut yidish biyemey ha-'Yontef Bletlekh' shel Peretz ve-Pinski." [In Hebrew.] In *Kovets Kenes Ha-Yesod.* Haifa: Haifa University, 1991.

Reyzen, Zalman. *Leksikon fun der Yidisher literatur, prese un filologye.* [In Yiddish.] Vilnius: B. Kletskin, 1926.

Reyzn, Avrom. *Epizodn fun mayn lebn: Literarishe erinerungen.* [In Yiddish.] Vol. 1. Vilnius: Vilner Farlag fun B. Kletskin, 1929.

Roskies, David-Hirsh. "Sifrut Yidish Be-Polin." [In Hebrew.] In *Kiyum Va-Shever*, edited by Israel Bartal and Israel Gutman, vol. 2, pp. 207–24. Jerusalem: Merkaz Zalma Shazar Le-Toldot Israel, 2001.

Ross, Nicham. "Hasipur hakhasidi keyetsira sifrutit: Dilema pedagogit u-fitrona." [In Hebrew.] *Mayim medalav* 18 (2007): 305–31.

———. *Margalit ṭemunah ba-ḥol: Y. L. Perets u-ma'aśiyot Ḥasidim* [Gem concealed in sand: I. L. Peretz and Hasidic tales]. Jerusalem: Hebrew University Magnes Press, 2013.

———. *Masoret Ahuva Ve-snu'a: Zehut Yehudit Modernit Ve-ktiva Neo-Khasidit Be-fetakh Hame'a Ha-esrim* [A beloved despised tradition: Modern Jewish identity and neo-Hasidic writing at the beginning of the twentieth century]. [In Hebrew.] Beersheba: Ben-Gurion University Press, 2010.

Rozentsvayg, Ayzik. *Der radikaler peryod fun Peretses shafn: Di yontef bletlekh.* [In Yiddish.] Kyiv: Melukhe-farlag fun di natsyonale minderhaytn, 1934.

Sadan, Dov. "Bontshe Shvayg un zayne Gilgulim." [In Yiddish.] *Folk un Tsiyon* 24 (1978): 15–18.

Sand, Shlomo, and Ernest Renan. *On the Nation and the "Jewish People."* London: Verso, 2010.

Shaked, Gershon. *Ha-Siporet Ha-Ivrit, 1880–1970.* [In Hebrew.] Vol. 1. Jerusalem: Keter, 1977.

Shatzky, Yankev [Jacob]. *Di geshikhte fun yidn in Varshe* [The history of the Jews in Warsaw]. [In Yiddish.] 3 vols. New York: YIVO, 1947–53.

———. "Paltiel zamoshtishens letters to Sholem Aleichem." *YIVO-bleter* 11 (1937).

———. "Perets-shtudyes." [In Yiddish.] *YIVO-bleter* 28 (1946): 40–80.

Shmeruk, Chone. "Harkeriyah lenavi: Schneour, Bialik, Perez veNadson" [Call to the prophet in Shne'ur, Bialik, Peretz, and Nadson]. *Ha-Sifrut* 2 (1969).
———. *Peretses yiesh-vizye: Interpretatsye fun Y. L. Peretses "Bay nakht oyfn altn mark"* [Peretz's vision of despair: Interpretation of I. L. Peretz's *At Night in the Old Marketplace*]. [In Yiddish.] New York: YIVO, 1971.
Sifre-agora. Warsaw: Ben-Avigdor, 1891.
Sokolow, Nahum. *Ishim.* [In Hebrew.] Tel Aviv: Stybl, 1935.
———. "Menahem the Writer: A literary picture by Ben-Avigdor" and "Rabi Shifra: A story by Ben-Avigdor." [In Hebrew.] *Ha-asif* 6 (1893): 213–24.
———. "Yosl the Crazy (Sketches from my memory)." [In Hebrew.] *Hatekufah* 26–27, 2nd ed. (1935).
Stuchkov, Nokhem. *Der oyster fun der yiddisher sprakh* [Treasure of the Yiddish language]. New York: Yidisher Visnshaftlekher Institut, 1950.
Trunk, Y. Y. *Poylen: Zilkhroynes un bilder.* Vol. 5, *Peretz.* New York: "Unzer tsayt," 1949.
Vakser, Menashe. "Dos lebn fun a yidishn dikhter." *YIVO-bleter* 12 (1937): 205–60.
Vintshevski, Moris. *Erinerungen.* [In Yiddish.] Moscow: Shul un bukh, 1926.
———. *Gezamelte verk.* New York: Frayhayt, 1927.
Weill, Claudie. "Russian Bundists Abroad and in Exile, 1898–1925." In *Jewish Politics in Eastern Europe: The Bund at 100*, edited by Jack Jacobs, pp. 46–55. New York: New York University Press / Żydowski Instytut Historyczny—Instytut Naukowo-Badawczy, 2001.
Werses, Shmuel. *Sipur ve-shorsho: 'Iyunim be-hitpatbut ha-prosa ha-'ivrit* [Story and source: Studies in the development of Hebrew prose]. Ramat Gan, Israel: Massada, 1971.
Weynig, N. "Poylishe lider fun Y. L. Perez fun yor 1874." [In Yiddish.] *YIVO-bleter* 12 (1937): 191–204.
Wolfssohn, Aaron. *Kalut da'at u-tsevi'ut: Rav. Ḥanokh ve-Rabi Yosefkeh.* [In Hebrew.] With an introduction by Dan Miron. Tel Aviv: Mif'alim 'Universitayim Le-Hotsa'ah Le-'or, 1977.
Yassour, Avraham. *Anarkhizm: Antologyah.* Tel Aviv: Resling, 2004.
Zuckermann, Ghil'ad. *Israelit safa yafa.* [In Hebrew.] Tel Aviv: Am Oved, 2008.

Additional Reference Sources

Historical Jewish Press online archive. National Library of Israel / Tel Aviv University. https://www.jpress.org.il/.
Steven Spielberg Digital Yiddish Library. Yiddish Book Center. https://www.yiddishbookcenter.org/collections/digital-yiddish-library.
Weinreich, Uriel. *Yiddish-English English-Yiddish Dictionary.* New York: YIVO, 1990.
YIVO Encyclopedia of Jews in Eastern Europe. YIVO Institute for Jewish Research, 2010. https://yivoencyclopedia.org/.

Index

Abramovitsh, Sholem Yankev (Mendele), 235n10
  Hebrew prose by, 11–12, 89, 91, 108. 239n80
  influence on Peretz, 111, 226n72
  on Jewish children's education, xvii
  language style of, 92
  use of poverty as subject, 22–23
  on a standard Yiddish literary language
  use of Yiddish-speaking narrators, xvii
  Yiddish prose by, 139, 246n175
Adler, Ruth, 47
Adorno, Theodor, 113, 196
"A Farshterter shabes" (A spoiled Shabbat) (Peretz), 50–52, 98
Agnon, Shay, 233n34, 252n48
"A kaas fun a yidene" (Anger of a Jewish woman") (Peretz), 47–52, 150, 184
Aleichem, Sholem, 38–39, 139, 226n17–23
  affinities with Peretz, 12, 15–16, 19
  almanac by, 240n89
  female characters in, 49
  fiction by, 11, 49
  and Jewish poverty, 23
  Peretz's letters to, xvi–xvii, 35
  Peretz's respect for, 215n8
  on popular Yiddish literature, 9–10, 12–13
  and realism, 16, 92

Altberg, Moyshe, 1
Amsterdam, Avrom, 62, 168
Anderson, Benedict, 205, 223n34
"An Edom" (Heine), 153
"A Night of Horror: A Research in Mental Disease" (Peretz), 106–11, 143, 183
An-ski, S., 162–63
antisemitism:
  in Europe, xxiii, 17–18, 26, 36, 75, 122, 217n29
  theme in Peretz's writing, 11, 18–19, 82, 122–24
Arbeter lider (Worker's poems), 135–36
Arbeter Ring (Workmen's Circle),, 207
Arbeter tsaytung (Workers' paper), 36, 141
"Argument, The" (Peretz), 86–87
Asch, Sholem, 174
Asefat khakhamin (Sages assembly), 75
At Night in the Old Marketplace (Peretz), 108
Atta Troll: A Midsummer Night's Dream (Heine), 152, 154
Atta Troll (Peretz translation), 152–53
"A volkn hot fardekt dem himl" (Peretz), 132–33
"Author as Producer, The" (Benjamin), 55, 68
Bar Kokhba, 60
Baron de Rothschild, 113

Barthes, Roland, 102
Bar-Yosef, Hamutal, 77–78, 97, 108–9, 130
Baudelaire, Charles, 96, 174
Bauer, Otto, xviii
"Baym fremdn khupe kleyd: A stsene fun varshever lebn" (By a foreign wedding dress: A scene from life in Warsaw) (Peretz), 139–45
Bekante bilder (Familiar pictures) (Peretz), 92–93
Ben-Avigdor (ne Avraham Leyb Shalkovitz), 240n91–92, 243n136
  aesthetic demands of, 91, 93, 94, 97–98, 102, 107
  and Hebrew literature's new realist movement, 91
  memories of Peretz, 81
  Peretz's attacks on, 90
  as publisher, 75, 92–95, 103
  writing by, 107, 239n76, 241n107
Benjamin, Walter, 174, 234n97
  critique of capitalism, 171
  on revolutionary art, xxv, 55, 68
Berdichevsky, Micha Josef, 96, 130, 162–63, 175–76, 188, 259n43
Bergelson, Dovid, 161
"Between two mountains" (Tsvishn tsvey berg) (Peretz), 176, 183, 198–204, 259n42
Bialer Rebbe, 198–99, 202–3, 206
Bialik, Haim Nachman, 86, 91, 96, 120–21, 130, 220n64, 239n80, 241n107, 245n171, 250n57
Bilder fun a provints rayze (Pictures from a travel journey) (Peretz), xix, xxi–xxii, 2–3, 7, 15, 21–22, 24, 29–34, 37, 65, 84, 104, 108, 111, 113, 126–27
"Bildung" (Peretz), xvii, 2–6, 9, 22, 54, 63, 65, 95, 114, 166–67
Bime'on kayitz" (In a Summer House) (Peretz), 102–7, 112, 114, 118
"Bimtsulot yam" (Depths of the sea) (Yalag), 123
"birth of Moses, the Giver of the Torah, The" (Peretz), 77–78
Blake, William, 133
Bloch, Ernst, 202–3
Bloch, Jan, 22, 221n12, 233n87
  Funding of *Bibliyotek*, 2
  Funding of Pale of Settlement study, xix–xx, 25–26, 29, 66
Bloch, Ernst, 202–3, 263n107
Bnei Moshe (society), 94.
Bodek, Menakhem Mendl, 194
"Bontshe" (play), 39
"Bontshe shvayg" (Bontshe the Silent) (Peretz), 36–41, 46–47, 49, 100, 118, 191, 206, 227n3, 228n15 Braynin, Reuven, 103
Börne, Karl Ludwig, 152
Bovshover, Joseph, 139
Braynin, Reuven, 198–99
Brisker Rov, the, 198–200, 202–3
"Bruria" (Mulder), 150–51
Buber, Martin, 163
Buch der Lieder (Heine), 117, 129–30
Bund, the, xxxi, 42, 72, 219n60, 260n53
  challenges facing (according to Peretz), 191
  figures associated with, 61–62, 168, 256n1
  history of, xxiii, 38
  initial purpose of, 41, 43
  Peretz's (intellectual/political) alignment with, 41–44, 67–68, 145, 178–79, 201
  Peretz's role in shaping, xviii, xxiv, xxvi, xxix, 36, 55, 95, 159, 205–7
  publications by, 63

Caplan, Marc, 28
Chamisso, Adelbert von, 103
Charney, Shmuel, xxvi, 219n58, 249n46
Choveve Tsiyon, 80–89, 94, 113, 213, 238n57
Class and Ethnicity in the Pale (Peled), xxiv
Collected Works, (Peretz), 182
"Crazy Idler, The" ("Der meshugener batln") (Peretz), 93, 108
"creators of chaos, The" (Sokolow), 78, 97
cultural autonomy, xviii, xxiii–xxiv, 68, 128, 216n14
Darwin, Charles, 64
Das Kapital (Marx), 41–42
"Date Palm, The" (Peretz), 120
"dead town, The" (Peretz), 201
"Dem rebns tsibek" (The rebbe's pipe), (Peretz), 182–86
Der balegole (The coachman) (Peretz), 134
"Der feter shakhne un di mume yakhne" (Uncle Shakhne and Aunt Yakhne) (Peretz), 50
Der Nister, 174
Der radikaler periyod fun Peretses shafn: "Di yontef bletlekh" (Rozentsvayg), xxv, 55
"Der Tannhäuser" (Heine), 153
Der yud (journal), 191
"Diary of a Madman" (Gogol), 108
Diaspora, the:
    as future Jewish home, xxiii
    Peretz's thoughts on, 3–5, 9, 81, 89, 148
Diaspora nationalism, xxvii, 9, 21, 81, 84, 163, 178
Dickens, Charles, 22, 25
Dickstein, Szymon, 41
"Die schlesischen Weber" (The Silesian weavers) (Heine), 154

Di kliyatshe (Abramovitsh), 10
Dinezon, Yankev, 39, 92–94, 162, 183, 211, 220n70
"Di royz" (The rose) (Peretz), 63
Di velt (publishing company), 63
Di yontef bletlekh (The holiday pages) (journal), 165, 192, 231n53, 232n73
    Peretz's articles in, 180–81
    Peretz's poetry in, 134–39, 141–44
    Peretz's production of, xiii, xxviii–xxix, 36, 55–86, 90, 94, 118, 121, 134, 139, 145–46, 154, 166, 205
    Peretz's stories in, 182
Die Weber (Hauptmann), 41, 46
Di yudishe bibliyotek (Peretz), xix–xx, 2–3, 26–27, 30–32, 60–61, 146, 153, 220n70, 224n50
"Dos eygentum" (Property) (Pereetz), 154
"Dos gebet" (The plea) (Peretz), 119–20
"Dos lid fun hemd" (Vintshevski), 139–40
"Dos shtrayml" (The fur hat) (Peretz), 182
Dostoyevsky, Fyodor, 22–23, 187, 200–1
Dos tsvansikte yorhundert (The twentieth century) (Reyzn), 66
Dovid, Yosef, 66
"Dray neytorins" (Three knitters) (Peretz), 134–40
Dr. Jekyll and Mr. Hyde (Conan Doyle), 109
Dr. Shtitser ("Dr. Supporter") (Peretz pseudonym), 63
Dybbuk, The (An-Sky), 260n53
"Dybbuk and the Crazy Person, The" (Peretz), 108
Eagleton, Terry, 16, 253n92
    on Marxism, 181–82, 189

on religion, 179–81
on Walter Benjamin, 55
Edelstadt, Dovid, 23, 139
Engels, Friedrich, 62, 118, 138
"Enlightened Carpenter, The" (Goyda), 75
Epshteyn, Shakhne, xxv
"Er un zi" (Peretz), 153
Er un zi (play) (Peretz), 153
"Eshet khaver" (A friend's wife) (Peretz), 49
"Europe with a Bow and Arrow (A Political Feuilleton)" (Peretz), 60, 66
"Even ve-even, eyfa ve-eyfa" (Stone and stone, double standards) (Peretz), 83–84
Faust (Goethe), 122
Feiner, Shmuel, 4
Fishke the Lame: A Story of Jewish Poor People (Abramovitsh), 23
Forverts (newspaper), 209
Frankel, Jonathan, xxiv
Frieden, Ken, 91, 93, 163, 168, 182–83, 199
"Friling" (Spring) (Peretz), 145
Frishman, David, xxvii, 70, 129–30, 239n32, 250n55, 255,127
Fun vos eyner lebt? (By what do we live?) (Dickstein), 41
Garrett, Leah, 153
Gautier, Théophile, 96
Gechtman, Roni, xxiv
Germany: A Winter's Tale (Deutschland: Ein Wintermärchen) (Heine), 153–54
Goethe, Johann Wolfgang von, 122, 128
Gogol, Nikolai, 108
Golde, Esther, 38
Golde, Julius, 38

Goldin, Ezra, 103
Gordon, Yehuda Leyb (aka Yalag), 47, 89, 122, 124–25, 229n30, 248n23
Goyda, Yitskhok (aka B. Gorin), 23, 36, 75, 94
Gozhansky, Shmul, 61–62
Gramsci, Antonio, xiii, xxii–xxiii, 218n41
Greaney, Patrick, 23–24
Groshen bibliyotek (Penny library), 93, 103
Ha-am, Ahad:
cultural Zionism, 94, 121
on Palestine's Arabs, 95
Peretz's quarrels with, xxix, 76, 87–88, 175–76
Ha-asif (almanac), 106–7
Ha-chetz (The Arrow) (Peretz), 69–73, 75–78, 85, 96–97, 107–9, 118–19, 121, 130, 172, 175, 234n1, 343n37
HaEmet (The truth), 74–75
"Ha-ir ha-ktana" (The little town) (Peretz), 126–27, 129
"Ha-isha Marat Khana" (The wife Mrs. Hanna), 49
Half Man, Half Monkey (Shomer), 15
"Ha-mekubalim"(Kabbalists) (Peretz), 165–6
Ha-melitz, 70
"Hanukah Candle, The" (Peretz), 135
Harel, Shlomo, 130
"Harp: An Arab Legend, The" (Peretz), 72, 75–77, 95, 107–8
"Ha-shutafut" (The partnership) (Peretz), 162–63
Hashakhar (The dawn), 74
Hasidic movement, 161–65, 178–79, 198, 201, 256n2, 260n58
Haskalah (Jewish Enlightenment), 70, 127
and education, 4, 123

hostility to Yiddish, xvii
integrationist model of, 114
and Jewish women's roles, 48
literature of, 6, 20, 47, 51, 54, 74, 91, 96, 100–1, 111–13, 120, 125, 130, 143, 145, 147, 150, 161–62
Peretz's attitude toward, xvii–xix, 4–5, 21, 78, 82, 87, 113, 164, 181
Ha-tsfirah (newspaper), 106–7
Ha-tzfira, 183
Ha'ugav (The Harp) (Peretz), 117–18, 120–21, 129–32, 152–53, 243n131
Hauptmann, Gerhart, 41, 46
Hayom (newspaper), 99
Hebrew:
 attacks on Peretz in, 70–71
 "blended" forms of, 91
 as elite/"holy" language, xvi, xix, 72, 75, 91, 93, 126
 as a spoken language, xvii, 90, 102
 Peretz's writing in, xiii, xv–xvii, xxi–xxii, xxix, 20, 34, 49, 53, 58, 60, 69–115, 117–134, 163–191, 194, 198, 205, 220n69, 233n80, 234n1, 243n137, 245n171
 as a popular literary language, 94
Hebrew literature:
and decadent literature, 96–97
expanding readership for, 92
Hebrew culture, xxiii
Hebrew poetry, 23
naturalist trends in, 101
"New Wave" of, 90–98, 102–7, 213, 239n77, 241n96
Peretz's concerns over, 96
Peretz's efforts to modernize, xxix, 104–7, 114, 121, 130, 133, 187–88

pseudoprophetic style of, 120–21, 139
and realism, 94
and Zionism, 89
"Hebrew Melodies" (Heine), 153
Hebrew press, 70–71, 74–75, 106–7, 223n34
"Heine and Peretz Feared and Doubted for Nothing" (Pomerantz), 156
Heine, Heinrich, 118, 246n2, 255n127
as muse for Peretz, xxi, 117, 125, 129–30, 152–56, 254n116
"Hekht" (a pike fish) (Peretz), 78–81, 84, 86
Herzl, Theodore, 26, 153, 241n100
Hever, Hannan, 121, 134, 152
"He who gives life, provides shelter" (Peretz), 186–89
Ḥibat Tsiyon poetry, 84–85
Hitchcock, Alfred, 110
"Hofenung un shrek" (Hope and fear) (Peretz), 156
Holiday Pages, The (journal), xxv
Holocaust, xxvii, 38
Hood, Thomas, 135–36, 139–40, 142
Horkheimer, Max, 28, 113, 196
Howe, Irving, 145
Huge, Victor, 22
Hutcheon, Linda, 183
Iber profesyonen (About professions) (Peretz), 2, 6–8, 65, 221n4
"If Not Even Higher: A Hasidic Story" (Peretz), 176, 191–97
I. L. Peretz and the Making of Modern Jewish Culture (Wisse), xxvii
Imber, Naphtali Herz, 84–85
"In eyrope un bay undz hintern oyvn" (Peretz), 86
"In postvogn" (In the mail-coach) (Peretz), 2–3, 9, 11–15, 18–21

"In the basement" (Peretz), 98
"In the City of Slaughter" (Bialik), 120–21
"In the days of commotion" (Abramovitsh), 89
"In the Mail Coach" (Peretz), 197–98
"In the Mail Coach" (Peretz), 100–1
Israel (modern nation), xxvii, 85
"I Won't Come to Your House" (Peretz), 130–31
jargon committees, 61–63, 72, 232n73
Jameson, Fredric, 105, 110, 146
Jewish intellectuals, xx, 3–4, 17, 179, 197
    Peretz's role as, xxii–xxiii, xxxi, 60, 71, 204, 207
    in Peretz's writings, 8–9, 54, 65–66, 111, 201
Jewish law (Halacha), 11, 14, 48, 86, 100, 170, 229n33
    in Peretz's stories, 48, 51, 121, 164, 175, 202, 230n38
Jewish nationalism, 123
    folk nationalism, xvii–xviii, 54
    hostility toward, xxiv, xix, 78, 125
    and language, xiv
    Peretz's style of, 13, 15, 19–21, 26, 30, 43–44, 54, 67, 78, 84, 121, 123, 131–32, 145, 163
    territorial nationalism, xxiii, 97
"Jewish poverty in the best works of our Yiddish writers" (Aleichem), 23
Jewish working class, 23, 118
    in America, 23
    ethno-class approach to, 202
    ethno-class consciousness among, xxiv–xxiv, 68, 205
    as ethno-class faction, 43–44, 134
    growth of, xix
    and Hebrew, 72
    jobs held by, xix

in literature, 75
Peretz's sympathy for, xiii, xxii–xxiii, xxvi–xxxi, 1, 3, 5–8, 39–46, 68, 71–72, 129, 134, 137–46, 163, 178, 186–87, 191, 195–96, 201–2, 205–7
"Kaddish, The" (Peretz), 97, 99, 163–65
"Kadru shamaym ka-ḥeres" (Peretz), 132–33
Katznelson, Berl, 37
"Khasene gehat: Detseylt fun a froy" (Married: As told by a woman) (Peretz), 52–55, 114 "Khayim Meshores" (Pinski), 61
"Kidush ha-shem" (Sanctification of the name of God) (Peretz), 123–24
King, Martin Luther, Jr., xxxi
"Kishron ha-ma'ase" (The ability to act) (Yahalal), 74
Klausner, Yosef, 77; 117–18, 130, 182, 236n28, 236–37n30
"Kotso shel Yud" (The tip of the Yud) (Yalag), 47
Kremer, Arkadi, 62
Kto z czego żyje? (By what do we live?) (Dickstein), 41
"Leah, the fish-monger" (Ben-Avigdor), 98
Legend of Peretz, The, viv
Les mystères de Paris (Sue), 187
Lestschinsky, Jacob, xix
"letter to agitators, A" (Gozhansky), 62
Lichtenfeld, Gabriel Judah, 122
Lieberman, Aaron S., 74–75
"Life of a Hebrew poet" ("Hayey meshorer ivri") (Peretz), 122–3 163
Lilienblum, M. L., 130
"Li omrim" (I am told) (Peretz), 124–25

Literature and life (Peretz), 88, 94
Literatur un lebn (Peretz), 36–37, 60–61, 81
"Little Stories for Big People" (Peretz), 79
Litvak, A., 62–63, 66–67, 72, 75–77, 168, 173
Litvakov, Moyshe, 174
"Lorelei" (Heine), 130
LTSFR (*Lets fun Redaktsye*) (Peretz pseudonym), 63
Luakh akhiasaf, 103
"Lutetia" (Heine), 154
Luxemburg, Rosa, xv
Lyesin, A., 62, 75
Ma'ase tsadikim (Story of tzaddiks) Bodek, 194
"Manginot Ha-zman" (The melody of our age) (Peretz), xvi–xvii, 82–85, 98, 125–27, 249n37
Mark, Yudl, xvii–xviii
Marmor, Kalman, 61, 79–80, 207, 231n60
Marx, Karl, 41, 118, 155, 177–81, 199, 203
Marxism, 189
 and the Bund, xxiii
 Jewish Marxists, xxiii, 179
 and Jewish workers, 35–36
 and literary interpretation, 96, 118, 163, 174
 and Peretz, xxvi, xxix, 96, 175
 proponents of, xviii, xxii, 163, 179, 205
 publications expounding, 41–42
"Masa duma" (The burden of duma) (Vintshevski), 120
"Mase Nemirov" (Peretz translation), 120–21
Maskilim (Enlighteners):
 and Jews' moral rehabilitation, 4
 and Jewish literature, 10, 124
 and Judaism/halacha, 51, 88, 161

 Peretz's attitude toward, 47–48, 111–114, 126, 162–63, 165, 167–68, 184, 192, 247n11
 in Peretz's writing, 82
 and Peretz's Yiddish folklore, 146
 on reaching the Jewish masses, 181
May Laws, xix
Medem, Vladimir, xxiii, 205–7
"Mekubolim" (Peretz), 165
"Menahem the Writer" (Ben-Avigdor), 94, 107
Menakhem Mendl (Aleichem), 49
Mendelson, Shlomo, 159
"Mendl Braynes" (Peretz), 50
"Mental Sickness among Writers" (Peretz), 108–9
"Messenger, The" (*Der meshulakh*) (Peretz), 93
"metamorphosis of a melody, The" (Peretz), 176
"Meyn nisht" (Do not think) (Peretz), 121, 157–59
"Mikhtav al dvar ha-khinukh" (Abramovitsh), 4
Minkov, Nokhem Borekh, 142
"Miracle of Chanukah, The" ("Nes khanike") (Peretz), 67
Miron, Dan:
 on *Bilder*, 30
 on Peretz and the *Haskalah*, 47
 on Peretz's Hebrew poetry, 130, 151
 on Peretz's legends/Hasidic stories, xxv–xxvii, xxix, 107, 113, 155, 159, 161–66, 168, 172, 181–88, 191–205, 204, 220n69, 258n26
 on Peretz's poetry, xxii
"Mishnat ḥasidim"/"Mishnes khsidim" (The teaching of Hasidim) (Peretz), 107, 172–77, 183, 198

"Monish" (Peretz), 125, 127–29, 134, 146–52, 215n4, 253n91
Montesquieu, 187
Mulder, Samuel I., 150–51
"Muser" (Moral) (Peretz), 51–52
"Mute, The" (Peretz), 98–106, 230n32
Nadson, S. I., 120
Nekrasov, Nikolai A., 23
Newman, Steve, 133–34
"New Movement, The" (Peretz), 63–66
Nietzsche, Friedrich, 201
   and Hasidism, 176
   influence on Peretz, 155, 175–76, 198, 202
Nomberg, H. D., xxvi
   Peretz's influence on, 10, 207
   on Peretz's writing, 166, 171–72, 174–75, 258n29, 263n114
Nordau, Max, 109
"Not an Idler" (nisht keyn batlen) (Peretz pseudonym), 60
Notes from the Underground (Dostoyevsky), 200–1
Nusinov, Yitskhok, 162, 174
Olgin, M., 161
"On Agitation" (Kremer), 62
"One guy swindles the other" (Peretz), 81–82
"Orphan of Nemirov, The" (Peretz pseudonym), 172
Ovnt blat (newspaper), 40
"Oysgeshtorbn" (Extinct) (Peretz), 141
pacifism, xix, 64, 217n24, 233n81, 233n87
Pale of Settlement, the, 38
   and the Jewish labor movement, 43
   Jewish wage workers in, xix, xxiv, 35
   Peretz's research on, xix–xxii, 22, 25–34
Palestine, xviii, 102, 164
   Ahad Ha-am thoughts on, xxix, 76, 87, 241n101,
   Peretz's thoughts on, xxix, 34, 76–77, 81, 83, 87–89, 95, 111
Parush, Iris, 21
"Passover is coming" (Peretz), 56, 58
Pat, Yankev, 207
Peled, Yoav, xxiv–xxv, 43, 205, 219n51–52
Penguin Book of Modern Yiddish Verse, The (Howe, Shmeruk, Wisse), 145
Peretz, I. L. (Yitskhok Leybush Perets):
advice for Yiddish-speaking Jews, 2
on the American dream, 186
anti-elitism, xxix, 10, 34, 87, 175–76, 200
and Arab Muslims, 76–77
arrest of, xxvii, 191–92
arrival in Warsaw, xv, xxii, xxviii, 83
and censorship, 39–40, 55–56, 60, 63–64, 66–67, 228n15
criticism of, xxvii, 70, 129–30, 239n32, 250n55, 255,127
on death and dying, 169–71
and the "decadent" tradition, 96–97
dubious opinions about, xxvi–xxix, 32, 97, 102, 165, 181, 186, 204–5, 207
early Yiddish writings, 9–21
on education for the masses (*folks-Bildung*), 44–45, 54–55, 93–94, 145–46
embrace of socialism, xxviii, 8, 28–29, 36, 39

on emigration to the United
    States, 1
on Enlightenment values, 78, 87,
    113, 189, 196
essays by, xxvi, xxviii–xxix, 1–4,
    9, 16, 22, 40, 54, 70, 73, 87,
    96–97, 103, 118, 154
fear of losing his artistic
    credibility, 36
feuilletons by, 60, 66–67, 86, 88,
    94, 107
gender politics of, 12–14, 16–17,
    20–21, 47–54, 100–2, 113, 138,
    140–41, 148, 164
Hasidic stories by, xxv–xxix, 107,
    113–14, 155, 159, 161–205,
    220n69, 247n15, 258n26,
    259n42, 262n86
and the haskalah (the Jewish
    Enlightenment), xvii, xviii–xix,
    53
influence on others, xv, xxvi, xxix,
    6, 24, 28, 41–42, 47, 63, 66–68,
    70, 85, 91, 102, 111, 125,
    128–29, 139, 141, 146, 152–53,
    155, 162, 173–75, 179, 198,
    207, 225n54, 236n22, 252n81,
    259n43, 263n106
influenced by, xv, 111, 125,
    129–30, 139–41, 152, 154–56,
    173–75, 198, 201, 203
Jewish folklore collecting,
    146–48
on Jewish identity, 3–4, 15
and the Jewish intelligentsia,
    xx, xxviii, 14, 16, 22, 26, 54,
    65–66, 72, 80, 87, 94, 128, 147,
    175, 181, 224n50
on Jewish "livelihoods," 6–8, 31
on Jewish migration, xviii
on Jewish poverty, xxi–xxii, 6,
    8, 11, 19, 22, 24–31, 34, 40,
    47–53, 65, 74, 100, 119, 123,
    140–41, 184, 188, 211, 220n69,
    236n28
and Jewish social realism (in
    literature), xxv, 15–16, 54,
    94–98, 103, 107, 142, 187
legal career of, xv, xxii, 1–2
letters written by, xvi–xvii, 1–2,
    35, 47, 63, 80, 87, 152, 162,
    183, 207, 211, 224n50, 240n94
on marriage, 46, 52–53, 112,
    138–39, 143, 145, 186, 251n78
memoirs about, xx
on modern education (*Bildung*),
    xviii, 2–6, 9, 22, 54–55, 188,
    216n11
and modernism, xxv, 10, 24, 77,
    95–100, 105–7, 121–22, 130,
    133, 145, 174, 183, 186
on "modernizing" Jews, xvii–xviii,
    2–6, 9, 21–22, 28, 32, 34, 37,
    93
plays by, 111, 245n171
poetry by, xxi–xxii, xxviii–xxix,
    49, 67, 74, 82–83, 103–7,
    115–45, 205
and Polish intelligentsia, xv
as Polish speaker, xv, xvii, 26, 81
"Polonization" of, xv
and progressivism, xiii, xxv, 3–5,
    12–13, 16, 18, 21–22, 24, 28,
    34, 47, 56, 66, 68, 85, 88–89,
    97, 109–112, 122, 134, 145,
    162, 181, 189, 191–92, 204
prophetic voice of, 76, 118–21,
    125, 139, 159
racist attitudes of, 94–95
radicalization of, xiii, xxiv–xxv,
    xxviii–xxix, xxxi, 35–58, 115,
    117, 201
as a "reactionary," xxviii–xxix, 19,
    163, 189, 204
on the "reactionary mindset,"
    189–91

readership of, xiii, xx, xxvi,
xxviii–xxix, 5, 7, 10, 21–22, 26,
32, 35, 39, 56, 61, 65, 120, 129,
168, 179, 181, 195
on religion as instrument of
control, 180–81
reputation of, xiii, xv, 191,
207
on romantic love, 19, 53–54, 100,
103–6, 110–11, 113, 117–18,
129, 132–33, 146
satires/parodies by, xxix, 15,
50–51, 58–59, 80, 81–84,
89–90, 113, 147–48, 151, 153,
163–68, 171, 182–86, 194, 213,
228n12, 239n74
Sephardic ancestry of, 28
on sexual themes, 50–51, 84, 101,
128, 151, 184–86
shift to romanticism, 84, 104–6,
114, 120, 163
on *shund* (lowbrow) writing, 10,
15, 93–94
and Socialism, xv, xx–xxii, xxv–
xxix, 1–8, 16, 28–29, 35–36,
38–44, 47, 56, 60–61, 66–67,
71–72, 89, 100, 107, 113–15,
120, 122, 124–25, 134–35,
139–41, 145–46, 152, 156–159,
162–63, 165–67, 175, 186, 192,
202
sketches by, 78, 84, 104, 112
speeches by, xxvii–xxviii, 177
as translator, 102–3, 120, 122,
135–36, 152–54
use of allegory, 39–40, 75, 78,
80–81, 84
use of epistolary genre, 40, 44–46,
49, 186–87
use of gothic elements, 107–10,
143
use of irony, 14, 15–17, 19–20,
31–34, 40, 54, 56, 58, 63, 98,
100, 112, 114, 126, 153, 168,
179, 183–84, 190–91
use of pseudonyms, 60, 63–64,
172
use of religious/ethnic stereotypes,
7–8, 15, 18, 20–21, 164, 167,
197–98
use of symbolist techniques, 108,
145, 174, 176–77, 220n69,
236n26
use of "traditional Judaism" to
promote Socialism, 6–7, 39–40,
56, 58–60, 181–87
writing in Polish, xvii, 122, 153,
197
as Yiddish speaker, xvii–xviii
on Yiddish writing as tool for
spreading modern ideas, xviii,
9
Peretz School, 207
Peretz Societies, 207
Peretz Square Park, 210
Perl, Joseph, 161, 187
Persian Letters (Montesquieu),
187
Pesakhzon, Yitskhok Mordkhe, 41
Pinski, Dovid, xx, 5, 36, 55–56, 59,
61–63, 68, 70, 73, 223n91
Plekhanov, Georgi, 174
Poezye (Peretz), 120
Polish Jewry, xix
Polish Socialist Party (PPS), 37,
41–42
Pomerantz, Alexander, 156
Poor Folk (Dostoyevsky), 187
positivism:
criticism of, 200–1, 259n47
and Jews, xvi, 6
Peretz's belief in, 2, 22, 36, 93,
100, 134
Peretz's criticism of, 181
In Poland, xv, 8, 215n, 241n104
postcolonial theory, 133, 205, 220n67

"Priest and a Prophet, A" (Ha'am), 121
"Prophet, The" (Pushkin), 121
Proudhon, Pierre-Joseph, 153
Psycho (Hitchcock), 110
Pushkin, Alexander, 121
Rabbi Akiva, 60
Rabbi from Bacharach, The (Heine), 153
Rabinovich, Alexander Ziskin, 75
Railroad Stories (Aleichem), 11
Rashi, 150, 153
"Realism and Love of Zion" (Peretz), 97
Reason, Faith and Revolution (Eagleton), 177
"Reb Khanine ben Dosa (a talmudishe zage)" (Peretz), 150
Reb Nachman of Bratslav, 172–73, 187, 236n22, 239n74
"Reb Yosl" (Mr. Yossel) (Peretz), 146–51
Renner, Karl, xviii
Revealer of Secrets, The (Perl), 187
Reyzn, Avrom, 10, 66, 174, 191, 197, 207
"R' Khanine Ben-Dose" (Mr. Hanina Ben-Dosa) (Peretz), 49
Romantsero (Peretz), 146, 152
Romanzero (Heine), 130
Rosenfeld, Morris, 139, 145
Roskies, David, 10, 175, 249n45
Ross, Nicham, 174, 176
Rozentsvayg, Ayzik:
  on Peretz's conservatism, 191–92, 204
  on Peretz's poetry, 125, 149, 151–52
  on Peretz's prose, 39–40, 53, 77
  on Peretz's radical turn, xxv–xxxvi, xxviii, 205
  on Peretz's readers, 168
  on Peretz's view of Hasidim, 162, 204

"R' Shifra" (Peretz), 107
Russian Empire, the, xix
Safa Brura (Clear Language), xvii
Sartre, Jean-Paul, 96–97, 241n108
"Scene (from Heine), A" (Peretz), 153
Schiller, Friedrich von, 105, 112
Schopenhauer, Arthur, 28, 241n104
Scott, Walter, 133
"Self-Sacrifice" ("Mesires-nefesh") (Peretz), 153
Shaked, Gershon, 114, 164
"Shalom al Yisrael" (Peace upon Israel) (Zweifel), 162
"Shamya gibor" (Peretz), 162
"Shem and Japheth on the train" Abramovitsh, 11, 89, 91
"Shinuy ha-arakhin" (Change of values) (Ha'am), 176
"Shmaya gibor" (Peretz), 183
Shmeruk, Chone, xxvi–xxvii, 145
"Sholom Bayis" (Domestic peace) (Aleichem), 49–50
Shomer, 10, 15–16, 222n17
shtetl Jews:
  in Peretz's writing, xxi–xxii, 10, 26–34, 98, 100, 111–13, 126–28, 142, 165, 167, 169, 183, 194, 198, 201, 226n66
"Shtraymel" (Peretz), 61
Shvartsberg, S. B., 70, 131–32, 234n2
Sifre-agora (Penny-books), 92, 94
Singer, I. B., 207
Slonimski, 183
Smith, Andrew, 109
Smolenskin, Peretz, 74, 101
Sokolow, Nahum, xv, 183, 217n32, 237n36–37
  agreement with Peretz, 107
  as editor, 106–7, 261n71
  impressions of Peretz, xx–xxi, 39
  memories of Peretz, xv
  people's confusion with Peretz, 97
  research by, xix
  on Zionism, 78

"Song of the Shirt, The" (Hood), 139–40
SPD (Sozialdemokratische Partei Deutschlands), 64
Spektor, Mordkhe, 23, 90–91, 191, 231n53
Spencer, Herbert, 64
Stalin, Joseph, 156, 191
Sternhartz, Nathan (Nosn), 172
Susati (Abramovitsh), 108
"Sweatshop, The" (Rosenfeld), 145
Świętochowski, Aleksander, xv
Talmud, the, 63
  in Peretz's writing, 6, 64–65, 150, 188, 230n38, 254n112
Tchernichovsky, Shaul, 96, 130
"To a Jewish Maiden Who Alienates Herself" (Peretz), 20
Taytsh-khumesh, 50–51
Terman, Moyshe, 62
"Thought, The" (Peretz), 72, 75–76, 107
"Tikavatenu" (Our hope) (Imber), 84–85
"Tip of a Yud" (Yalag), 122
"Tmunot me-olam ha-tohu" ("Scenes from Limbo") (Peretz), 111–14
Torah:
  in Peretz's writing, 6, 48, 50–51, 77–78, 81–82, 119, 148, 150, 173–74, 187, 202, 236n22
"Torat Ha-no'ar" (Smolanskin), 108
"To the Lovers of Hebrew and Its Literature" (Ben-Avigdor), 92
"Treyst mayn folk" (Take comfort my people) (Peretz), 145
Tsene-Rene, 148
Tsinberg, Y., 152
"Us and Peretz" (Medem), 205–6
"Veber-libe: Dertseylung in briv" (Weaver-Love: Story in letters) (Peretz), 40–46, 100, 128, 138, 142, 186–87, 212–13

Vintshevski, Morris, 74–75, 120, 139–41, 235n18, 247n14
von Suttner, Bertha, 63
Vorwaerts! (Journal), 154
"Vos viln mir?" (What do we want?) (Peretz), 81
"Vos zol ikh veln?" (What should I want?) (Peretz), 67, 85
Wagner, Richard, 153
Warsaw Positivism, 5, 17
Werses, Shmuel, 102
Wessely, N. H., 150
West, Cornel, xxxi
"What Do I Want?" (Peretz), 180–81
What is Property? Theft! (Proudhon), 154
"What Is Soul?" ("Vos heyst neshome?") (Peretz), 93
"Wife Mrs. Hanna, The" (Peretz), 111
Winter Notes on Summer Reflection (Dostoyevsky), 200
Wisse, Ruth, xxvii, 67, 145, 156
Wolff, Frank, xxiv
"woman's wrath, A" (Peretz), 98
Wordsworth, William, 133
World of Sholom Aleichem, The (play), 38–39
Yahalal (i.e. Yehuda Leib Levin), 74, 139
Yehoyesh, 93
Yiddish:
  as common language/"people's language," xiii, xix, xv–xvi, 14, 72, 92–93, 125, 128, 130
  curses in, 91
  epistolary literary genre, 49
  as "feminine" language, xix
  highbrow literature in, 93
  Jewish writers' preference for, xvii
  and the Jewish workers' movement, xxiii, 35–35
  as a literary language, xviii, 102

low status of, 3, 129
as marker of spiritual value, 43
Peretz's "fondness" for, xv–xix, 43, 128
secular Yiddish culture/yidishkayt, xxiii–xxiv
standardization of, xviii
"symbolic capital" of, 146, 179
as unifying force for Jews, 17, 21, 34
Yiddishized Hebrew, 98, 102
Yiddish press, xviii, 36, 62, 227n4
Yiddish schools, xxiii–xxiv
"Yokhanan the Melamed's stories" (Peretz), 186–91
Zakreski, Patricia, 140–41
Zeitlin, Aaron, 207
Zionism:
and Aḥad Ha'am, 175–76
and Bialik, 120–21, 220n64
figures associated with, 37
and Herzl, 153
historiography of, xxiv
and the Holocaust, xxvii
hopefulness of, xxiii
and the narrative of "return," xviii
Peretz's attitude toward, xxix, 3, 58, 70, 78–89, 94, 97, 111, 114–15, 117
and Poland, 13
political Zionism, 191
proto-Zionism, 58, 76, 111, 113
and territory, 9
Zionist press, xxvii, 89, 103, 191, 213
Zweifel, Eliezer, 162, 176

www.ingramcontent.com/pod-product-compliance
Lightning Source LLC
Chambersburg PA
CBHW021647230426
43668CB00008B/543